advanced
JAVA
Development for Enterprise Applications

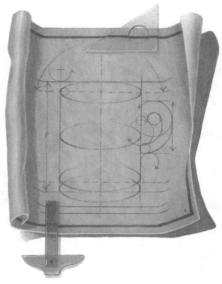

CLIFFORD J. BERG

D1249347

Prentice Hall PTR
Upper Saddle River, New Jersey 07458
http://www.phptr.com

ISBN 0-13-080461-4

90000

9 780130 804617

Library of Congress Cataloging-in-Publication Data
Berg, Clifford J.
  Advanced Java development for enterprise applications / by Clifford J.
Berg.
     p. cm.
  Includes index.
  ISBN 0-13-080461-4 (pbk.)
  1. Java (Computer program language)   2. Application software-
-Development.   I. Title
QA76.73.J38B478   1998
005.13'3--dc21   98-18367
                              CIP

Acquisitions editor: *Mary Franz*
Editorial assistant: *Noreen Regina*
Marketing manager: *Dan Rush*
Editorial/production supervision
      and composition: *Eileen Clark*
Manufacturing manager: *Alexis Heydt*
Cover design: *Anthony Gemmellaro*
Cover design director: *Jerry Votta*

© 1998 by Prentice Hall PTR
Prentice-Hall, Inc.
A Simon & Schuster Company
Upper Saddle River, New Jersey 07458

Prentice Hall books are widely-used by corporations and government agencies for training, marketing, and resale.
The publisher offers discounts on this book when ordered in bulk quantities.
For more information, contact:
        Corporate Sales Department
        Phone: 800-382-3419, Fax: 201-236-7141
        E-mail: corpsales@prenhall.com
Or write: Prentice Hall PTR
        Corp. Sales Dept.
        One Lake Street
        Upper Saddle River, NJ 07458

Printed in the United States of America
10 9 8 7 6 5 4 3 2

ISBN 0-13-080461-4

Prentice-Hall International (UK) Limited, *London*
Prentice-Hall of Australia Pty. Limited, *Sydney*
Prentice-Hall Canada Inc., *Toronto*
Prentice-Hall Hispanoamericana, S.A., *Mexico*
Prentice-Hall of India Private Limited, *New Delhi*
Prentice-Hall of Japan, Inc., *Tokyo*
Simon & Schuster Asia Pte. Ltd., *Singapore*
Editora Prentice-Hall do Brasil, Ltda., *Rio de Janeiro*

To my beloved and wonderful daughter,
Ariane

Contents

Chapter 7

JavaBeans for the Enterprise, 455

Introduction

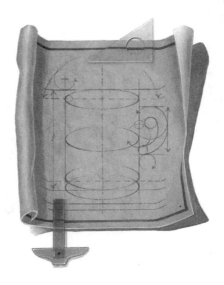

The development of computers brought great expectations for what they might enable people to achieve. In fact, computers have enabled us to achieve incredible things. The ability to perform large numbers of calculations reliably and quickly made Project Apollo possible. Computer simulations enable scientists and engineers to analyze and understand complex physical systems, such as the birth of stars and even the beating of the human heart.

Complementary gains have been expected in business and information processing. People have long anticipated a paperless office, in which all information is stored in computers and moves electronically to wherever it is needed at any moment, and is useable from any device. Unfortunately, while computers are omnipresent in business and government today, they have failed to bring the productivity gains that people predicted. The paperless office has still not arrived; software is increasingly complex and hard to install and use; and while the Internet is solving the data accessibility problem, there is still no software infrastructure today to allow information to be equally accessible wherever you go.

There is much debate on the subject of why this might be, but at the heart of all these arguments lies the common recognition that computer software is still to this day expensive to build, deploy, and maintain, and this cost offsets the operational gains that its installation brings about; multiuser programs needed by organizations are even more difficult to build. The range of computing devices in use are still too incompatible, making it inconvenient if not impossible to universally

transport or deploy software wherever there is data that needs it; and security problems associated with global data accessibility need to be solved before this can even be considered.

Java is poised to remedy all this. Java provides a component-based software model that works, and there are already software component sets (such as Lotus e-Suite and many others) which demonstrate that it is possible to create modules which can be plugged together without programming. This is the Holy Grail of computing, and it is within our reach.

Java programs are also platform-neutral, and the range of systems on which Java can run is growing rapidly. This is an extremely important issue for large organizations, especially international ones. While in the U.S. the main operating systems are UNIX and Windows, outside the U.S. many large multinational corporations rely on other operating systems, proprietary to Japanese and European manufacturers. The world speaks more than just Windows and UNIX. Furthermore, it is hard to imagine that these will reduce to a single proprietary operating system at some point: the ramifications of this occurring are great. It would spell the end of competition within the software industry, and governments would have no choice but to intervene. It is unlikely for other reasons, however. While Windows gets better and better, the alternatives get better too. The industry is changing rapidly in unexpected ways, and Java is one example of such a change; there will be others. This makes platform neutrality even more important for those making an investment in software development.

Java is particularly well suited as an enterprise platform for many other reasons. Its platform neutrality simplifies deployment issues; and Java has many natural automated deployment options, including web-based deployment using browsers and self-updating desktop-based deployment using replication protocols.

Java's simplicity is a great strength in a tool for developing applications. The programming model of the Java language distills the best features of object-oriented languages into a practical subset that is easy to program with, produces programs that are easy to understand and inexpensive to maintain, and yet is powerful, compact, and efficient. Java sacrifices little or no performance for these advantages. In addition, the Java programming packages, called "APIs" (application programming interfaces), which are included as standard components of any Java development kit, constitute a programmer's library of unprecedented power for developing wide-ranging applications for business, which are nevertheless runnable as they are on any computer operating system that supports Java, and which make possible things that developers previously had to use operating-system-dependent techniques for. These APIs have extensive support for building distributed applications, and components which can interoperate across a network.

The "JavaBeans" software component model provides a framework for building reuseable program modules. This has two advantages: it allows companies to choose from the full range of software component toolkits, and know that the components will be useable in the organization's development tools; and it also enables an organization to develop its own reuseable components, reducing the maintenance and lifecycle cost of software. The Enterprise JavaBeans framework takes this many steps further, and breaks new ground by defining a standard architecture for applications servers, delegating to vendor-provided components most of the complexity of building transactional applications and applications that are interoperable across products from multiple vendors.

Finally, but perhaps most importantly Java addresses security issues in a comprehensive and fundamental way, taking advantage of its virtual machine design to provide an insulating layer between an application component and its environment. It is now possible to deploy applications without fear that they might corrupt or compromise the local environment. This is an important feature for applications that might need to interoperate with components outside the organization, or traverse public networks in so-called extranet applications.

This book will explain Java-related technologies of particular importance to organizational software development. This book is not intended to be an in-depth treatment of all enterprise subjects. In fact, the topic of enterprise application development is so broad that it would require a library of books to cover each area in depth. I therefore do not promise to even mention every topic that is relevant, much less cover each in depth. However, an advanced programmer needs to have a working knowledge of most aspects of a system in order to understand the entire system. For example, a developer working on a secure socket service to be used for an extranet RMI application does not need to know all about every aspect of RMI, but does need to know fundamental RMI issues as well as the issues related to security. This book tries to provide a big picture, in a highly practical manner that is immediately useful to most developers, regardless of what their particular expertise is. I will avoid most user-interface-related topics, because those are covered extensively in other books.

The readers of this book are expected to be advanced, but with varied backgrounds. I assume that most know basic Java programming, but that some will know some aspects of Java and not others. Since Java and its related technologies are so new, many Java developers today have great expertise in software engineering, but not necessarily with these particular technologies. One should not have to read books on JavaBeans, CORBA, Java threads, Java networking, and other APIs just to get started on an enterprise-scale project. An emphasis is placed on showing actual implementation details, with real products used in examples. This is done to give advanced developers an immediate feeling for what the code might really look like, without having to read lots of explanatory text.

This book covers both Java 1.1 and 1.2. At the time of this writing, Java 1.2 is in beta release, but will probably be in a final release when this book is in print. In most cases I do not separate discussions of 1.1 and 1.2, but mention where there are differences. Since some of the 1.2 API is not finalized at the time of this writing, there may be some differences between the 1.2 features presented here and the final release, although differences should be few.

In this book I have tried to avoid Java technologies that depart from Java standards. It is my feeling that standards are extremely important for large applications and large organizations. The success of Java hinges on its acceptance as a standard, so it is illogical to embrace nonstandard Java implementations. Furthermore, the market forces behind the establishment of standards for this technology are so great that, in the long run, any resistance to standardizing it has to yield to the greater needs of all the companies now building Java-based products and solutions and the customers that will be depending on them.

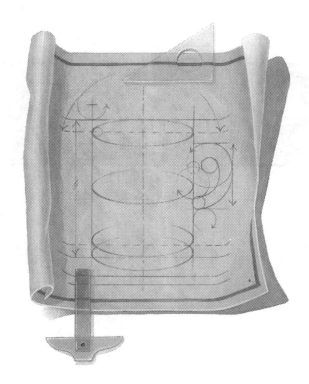

CHAPTER 1

- Risk Management
- Quality Assurance
- Design
- Coding

Java Project Lifecycle

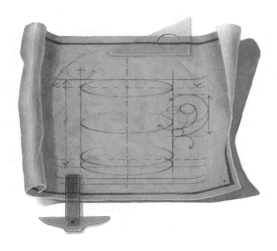

A Java software development project enjoys many advantages over a non-Java project, because Java is an object-oriented language, so object-oriented design methodologies map easily to a Java implementation; and also because the Java language and object model are simple and intuitive, so the implementation language does not itself introduce additional complexity that is not present in an application model or logical design. A Java development project can anticipate a fast track from requirements to design and implementation, and a high level of productivity for staff.

These advantages do not eliminate the need for traditional quality assurance or design methodologies. In fact, they make these methodologies more effective, by reducing the "impedance mismatch" between object-oriented design methodologies and the software implementation. Object-oriented data models can be mapped almost automatically into Java object database schemas, further reducing the translation that must occur when transitioning from design to implementation. As discussed in the chapter on databases, Java has made object-oriented databases practical by making them portable.

On the other hand, this simplified and more practical object-oriented development model brings with it new risks. Technology is changing more quickly now than ever before, and this applies to Java and non-Java-related technologies. The days when you could wait a few years for a technology to mature, and then pick a product and stay with it for ten years, are gone—and will likely never return. We are now in an era when there are major technological upheavals continually, and all development nowadays carries technological risk as a result.

Rather than provide a comprehensive treatment of software project development and lifecycle issues, which can be found elsewhere, I will focus on those aspects that are of special importance to Java technology projects. I will try to answer questions such as

- What are the issues that come up in a Java project?

- How are these issues different from other kinds of projects?

- What steps can you take to minimize risk in a Java project? How are Java projects different?

- How should you fine-tune your development methodology?

- What design guidelines should you use? Coding guidelines? Testing techniques? Measurement techniques?

I will also try to provide software developers with an overall understanding of the issues that quality assurance staff must deal with, and what a developer must know in order to assist in and be part of the quality assurance process.

Risk Management

Development using Internet technology—Java or otherwise—is characterized by these features:

- New technology abounds, seemingly in every area of the project.

- Rapid delivery is required—people can't wait nowadays.

- Many disparate elements are required, often from multiple vendors.

As if project development were not hairy enough, these wildcards have to be tossed in!

It seems like every six months there is an entire new *class* of products and APIs, designed to fill spaces unaddressed by those from before. Many server vendors also now make major enhancements to their core products more than once a year. This makes it hard to build a system, because there is the risk that the products are unreliable or have unanticipated behavior, or advertised features are not quite ready.

Some times it is wise to forego a new class of products or a new API until it has matured. The problem is, you never get to that state anymore. If something is so mature that it is no longer evolving, it is dead. The problem is not that products evolve; it is the *rate* of evolution that has sped up, as a result of the tremendous growth of the Internet and the spread of computers to mainstream and even home use.

The Java core API is a good example of an evolving technology. The hunger for enhancements is so great that people are usually willing to put up with bugs in order to use the new features. Take the Swing API. When Swing was in beta 0.5, we already had clients using it for mission-critical applications. They could not be dissuaded. The reason was that, even though it was buggy then, it would become stable by the time it was officially released, and they wanted to base their development on a standard. Swing was also so much nicer than its predecessor, the AWT, that staying with the AWT was not even an option. One could say that this is a special case, because the AWT was flawed, but in fact it is not a special case, because in every corner of Internet technology you see this—a constant outcropping of things so new and so different that they cannot be dismissed.

Not all of these new inventions have staying power, however. When "push" technology first appeared, it was touted as the new wave that would drive our desktops from now on. As it turned out, this technology's strength is in the deployment of applications, as opposed to dynamic desktops. In only one year, the entire perception of how this technology should be used made a complete turn. It is a major challenge for a manager to sort the promising technologies from the doubtful ones, and move cautiously but at the same time without fear of using something new—because everything is new.

The viability and professionalism of the provider of a technology must also be considered when making a selection. A great many Java product companies are startups, or small organizations recently acquired by larger ones. Of course, all companies start small; in the mid-80s Oracle was a fledgling company and an underdog, battling against mainframe Codasyl and IMS databases, so smallness itself should not be a handicap. It is a red flag, however. In a recent project, an object-oriented "blend" product was selected to provide an object-oriented layer for a relational database. Many vendors were evaluated, and since the Java binding of the ODMG standard for object-oriented databases was fairly new, not all vendors had incorporated it into their products. As a result, there was quite a bit of disparity between the model used by the different vendors. The vendor that was finally selected was persuaded to agree to accelerate their schedule for certain feature enhancements of interest to the project, at the expense of others. Since they were a small vendor, and this was a large customer, convincing them was easy. They made the changes, but when the product started to be used, other unanticipated limitations were discovered. Luckily, this was during a prototype stage for the project, because the limitations necessitated reconsideration of the project's core architecture.

The constant change of technology is a major problem for staff training. It is virtually impossible to staff a project with people who have experience in all the things you want to use. In February 1996 I recall seeing an ad in a newspaper, for a programmer with "2+ years of Java development experience." Apparently the human resources person who wrote the ad was not aware that at the time there were perhaps 20 people in the world who fit that description, and they were very busy.

The cost of obtaining specialized talent can also be a factor that reduces flexibility if not increasing risk. One project I consulted on originally had decided that the best technology to implement their application in was Lotus Notes. However, Java was selected because it was calculated that while Lotus Notes developers could be found, the cost of obtaining them in the required numbers would double project costs compared to using C++ programmers and training them in Java.

The incentive to tolerating these risk factors is that these new technologies promise lower-cost development, much wider deployment and end-user productivity and functionality, and greater adaptability. In order to get control of the risks so that these gains can be realized, a strategy is needed with new emphasis on rapid delivery in a core-capability-driven manner. To this end, I propose three rules to comprise this strategy. Surely you have heard these rules before, but I am putting them at the top of the list.

The first rule is, ***keep each component simple***. By keeping things simple, you can get quick turnaround in development—this is important so that you discover quickly if the project is going to have technological difficulties. Do not create unnecessary layers. Make sure each layer has a well-defined purpose that is easy to conceptualize. Otherwise, your best staff resources will be spent creating advanced local architectures, instead of understanding and applying the plethora of new technology. Also, with things changing so rapidly, you don't want to invest too much effort in in-house designs that may become obsolete or replaced by components available in the marketplace. True component-based software is finally appearing. Don't worry that staff won't be challenged—it is a tremendous challenge to understand, evaluate, assemble, and apply all these new technologies, even if custom programming is kept simple.

The second rule is, ***focus on the primary mission of the application, and make that work really well***. Concentrate on what the application has to do most of the time. Tune the system for that. A system that does everything equally well is either overfunded or in fact does everything in a mediocre manner. If the primary mission is processing orders, design the system for that. If the primary mission is checking patient records, design the system for that. In large systems that are built in stages, sometimes the wrong piece is built first and then drives the rest of the design. For example, if the system must interface to an external system, a data loading mechanism might be built early on, and the system's primary features added later. Unfortunately, when this is done, there is a risk that the system will be tuned for the data loading process, which is not the primary purpose of the system. The result is a system that may load data well, but has poor response time for calling up data—the primary mission and success criterion of the system.

The third rule is, *if using new technologies, build a prototype*. You cannot avoid using new technologies today, and things are changing all the time. The best way to deal with this unstable situation is to move quickly, to avoid obsolescence, but prudently, in measured steps, to manage the risk of using new features. Don't commit to an architecture without building a prototype that tests the core mission-critical functionality using the new technologies. That is the only way that technology limitations will be exposed so that a successful full-scale architecture can then be designed. Further, it takes someone with a great deal of experience with these technologies to judge where the risks might be, and what features prototype development should focus on.

Quality Assurance

Quality assurance is a process, and it must be an integral part of development, not subservient to it. A quality assurance process consists of a set of procedures, criteria, and guidelines which ensure that developed code works and agrees with specifications, and that the resulting system meets all requirements.

In order to achieve this, it is clear that the quality assurance process must be built into the development process, so the development lead must play a major role in designing the QA process; it cannot be completely delegated, because only the development lead or management have the authority to mandate the required procedures and checkpoints. Also, because of the tight integration of the QA process with development, designing a complete QA process requires intimate understanding of the workflow process being used. The development and QA process constitute a system, and someone must design the system, and then have the authority to institute it and subsequently work out the kinks.

The first order of business for the lead development engineer, therefore, is to approach the development of a quality assurance process and its components (test suites, scripts, test databases, etc.) as a design and implementation task that is closely integrated with all other modules being designed and built, and the specification and implementation of these should ideally precede the actual system being built.

All of the products of the analysis, specification, design, and implementation processes should be placed under configuration control, using a source-code control system, and be made available project-wide via a shared directory on a LAN. When the project transitions from one phase to the next (e.g., from design to development), the final versions of the documents produced in the prior phase should be published in an easily accessible form, such as an internal web site. A web site administrator would be responsible for publishing any updates to these otherwise frozen documents, and in general making sure they are current. Nevertheless, the documents of prior phases should be maintained under configuration control at least until the system is released, in case deleted material needs to be recovered.

The Phases of Development

The normal phases of a development project are requirements specification, logical design, detailed system design, implementation, final testing, deployment, and post-deployment maintenance and enhancement. Different methodologies may call these phases by different names, but they are always present. Each phase has its own products, which may be documents, code, or test results.

Sometimes in large projects the requirements phase is also separated into a user-view phase, producing use cases or their equivalent, and a requirements specification phase, in which the requirements embedded in the use cases are recast as a features list. The main justification for doing this is that the features list embodies a checklist which can be used as a basis for test plan development and acceptance testing. Also, if a domain team produces the use cases, and a separate development team produces the requirements list, it is a way of forcing the developers to digest and understand the system requirements, by expressing them in their own terms.

A logical design partitions the system into conceptual components and specifies their behavior. It is important that as much information about the problem domain be reflected, and that minimal attention be paid to considerations having to do with performance, platform, or technology choices, unless these things are constants and known ahead of time, or are key choices that affect the functional capabilities. The reason is that this postponement allows choices of platform and technology to be deferred and left for implementation experts. The important goal of the logical design phase is to synergize the knowledge of application experts and implementation experts to produce a logical model of the system which could be implemented and would work, but perhaps not optimally.

If the system has transactional behavior, transaction partitioning should be addressed in a logical sense (what are the transactions), but not the implementation (e.g. whether DBMS locking is to be used, or implemented with an optimistic policy or checkout). This does not mean that no thought should be given to such issues; in fact, judgment about the likely technical challenges of the alternative logical designs is crucial to coming up with a design that can be built within the project's budget. Pinning down specific implementations is probably premature, however, since at this point a prototype has not even been built, and regardless the focus should be on making sure all the application's functionality is addressed.

A prototype should be developed during the logical design phase if possible. If there are new technologies involved—which is almost inevitable nowadays— what are their limitations? Do they perform as advertised? What surprises do they have in store? Scale prototyping and testing should also be performed in an investigatory manner during this stage. Note that bugs such as memory leaks in key third-party components may not show up until the system is tested at scale.

The detailed design phase modifies the logical design and produces a final detailed design, which includes technology choices, specifies a system architecture, meets all system goals for performance, and still has all of the application functionality and behavior specified in the logical design. If a database is a component of the system, the schema that results from the detailed design may be radically different in key places from the one developed in the logical design phase, although an effort should be made to use identical terminology and not change things that do not need to be changed. The detailed design process should document all design decisions that require schema changes, or in general any changes to the logical design, and the reasons for the change. The project manager's challenge will be to again disseminate understanding of the new design, which is replacing a logical design that had achieved credibility and consensus. This is the reason why all changes need to be well documented, so there is a clear migration, and the changes do not seem radical or arbitrary.

If a features list approach is used, it is easy to separate the project into builds, and make the detailed design and implementation phases of each build iterative. The systems's features can be analyzed for dependencies and resource requirements, and assigned to project builds based on these dependencies, critical path, and priority. The minimum set of features for a testable bootstrap system can then be determined. For each build, additional features are added, and all tests are rerun, resulting in a working system after each build with increasing functionality and reliability. During each build, a detailed design of each feature can be performed, identifying the packages and classes affected, and with roughcut and then detailed updates to the specifications being produced, possibly in an iterative manner, and finally actual implementation in code. I have seen this technique work extremely successfully on many compiler and other projects with which I have been involved, and it is directly applicable to all kinds of systems.

Once a detailed design for a build is agreed upon, the implementation phase should make very few changes to the system design, although some changes are inevitable. It is critical for maintainability that all changes be incorporated back into the design specifications. Otherwise, the value of the system design will be lost as soon as the system is released, and the only design documentation will be the code. A system documented only by its code is very hard for management to understand and upgrade, outsource, or disseminate.

A Java-specific reason to incorporate changes back into specifications is that JDK 1.2 introduces the concept of package versioning. A package is viewed as a field-replaceable unit, and besides its name has two identifying pieces of information associated with it: its *specification version* and its *implementation version*. Two versions of a package that have the same specification version are implemented according to the same specifications, and should therefore be field-replaceable; the only difference between them should be that one has bug fixes which perhaps the other does not. A user might choose one implementation version over another if the user has instituted workarounds for certain known bugs; otherwise, the latest implementation version should be the most desired one. You can see that in order for this methodology to work, there must exist a well-defined set of specifications for every package, and those specifications should have a version number associated with them.

Some methodologies view final QA testing as a separate phase of its own. This is a legitimate way of looking at final testing. However, developers are still busy during this period. They are not adding new functionality; instead, they are responding to bug reports from the QA group. The workflow is not any different, and all feedback mechanisms for changes and notification must still be in place. It is not clear, then, if distinguishing between development and final testing is of much value, except to clearly mark a cutoff point for adding new features and begin testing the packaging and deployment system. The QA group will likely make a "frozen" copy of the project code and test it in complete isolation, but testing of "frozen" code in this way still does not obviate feedback to the developers to subsequently fix reported problems. In fact, generating frozen releases is part of the normal build process, even though it may receive increased emphasis in the final build.

Throughout all these phases, continuity is essential. A project that assigns domain analysis tasks to analysts and then reassigns those analysts during the implementation phase is operating with a severe handicap, if not doomed to failure.

Domain expertise must remain within the project throughout its lifecycle. The dilemma is that once up-front analysis is complete, the analysts have less work, and their role becomes more passive. Often this cannot be justified, and these people are valuable to the business and are needed elsewhere. A solution that often works well is to keep a few domain experts assigned full time, and give them the permanent role of *facilitator*. In this capacity, they perform domain analysis, and execute all change requests to requirements specifications. They also develop user-oriented test plans, and construct system documentation. Their role therefore remains an active one, and their knowledge about the application, and contacts within the organization, can still be tapped when questions arise during development.

Design Walkthroughs

Walkthroughs are usually performed for program code, but regrettably often not for designs. For a complex system, it is extremely valuable that a walkthrough be performed for a design as well as implementation code. The walkthrough can occur as part of the design process, if it is done as a group modeling and scenario development exercise; or it can be done in a traditional sit-down walkthrough of a design spec produced by an individual, or both. Regardless, there must be a design to review, on paper or in a computer, ideally with procedural components, because they are the easiest to review in a group setting.

The purpose of a walkthough is

- To disseminate knowledge about a design in a participative way so that people absorb and understand it.

- To discover logical errors, or design flaws. An "issues list" is normally produced to identify items that need resolution.

- To discover incompatibilities between subsystems being developed by different people. A "related issues list" may be produced for distribution to potentially affected parties for future resolution.

- To verify adherence to coding or design standards.

- To boost morale and develop team spirit.

Management should participate in initial walkthroughs, and then leave them to senior engineering staff to manage. Development staff must feel uninhibited in a walkthrough to voice opinions. Staff should be advised ahead of time that having a defensive attitude is not permitted. A designer's or programmer's performance should not be evaluated based on the number of problems discovered in walkthroughs, but by a trend of fewer problems over time.

It is interesting and challenging that while a major purpose of a walkthrough is to create team spirit, the other purposes involve problem discovery, that is, finding fault with someone's design or implementation. Handling this is not an easy matter. It is the primary task of the person managing the walkthrough to transform this discovery process into a positive and productive exercise, which leaves the team feeling energized and that they now have a solid design and are on the right track, and that no one was reprimanded or made to feel incompetent. Humor and a pre-walkthrough pep talk are often helpful in this regard. Bringing doughnuts also helps!

Configuration Control Issues

Change notices (CNs) and change requests (CRs)—which may collectively be referred to as change vehicles (CVs)—are documents that provide notice about a change or a request for a change, respectively. These may be e-mail documents, possibly composed with a web form, and are used to control and track changes to parts of a design that are deemed stable. They are normally used once a stable specification of some kind exists. They provide a means to change the product of a previous phase of development. A change notice contains an announcement of a change made to some document or piece of information product, and a change request contains a request to make a specified change; both contain reference, routing, and tracking information, the originator, reason, and so forth.

During detailed design or coding, it is not useful to use CNs or CRs for most changes to that phase's product. Everything is in a state of flux, so everything would need a CV. However, a change vehicle should be used for changes to behavior that deviate from the specification (so the specification will need to be changed as well; this should be ideally handled in the same CV). A change vehicle should also be used for a change that affects anyone else, in particular changes to implementation interfaces or protocols that may or may not be part of the specification. Of course, if someone else is currently responsible for a package or a class, a CR should be used to initiate a change, rather than checking it out and making the change when they are not looking!

Sometimes within a project it will be convenient to assign a particular class to a developer for development or enhancement. At other times, an entire package may be assigned. In general, it is preferable to make packages the level at which task responsibility assignments are made, since Java specification versions apply to a package, but sometimes the package may be too large or general-purpose for this to be practical. The decision of task granularity therefore has to be made on a case-by-case basis.

Regardless, from the beginning all work should be set up under an automated version control system, including all documentation.

The CV mechanism should be as automated as possible. It may make use of an e-mail mailing list with aliases set up for the groups responsible for different packages. A private news server may also be used to provide a viewable history of changes, notices, and communication about packages and development issues.

A CR should be routed to the person/group currently in charge of the component. It should also get posted on a newsroup for the package and any affected packages. The CR should be either be approved or rejected, and, if approved, someone assigned to make the change.

When the change has been made, a change notice should be initiated. This should be routed to the original initiator of the CR and all interested or affected parties, and a news item about the change posted, attached to the original CR. Optionally, CRs and change notices may automatically go into a database, with a query to provide status information based on the CV number, author, package, or class.

If development teams are not located in the same office or geographic region, it is still possible to integrate the teams so that they operate almost as if they were co-located. In this case it is even more important to divide design and implementation responsibility into packages, so that a site knows exactly which packages it is responsible for. There is no reason a site's packages cannot be subpackages of any given higher-level package—packages are just a naming hierarchy, and subpackages may be named in any way that makes sense, even across teams or locations.

If the project is fortunate enough to be able to implement a virtual private network (VPN) with acceptable bandwidth, then all locations can use the same version control system for accessing software. Generally, however, at least a T-1 connection is required to make this practical, since most version control systems move large amounts of data when computing deltas and source versions. Depending on the version control system being used, this should be tested.

If using the same version control system is not practical, either because of the lack of a VPN or lack of bandwidth, then transporting code deltas between sites may be possible, if the source code control systems support this, and if each site only modifies its own packages. To make this possible, the version control system must support the import of deltas, and most do not have this feature. Alternatively, each site can be implemented as a separate project within the version control system, and the integration of projects can be achieved by encoding the checkin and extractions into the overall project makefile.

Most projects have a data layer of some sort. A database administrator is the party responsible for the data layer component. This should be a highly stable component before coding starts. Build increments for the data layer should be handled as a special case, and performed with less frequency than other project components, and be followed by testing to establish a new baseline. The data layer will also have to be loaded with test data. Generally, at least two versions of the data layer's test data need to be maintained concurrently: a small version for development and unit testing, and a fully loaded mock-up database for full system and scalability testing. It is usually not practical to develop using a fully loaded database, due to increased load and query times, and yet a small version does not stress the system. Thus, both are needed to satisfy development and testing requirements.

If the coding process discovers an error in a specification, the same procedure should be used to change a specification as to change code. Ideally, design specs should be integrated into the code, so the entire issue of synchronization of code and specifications goes away (although the need to approve, document, and disseminate specification changes does not, and integrating specs with code introduces the possibility that specifications may be changed without authorization). Depending on the development tools, the physical integration of specifications with code may not be possible. Diagrams are especially problematic. One very enterprising group I worked with photographed and scanned all sketches produced in design meetings and posted them on the internal development group's web site. Eventually, these highly meaningful sketches were replaced with high-quality renderings. Code comments can refer to online diagrams, by including HTML tags that embed graphic images, or by embedding PDF or other document formats that have diagrammatic capability. Having entry level staff render design sketches into online documents is a way to help get the new staff up to speed on the key aspects of the design.

The ideal development environment therefore would work from web-viewable source formats; separate design and implementation components but integrate them by reference, including embedded diagrams within source specifications and source code; allow integrated viewing via web publishing; provide automatic generation or extraction of "webified" documentation and specifications; and control access to all components via a version control system. At this time I am not aware of a product that meets all these requirements, but some of the specification design environments which will be discussed later come close.

It is extremely important that detailed actual specs be maintained in sync with the code; otherwise, a "guru" system will result, with the knowledge only in the heads of key developers, and there is the possibility that management will lose control of the system and be unable to make technical judgments without relying on guru staff who have an interest in making the system more and more complex. Staff should not be blamed for this tendency: it is the natural tendency of good developers to want to tackle interesting problems; the best business solution is often the simplest, however. The real problem is making sure that the system is well documented and understood by all.

Testing

There should be a testing/QA process for ensuring that documentation and software match, and that these match the specs. Deviations discovered during this methodical testing should result in bug reports. There needs to be a procedure for allocating bug reports to engineers for investigation and bug fixing. A bug fix will not normally trigger a CV unless the change meets normal criteria for generating a CV, such as a change to a system specification, or to system interfaces, external behavior, or subsystems currently being maintained or enhanced by another group. In the last case, in which bugs are being fixed for a deployed system version in parallel with work on a new and enhanced system version (which has a new specification, according to the JDK 1.2 versioning concepts), a CV would also be generated against the new system, since the responsibility for fixing bugs to the deployed system version is a different responsibility than that of building the new system version.

There should be a streamlined and automatic bug reporting process, accessible online to programmers and analysts. Bug reports should go into a database so that they do not accidentally collide (two different reports get assigned the same bug number), and also so that they can be tracked and analyzed. Test results, bug reports, and fixes follow statistical trends (so do CVs), and analyzing this trend (both during the project as well as making historical cross-project comparisons) is valuable to management. This is difficult for developers to understand sometimes, because developers are close to the system and do not see the components in a statistical way, just as parents do not see their children as statistics. Graphing progress in fixing bugs and posting those graphics helps to crystallize the goal for development staff during final stages of development and testing, which is to get the system as near bug-free as possible.

The bug reporting process should generate a notice to the parties responsible for the suspect module and all affected modules. A news item should also be posted. A bug report should identify the class and, if applicable, the method or construct involved. It should identify the system build. It should possibly identify the line numbers involved, if known, and the nature of the incorrect behavior. It may recommend a fix. It should also, if practical, identify a test program that demonstrates the error; this may be attached or referenced by a file URL.

Test suites either can be based on functional requirements, such that each atomic requirement of the system is tested, or code-coverage-based, such that every logical pathway and system component is exercised, or both. Functional tests generally are used for most systems; code coverage tests are used to augment testing for systems that have stringent reliability requirements.

Some systems, such as compilers, are amenable to batch testing. This is a highly efficient way to test a system, since a test suite can be rerun every night, and progress is easy to assess, since each night the test suite should turn up fewer bugs. Tracking progress is easy, because there is a well-defined set of tests which cover the entire scope of the system's requirements, and test passage or failure is automatically determined by the test. The process of rerunning test suites and comparing the results is known as *regression testing*. It is not uncommon for compiler test suites to have tens of thousands of tests, depending on the complexity of the language translated by the compiler.

Interactive systems, on the other hand, must often be tested manually. There are tools that can be used to simulate a human user, generate mouse events, and so on. These can be used for automatic testing; but in many cases it is more practical to run the system through a test procedure with a human at the helm. This will turn up previously unobserved quirks that an automatic test cannot.

Developing user simulation tests is also very time-consuming, and the time may be better spent in actual human-run testing. It boils down to the comparative cost of performing the test suite manually, versus the cost of developing automatic tests and then running them automatically the same number of times, which likely has negligible cost compared to running the tests manually. A strictly analytical way of looking at it is:

If

```
cost_of_developing_auto_tests <

(no_of_times_test_suite_is_run) x
   (cost_of_running_same_tests_manually)
```

then develop automatic tests.

However, even if automatic tests are developed, some manual testing still needs to be done to catch unanticipated problems. Two other considerations are that, having developed an automatic test suite, it will have to be maintained; on the other hand, it can be used and added to for every future release.

There are many Java-based automatic testing tools. SunTest (www.suntest.com), a Sun Microsystems division, has a suite of high-quality testing tools, including JavaStar, for building automated test suites for UI-based applications; JavaSpec, for constructing high-coverage test suites for noninteractive code; and Java-Scope, for test coverage analysis. On the subject of test coverage, a new entry at this writing is DeepCover, from Reliable Software Technologies (www.rst-corp.com). While this is a new Java coverage tool, RST has long experience in test code coverage analysis, originating with work for the Department of Defense, and has adapted their technology to Java. Also, their AssertMate product allows you to specify correctness assertions without modifying your source code. Another coverage tool is TCAT for Java, by Software Research, Inc. (http://www.soft.com), designed for testing Java applets running in browsers.

Even if you execute user tests manually, most systems have a data layer or service layer core for which automated procedural tests can be developed. If this layer is automatically generated, based on a schema, creating a test suite for it may not be necessary. If the layer is manually coded, developing a regression suite for it is strongly recommended.

The importance of developing a test suite for a data layer component depends on the potential cost of observed and unobserved failure. Errors in a data layer may often go undetected. However, it is not difficult to develop a regression suite for the core layer, and it will have the side effect of enhancing the understanding of the system. It can be run periodically to make sure that the core system's behavior is not changing over time and deviating from specifications. Tests can be added to the regression suite throughout the system's lifetime, and the test suite's value will increase. The regression suite, in effect, becomes the proof that the system has certain characteristics. For example, if one wanted to test for year-2000 compliance, it likely would not be hard to find the tests in the regression suite that have to do with manipulating dates and times, and merely add a few tests to see if the year 2000 can be handled. The existence of a regression suite makes it easier for management to evaluate the cost of changes in future versions of the system, possibly only because of the increased precision with which the system is implemented and conforms to specifications. The suite can also be used to evaluate the impact of technology substitutions within the data layer.

Test programs and procedures should be treated as a system component and put under revision control, with changes handled by the same CR and change notice procedure as the system itself. The test suite should also include scalability testing, which is often forgotten for middle-range applications and even for large ones.

Design

Design is the process of producing a specification for constructing something. A "logical design" focuses on a system's behavior, which may include details of external interfaces, but overlooks many of the internal workings of the system. A logical design is different from a requirements specification in that a design begins to address *how* requirements are accomplished. It need not (should not) reiterate those requirements.

A design needs to precisely specify what the system does, however—the inputs and outputs, and the transformations or algorithms that are relevant to the application. These may appear in the system's requirement. The design makes decisions about how the requirements are to be implemented. If the requirements contain algorithm specifications or procedures, the design addresses the form these will take in the system. The design will specify components which provide these algorithms or procedures.

A logical design is merely an abstraction of the system, with many details left out. In a logical design many decisions about implementation are postponed, in order to create a first-cut design that can be understood and verified by domain experts, and serve as the basis for a prototype. There is really no other qualitative or substantive difference between logical and detailed system designs, except the level of abstraction and postponement of decisions which hinge on detailed design analysis and technology choices. A logical design may therefore be viewed as a model, since it describes a hypothetical and simplified implementation.

Most projects employ a "detailed design" phase prior to coding. In a detailed design, features and terminology should match actual components and constructs in the real system to be built, and for this reason a detailed design is sometimes referred to as a "physical design." In contrast, only the behavior of the major components of a logical model need match the actual system. A detailed design begins with a specification of the actual top-level physical architecture of the planned system. A detailed design specification must also include decisions on issues that are postponed in a logical model; in a detailed design, no major issues are postponed. The level of detail to be included in the logical and detailed design—and even whether to separate these tasks or combine them—is a critical decision. It has been my experience that if a proof-of-concept and technology evaluation prototype is developed during the logical design phase, the knowledge gained can be used to produce a highly complete detailed design, and drastically reduce risk for the project.

UML—A Universal Modeling Language

We are fortunate that there has finally been a convergence in the various object-oriented system modeling notations. Universal Modeling Language (UML), which has rapidly become the accepted standard for specifying object-oriented systems, defines a set of diagrammatic conventions for representing virtually every aspect of a system. The different kinds of diagrams specified by UML are:

Use case diagram—Identifies actors and the functions (use cases) they perform in a diagrammatic manner. Useful for showing the roles users play in a system, in terms of which use cases they interact with. Appropriate for giving an overview of work processes.

Class diagram—Identifies interfaces and classes, their attributes and operations (i.e., methods), and the cardinal, compositional, and derivational relationships between them. Most applications will have a core object model expressed with class diagrams. In a database application, certain classes will be labeled persistent.

Sequence diagram, collaboration diagram—Time-based diagramming techniques to show the messaging behavior of a system. A sequence diagrams is a two dimensional chart showing the flow of messages between objects versus time. A collaboration diagram does not impose a two-dimensional organization, but identifies the sequence of message flows by assigning them numbers that increase with time. A collaboration diagram has somewhat the appearance of a data flow diagram, and can be used effectively to give a high-level view of what is happening in a system. Often object instances will be represented instead of classes, to show a "typical" scenario.

Package diagram—Shows system partitioning. This is directly applicable to a Java application, since Java has a very analogous package construct. This is perhaps the hardest diagram to do right, although on the surface it looks like the simplest kind of UML diagram. The challenge is that in many systems—even some well designed ones—everything uses everything, and one can end up with a package diagram that has lines between every component.

Implementation diagram—Similar to a class diagram, but for large-grain components. This can be used to show communication between large-grain components, such as a server object and clients. It can also be used to show how a software system is configured or deployed, in terms of which components reside in which machines.

Activity diagram, statechart diagram—State-based diagramming techniques for showing concurrent behavior. These are very useful for specifying aspects of a design that uses multithreading.

Let's now look at what goes into a Java design, and which of these modeling diagrammatic formats can help.

What Does a Java Design Spec Look Like?

A design specification for a software system to be developed in Java may contain some or all of the following. Depending on the complexity and requirements of the system, some aspects will be more important than others; I am assuming that use cases or requirements, or a features list (or all of these) have already been documented. A detailed design will address all of the following areas, except those that are not applicable to the system; a logical design will address fewer areas. By having matching sections, it is possible to map the changes from a logical design to a detailed design. A detailed design document should also explain decisions that were made that led to differences between the logical and detailed design. (Recall that differences between a logical and detailed design do not necessarily represent inconsistency; the physical model need not have the same objects as the logical model.)

- *Design description:* An overview of the design, explaining how components interact and the primary logical flow. Recommended format: informal.

- *Object model:* An object model, which identifies interfaces, classes, and their cardinalities, and identifies the composite objects that will form the basis of transactions. In a logical design, it would be advisable to postpone the specification of concrete classes and leave classes abstract. Recommended format: UML class diagrams.

- *Member specification:* An exact specification (well-commented interfaces and classes) of the methods, attributes, and associations in each of the interfaces and classes, and the purpose of each. Ultimately, you want to express these in Java so that these specifications can be incorporated into the code. Consider using "javadoc" code commenting conventions, and embedding diagrams via HTML tags. An alternative, however, is to fully annotate the object model and generate these specifications automatically, using a tool such as Rational Rose or Together Java. The challenge is that the specifications are likely to be many paragraphs if not more per method, and the tool must accommodate this. For methods, these specifications should say what the methods do, and optionally how; see *Functional specifications* below.

- *Environment specification:* A specification of the planned deployment environment(s), and the approximate expected usage pattern, volume, and other characteristics—don't leave scalability considerations for a later phase. Format: text, UML implementation diagrams, use case diagrams, tables, and charts.

- *Design concepts:* Decisions about key issues, such as transactional behavior. (See the chapter on databases.) Format: informal text and diagrams, UML collaboration or sequence diagrams, activity or statechart diagrams, and class diagrams.

- *Functional specification:* Pseudocode or scenarios for key behavior. This can be incorporated into the member specification if desired. If the application contains visual components, their layouts and designs should be specified in this section. Applicable formats: UML collaboration or sequence diagrams, Java pseudocode, activity or statechart diagrams, and screen shots. If the system requirements include a features list, all items in it should be referenced by the functional specifications.

- *Package specification:* What the packages will be (the major ones); and a description of the purpose of each package, which packages are reusable, which packages are independently deployable, and the primary dependencies between the packages. Format: text, Java, and UML package diagrams.

- *External interfaces identification:* Any other schemas or components that may be required to interact with external systems. Format: text, IDL, tables, and diagrams appropriate for the external systems, class diagrams for the interfacing components in this system; collaboration, sequence, activity, or statechart diagrams; UML implementation diagram.

- *Exception specification:* Primary kinds of exceptions, and strategies for generating and handling exceptions. This should be a text document, with class diagrams, which identifies the base Java exception classes (modeled as a "signal" in UML—see below), from which all project exception classes will derive. It also specifies what information will be encoded in exception messages, and criteria for deciding at what levels of code exceptions should be handled, propagated, or converted.

- *Resource specification:* Primary categories of properties, messages, resources, and basic components and strategies for accessing and managing them. This is a textual specification; an exact specification of resource adapter classes, if any, is provided in other applicable sections as for any other system component, and may be referenced.

- *Naming specification:* Naming conventions to be followed for all named elements in the implementation. You can fold this specification into the sections above that apply to each type of named element, keep it separate, or place it in a coding style guide (see below). It is a good idea to follow and extrapolate from the naming conventions in the JavaBeans specification. (See the JavaBeans chapter.)

- *Coding style guide:* Aesthetic guidelines for the implementation code and scripts.

- *Test specification:* A set of tests to be performed and test systems to be constructed. Format: text, or a test-tool-specific format.

- *Deployment specification:* A specification of the tools required, means, and manner in which the system is to be put into initial operation. This is not to be confused with the environment specification, which defines the operational environment; in contrast, this specification defines the system and procedures for installing and bringing the system into operation. Format: text, UML implementation diagram, and other charts and diagrams as appropriate.

A question that arises is, can Java be used as a modeling or domain specification language? And, if so, should analysts learn Java? My own feeling about this is mixed. Java is a low-level language, but it is object-oriented. It is not productive for domain experts to spend time learning how to code Java statements. However, it is useful for analysts on a Java project to understand the specifics of Java's object-oriented features, such as classes and interfaces. Having a concrete understanding of these helps enormously when dealing with UML abstractions. It also facilitates communication between developers and analysts.

The Object (Class) Model

Java is an object-oriented language. As such, a Java program is itself a precise specification for an object-oriented system, which a Java compiler can translate into an actual system. The primary elements of a Java object model are

- Packages
- Interfaces
- Classes

Packages

A package should serve a well-defined purpose. This purpose should be clearly documented in the package's specification. Unfortunately, Java does not have a standard way to document packages. However, most design tools provide this. It is good practice to assign a package to a single developer, and not have more than one person modify a package at a time. Subpackages can be created if necessary or convenient, to allow for delegation. Assigning a package to a single developer gives the developer a well-defined mission, as long as the package has a well-defined purpose.

A package also constitutes a field-replaceable unit, and has a version associated with it for deployment configuration control. (See the chapter on deployment platforms and techniques.) Viewing it this way provides some guidance about deciding how to partition a design into packages. For example, consider the following diagram (Figure 1–1):

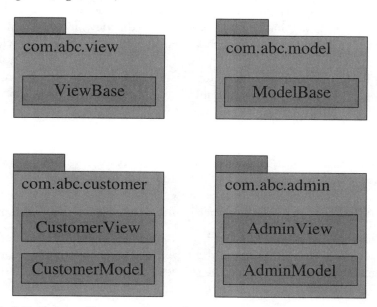

Figure 1–1 Packages allow a system to be partitioned into generic and application-specific components.

Figure 1–1 shows an example of partitioning a small GUI-based system into packages. Note that UML identifies a package by giving it a little tab (I've bent the standard a little, by using Java syntax for the package names—UML uses "::" instead of "." to separate package name components). This diagram shows four packages: com.abc.view, com.abc.model, com.abc.customer, and com.abc.admin.

In this example, common types and behavior are abstracted out into generic layers for user interface components and data access components, and each of these is put into a separate package. There are also packages for the specific application subsystems to be developed and deployed: a customer application subsystem and an administration subsystem. The customer subsystem has two classes (or interfaces), and the administration subsystem has two classes (or interfaces) as well. The customer subsystem probably uses components from both the view package and the model package; and the administration subsystem is likely to use components from both the view and the model packages.

An alternative arrangement would have been to consolidate all of the "view"-related components into one package: a package containing ViewBase, CustomerView, and AdminView; and likewise consolidate the "model"-related components into a package that contains ModelBase, CustomerModel, and AdminModel. The problem with doing this is that every time a new kind of subsystem is created, it impacts every package: since a subsystem will likely need both a view and a model, components will have to be added to both the view and model packages, requiring redeployment of every package. Furthermore, the role of the view and model packages is then unclear: they provide services that span the breadth of the entire application. It would be far better to isolate the discrete service components of the application, especially the reusable ones. Packages are the ideal mechanism for this.

Interfaces

Java interfaces define roles. The roles of the elements of a system are naturally the first things that get defined, because to define an object without defining its role is to create an object which has no known purpose. It makes sense to define the roles of the elements in the system first, and then define classes that can take on those roles.

Using interfaces also helps to decouple the parts of a system. If the system's behavior is defined in terms of interface types instead of concrete types, the system's designer is free to repartition the system into different concrete classes, with minimal impact.

Interfaces serve as the specification that subsystems use to communicate. In Java, a subsystem is manifest by a package. The interfaces, along with the documentation specifying the semantics of their methods, constitute the package's contract with other packages. Since all methods defined in an interface are public, defining behavior in terms of interface types guarantees that members inappropriately declared public within classes will not be accessed by other packages. If the interfaces are well defined and do not change much during a project, programmers are largely protected from implementation changes.

UML has its own concept of an interface, which is very closely aligned with the Java concept. One difference is that UML interfaces cannot contain attributes—any attributes. Java allows interfaces to contain static final attributes.

Classes

Even if you use interface types extensively in your application, packages are still not completely protected from changes to other packages. Interfaces cannot have constructors, so in order to instantiate instances of classes defined elsewhere, you will have to reference a concrete class type.

You can isolate your code from making an explicit reference to a concrete class in another package by identifying the class via a property, and then manufacture an instance of that class by using

```
String myClassName =
   System.getProperty("com.mycorp.myproj.myproperty");

MyInterfaceType instance =
   (MyInterfaceType)(Class.forName(myClassName).newInstance());
```

or, if the class is a bean,

```
String myBeanClassName =
   System.getProperty("com.mycorp.myproj.myproperty");

MyBeanType bean =
   (MyBeanType)(Beans.instantiate(getClass().getClassLoader(),
   myBeanClassName));
```

For this to work, the class must have a default constructor. Another solution is to use a factory:

```
String myFactoryClassName =
   System.getProperty("com.mycorp.myproj.myfactory");

MyFactoryType factory =
   (MyFactoryType)(Class.forName(myFactoryClassName).newInstance());


MyInterfaceType instance = factory.createInstance(...);
```

where MyFactoryType is a class you have defined that has a method createInstance()—or any method—that has the function of creating an instance based on runtime or configuration criteria such as property settings.

The reason I am making a big deal about this is because it is important to isolate packages from each other, and constructors are the leaky faucet in that house. One language I worked with years back solved this problem by requiring all classes to have an interface, and allowing you to defer the selection of an implementation class until link time, or even runtime. This way, alternative implementations could be used (e.g., a test stub package or the actual package) without affecting the code.

Abstract classes do not solve this problem, because abstract classes, while they have constructors, cannot be instantiated. They can have static factory methods, but you will still need a property or some mechanism to identify the concrete class to be instantiated.

Relationships between Elements of the Object Model

The kinds of relationships between packages, classes, and interfaces that may be specified explicitly in a Java object model using Java syntax are:

> *Package membership*—The package to which the class or interface belongs . We have already seen an example of how this is represented in UML.

> *Implements*—A class can implement zero or more interfaces.

> *Extends*—A class can extend the implementation of another class. An interface may also extend zero or more other interfaces.

In addition, for modeling our system, we would like to be able to specify:

> *Instance cardinality*—Conveys cardinality semantics between instances of the connected classes or interfaces

> *Instance composition*—An object connection which indicates a "compositional" relationship, such that instances of a class are logically composed of one or more instances of another class or interface, meaning that the class is an owning or controlling class for these subordinate instances

> *Arbitrary constraints and semantics*—Enables annotated relationships, and definition of custom types of relationships

There are, in fact, symbols in UML class diagrams for all of the above relationships. Let's look at a UML class diagram as an example (Figure 1–2).

This diagram depicts one interface and three classes, one of which is labeled as abstract. Note that the kind of box used for the interface is the same as for a class, except that the interface has a UML "stereotype" symbol that says "interface" in it—a stereotype is a special role modifier that is written inside of double-angle-brackets (called "guillemets"). The abstract class is labeled as abstract using a different kind of label, a UML "property string." There are predefined stereotypes and property strings in UML, but you can define your own as well, unique for your application. Your design tool may have its own properties and stereotypes defined as well.

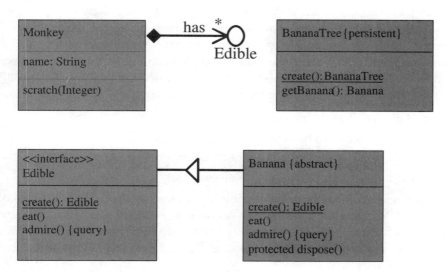

Figure 1–2 A UML class diagram showing interface, abstract, and persistent types.

In Figure 1–2, the class Banana implements the interface Edible. This is depicted by the large triangle embedded in the line extending from Banana to Edible; the triangle points from the special to the general, or, in Java terms, from the implementor to the implementee. The same symbology is used for inheritance: if one class extends another (or several—multiple inheritance is permitted in UML, but you should avoid it for classes if your application is in Java), the triangle points from the specialized class to the class from which it extends.

Cardinal and role relationships between entities are shown by an association line connecting them, with various symbols attached. In our example, there is an association between Monkey and Edible. Edible has a stand-in, a circle with the label "Edible." This can be used anyplace the interface Edible is needed, so we don't have to repeat the Edible interface in its entirety on every diagram where a class implements it. The line is labeled "has" to indicate the semantic relationship between the monkey and the edible, and the arrow points in the direction required by that relationship. The "*" is an indication of cardinality between a Monkey and an Edible in this relationship: "*" is shorthand for "0..n." Other possibilities are "1," "1..2," "1..n," and so on.

The diamond on the Monkey side of the association line tells us that this is an aggregation relation: it means that an instance of Monkey has several Edibles. Well, we knew that by the "*" symbol. However, there are two forms of aggregation: simple, and composite. If the diamond is hollow, it represents simple aggregation and is merely stating that a Monkey references multiple Edibles. If the diamond is solid, as in our example, it represents composite aggregation, and means that the Monkey owns the Edibles—they are logically part of the Monkey instance to which they are attached. This is a very important distinction for defining transactions on persistent objects, as will be seen in the chapter on databases.

The kinds of modifiers defined in Java for classes and interfaces are:

> `final`—May not be extended
>
> `abstract`—May not be instantiated without subclassing
>
> *Scope* (`public`, `package`)—Accessibility

These can be specified simply by labeling the classes or interfaces in the class diagram with UML property annotations. As we have seen, {abstract} is a property that is predefined in UML. You can define your own, however, so if, for example, security considerations mandate that a class be final, you can designate it as such using a {final} property.

It would also be nice if we could specify these characteristics:

> *Persistence*—Is the type persistent, via a persistence mechanism? If so, is it indexed?
>
> *Mutability*—Once constructed, can instances of this type be modified? Can members of this object be modified? Can they only be self-modifying, or modifiable by other instances of this type? Note that the object may be a composition of objects that are of third-party types, so we may not have control over which fields or accessors are private, and have to specify mutability policies at a composite level.

There are no built-in modifiers in UML for these characteristics, but again, we can simply label classes as such to identify them as persistent or immutable. In the example, the BananaTree class is labeled with a {persistent} property. The importance of these two characteristics is discussed in the chapter on databases.

The modifiers that may be specified in Java for methods and fields are:

> *Scope* (`public`, `private`, `protected`, `package`)—Accessibility
>
> `abstract` (methods only)—Not implemented in this class
>
> `static`—Belongs to the class instead of an object instance
>
> `final`—Cannot be overridden (methods) or changed once set (attributes)
>
> `synchronized` (methods only)—Requires an object instance (for non-static methods) lock or class (for static methods) lock for entry
>
> `native` (methods only)—Implemented by non-Java code

Of course, we don't necessarily want to specify implementation attributes in the object model—certainly not in early stages of design. On the other hand, the model should allow us to specify them when they are important for a design. We may also want to annotate the detailed design with these properties as these implementation decisions are made. UML class diagrams support method and attribute scope, using the same keywords as in Java: public, protected, and private. (There is a slight difference in semantics for "protected.") A static method or attribute is underlined in UML. UML does not have a keyword for indicating constants, but defines the {frozen} property for attributes that are unchangeable, (i.e., final). Note also the {query} property shown in the example for the admire() method. This means that the method has no side effects; it does not change the state of the instance on which it is called, or of the system.

UML defines the property strings {sequential}, {guarded}, and {concurrent} for specifying the concurrent behavior of methods. {sequential} is the default and indicates an ordinary unprotected method. {guarded} is equivalent to Java's synchronized keyword, and {concurrent} means the method is fully reentrant and does not need to be synchronized.

Exceptions

The reliability of the system is greatly affected by the way exceptions are handled, and how consistent the system is in dealing with exceptions. Even though Java cannot (assuming a bug-free VM or JIT, and that all native code is bug-free) cause a protection fault, things can still go wrong, and it is up to the programmer to trap them in an appropriate way, and also to anticipate what kinds of exceptions might occur—especially unchecked exceptions.

Java divides exceptions into three categories (at last, something that there are not "two kinds" of!): runtime exceptions, errors, and application exceptions. Runtime exceptions are those that extend from the base type RuntimeException; these represent programming errors that should never occur in the lifetime of the system. They are the equivalent of the "bomb" symbol that displays on an Apple Macintosh when a severe error occurs, causing a program to terminate. Errors extend from the base type Error, and represent system configuration error conditions. An error does not indicate a bug in the software, but rather that something was not set up right (e.g., perhaps you have the wrong version of something). That is what errors are *supposed* to be for. The last category, application exceptions, are those that extend from Exception but do *not* extend from RuntimeException. Application exceptions are generally for user errors and anything you as the programmer want to define as an exceptional condition that should cause the program to deviate from its normal flow and back out of what it is doing.

Alas, these three categories of exceptions can be separated into two groups: checked and unchecked. Application exceptions need to be declared by your code; it will not compile unless you do. The other kinds, runtime exceptions and errors, are unchecked and do not need to be declared, and so can occur at any point. Just because you don't have to declare it, however, does not mean you do not need to be prepared for it.

In most applications, it is undesirable for the application to crash. The Java equivalent of a program crash is a stack trace, followed by program termination. To prevent this when an unchecked exception occurs you can create an exception "firewall"—an outer level throws clause that catches Throwable—the base type of *all* exception types. (More precisely, I should say it is the base type of all "throwable" types, but let's not get hung up on terminology.) You will need to do this in the outer level routine (main() or run() most likely) of every thread your program creates. It is up to you what to do when an unexpected exception occurs—perhaps you will display a window with a bomb! More likely you will want to give the user some information, such as a message to contact the system administrator. You may even give them an option to commit what they are doing, if you dare. At least they don't have a blank screen, however.

It should be noted that not all error conditions cause exceptions. For example, numeric overflows do not. In that case, you will simply get incorrect results! Thus, you should be extra careful about calculations with large numbers.

There are also some classes of exceptions that get *converted* into other kinds. For example, any exceptions that occur during static initialization of objects get caught by the system and a new ExceptionInInitializerError is thrown. In order to get the original exception, you can call the getException() method on this error object.

Java does not have an assert statement, but you can achieve the same effect by creating a method that takes a boolean and, if the value is false, throws a RuntimeException. This will propagate out to your exception firewall, or to the first catch clause that catches the RuntimeException.

Exception classes should be given the URL stereotype <<signal>>.

Properties and Messages

You will want to define project-wide standards for defining resources and messages. If your application is ever to be internationalized, you cannot embed text strings in the code. All strings should be defined in resource files or classes. Resources should be associated with the package in which they are used, or in a resources package if general-purpose. See the "Resources Chapter" for more details on this.

In addition, all system configuration parameters should be defined as properties. The system design document should maintain a list of these properties. It is a good policy to name properties according to the class or package with which they are logically associated. Thus, for example, if your application's main class is called "com.mycompany.myproject.main.Main," and you need a property to hold the value of the startup directory for the program, you could name the property "com.mycompany.myproject.main.Main.startup," or "com.mycompany.myproject.startup." If you have a utility package, say "com.mycompany.util," and it has a class that needs a property to set a start-date value, you could call that property "com.mycompany.util.startdate." This convention helps to avoid collision of property names.

Design Tools

Object-oriented software design tools allow you to define an object model in a graphical manner, and then automatically generate program code that implements the model. Nowadays, most of these tools support Java code generation; in fact, Java is gaining if not taking the lead over C++.

One such tool is Together Java by Object International (www.io.com). This is a very elegant tool, developed by Peter Coad's company. When I first saw the Java version demonstrated before it was released, I was truly amazed at how snappy and well engineered the product was. This tool itself is an example of one of the nicer Java products available. You use the tool to construct an object model, and it generates Java code automatically, allowing you to edit method implementations. It will generate an object model even for existing code, from class files. I am told that it took only a few minutes to generate an object model for the entire Java API! It also has the capability to integrate tightly with Borland's JBuilder and Symantec's Visual Cafe.

There is also Rational Rose, from Rational Software (www.rational.com). These folks were instrumental in pushing the development of UML, which is now an OMG standard.

Another UML- and Java-centric entrant is LOREx2 for Java, by Elixir Technology Pty. Ltd., http://www.elixir.com.sg.

Coding

Coding is viewed by programmers as the "real work." However, if a detailed design is done properly, coding is merely execution. "Merely" is a loaded word. It is as though once having divided the canvas into tiny spaces and labeled them with colors, Rembrandt declared, "Now it is merely execution."

Coding is actually a highly creative exercise, and creativity, ingenuity, fore-thought, and experience are all necessary to fill in the gaps and convert even the most detailed design into a well-designed and well-running program. That is why it is important that the creative aspect not be managed out. Good programmers are not a commodity; in the end, it is the talent of the programmers that makes the critical difference.

Compiling and Development Environments

Here are some tips for getting the programming effort off to a good start.

- Make sure everyone uses the same versions of tools, by putting them in a central location and using shared copies. In particular, you don't want people using different versions of packages or the JDK.

- You must decide where to put source and output. In general, keep source and class files in different directory trees, and compile from a third location. If you are using the JDK compiler, use the "-d" option to specify where to place the source. Use the "-depend" option if you have recursive dependencies between classes or packages.

- CLASSPATH confusion: *don't set a system classpath*. For development, set your project classpath in your current shell, using a command script, or simply pass it as a parameter to command line tools you run or as a project setting in an interactive tool. The reason is that if your *system* has a classpath, you cannot reproduce the end user's system environment, which will probably not have a classpath set. If your development tool inappropriately requires a classpath to be set for your system, try invok-ing the tool from the command line. When you install tools, check if they have set a classpath, and unset it if they have. If you simply *must* set it automatically, set it in a user-specific script or, on NT, in the user-specific environment settings, and use a different user logon for testing.

- Compiling with a JIT, testing with the interpreter. If you are using the JDK, you can make the compiler—which is written in Java—run much faster by using the JDK's JIT. To do this:

    1.   First, install the JIT (see the "Platforms" chapter)

    2.   Use this command line to compile:

        ```
        java -Djava.compiler=symcjit sun.tools.javac.Main
          <javac-args>
        ```

    3.   For testing without the JIT, simply run the Java interpreter in the normal way.

- Use makefiles or a build configuration tool; they allow you to "clean" builds, build schemas, persistify classes, and so on, in an automated way. (*Make* and other UNIX tools are available free with optional fee-based support from Cygnus.) Cleaning is important because sometimes class or even package names may change during development, and you need a way to purge things—remember, name resolution is done by the compiler. One problem you may run into with make is that Java inner classes compile into class files that contain a dollar sign ("$"), and make treats this symbol in a special way. If you refer to a class file explicitly, you can escape this symbol to prevent make from interpreting it. However, if you use wildcards in the makefile, the list of class files is generated by make, and so you cannot escape the "$" symbol. One of my engineers got around this by using an expression to first build a list of class files, and then inserting escape sequences into the list before handing it back to make.

- Use a source code control system for everything that is not automatically generated.

- What about debugging? As it turns out, most people who program in Java do not use a debugger. I am included in this category. When I used to develop compilers in C and C++, I spent most of my day hopping between an editor, a shell, and a debugger. Java greatly reduces the need for a debugger, because the VM catches all error conditions. Still, debuggers can be useful, especially with problems that are hard to repeat. Furthermore, many development environments for Java come with a debugger built in. You can also get an excellent standalone Java debugger called JWatch from Intermetrics (http://www.intermetrics.com—a former employer of mine). Its main selling point is that it can debug multiple programs at once running in different VMs, even on different machines, and it does not impose a development environment on you.

Optimization

Do not try to optimize code during first-time development. The first order of business should be to get the code working and meeting functional specifications. However, while programmers work they notice opportunities to make improvements later. You do not want to lose these thoughts, so encourage programmers to embed comments regarding potential optimizations, and use a project-standard way to mark such comments with searchable keywords.

Most of the time, the areas that need optimization can be pinpointed later on with a profiling tool. One such tool (fairly new at this writing) for Java applications is JProbe from KLGroup (www.klg.com). Another is OptimizeIt from Intuitive Systems (www.optimizeit.com).

I am often asked if Java's object-oriented nature makes it inefficient. It is well known that there is a performance penalty for many object-oriented features; for example, virtual method calls require runtime table lookups. Also, using object-oriented design techniques, such as accessor methods, results in a penalty: tests I have run show a fourfold time overhead in using accessors over simply referencing a variable, as a result of the VM performing an invokevirtual operation instead of a getfield operation. On the other hand, Java is a highly productive language, and using a profiler and tuning the code can result in very good performance. Well-designed Java applications are indeed very snappy. If a Java application performs poorly, it is probably not designed well.

Using Code Metrics

A code metric is a statistic that reflects a frequency or ratio of occurrence of some kind of construct or syntactic relationship within a program. Metrics can be useful in discovering areas to examine for possible improvement, from the point of view of either reliability or performance. Here are some revealing metrics for a Java package or system.

- *Class size*—A high value may indicate that the class could be decomposed further, or that some generic behavior could be abstracted out.

- *Numbers of public, protected, and private methods per class*—A large number of public methods may indicate that the interface should be simplified and some methods made protected. General-purpose reusable classes will have more public methods than application-specific ones.

- *Number of inner classes in a class*—GUI-oriented components will have lots of inner adapter classes. Still, lots of inner classes may indicate that the class should be decomposed into several smaller classes, or reusable components abstracted out.

- *Average number of parameters per method*—A large number of parameters per method may indicate that the states of the system are poorly defined. Reusable components will generally have several variations of a method, which take different numbers of parameters, providing flexibility.

- *Ratio of interfaces and abstract classes to concrete classes*—A small number of interfaces or abstract classes may indicate a system that will be hard to extend.

- *Depth of inheritance*—The expected level of depth of inheritance depends on the complexity of the system. A shallow system may indicate limited reusability; conversely, a deep system may indicate over-abstraction and a design with poorly defined layers, since when programmers find they cannot get what they need from existing layers, they tend to create another.

- *Interclass attribute coupling*—In general, interclass attribute coupling should be minimal, limited to either intrapackage references, or inter-package references of final values. A small value should be expected of a good design.

- *Interclass method coupling*—A low value may indicate a monolithic design that is hard to extend.

- *Average depth of nesting of constructs within a class's methods*—Indicates the complexity of an implementation. A deeply nested section of code may indicate poor decomposition or lack of delegation.

- *Total number of interfaces and classes in a package or system*—A very large number may indicate that the system could be partitioned into more packages for better workflow management, maintainability, and understandability.

- *Ratio of internal classes to public classes within a package*—A small ratio may indicate a small number of monolithic classes; a very large ratio may indicate that the system will not be extensible.

- *Average number of classes extended or interfaces implemented per class in a package*—Indicates sharing of roles among objects. A small number may indicate a hard-wired design that combines object types with specific implementations. A large number may indicate a muddy design in which "everything can potentially do anything."

Absolute values do not indicate much, because applications are so different. It is more useful to compare values for different packages within a system. Values far from a project average should be analyzed, but may simply indicate that that package has different needs than other packages.

Of course, thinking about metrics is not useful unless you have a way to measure them. Reliable Software Technologies (www.rstcorp.com) makes such a tool, called TotalMetric.

Developing Coding Standards

Coding standards are the rules by which programmers on a project must live. Most programmers hate coding standards, because invariably they include rules that go against one's own aesthetic sense. Programmers take a great deal of pride in their work, and want to be able to identify a piece of work as their creation.

For this reason I don't like to go overboard in mandating a specific style. Maintainability is the goal, not uniformity except when it enhances maintainability. Uniformity is not a good thing in itself. Each rule in a standard has to have a business reason for being there. Do not make too many rules; programmers have enough to remember. Rules should have significant value to be in a guideline; a guideline should not have any rules that are there just for the sake of making rules. Thick coding standards do not get read. Coding standards that address tangible programming issues are interesting, and not only get read, but get discussed over lunch.

You should develop criteria for what to make beans. Decide how completely you will follow the bean introspection guidelines, since following them to the letter and in entirety is very burdensome if applied for all work. How "bean-like" you should make something depends on what its role will be in your organization over time. (See the "Beans" chapter for more details on this issue.)

You should develop your own coding standards, but you may use the following list as a guide or starting point.

- Standard headers—Define the standard header for all your project's code. If you have legal rights to protect, state them in the header. The header can also include contact information and change history.

- Package names—Package names should be all lower case, and be prefixed with the Internet domain of your organization, but with the components of the domain name in reverse order. For example, a for-profit organization with a domain "ourcompany.com" should create packages with names like "com.ourcompany.ourproject," "com.ourcompany.anotherproject," and "com.ourcompany.ourproject.packageabc." Do not use capitals for the class A prefix (e.g., COM); this was a bad recommendation in early Javasoft documentation and is being abandoned in favor of all lower case.

- Creating a package description—See the section "Packages Are Field-Replaceable Units" in the chapter on deployment platforms and techniques for a description of manifest package descriptions.

- Using "import" v. explicit scoping—Be conservative in how many packages you import with a wildcard. In general, import package classes explicitly.

- Use interfaces to shield against change, to allow overlapping of roles, and to allow for alternative implementations.

  If you must extend a class that has an interface, consider doing it like this:

  ```
  interface A {}

  class AImpl {}

  interface APlus extends A {}

  class APlusImpl extends AImpl implements APlus {}
  ```

or

```
class APlusImpl implements APlus {}
```

This makes it possible to largely hide the existence of the APlusImpl concrete type from the rest of your code. The only dependence might be when a constructor must be invoked.

- Avoid using nonfinal static data. Browsers use the same class loader instance for applets that have the same codebase, so one applet can clobber another's static data. (This is also a potential security weakness for signed applets.)

- Do not use public variables unless you need to for some reason, or if they are final. Also, remember that unlike methods, variables are statically bound (i.e., they are not virtual), so there is no advantage to overriding them—so declare them private, not protected.

- Declare methods public or protected. Use no modifier at all if you want other classes within the package to be able to call the method, but not classes outside the package.

- Decide where to put braces and indentation within a block, and be consistent for all kinds of constructs.

  This is by far the most "personal" issue for programmers. The location of braces affects the appearance and to some extent the organization of a program. The two most popular alternatives are:

  Keep matching braces in the same column.

```
void m()
{
}

class C
{
}

try
{
}
catch (Exception e)
{
}
```

...and so on...

Start the first brace on the same line as any leading construct or token, and line up the ending brace with the start of that construct or token.

```
void m() {
}

class C {
}

try {
}
catch (Exception e) {
}
```

Most programmers indent one tab for constructs appearing inside braces.

I will not go into all the possible nuances, variations, and minor issues, because they *are* minor and I suggest your guidelines not go into purely style details either, such as whether the "catch" token should be on the same line as the preceding brace. These kinds of rules frustrate programmers primarily because they impose restrictions with no real gain, and often the right choice depends on the complexity of the code in which a construct is used.

However, sometimes indentation is important, especially if there are many nested constructs. Consider the case of an expression that creates a new instance of an anonymous class, whose constructor takes some kind of adapter class as an argument, which must also be anonymous.

```
MyClass c = new MyClass
(
   new MyAdapter()
   {
      {
         ...initialization code goes here, since an
         anonymous class cannot have a constructor...
      }

      ...methods and variables...
   }
);
```

Using the alternative style discussed above, this would look like

```
MyClass c = new MyClass(new MyAdapter() {
   {
```

```
        ...initialization code goes here, since an
          anonymous class
        cannot have a constructor...
    }


    ...methods and variables...
   });
```

While this uses less indentation, less is not always better. It is not clear what the rules should be for a brace following another brace, and parentheses following a brace. Furthermore, with deep nesting, it is hard to match braces up unless there is a clear visual clue, such as requiring that starting and ending constructs of all kinds be placed in the same column, unless they are able to be placed on the same line.

There is also a style that is used frequently, even by JavaSoft programmers, which surprises me greatly. I personally find it so hard to read that whenever I have to read code which uses this style, I first put it into a word processor so that I can highlight sections to remind me where they begin and end. The style uses no indentation for classes or method implementations. For example,

```
public class HardToRead {
/** Hard to read method.
 * We'll try to make this method as hard to find as
 * possible.
 */
public int hardToFindMethod() {
// This is code inside the method.
int x = 0;
if (x == 0) {
   System.out.println("Always true");
} else {
   System.out.println("Never will happen");
}
}
}
```

Ouch! Yet one sees it a lot, or variations of it. Without getting into aesthetics at all, the problem with this style is that it is extremely hard to locate features. For example, finding where a method begins is difficult because method beginnings occur in the same column as variable declarations, so columns cannot be used as a visual cue. The same holds true for braces. This kind of reminds me of Fortran-66, in which every line began in the same column. Needless to say, I do not recommend this style.

- Use parentheses in expressions. Do not rely on operator precedence or association rules, primarily because most programmers do not remember all these rules offhand, and it makes reading code difficult.

- Do not impose excessive ordering on items declared in classes and methods.

  Different ordering is appropriate for different designs. However, it is helpful to group overridden methods according to the superclass or interface in which they are originally declared.

- Naming: You would be advised to use the Beans naming conventions (see the chapter on beans), regardless of whether a class is intended as a bean or not. There are some naming issues that are not addressed in the beans spec. These include:

  > Naming of interfaces

  > Naming of implementations

  > Naming of event signaling (generating) methods

  However, for implementations there is an RMI convention in which a concrete class that implements an interface is usually named after the interface, with the suffix "Impl." Also, most beans name event signaling methods by prefixing the event name with "fire." Interfaces represent base types, so they should have names that look like types, not specific implementations. I therefore do not prefer using special prefixes or suffixes on interface names. It is also a Java convention that type names begin with a capital, and instance variables begin with a small letter, and both use mixed case.

- If you create an exception, throw it from the same line. The reason is that the constructor for Throwable fills in the stack trace information, and if you throw the exception from a different line, this information will not reflect the line from which the exception was thrown.

- Distinguish between these categories of error conditions:

  - Non-Runtime Exceptions: normal "lifecycle" exceptions that represent user errors and other conditions which can be expected to occur during the lifecycle of the system, and the cause of which can be determined in the program.

  - RuntimeExceptions: Error conditions that should never occur, and for which the explanation cannot be deduced within the code; for these, throw a RuntimeException. Catch RuntimeExceptions at the outermost level, in a Throwable "firewall"; for RuntimeExceptions, display a dialog indicating a fatal error and possibly allowing the user to attempt to save data or commit or abort transactions. A method which can throw a RuntimeException does not have to declare that exception in its throws clause.

- Errors: Error conditions that represent a misconfiguration of the environment, but do not represent a programming error, and for which there is no recovery. For example, a database manager might throw an error indicating that the schema is out of sync with the application; this may be unrecoverable in most cases, but not if the application is designed to deal with this by deploying new up-to-date application code. If an application is not prepared to deal with an error, it should perform any cleanup and let the error propagate out to the Throwable firewall. Errors do not have to be declared in the throws clause.

- Inside a `finally` block, catch all possible exceptions that might occur within the block.

- For an interface method, anticipate the most general kind of Exception an implementation might throw. Consider throwing Exception in interface methods that might have unanticipated implementations. Recognize that if your interface methods do not declare a fundamental enough exception type, implementors will not be able to throw exceptions.

- Comments

  The most important thing is that a comment say more than the obvious. For example, a method called "setX()" should not be documented as "Sets the value of X." It should say what the intended purpose of the method is, for example, if it is merely an accessor or has other side effects; that is, the role the method or construct plays. Do not be concerned with grammatical issues unless you plan to hire someone to proof the code for linguistic correctness. Programmers should spend their time thinking about program correctness, not grammatical correctness. However, programmers should endeavor to be precise when writing comments.

  Comments on major features like classes and methods should give additional information. The javadoc guidelines serve as a standard for this. I feel this standard is defective for the reasons outlined below. In the absence of something better, the javadoc comments are workable, but if you are using an IDE and do not need to use javadoc, you might consider ignoring the javadoc guidelines. Choosing this path, you should take the best of javadoc and leave the worst behind. Specifically, comment headers should include an overall description of the method, including its purpose and constraints for use, references to related items, and possibly author and version, although the latter should perhaps be used only for the entire file or class during initial development, and used at the method granularity during later maintenance phases. Comments for parameters and exceptions can be placed side by side with the associated items. This can even be done for the return value, if desired, rather than putting it in a header, far removed from the place of definition. For example consider the following fictitious method definition:

```java
/**
 * Perform any spanking that may be warranted. This is a complete
 * operation, which
 * actually invokes the spanking paddle driver to complete the execution
 * of the spanks.
 * Spanking occurs synchronously in the calling thread; i.e., this
 * method blocks until the
 * spanks have been delivered. This method is part of this class's
 * public interface, and is
 * intended to be called by any StaffManager client.
 *
 * See also:
 * computeNumberOfSpanks()
 * SpankDriverFactory.getSpankDriver()
 * SpankDriver.spank()
 */
public int doSpanking        // returns the number of spanks actually
                             // delivered
(
    int hours,               // hours since arrival; must always be positive.
                             // The input value is checked, and a
                             // BadValueException
                             // is thrown if it is not positive.

    boolean spank            // If true, the user should be spanked if they
                             // are late logging on; i.e., if hours >
                             // StaffManager.GRACE
)
throws
    BadValueException,       // Thrown if hours is not valid
    CannotSpankError         // Thrown if a device driver error - we do not
                             // have to declare
                             // this, but want to force calling code to
                             // handle it
{
    ...
}
```

This is far better than having to retype (and maintain in sync) all parameters and exceptions redundantly, far from where the parameters and exceptions are declared. A well-designed document generator would easily be able to extract the comments from this method definition and associate them with the appropriate constructs; it might even be able to generate a list of "see-also" items, based on references in the method body (which could perhaps have special comment tags next to them, directly where used). [Note: some day, if I have time, I am going to write a *real* code documentation generator for Java.]

The javadoc program is not able to do any of this, and requires you to retype parameter names and exceptions in the header, after you have typed them where they are defined, and use an arcane and unnecessary syntax using @ symbols. Unfortunately, the javadoc guidelines some-how found their way into the Java language specification. This does not mean, however, that one has to follow them. Again, if you have an alter-native means of generating documentation, you do not need to adhere to javadoc's ridiculous redundancies.

Comments should also include what the assumptions of the program-mer are, what side effects occur, and the protocol of use for any con-struct. Can a method be called more than once? Does it rely on anything else occurring first, or is it completely self-contained? Does it modify any of its input parameters? If the return type is an object, is the object freshly constructed, or is it merely a reference to something passed in? Is the effect of the method "deep" (its effect immediately propagates and is complete) or "shallow" (the method is just an accessor, and other methods need to pick up where this one leaves off to complete the oper-ation)? If the method is a constructor (especially a default constructor), under what circumstances can the constructor be used with new to cre-ate a valid instance?

If a method implements a method specification from an interface, or overrides a method from a superclass, the method's header comment should say so. Even better, you should group methods together accord-ing to which superclasses they override or interfaces they implement. For example,

```
interface A
{
   public void a();
}

interface B extends A
{
   public void b();
}

class CB implements B
{
```

```
// From B:

public void b() {}

// From A:

public void a() {}
}
```

- When returning a mutable type, never return something that was passed in unless the usage of the method specifically requires that (i.e., the method's purpose is to transform an argument). Violating this can lead to bugs that are difficult to locate because if code calls a method which returns an object, and the code thinks it is the only holder of that object and it is not, the object might change unpredictably.

- Put code that is enabled or disabled by program configuration switches in separate classes, so they do not need to be loaded if the associated switches are turned off.

- All instantiable reusable classes should override the Object methods equals(), hashcode(), and clone(). A shortcoming of the Java language is that there is no way to specify that an implementation *must always* be overridden in every subclass. Classes that override clone() as a public method should implement the Cloneable interface.

- Make all classes implement Serializable, unless there is a specific reason not to. (If a base class implements Serializable, however, derived classes retain the implementation.)

- Adhere to Beans guidelines for what should be transient.

- Only call final methods in a constructor. Unfortunately, Java does not let you specify a constructor that all subclasses automatically inherit (except for the default constructor). As a result, you may sometimes end up creating an initialization method of your own, and calling it in constructors. If you do this, you will want to make sure that this initialization method is final so that subclasses cannot override it and unwittingly change the way super() behaves.

- Don't rely on finalize().

- Watch for multiple thread access to unsynchronized objects, especially in UI adapter classes; every method that modifies a class variable (as opposed to a method variable) is suspect. Every wait() should have a corresponding notify(), and vice versa, unless proven otherwise. Always obtain object locks in the same sequence when multiple locks are needed. (See the "Threads" chapter for details.)

- Don't kill running threads without forcing them to block in a well-defined state—or at least do so with care. Remember that when you kill a thread, it releases its locks, even if it was not done updating an object.

- Watch for runaway object creation. Nullify references no longer used.

- Explicitly close or dispose of resources such as server connections. When using socket connections, close any buffered stream objects, as well as the primitive socket object, since many implementations leave the socket open even after you close the buffered stream object.

- Define all constant values in resource files or classes.

- Define properties for all configurable values, and properties to point to all resources.

- Do not rely on object serialization for long-term storage of objects, unless you are confident that the classes involved will not change over time, or that changes will be compatible. In general, changes which add attributes and new class types are compatible, and changes which remove attributes and change structure are not.

CHAPTER
2

- **Characters**
- **Converting from Other Latin-Character-Mapped Representations**
- **Multinational Font Support**
- **Locales**
- **Formatting and Parsing of Localized Values**
- **Resources**
- **Resource Bundles**
- **Parameterized Resources**
- **Keyboard Entry**

Properties, Resources, and Internationalization

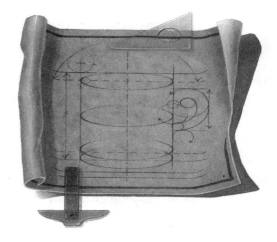

Applications that are to support many users in a global scenario need to be internationalized to support localized currencies, time and date representations, and number formats. Such applications need to be configurable for a locale by external means without the need to change code and recompile. They also need to be easily deployable, in such a way that moving the application does not break assumptions about the locations of resources needed by the application. These are issues addressed by the Internationalization and Resource APIs.

Characters

In order to understand strings, fonts, and international character sets, you first have to understand characters. A character is represented by a "code point"—a numeric value which uniquely identifies that character. Java uses the Unicode character set for all character representations. This standard defines a Universal Character Set (UCS) consisting of 16-bit characters. It is identical to the ISO 10646 UCS-2 (16-bit) character standard. The ISO standard also defines four-byte characters, UCS-4, but that is not included in Unicode.

A character is visually depicted by a "glyph," a graphic representation. This has nothing to do with Unicode, which does not address glyphs or character fonts. A "font" is a glyph set. It can cover any range of code points chosen by the font's supplier (usually a commercial font vendor). A font is a graphic and stylistic rendering of all the characters within a code point range chosen by the font supplier.

A given font may also have variations—called "faces"—to represent bold, italic, and other character styles. When you obtain a font, you are obtaining someone's artistic implementation of a particular code point range.

Java 1.2 lets you specify fonts by the vendor-supplied font names; or you can specify a "logical" font name. The logical name specifies a generic font that is universal for all Java platforms, and therefore completely portable; each Java installation maps system fonts to these logical names via the font.properties file. You can also specify a vendor-specific font name using the Java 1.2 GraphicsEnvironment.getFont() method. In either case, a particular vendor font is selected, which maps some code point range to displayable glyphs. This has nothing to do with the language intended for display, except that the selected font may include Unicode ranges which represent the code points used by a particular language.

In the Unicode world, you do not get a font "for a language." The Unicode code point space is not divided by language. While some languages are represented primarily by a certain range, others share ranges. For example, the Latin-1 range, 0-255, is a set of characters shared by most Western languages. A group of related characters is called a "script," and the range of contiguous Unicode values that represent that script is called a "code block."

Unicode allows for more than one representation of certain characters. For example, composite characters such as "ü" and "ll" can be represented either by a single Unicode character or by a pair of characters, consisting of the base character followed by a "nonspacing" character to add the additional feature, such as the umlaut in "ü." Unicode defines a mechanism for transforming composite characters into base and nonspacing character pairs so that the base character can be retrieved if it is needed for operations which treat the base character and composite character the same, (e.g., if "u" is to be treated the same as "ü"). Unicode has special control characters for modifying the direction of character presentation, switching from left-to-right to right-to-left midstream.

Converting from Other Latin-Character-Mapped Representations

Characters in Java are represented in Unicode, but most computing platforms do not use Unicode as their normal means of storing character data in files. It is good to use the platform's normal format, because then you can exchange data with other programs more easily.

In order to support the conversion of character data native formats and Unicode, Java provides two kinds of classes:

    `Reader`—transforms an external character source to Java representation (i.e., Unicode)

    `Writer`—transforms Java character representation to an external form

There are concrete implementations of these for different data sources, including FileReader, PrintWriter, and others, as well as generic InputStreamReader and OutputStreamWriter classes.

In many cases, the encoded value of a character is a value that identifies a glyph in the font sets supported by a particular platform. For example, Latin-1 font sets use the Latin-1 encoded values to identify a character within the font set for display. It is important to understand this, that encodings are usually font values, but not always—it depends on the kind of encoding, and if there are font families that support that encoding.

Most 8-bit encodings such as Latin-1 have the disadvantage that characters not representable by the encoding are lost whenever Unicode characters are written in the format. Nevertheless, it is necessary to have encoders for the 8-bit formats supported by the platform, and any platform for which you have to generate output or read input.

An 8-bit encoding that does not have this loss of information deficiency is UCS Transformation Format (UTF)-8. This format is defined in the Unicode standard as a way to represent Unicode data in a manner that is backward compatible with 7-bit ASCII.

UTF-8 represents 7-bit ASCII values (which are also identical to Latin-1 values in the 7-bit range 0–127) in their normal way. However, if the high bit is not zero, the byte is understood to begin a non-ASCII multibyte character: the number of "1" bits that occur before the first "0" bit indicate the number of bytes in the multibyte sequence. Using this scheme, the representation of a stream of ASCII-7 characters is identical to a UTF-8 stream containing the same characters. If a non-ASCII character needs to be represented, the escape sequence just described is used. UTF-8 is described in RFC 2044.

When you construct an InputStreamReader, you can choose between two forms of the constructor:

> `InputStreamReader(InputStream is, String encoding)`—Construct an input stream reader, for the specified stream encoding.

> `InputStreamReader(InputStream is)`—Construct an input stream reader, but use the default encoding for the platform

The second form calls sun.io.ByteToCharConverter.getDefault() to get the platform's default encoding. This is determined by the system property "file.encoding," or the default value of "8859_1" (which is Latin-1) if the property is not set.

In order to actually find the decoder, the constructor then calls

```
sun.io.ByteToCharConverter.getConverter()
```

This method uses the property "file.encoding.pkg" to construct the full package-qualified name of the byte-to-char converter class, using the template

```
<file-encoding-package>.ByteToChar<encoding>
```

For example, the name of the installed UTF-8 encoding is "UTF8," and the default value of the "file.encoding.pkg" location is "sun.io", so the converter is in sun.io.ByteToCharUTF8. Thus, to install your own decoder package, you can set the system property "file.encoding.pkg" and put all your decoder classes in there. This is a little bit inflexible, because doing so causes you to lose access to the installed decoders, so this technique may be refined in the final 1.2 or future Java releases.

The encodings supported (conversions to and from these are installed in package sun.io) in Java 1.1 are as follows. You can look in package sun.io to see if there are any additional ones in your Java release.

```
UTF8—Standard—UTF-8
8859_1 - ISO Latin-1
8859_2 - ISO Latin-2
8859_3 - ISO Latin-3
8859_4 - ISO Latin-4
8859_5 - ISO Latin/Cyrillic
8859_6 - ISO Latin/Arabic
8859_7 - ISO Latin/Greek
8859_8 - ISO Latin/Hebrew
8859_9 - ISO Latin-5
Big5 - Big 5 Traditional Chinese
CNS11643 - CNS 11643 Traditional Chinese
Cp1250 - Windows Eastern Europe / Latin-2
Cp1251 - Windows Cyrillic
Cp1252 - Windows Western Europe / Latin-1
Cp1253 - Windows Greek
Cp1254 - Windows Turkish
Cp1255 - Windows Hebrew
Cp1256 - Windows Arabic
Cp1257 - Windows Baltic
Cp1258 - Windows Vietnamese
Cp437 - PC Original
Cp737 - PC Greek
Cp775 - PC Baltic
Cp850 - PC Latin-1
Cp852 - PC Latin-2
Cp855 - PC Cyrillic
Cp857 - PC Turkish
Cp860 - PC Portuguese
Cp861 - PC Icelandic
Cp862 - PC Hebrew
```

```
Cp863 - PC Canadian French
Cp864 - PC Arabic
Cp865 - PC Nordic
Cp866 - PC Russian
Cp869 - PC Modern Greek
Cp874 - Windows Thai
EUCJIS - Japanese EUC
GB2312 - GB2312-80 Simplified Chinese
JIS - JIS
KSC5601 - KSC5601 Korean
MacArabic - Macintosh Arabic
MacCentralEurope - Macintosh Latin-2
MacCroatian - Macintosh Croatian
MacCyrillic - Macintosh Cyrillic
MacDingbat - Macintosh Dingbat
MacGreek - Macintosh Greek
MacHebrew - Macintosh Hebrew
MacIceland - Macintosh Iceland
MacRoman - Macintosh Roman
MacRomania - Macintosh Romania
MacSymbol - Macintosh Symbol
MacThai - Macintosh Thai
MacTurkish - Macintosh Turkish
MacUkraine - Macintosh Ukraine
SJIS - PC and Windows Japanese
```

Multinational Font Support

As explained earlier, in a theoretical sense you do not install a font "for a language." However, in a practical sense you do, because usually a given font will contain glyphs for code point ranges that fall within the range used by a particular language. In fact, the font implementation will likely use a non-Unicode encoding for its code points, and a conversion class will be needed. The conversion class is specified in the font.properties file. The font.properties file therefore contains primarily two kinds of entries: mappings from the Java "logical" fonts to actual vendor fonts (which may be designed to contain glyphs for certain languages), and the character encoding class to use for each logical font. Thus, in the implementation available at this writing, for a given logical font all encodings must be the same.

If you use logical font names, the system uses the encoder specified in the font-properties file to convert from Unicode representation to the font code representation. However, if you specify a vendor font explicitly, the system must map between Unicode values and vendor font glyphs. At the time of this writing, the implementation of this is still being finalized.

Locales

A "locale" is a combination of language and geographic location. Based on a locale, it is possible to select a set of characters—hopefully contiguous—which can represent all the symbols needed by that locale.

It is up to the application or individual classes to make use of locales. However, the AWT components have a locale attribute, so that they can be localized:

```
Component comp = new Button();
comp.setLocale(java.util.Locale.US);
```

Below we will see how to make use of this.

Specifying a locale does not automatically cause different fonts to be used, and so on. The whole idea of Unicode is that you can display any character. Characters are not language-specific. Unicode defines a uniform character space. It is therefore up to the application to obtain different strings or graphics (i.e., resources) to use, depending on the locale.

There are two versions of the constructor for locale:

```
Locale(String language, String country);
Locale(String language, String country, String variant);
```

The language parameter is a string containing the (lower case) two-letter ISO-639 code for the language. (These codes are listed in the language code table at the end of this chapter.) The country parameter is a string containing the (upper case) two-letter ISO-3166 code for the country. (These code values are listed in the country code table at the end of this chapter.) If country is an empty string, the default country for the language is used. The variant parameter is provided for situations in which there may be language (or currency, etc.) variants within a region. Use Locale.getDefault() to get the system default locale.

Formatting and Parsing of Localized Values

Once you have a locale defined, you can use Java's built-in locale-sensitive number, currency, and date-time formatters, from package java.text.

Numbers

A number formatter can be used to parse and display numeric values in different formats in a locale-sensitive manner. Different locales have different ways of representing numbers. For example, while in the United States the number "one-thousand-three-hundred-point-three-zero" would be represented as "1,300.30," in some European countries it would be represented as "1.300,30." Here is an example of getting a locale-specific number formatter, using it to parse a number value from a string, and then formatting the same value for output again:

```
NumberFormat nf = NumberFormat.getInstance(locale);
double d = nf.parse("1.2005e+3").doubleValue();// parsing input
String s = nf.format(d);                    // formatting for output
```

Currencies

Currency values are represented differently in different locales, including the unit of currency symbol, and the decimal location and style. Here is an example of getting a locale-specific number formatter, and using it to parse a currency value for that locale, and then format the value again for output for the locale:

```
NumberFormat cf = NumberFormat.getCurrencyInstance(locale);
double d = cf.parse("$1,200.50").doubleValue();// parsing input
String s = cf.format(d);                    // formatting for output
```

Date and Time Values

Dates and times are represented differently in different locales. You use the Calendar class to perform most date and time operations. Here we get the current date-time, and then use a Calendar object to get the current hour value:

```
Date d = new Date();
Calendar c = Calendar().getInstance();
int h = c.get(Calendar.HOUR);
```

Use the DateFormat class to parse and format dates:

```
DateFormat df = DateFormat.getDateInstance(locale);
Date d = df.parse("12 Jan 2012");// parsing input
String s = df.format(d);// formatting for output
```

Resources

A "resource" is a collection of information which can be retrieved by name, and which relocates automatically with the program. A resource can therefore be packaged with an application, and there is a well-defined mechanism for retrieving it within the program. Some examples of resources include:

- **Image files**
- **Image icons**
- **Text**
- **Fonts** (see the Swing font use categories)
- **Serialized Java objects**
- **Audio files**

The class loader knows how to find a resource based on a location relative to where it loaded its classes from. For example, the following call to getResource() looks in the class's codebase for the image resource's URL:

```
URL imageUrl = getClass().getResource("IMAGE.GIF");
```

Once you have the URL, you can use the Applet.getImage(URL) method if you are in an applet, or the Toolkit.getImage(URL) method if you are not in an applet. For resources for which a URL is inappropriate, use the getResourceAsStream() method, which returns an input stream.

A resource name is just a string, however. If you name a resource "abc.def," it does *not* interpret the "abc." as meaning package abc.

There are also other resource-retrieval mechanisms, as discussed in the chapter on Java Beans.

Resources in Subdirectories

Resources obtained via the class loader are located relative to the codebase from which the class was loaded. If the class is in a package, it will look in the subdirectory associated with that package, again relative to the codebase of the class. This is default behavior; class loaders for specific purposes (e.g., Castanet's class loader) are free to override this behavior; the only common aspect is that the application should not need to specify a hard location—it should be relative to the current class. A class loader treats JAR files just like directories, so you should put your resources into the appropriate package subdirectory before creating the JAR file.

You can refer to a resource in another package by giving a fully qualified name, using URL syntax, with a leading "/" indicating the codebase, such as

```
/package1/package2/resources/IMAGE.GIF
```

For example, the following program, which belongs to package "p", accesses an image resource in package "q," which is parallel to p in the package hierarchy:

```
package p;
import java.awt.*;
import java.net.*;
public class C extends Canvas
{
  public static void main(String[] args)
  {
    Frame f = new Frame();
    f.setSize(150, 100);
    f.show();
    Toolkit k = f.getToolkit();
    C c = new C();
    URL url = c.getClass().getResource("/q/image.gif");
    i = k.getImage(url);
    f.add("Center", c);
    f.validate();
    f.repaint();
  }

  public void paint(Graphics g)
  {
    g.drawImage(i, 10, 20, this);
```

```
    }

    static Image i;
}
```

If placed in a JAR file, the JAR file structure might be

```
MANIFEST.MF        META-INF\
C.class            p\
image.gif          q\
```

To run this program from the command line, all you need to do is put the JAR file in your classpath and type "java p.C". The image should display, regardless of which directory you are in when you run the program. Thus, the getResource() method interprets "/q/image.gif" as meaning file resource "image.gif" in subdirectory "q" relative to the codebase of the class that getResource() is called for.

Resource Bundles

A "resource bundle" is a collection of resources or resource names, representing resources associated specifically with a given locale. The class ResourceBundle has a method, getBundle(), used to obtain a resource bundle of a given name for a given locale.

There are two kinds of resource bundle; the getBundle() method looks for one kind, and then, if it does not find it, looks for the other kind. You can therefore implement your resource bundles in either of these two manners. The two kinds are

- A subclass of ResourceBundle, according to certain naming conventions

- A resource .properties file, according to naming conventions

You can therefore provide a concrete class that has the ResourceBundle methods "hard-wired" for your application; or you can use the resource property file mechanism provided with Java. If you do the former, your bundle class name must follow the convention <bundle-name>_<locale>, where "locale" is the string representation of the locale obtained via toString(). A resource property file must be named in a similar manner, but ending in ".properties."

For example, suppose we have a resource properties file called "MyResourceNames_en_US.properties." According to the naming convention for property files, this file is for the locale whose string equivalent is "en_US"; that is, the English language as written in the United States. (We could also have used simply "US"—it would have recognized "US" as a country code, and applied the default language for that region.) To obtain the bundle called "MyResource-Names" for the US locale, we could do the following:

```
ResourceBundle bundle =
  ResourceBundle.getBundle("MyResourceNames", locale);
```

The getBundle() method will first look for a property class, named according to the conventions, and if it does not find one, will look for a .property file and use it to construct an instance of PropertyResourceBundle, which is a subclass of ResourceBundle and takes an input stream as input: the .property file. This two-step search allows you to defer the decision of which bundles to implement with ResourceBundle classes, which are potentially more efficient.

Property files contain name-value pairs. Suppose our property file contains

```
myclass.image.filename=\\images\\MYFILE.GIF
```

This line defines the property "myclass.image.filename" to have the value "\images\MYFILE.GIF." Note that the backslash character is treated as a Java escape character (this is how you can enter Unicode values, if you do not have a Unicode text editor), so we must use two in sequence to represent one literally. (The use of a backslash in a file path looks as if it is file-system dependent, but actually it is not, because if the application is deployed in a JAR file, the JAR API will interpret it as meaning a subdirectory, regardless of what kind of system the program is executing on.)

Once you have a reference to a bundle defined in a property file, you can obtain the value of a name value pair by using the getString() method. For example, here I get the value of the "myclass.image.filename" name-value pair:

```
String imageName = bundle.getString("myclass.image.filename");
// Gets the image file resource name specified in the bundle
    property file
```

We can then get the actual resource, as already demonstrated:

```
URL imageUrl = getClass().getResource(imageName);
```

While the above resource name looks like a property and it is stored in a file that ends with a ".property" suffix, I hesitate to call it a property because we have not created any Java Property objects. This mechanism has nothing to do with Java system properties (obtained via System.getProperty()) or any Java Property object. You are free, however, if it is convenient for you, to create a Property object to contain the values obtained from the bundle, but this is not done automatically. (Note that the values of many Java system properties are defined in special property files. These files generally do not use the PropertyResourceBundle mechanism, and the mechanism for loading them is unique to the class of properties.)

Creating a Resource Bundle Class

If you prefer a class implementation over a .property file, you can implement your resource bundle as a class quite easily. You can either extend the ResourceBundle class and implement the handleGetObject() method, or you can extend the ListResourceBundle class, which provides a handleGetObject() method implementation.

The following example creates a resource bundle base class, which is used when the specified locale cannot be found, and a German-language version of the class, which extends from it. The private Object array contains the actual resource values that are returned when a resource is asked for by name. Note that one resource is an object of a user-defined type ("StartState"), and the other is a string. In the German case, the string contains a Unicode value—the two-byte hexadecimal value for "ö," which is 0x00f6.

```
public class MyResources extends ListResourceBundle
{
   public Object[][] getContents()
   {
     return contents;
   }
   private static Object[][] contents =
   {
      { "com.ourco.ourproj.startstate", new StartState() },
      { "com.ourco.ourproj.title", "Today is a beautiful day" }
   };
}
public class MyResources_de extends MyResources
{
   public Object[][] getContents()
   {
     return contents;
   }
   private static Object[][] contents=
   {
      { "com.ourco.ourproj.startstate", new GermanStartState() },
      { "com.ourco.ourproj.title",
        "Heute ist ein sh\u00f6nes tag" }
   };
}
```

Encapsulating Resource Bundle Access

A useful technique for encapsulating access to the correct resources bundle and associated resources is to create a single utility class which accesses the bundle and all resources in a uniform way. Such a class is often referred to as a "resource adapter". This class implements the application's policy for determining which locale is used (e.g., by using the default locale for the platform, or by reading the locale from a property), and provides a convenient interface for retrieving specific types of resources with specialized methods. For example, a resource adapter might have a getMessageString() method, which retrieves a particular message for the locale, according to the application's message display requirements. Other possible methods might include getImage(), getHelpURL(), and getTooltip(). In each case, the application code does not have to perform the work of determining the locale, getting the resource bundle, and extracting the required resource—this is all done by the resource adapter and its specialized methods.

Parameterized Resources

You can create parameterized resource strings, and then effect parameter replacement with the MessageFormat class. For example, suppose our resource .property file contains

```
myclass.message=Please select {0} or more recipes from {1}...
```

Once we have the bundle, we can get the resource string using

```
String message = bundle.getString("myclass.message");
```

This string contains "Please select {0} or more recipes from {1}...". We can perform substitution on this as follows:

```
Object[] a;
String[] s1 = { "3", "the handy book" };
String[] s2 = { "4", "the big book" };
if (hunger.equals("moderate")) a = s1;
else a = s2
String substitutedMessage = MessageFormat.format(message, a);
```

In this example, the String array is used to obtain values to substitute into the message string.

The MessageFormat class has much more power than this, however. You can use it to perform type-specific formatting (e.g., to format date and time values) and to perform conditional formatting. As an illustration, suppose our message string contains

```
"Please select {0} or more recipes from {0,choice,0#the handy
    book|2#the big book} ...";
```

The syntax "{0,choice,..." indicates the start of a choice expression, sort of like an inline switch statement; the "0#..." provides the expression to use if the {0} parameter value is 0, and the "2#..." following the " | " provides the value to use if {0} evaluates to anything greater than or equal to 2. Thus, the following code will produce "Please select 0 or more recipes from the handy book..." when "hunger" equals "moderate"; it will produce "Please select 1 or more recipes from the handy book..." when "hunger" equals "good", and "Please select 3 or more recipes from the big book..." when "hunger" is anything but "moderate" or "good":

```
Object[] a;
if (hunger.equals("moderate")) a = new Integer[] { new
  Integer(0) };
else if (hunger.equals("good")) a = new Integer[] { new
  Integer(1) };
else a = new Integer[] { new Integer(3) };
String substitutedMessage = MessageFormat.format(message, a);
System.out.println(substitutedMessage);
```

This feature is most often used to implement conditions where a choice needs to be made between using words such as "one," "both," and single versus plural forms.

Keyboard Entry

Operating systems usually come in localized versions, which provide character fonts for the locale and resource files with localized messages. It is up to the application to make use of these, and many native applications come in locale-specific versions. An internationalized Java application will have resource files for the locales in which it is deployed or viewed. If the user wants to enter data, they likely have a keyboard specific to their locale, and their system's keyboard mappings will be set accordingly. As long as the application uses localized resource files using Unicode characters, the user should be able to see locale-specific messages in a font in their language.

This approach works fine for European languages, which have small alphabets. It does not work so well for many Asian languages, which have large sets of symbols. For these languages, it is necessary to provide special functions for choosing from symbol candidate lists. Entering a single symbol may require several steps using a standard keyboard.

A utility for allowing the user to enter and choose symbols in this way is called an "input method tool." Asian language versions of operating systems such as Windows come with input method tools. There are also third-party tools which use the operating system's input method API to implement additional functionality, or perhaps provide a different style of input. A popular one for Chinese is called Chinese Star. It allows the user to enter han-yu-pin-yin Latin-character representations of Chinese symbols, and maps them to the corresponding Chinese symbols. For example, if you have Chinese Star, you can use it to enter Chinese characters into an AWT text field or text area.

The Java Input Method Framework (JIMF) is designed to accommodate Asian symbol entry. It allows you to receive events from the system's input method tool, and from those events obtain inputs generated by the user using the tool. Using this interface, it is possible to bypass the standard ways components respond to text input. The eventual goal of the framework is to enable "on-the-spot" editing, in which Asian characters can be entered, selected, and edited in place in ordinary text components, instead of in a special side window (called a "root" window). At the moment, the framework requires use of the host's native input method tool, which then generates the required Java events to notify the component when new characters have been selected.

There are two primary aspects to this scenario: receiving notification of text input events from the input method tool, and responding to requests for display-related information from the input method tool. The input method tool may want to know, for example, what section of text is currently highlighted in the component. To support this, all components (as of Java 1.2) have a method called getInput-MethodRequests(). This method returns an object that implements java.awt.im.InputMethodRequests which has the required callback methods. These methods are:

```
public Rectangle getOffsetLocation(TextHitInfo offset)
public TextHitInfo getLocationOffset(int x, int y)
public int getInsertPositionOffset()
public AttributedCharacterIterator getCommittedText(
  int beginIndex, int endIndex, String[] attributeNames)
public int getCommittedTextLength()
public AttributedCharacterIterator
  cancelLatestCommittedText(String[] attributeNames)
public AttributedCharacterIterator getSelectedText(String[]
  attributeNames)
```

Since all components implement this method, you only need to override it if you are providing your own version of this object, in order to respond in a custom way to requests from the input method tool. This would be necessary to implement on-the-spot editing, for example.

If you merely want to override how the component responds to new input, you only need to provide an InputMethodEvent adapter by implementing java.awt.event.InputMethodListener, which has these methods:

```
void inputMethodTextChanged(InputMethodEvent event)
void caretPositionChanged(InputMethodEvent event)
```

Add the adapter to your component by calling addInputMethodListener(), and the component will then receive text events from the input method tool. Input method editing has to be enabled, however, and for that you call the enableInput-Methods() method with an argument of *true*. Here is a simple example:

```
import java.awt.*;
import java.awt.event.*;
public class Demo extends Panel
{
```

```
   private TextArea ta;

   public Demo()
   {
      ta = new TextArea();
      ta.setSize(500, 200);
      add(ta);
      ta.enableInputMethods(true);
      ta.addInputMethodListener
      (
         new InputMethodListener()
         {
            public void inputMethodTextChanged(InputMethodEvent
             event)
            {
            System.out.println(event);
            // Just return if we want the component's default
            // processing for this event; otherwise, we need to
            // call event.getText(), and process the event
                ourselves,
            // and call event.consume().
            }
            public void caretPositionChanged(InputMethodEvent
             event)
            {
            System.out.println(event);
            // Just return if we want the component's default
            // processing for this event; otherwise, we need to
            // call event.getCaret(), and process the event
                ourselves,
            // and call event.consume().
            }
         }
      );
   }
}
```

InputMethodEvent has these public methods:

`AttributedCharacterIterator getText()`—Allows you to get an iterator for retrieving the text obtained by the input method or root window.

`int getCommittedCharacterCount()`—Get from the input method the number of characters the user has committed.

`TextHitInfo getCaret()`—Get a caret object, describing the caret position and direction of editing.

`TextHitInfo getVisiblePosition()`—Get the position that should be visible—most likely what is being edited.

`void consume()`—Consume this event so that default processing does not occur for the component using the committed input.

`boolean isConsumed()`—Return true if the event has been consumed.

To provide on-the-spot editing, you implement the java.awt.im.InputMethodRequests interface (either in the component or as an adapter object). You also override getInputMethodRequests() in your component and return your object, which implements InputMethodRequests.

Unfortunately, you will not be able to try this unless you have an operating system version which supports input method tools, such as an Asian version of Windows.

Language Codes

aa	Afar	es	Spanish
ab	Abkhazian	et	Estonian
af	Afrikaans	eu	Basque
am	Amharic	fa	Persian
ar	Arabic	fi	Finnish
as	Assamese	fj	Fiji
ay	Aymara	fo	Faroese
az	Azerbaijani	fr	French
ba	Bashkir	fy	Frisian
be	Byelorussian	ga	Irish
bg	Bulgarian	gd	Scots Gaelic
bh	Bihari	gl	Galician
bi	Bislama	gn	Guarani
bn	Bengali; Bangla	gu	Gujarati
bo	Tibetan	ha	Hausa
br	Breton	he	Hebrew
ca	Catalan	hi	Hindi
co	Corsican	hr	Croatian
cs	Czech	hu	Hungarian
cy	Welsh	hy	Armenian
da	Danish	ia	Interlingua
de	German	id	Indonesian
dz	Bhutani	ie	Interlingue
el	Greek	ik	Inupiak
en	English	is	Icelandic
eo	Esperanto	it	Italian

Language Codes (continued)

iu	Inuktitut		rn	Kirundi
ja	Japanese		ro	Romanian
jw	Javanese		ru	Russian
ka	Georgian		rw	Kinyarwanda
kk	Kazakh		sa	Sanskrit
kl	Greenlandic		sd	Sindhi
km	Cambodian		sg	Sangho
kn	Kannada		sh	Serbo-Croatian
ko	Korean		si	Sinhalese
ks	Kashmiri		sk	Slovak
ku	Kurdish		sl	Slovenian
ky	Kirghiz		sm	Samoan
la	Latin		sn	Shona
ln	Lingala		so	Somali
lo	Laothian		sq	Albanian
lt	Lithuanian		sr	Serbian
lv	Latvian, Lettish		ss	Siswati
mg	Malagasy		st	Sesotho
mi	Maori		su	Sundanese
mk	Macedonian		sv	Swedish
ml	Malayalam		sw	Swahili
mn	Mongolian		ta	Tamil
mo	Moldavian		te	Telugu
mr	Marathi		tg	Tajik
ms	Malay		th	Thai
mt	Maltese		ti	Tigrinya
my	Burmese		tk	Turkmen
na	Nauru		tl	Tagalog
ne	Nepali		tn	Setswana
nl	Dutch		to	Tonga
no	Norwegian		tr	Turkish
oc	Occitan		ts	Tsonga
om	(Afan) Oromo		tt	Tatar
or	Oriya		tw	Twi
pa	Punjabi		ug	Uighur
pl	Polish		uk	Ukrainian
ps	Pashto, Pushto		ur	Urdu
pt	Portuguese		uz	Uzbek
qu	Quechua		vi	Vietnamese
rm	Rhaeto-Romance		vo	Volapuk

Language Codes (continued)

wo	Wolof	za	Zhuang	
xh	Xhosa	zh	Chinese	
yi	Yiddish	zu	Zulu	
yo	Yoruba			

Country Codes

AFGHANISTAN	AF	BRITISH INDIAN	
ALBANIA	AL	OCEAN TERRITORY	IO
ALGERIA	DZ	BRUNEI DARUSSALAM	BN
AMERICAN SAMOA	AS	BULGARIA	BG
ANDORRA	AD	BURKINA FASO	BF
ANGOLA	AO	BURUNDI	BI
ANGUILLA	AI	CAMBODIA	KH
ANTARCTICA	AQ	CAMEROON	CM
ANTIGUA AND BARBUDA	AG	CANADA	CA
ARGENTINA	AR	CAPE VERDE	CV
ARMENIA	AM	CAYMAN ISLANDS	KY
ARUBA	AW	CENTRAL AFRICAN	
AUSTRALIA	AU	REPUBLIC	CF
AUSTRIA	AT	CHAD	TD
AZERBAIJAN	AZ	CHILE	CL
BAHAMAS	BS	CHINA	CN
BAHRAIN	BH	CHRISTMAS ISLAND	CX
BANGLADESH	BD	COCOS (KEELING) ISLANDS	CC
BARBADOS	BB	COLOMBIA	CO
BELARUS	BY	COMOROS	KM
BELGIUM	BE	CONGO	CG
BELIZE	BZ	COOK ISLANDS	CK
BENIN	BJ	COSTA RICA	CR
BERMUDA	BM	COTE D'IVOIRE	CI
BHUTAN	BT	CROATIA (local name: Hrvatska)	HR
BOLIVIA	BO	CUBA	CU
BOSNIA AND		CYPRUS	CY
HERZEGOWINA	BA	CZECH REPUBLIC	CZ
BOTSWANA	BW	DENMARK	DK
BOUVET ISLAND	BV	DJIBOUTI	DJ
BRAZIL	BR	DOMINICA	DM

Country Codes *(continued)*

DOMINICAN REPUBLIC	DO	HEARD AND MC DONALD ISLANDS	HM
EAST TIMOR	TP	HONDURAS	HN
ECUADOR	EC	HONG KONG	HK
EGYPT	EG	HUNGARY	HU
EL SALVADOR	SV	ICELAND	IS
EQUATORIAL GUINEA	GQ	INDIA	IN
ERITREA	ER	INDONESIA	ID
ESTONIA	EE	IRAN (ISLAMIC REPUBLIC OF	IR
ETHIOPIA	ET	IRAQ	IQ
FALKLAND ISLANDS (MALVINAS)	FK	IRELAND	IE
		ISRAEL	IL
FAROE ISLANDS	FO	ITALY	IT
FIJI	FJ	JAMAICA	JM
FINLAND	FI	JAPAN	JP
FRANCE	FR	JORDAN	JO
FRANCE, METROPOLITAN	FX	KAZAKHSTAN	KZ
FRENCH GUIANA	GF	KENYA	KE
FRENCH POLYNESIA	PF	KIRIBATI	KI
FRENCH SOUTHERN TERRITORIES	TF	KOREA, DEMOCRATIC PEOPLE'S REPUBLIC OF	KP
GABON	GA	KOREA, REPUBLIC OF	KR
GAMBIA	GM	KUWAIT	KW
GEORGIA	GE	KYRGYZSTAN	KG
GERMANY	DE	LAO PEOPLE'S DEMOCRATIC REPUBLIC	LA
GHANA	GH		
GIBRALTAR	GI	LATVIA	LV
GREECE	GR	LEBANON	LB
GREENLAND	GL	LESOTHO	LS
GRENADA	GD	LIBERIA	LR
GUADELOUPE	GP	LIBYAN ARAB JAMAHIRIYA	LY
GUAM	GU	LIECHTENSTEIN	LI
GUATEMALA	GT	LITHUANIA	LT
GUINEA	GN	LUXEMBOURG	LU
GUINEA-BISSAU	GW	MACAU	MO
GUYANA	GY	MACEDONIA, THE FORMER YUGOSLAV REPUBLIC OF	MK
HAITI	HT		
		MADAGASCAR	MG

Country Codes *(continued)*

MALAWI	MW	PAKISTAN	PK
MALAYSIA	MY	PALAU	PW
MALDIVES	MV	PANAMA	PA
MALI	ML	PAPUA NEW GUINEA	PG
MALTA	MT	PARAGUAY	PY
MARSHALL ISLANDS	MH	PERU	PE
MARTINIQUE	MQ	PHILIPPINES	PH
MAURITANIA	MR	PITCAIRN	PN
MAURITIUS	MU	POLAND	PL
MAYOTTE	YT	PORTUGAL	PT
MEXICO	MX	PUERTO RICO	PR
MICRONESIA, FEDERATED		QATAR	QA
STATES OF	FM	REUNION	RE
MOLDOVA, REPUBLIC OF	MD	ROMANIA	RO
MONACO	MC	RUSSIAN FEDERATION	RU
MONGOLIA	MN	RWANDA	RW
MONTSERRAT	MS	SAINT KITTS AND NEVIS	KN
MOROCCO	MA	SAINT LUCIA	LC
MOZAMBIQUE	MZ	SAINT VINCENT AND	
MYANMAR	MM	THE GRENADINES	VC
NAMIBIA	NA	SAMOA	WS
NAURU	NR	SAN MARINO	SM
NEPAL	NP	SAO TOME AND PRINCIPE	ST
NETHERLANDS	NL	SAUDI ARABIA	SA
NETHERLANDS		SENEGAL	SN
ANTILLES	AN	SEYCHELLES	SC
NEW CALEDONIA	NC	SIERRA LEONE	SL
NEW ZEALAND	NZ	SINGAPORE	SG
NICARAGUA	NI	SLOVAKIA (Slovak Republic)	SK
NIGER	NE	SLOVENIA	SI
NIGERIA	NG	SOLOMON ISLANDS	SB
NIUE	NU	SOMALIA	SO
NORFOLK ISLAND	NF	SOUTH AFRICA	ZA
NORTHERN MARIANA		SOUTH GEORGIA AND THE	
ISLANDS	MP	SOUTH SANDWICH ISLANDS	GS
NORWAY	NO	SPAIN	ES
OMAN	OM	SRI LANKA	LK

Country Codes *(continued)*

ST. HELENA	SH	VATICAN CITY STATE	
ST. PIERRE AND		(HOLY SEE)	VA
MIQUELON	PM	VENEZUELA	VE
SUDAN	SD	VIET NAM	VN
SURINAME	SR	VIRGIN ISLANDS	
SVALBARD AND		(BRITISH)	VG
JAN MAYEN ISLANDS	SJ	VIRGIN ISLANDS (U.S.)	VI
SWAZILAND	SZ	WALLIS AND	
SWEDEN	SE	FUTUNA ISLANDS	WF
SWITZERLAND	CH	WESTERN SAHARA	EH
SYRIAN ARAB REPUBLIC	SY	YEMEN	YE
TAIWAN, PROVINCE		YUGOSLAVIA	YU
OF CHINA	TW	ZAIRE	ZR
TAJIKISTAN	TJ	ZAMBIA	ZM
TANZANIA, UNITED		ZIMBABWE	ZW
REPUBLIC OF	TZ		
THAILAND	TH		
TOGO	TG		
TOKELAU	TK		
TONGA	TO		
TRINIDAD AND TOBAGO	TT		
TUNISIA	TN		
TURKEY	TR		
TURKMENISTAN	TM		
TURKS AND CAICOS			
ISLANDS	TC		
TUVALU	TV		
UGANDA	UG		
UKRAINE	UA		
UNITED ARAB EMIRATES	AE		
UNITED KINGDOM	GB		
UNITED STATES	US		
UNITED STATES MINOR			
OUTLYING ISLANDS	UM		
URUGUAY	UY		
UZBEKISTAN	UZ		
VANUATU	VU		

CHAPTER
3

- JAR Files
- JRE
- The Java Activator (aka Java Plugin)
- Self-Updating Deployment
- Servlets

Deployment Techniques and Platforms

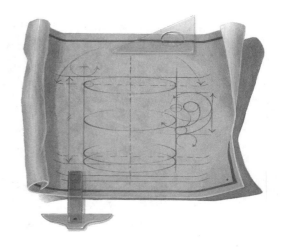

In 1997 a semantic battle ignited between Sun Microsystems and Microsoft, over whether Java was a platform or a language. The interpretation centers around whether Java constitutes a mere syntax for the representation of programs using technologies, or if it encompasses a binding for those technologies, and perhaps is a technology itself. Microsoft prefers the language interpretation, because it views Windows and Windows NT as the only platforms one should use, and does not want a new detractor from that viewpoint. Sun contends that Java is a platform, because programs written for the Java core API can access a large set of technologies in a consistent way, on all operating systems; therefore, that API constitutes a platform.

Java is, of course, a platform. Whether it represents an interface to host facilities or includes facilities itself is moot, because it depends on how a particular Java port is implemented and on the operating system and is transparent to the application. Furthermore, operating systems depend themselves on third-party components, such as device drivers, which are accessed through a consistent "platform" API. Java is a platform because the set of core APIs is comprehensive enough to write most programs, and therefore applications can be developed "for Java" without regard to which specific brand of system they will actually run on. It is the comprehensiveness of the API that makes it a platform and not just a language. If the core API were merely a set of collection, IO, and utility classes, then it would be a language —but the API's go way beyond that.

Despite the neutrality of the API, a developer still must be cognizant of the kinds of systems on which a program will run. The issue of deployment for the target set of platforms must also be considered, as different platforms have different deployment options, and deployment requirements may be an important part of the application.

Java's early and rapid acceptance originates from its ability to use web deployment. Java applets running in browsers were the first kinds of Java programs to be popularized, and this mode of deployment was used so much that many people came to think that Java could or should only run in browsers. I remember a discussion with a technical manager in 1995 in which he asserted that while a standalone Java application was interesting, you would "never use it that way."

While the applet model has many advantages for consumer applications, it has severe shortcomings for intranet applications, and there are other superior alternatives, which I will discuss. Java is an extremely powerful technology for building and deploying intranet and extranet applications. This is due to its powerful API, the high level of productivity achieved with Java software development, the high level of maintainability of that software, and the ability of Java to meld together applications from different sources. In addition, the truth is finally being disseminated about Java security: Java is by far the most secure solution for application development. An organization that is worried about security may react by shying away from new technologies such as Java, and some firewall and VPN vendors have used ActiveX and Java with scare tactics to sell more products; however, Java should be an important part of a security *solution* for most organizations. Today, many IS managers are uncertain about Java because it is new, and they do not know how to evaluate the risk of allowing automatically deploying software. What is overlooked, however, is that this must be compared with the alternative: users routinely download binary software on their own from Internet sites, and this is the origin of many viruses. The automatic deployment of Java is therefore not a liability, but a strength, because since the process is automatic it can be controlled, managed, and made secure.

In this chapter I will discuss various techniques for Java software deployment and compare them. I will give you the information to help you to decide which techniques are best for your application, and show you how to write programs that can utilize these techniques. I will focus primarily on the platforms suitable for mainstream enterprise applications, as opposed to specialized or embedded platforms.

JAR Files

For deploying Java software, the standard container is a "JAR" file, which stands for "Java-ARchive." A JAR file is a file which contains other files. If you are familiar with ZIP files you are familiar with JAR files, because they have the same format. In addition to using the ZIP format, a JAR file contains some special files to allow a JAR to fulfill its purpose of acting as a container for Java code distribution.

The JAR format has these purposes and advantages:

- A transportable and platform-independent container for a collection of related or dependent code and resources. May constitute an executable unit as well.

- Supports hierarchical directories (again, in a platform-independent manner).

- Allows a package to be transferred more efficiently, via a single network connection.

- A package field-replaceable unit (see below)

- Self-describing, via a manifest file, which can contain arbitrary attributes, descriptions, and digital signatures for the archive's contents.

- Contents can be compressed (on a file by file basis), allowing for efficient transfer.

A JAR file may contain files of any type. Generally, it consists of Java class files and resource files (e.g., image and sound files, and property files) in either a flat structure or Java packages. It may even contain native code, although the application will have to know how to move binary code into the system's path, since that is where the loadLibrary() method looks, or have to use the load() method instead of the loadLibrary() method). In addition, a JAR file contains a directory, called "META-INF," which contains a "manifest" file. The manifest file contains an attributed list of all of the files in the JAR file, and base-64-encoded MD5 and SHA-1 digital hashes of each of the JAR file's contents. (See the "Security" chapter for a description of hashing algorithms.) The manifest file therefore contains, in effect, a fingerprint of the JAR file's contents. The manifest is in ASCII format, and so is human-readable and editable.

Like ZIP files, JAR files can contain directories. In fact, a JAR file must have at least one directory: the directory containing the manifest file. This is "META-INF." If the JAR file is signed, this directory also contains signature instruction files and actual signature files. Signing will be discussed later.

When building a JAR file, if you are including packages from third parties, you will want to remove classes you do not use. Some IDEs have a tool to do this automatically for you. If you do not do this, you will be forcing users to download code they never execute.

How to Create a JAR File

To create a JAR file, you can use a ZIP tool to create the initial contents and then use JavaSoft's "jar" tool to add the manifest, or you can use jar to do the whole thing. The jar tool is invoked in a similar manner to the UNIX tar command. In the basic case of creating a new JAR file, this is

```
jar cf <jar-output-file> <class-files...>
```

For example, the following command creates a JAR file from the specified list of class files:

```
jar cf MyJarFile.jar ClassA.class ClassB.class
```

To deploy a Java applet encapsulated in a JAR file, use the archive attribute in the applet tag:

```
<applet
  code="MyApplet"←or use "MyApplet.class"
  archive="archive.jar"
  width=100 height=100
  codebase="http://somewhere.com/mystuff/"←optional
>
</applet>
```

In order to find the class MyApplet, and all subsequent classes, the class loader will look in the JAR archive. You can also specify a list of JAR archive files, in which case the class loader will look in each until it finds what it wants. If it does not find a needed class or resource in any of the listed JAR files, it looks in the location from which it got the JAR file from (the codebase). The syntax for specifying a list of JAR files is as in the following example:

```
archive="archive1.jar, archive2.jar, archive3.jar"
```

Thus, the archive attribute behaves much like a classpath which contains only JAR files, and has the codebase implicitly as the last entry.

Signed JAR files

A JAR file can be signed multiple times, possibly using a different encryption algorithm each time. The reason for doing this is that you will want to sign a JAR file with a superset of the algorithms your anticipated end users will have installed on their Java platforms. For example, Netscape Navigator comes with RSA encryption installed as an available algorithm for its Java clients. This is achieved by setting a Java security property to point to the RSA provider class that implements those algorithms. (See the "Security" chapter for an explanation of this.) Other browsers may not have the RSA provider installed, and may only have the default DSA provider. Therefore, you should sign your JAR files with DSA, and possibly with RSA as well.

A signature instructions file is essentially a list of the files to sign, and also a hash of the manifest entries of the files to be signed; and, as already explained, these entries themselves contain hashes of the actual files. It is actually the signature instructions file which gets signed. (Talk about being indirect!)

The signature instructions file is therefore derived from the manifest, which is derived from the files in the archive. This derivative relationship therefore makes signing the signature instructions file equivalent to signing the actual files themselves.

The signature instructions file is signed by encrypting a hash of it with a specified algorithm and placing the encrypted hash in the archive. The signing process also includes a digital certificate, and these are placed in a file that has the same name as the instructions file, but with the name of the signing algorithm appended as a file extension. There can be a multiple of these files—one for each algorithm that is applied. There can also be multiple instruction files—one for each subset of files to be signed. See the "Security" chapter for more information on digital signatures.

Signing with JDK 1.1

(See the "Security" Chapter for a discussion of certificates, and public and private keys.)

javakey produces X.509 v.1 certificates, which are not compatible with Netscape Navigator (which requires v.3). Therefore, use Netscape's own signing tool, "signtool" (discussed below) when creating certificates to be used by Navigator or Communicator.

You can use javakey for creating certificates to be used by HotJava and applet-viewer; or you can obtain a certificate and key pair from a CA and add those to your javakey database and use them to sign your JAR files. To do that, you must have a security provider implementation installed that matches the algorithm used by the CA. (See the "Security" chapter for a discussion of adding a provider.)

To add a certificate and key pair to your javakey database, these are the steps:

1. Enter yourself into your javakey database. This creates an identity in the database which you will use to refer to the certificate and key pair associated with this identity. For example, to create an identity called "ourcompany,"

```
javakey -cs ourcompany true
```

The "true" specifies that this is a trusted identity—the trust attribute is maintained in the javakey database so that applications like appletviewer can determine if certificates associated with this identity are trusted, and therefore if objects such as JAR files signed by this certificate should be trusted as well.

2. Obtain a new certificate and key pair from a source that is trusted by your target audience—either a CA or your company's certificate server.

3. Import your certificate and key pair into your javakey database; for example,

```
javakey -ic ourcompany our_certificate.cer
javakey -ikp ourcompany our_pubkey.der our_privkey.der
```

The first line imports a certificate from the file "our_certificate.cer" and associates it with the identity "ourcompany." The second line imports the public and private key pair associated with the certificate. You need both the private key and the certificate in your database to sign a JAR file.

4. Use your certificate and key pair, with javakey, to sign the JAR file:

First create a signing directives file. Here is an example, which I will store in a file called "signing.directives":

```
signer=ourcompany
cert=1
chain=0
signature.file=SIF
```

The first line specifies the identity. This must match the subject name in the certificate (see below). The second line specifies which certificate in your javakey database to use for the signing. You can list the certificates in the database with the javakey -ld command.

The third line has to do with certificate chaining (see the "Security" chapter for an explanation of certificate chains), and is not used. The last line specifies the base name to use for the signature instructions and signature files in the JAR file; it must have no more than eight characters.

To sign the JAR file, use a command such as the following:

```
javakey -gs signing.directives OurJarFile.jar
```

All of the above assumes you have obtained a certificate from a third party. To create a certificate (instead of obtaining one), steps 2 and 3 would be replaced with:

2. Generate a public/private key pair using javakey. For example, to generate a 512–bit DSA key pair,

```
javakey -gk ourcompany DSA 512 our_pubkey.def our_privkey.der
```

3. Generate a certificate using javakey.

To generate a certificate from the key pair, you need to create a directives file for javakey. Suppose it is called cert.directives, and it contains this:

```
issuer.name=ourcompany
subject.name=ourcompany
subject.real.name=Our Great Company
subject.org.unit=Special Projects Division
subject.org=Our Great Company
subject.country=US
start.date=1 June 2000
end.date=1 Dec 2000
serial.number=1001
out.file=ourcompany.cer
```

This is the information javakey uses to create an x509 v.1 digital certificate. Note that the issuer name and subject name are identical. That is because this is a self-signed certificate. If you obtain a certificate from a certificate issuer, they would be the issuer and you would be the subject. The start date and end date define when the certificate becomes valid and when it ceases to be valid. The serial number uniquely identifies the certificate, and is assigned by the certificate issuer. The certificate will be created and placed in the specified output file, "ourcompany.cer."

To actually create the certificate, use a command such as the following:

```
javakey -gc cert.directives
```

The certificates produced by javakey are X.509 v.1 certificates, which do not distinguish between signing or authentication uses. The usage being discussed here is for signing. The normal procedure for obtaining a signing certificate from a CA is to go to the CA's web site with your browser and provide the requested information. The browser will automatically generate a key pair and blank certificate, store those in its database, and send the certificate as a certificate signing request (CSR) to the CA over the web. The CA will sign the certificate and send it back, again over the web or via email.

javakey does not itself have a means of generating a CSR. You could use the browser based procedure to get a CA-signed certificate, except that you would not be able to use the certificate for signing by javakey, since the browser will install the private key in its database, and so it will not be accessible to javakey. JDK 1.2's keytool provides a way to generate a CSR directly, without using a browser.

Signing with JDK 1.2

JDK 1.2 replaces the javakey tool with two new tools: keytool and jarsigner. They are refreshingly easier to use than javakey (you don't have to create directive files), and much more practical for broader use, since you can generate a CSR. In addition, the javakey database is now known as a "keystore." (See the "Security" chapter for a discussion of keystores.)

Entering a Signing Certificate into the Certificate Keystore—Keytool

keytool lets you:

1. Insert a certificate from an external source into the keystore, and define it as a trusted certificate.

2. Create a new private/public key pair. The private key is stored in a specified keystore; a certificate is created, containing the public key, and put in the keystore also.

3. Create a CSR to send to a CA.

4. Import a certificate received from a CA in response to your CSR.

If you are setting up a keystore, you will need to do step 1 to define a set of trusted certificates. This is because, unlike JDK 1.1's javakey, keytool does not let you define certificates as trusted or untrusted; it assumes all certificates in it are trusted, and verifies a certificate when it is entered by checking its signature and seeing if it is signed by another certificate in its database. Self-signed certificates are a special case: they are implicitly trusted. You must therefore be certain that any self-signed certificates you import are authentic.

Here is an example of importing a trusted CA certificate:

```
keytool -import -alias verisign -file verisign.cer
```

You will be prompted for a password to grant you access to the keystore. If the keystore does not yet exist, the password you enter will be the one it uses from then on. You will also be prompted for a password used to encrypt and unencrypt the private key created for the alias. The term "alias" is somewhat misleading—it identifies an entity within your keystore; it is called an alias because it is not a globally defined name, such as the certificate holder's distinguished name. The alias is the name by which you refer to all information about the key pair and certificate you are creating.

If you are testing an application, you will need to also do step 2; for example,

```
keytool -genkey -alias ourcompany -file ourcompany.cer
```

At this time, the default implementation included with JDK 1.2 includes only the DSA signing algorithm. Thus, the key pair generated will be DSA keys, with a default key size of 1024 bits unless you specify otherwise (e.g., you could specify 512). In order to create a key pair using the RSA algorithm, you would have to install an RSA provider class implementation (this is discussed in the "Security" chapter).

You might be tempted to bypass all this and obtain a signing certificate by other means; the difficulty then is that you will not be able to use jarsigner, since jarsigner relies on your keystore: it uses the private key created by keytool and stored in your keystore to sign a JAR file. Unlike with the JDK 1.1 javakey tool, there is no way to import a private key into keytool. Therefore, if you obtain a certificate without using keytool, you will have to use another tool for signing your JAR file (e.g., Netscape's signtool tool, discussed later). Javasoft plans to include the ability to import externally generated key/certificate combinations in the final Java 1.2 release or a future release.

The certificate you create is valid for a default period of 90 days, unless you override the default with the "validity" option (e.g., "-validity 365" would make it valid for a year).

If you are deploying a final end-user application, you will need to also do steps 3 and 4 to get an actual signed certificate from a CA (or a certificate server) that uses your public key, and install that certificate in your keystore so you can use it to sign your JAR file, for example,

```
keytool -csr -alias ourcompany -file ourcompany.csr
```

The file ourcompany.csr is the output file. This is the file that needs to be sent to a CA for signing. At this time, however, you may have to make special arrangements to get the CSR processed, since most CAs are set up to do this over the web using a browser or other automated CSR exchange software, and are not accustomed to receiving the CSR as a standalone file.

After processing the CSR, the CA will then send you a new certificate. This certificate contains your public key, and assumes you have the corresponding private key stored in your keystore (or somewhere). Suppose they send you a file called ourcompany.cer; you can import this CA-signed certificate into your keystore as follows:

```
keytool -import -alias ourcompany -file ourcompany.cer
```

It will replace the self-signed certificate that was there before.

(Note: You do not need to send your certificate to users of the JAR file you sign; the certificate is automatically included in the JAR file by the signing process.)

keytool cannot yet handle chained certificates (certificates must be flat), but will in a future release. Make sure your CA does not send you a chained certificate. They will also want to know if you want a signing certificate or a server certificate: that depends on what you plan to use the certificate for. For signing a JAR file, you want a signing certificate. It is up to the application to decide whether it wants to be picky about this detail, which is a v.3 extension.

keytool produces x.509 v.1 certificates. It can import and use v.3 certificates, however. You cannot use it to produce certificates for Netscape Navigator, SSL servers, and other server products, in general, since they require v.3 certificates; but you can use v.3 certificates obtained from your CA via the CSR process described here.

Signing the JAR File—Jarsigner

Once you have a certificate and key pair in your keystore, you can sign your JAR file with the certificate's associated private key (which you created in step 2) using the jarsigner tool. You can do this as follows:

```
jarsigner OurJarFile.jar ourcompany
```

You will be prompted for the keystore's password and for the alias's (ourcompany) password. The JAR file will be signed with the private key stored in the keystore for ourcompany according to the algorithm corresponding to that key. Thus, you do not need to specify the signing algorithm here.

The signature instructions file will be automatically generated by jarsigner, and list all the contents of the JAR file. Thus, if you plan to add unsigned contents, add that after you sign it.

The type of key determines the algorithm that will be used to sign the JAR file. You must have that algorithm installed as a security provider.

Packages Are Field-Replaceable Units

JDK 1.2 adds a new dimension to Java packages and JAR files. It views a JAR file as primarily a collection of packages, and views a package as a *field-replaceable-unit*—an entity which has an identifiable version number, and can be distributed and replaced as a unit for upgrades or bug fixes.

In addition to an entry for each file contained in the archive, a JDK 1.2 JAR manifest should contain an entry for each Java package represented in the JAR archive. A package entry should have the following attributes:

Name—The name of the directory within the archive that contains the package's class and resource files

Specification-Title—The title of the API specification to which this product adheres

Specification-Version—The version sequential number of the API specification

Specification-Vendor—The vendor who owns the specification.

Package-Title—The Java package name

Package-Version—The version identification of this package build; merely a string, need not be sequential in any way

Package-Vendor—The organization that supplies this package

Here is an example:

```
Name: /com/acmeapi/ourproduct/
Specification-Title: "Our Great Product"
Specification-Version: "2.0"
Specification-Vendor: "Acme API Writers, Inc."
Package-Title: "com.acmeapi.ourproduct"
Package-Version: "2.0_bugfix3"
Package-Vendor: "Show Me The Money, Inc."
```

The concept is that a package is an implementation of a specific release of a *specification*. Packages that implement the same *specification* version should be logically interchangeable, assuming a bug-free world. A *package* version, on the other hand, is a particular release of an implementation, possibly a bug-fix release. Different package versions for the same specification version must implement the same API and functionality.

When a user upgrades by incorporating a JAR file that implements a newer specification, the user can expect to receive new and possibly different functionality. When upgrading to a newer package version, however, no new functionality is expected, but behavior may change as a result of repairs to the implementation. The user should retain final control over whether to accept this upgrade, and perhaps return to an earlier package version if the changes have other side effects that are unexpected or not desired. For example, a newer package version might have improved performance, but introduced a new bug that was not there previously. In this case, the user may want to uninstall the new package and reinstall the earlier version. To do this, the user needs to be able to ask the application what version of each package it is using, and instruct the environment to uninstall or install specific package versions. It is up to the environment or application to provide this dynamic installation capability.

Note that this model is appropriate for web-based deployment, and traditional diskette-based modes of deployment as well, but not for a code replication channel such as Castanet (see self-updating deployment later on). A replication channel addresses version compatibility by ensuring that every client has the latest version; there is no concept of rolling back to an earlier version, and to do so would require having a separate channel for each version available at any time; one could, for example, have three channels, for the current and previous two versions. If a person wanted to go back to an earlier version, they would have to unsubscribe to the channel representing the latest version, and subscribe to a channel representing the earlier version. The channel administrator would have to stagger updates to these channels, to maintain the three versions. These versions could represent specification or package versions, depending on whether they implement the same functionality and interfaces. An alternative approach is to add logic to the channel application that allows the user to choose between different packages, which can be saved in a channel profile for the user.

So which way should you do it? The single-version Castanet approach is more appliance-like, and is more appropriate for strictly hands-off users who cannot be expected to get involved in any application maintenance or administration activities. Providing users with version information, and allowing them to choose between versions, adds flexibility, and may be appropriate for sophisticated users and applications. For example, for a very complex application some users may want to postpone upgrades for awhile, especially if they have created data using an earlier version. This can still be done with Castanet, but whether you do it with Castanet or not, it requires adding to the application the ability to choose between package versions.

Creating an Executable JAR File

A JAR file can be made executable by designating one of its classes as a "main" class. The JAR file can then be selected by the `java` or `jre` interpreter, without having to specify the internal class name to run. To make a JAR file executable, you must modify its manifest file. To extract the manifest,

```
copy <your-archive>.jar \work
cd \work
jar xvf <your-archive>.jar
copy META-INF\MANIFEST.MF .\<your-archive>.mf
del META-INF\*.*
rmdir META-INF
```

Edit the manifest with a text editor, and give the main class a property of

```
Main-Class: <your-main-class>
```

For example, suppose a manifest contains one entry, for a file called "C.class":

```
Manifest-Version: 1.0

Name: C.class
Digest-Algorithms: SHA MD5
SHA-Digest: FMpaHnSoID9J/w37tqwR7YFSISO=
MD5-Digest: pOOLP5/aOPs7buzEud4L3Q==
```

You would then add the Main-Class attribute, and the resulting manifest would then contain:

```
Manifest-Version: 1.0
Main-Class: C.class

Name: C.class
Digest-Algorithms: SHA MD5
SHA-Digest: FMpaHnSoID9J/w37tqwR7YFSISO=
MD5-Digest: pOOLP5/aOPs7buzEud4L3Q==
```

Then rebuild the JAR file with the new manifest:

```
jar cmf <your-archive>.mf <your-archive>.jar <extracted
  directories or files...>
```

Now you can specify the JAR file as if it were a Java program,

```
java -jar abc.jar
```

or, if you are using the Java Runtime Environment (described below),

```
jre -new -jar abc.jar
```

The "-new" option is required for the JRE 1.2 release, but may not be required in the future. To execute this JAR file from a program,

```
JarFile jf = new JarFile("<JAR-file-name>");
jf.exec(<args>);
```

or from the command line,

```
java <JAR-file-name>
```

or

```
jre -classpath <classpath> <JAR-file-name>
```

Netscape: Creating and Deploying a Signed JAR File for Netscape

The Netscape Capabilities API

Unwilling to wait for Java 1.2, Netscape has implemented its own domain security model. (See the "Security" chapter for a description of Java 1.2 security domains.) In order for a code source to leave the Java sandbox and access a protected capability, the code must be signed, and the thread performing the access must take responsibility for the access by calling the netscape.security.enablePrivilege() method and explicitly requesting the specific capability. Assuming the capability is granted (i.e., the code is signed, and the user does not respond negatively to a dialog that asks for approval), the code will be able to access that capability until it either exits the static scope in which the enablePrivilege() call was made (usually returning from a routine), or until the revertPrivilege() or disablePrivilege() method is called.

Let's consider an example. Suppose your applet wants to access the system clipboard. Doing so is normally restricted for applets, and will result in a security violation. However, if the applet is signed and makes an enablePrivilege() request to obtain permission, it may access the clipboard as follows:

```
// Request privilege to get the clipboard
try
{

  PrivilegeManager.enablePrivilege("UniversalSystemClipboardAccess");
    showStatus("Privilege granted to access system clipboard");
}
catch (Throwable t)
// either NoSuchMethodException or NoSuchMethodError
{
    // Probably not Netscape; assume we do not need
    // capabilities...
    showStatus("Error requesting capability; proceeding anyway");
}


// Get the clipboard
Clipboard clipboard = getToolkit().getSystemClipboard();
```

The PrivilegeManager class is part of package netscape.security (which, of course, must be imported or referenced explicitly), which implements Netscape's Capabilities API. (You can obtain this package for compiling from Netscape's developer.netscape.com site, or extract it directly from Netscape's browser archive files.) If an applet that contains calls to Netscape Capabilities API occurs in a non-Netscape browser, it will throw a NoClassDefFoundError. You can catch this error, and either abort what you are doing or proceed cautiously anyway, hoping that the browser will still let you do what you are trying to do. For example, Internet Explorer merely requires that an applet be signed and does not require any capability requests so it will allow clipboard operations for signed applets. Thus, the above code will work in either Netscape or IE.

The string parameter in the enablePrivilege() call is a capability "target"— a resource or capability that is protected by the security manager. The targets Netscape has defined that pertain to Java are listed below:

```
UniversalAwtEventQueueAccess
UniversalBrowserRead
UniversalBrowserWrite
UniversalAccept
```

```
UniversalConnect
UniversalExecAccess
UniversalExitAccess
UniversalFileDelete
UniversalFileRead
UniversalFileWrite
UniversalLinkAccess
UniversalListen
UniversalMulticast
UniversalPrintJobAccess
UniversalPropertyRead
UniversalPropertyWrite
UniversalSetFactory
UniversalSystemClipboardAccess
UniversalThreadAccess
UniversalThreadGroupAccess
UniversalTopLevelWindow
```

Creating the Signed JAR File Using Netscape Signing Tool (formerly "zigbert")

To create a signed JAR file for Netscape, you should use Netscape's "signtool" tool (available from Netscape's developer.netscape.com site). signtool works a little differently than the corresponding Javasoft tools. To create a signed JAR file with signtool, these are the steps:

1. Put the contents to be signed (Java class files, etc.) in a working directory.

2. Run the signtool on that directory; signtool produces a manifest and signature instructions file, and signature files.

3. Package the directory contents in a ZIP file using a ZIP tool, and name the ZIP archive with a .jar extension.

Before you can use signtool to sign a JAR file, you must have a signing certificate. For testing, you can use signtool with the -G option to create a self-signed certificate. You can use a self-signed certificate for signing until you obtain a CA-signed certificate for signing your final deployable JAR file. A CA-signed signing certificate can be obtained from a certificate authority such as Verisign (http://digitalid.verisign.com/nosintro.htm) or Thawte Certification (http://www.thawte.com), or from a certificate server product.

Netscape has its own certificate and key database. Certificates are kept in a file called "cert7.db," and keys in a file called "key3.db." Any certificates imported via the Netscape browser will have been installed in these files. Copy these files to your current directory (above your work directory). Copying them is important, so that you do not accidentally clobber them while attempting to create your JAR file. Once you have copied them to the current directory, use the command,

```
signtool -L -d.
```

This will list the certificates in the cert7.db file; those which have corresponding private keys in the key3.db file and are designated as a signing certificate will appear with an asterisk next to them,

```
signtool -k ourcompany -Z ourjarfile.jar workdir
```

where "workdir" is the directory containing the content to be signed. You will be prompted for the password to the key3.db database. (The value of this password is set in Navigator in the Security preferences in the Passwords tab.)

The signed jar file, "ourjarfile.jar," has now been created.

If you have created an applet that performs privileged operations and uses the capabilities API, you will need to package the applet in a signed JAR file for deployment. It is possible to test the applet, however, without doing this. You can disable the requirement to have a certificate by editing the Netscape prefs.js file located in the user directory. Make sure that Netscape is not running when you edit this file, since Netscape overwrites this file based on values it has stored in memory. In the prefs.js file, add this line:

```
user_pref("signed.applets.codebase_principal_support", true);
```

You will then be able to test applets that are not signed. However, *make sure that you do not leave this setting in the prefs.js file, as it leaves your system vulnerable to unsigned applets that will be able to execute outside of the Java sandbox!*

One final note: when compiling your Java classes, if you are using JDK 1.1, do not use the -O option, because the optimization used generates class files that are unusable by Netscape's class verifier. This incompatibility has been fixed in JDK 1.2.

Microsoft CAB Files

In this book I have tried to avoid proprietary technologies that go against open standards. I am willing to make a few exceptions, however. Microsoft's Internet Explorer is used as a standard browser and Java platform by many corporations. Organizations using that browser should be careful about using Java language and package extensions that might affect portability to a non-IE Java platform.

Microsoft does not support the JAR file standard, and has its own software packaging technique called CAB ("cabinet") and very recently renamed distribution units (DUs). I will briefly explain how to create a CAB file, with the caution that you should make sure that software developed for IE runs under the Java Activator, as part of your QA process before you package it in a CAB file.

CAB files provide similar advantages to Netscape's Smart Update feature (discussed later), which uses JAR files. This includes permanent installation and version management. In addition, CAB files can be compressed a little more than JAR files, because the entire CAB file is compressed as a unit, instead of file by file.

Creating a Signed Self-Installing CAB File

First put all the files to be packaged into a work directory.

For client installation, you must create a .INF file (e.g., OurSetupFile.inf) in the work directory. For example, assuming that the CAB file is to be called OurCAB-File.cab, you can use a .INF file like this:

```
run=extract32.exe /e /a /y /l %49000% OurCABFile.cab
ClassId="{2CDCA141-0029-A32B-CC6B-00528E3624D0}"
HKLM, "SOFTWARE\Classes\CLSID\%ClassId%\InstalledVersion",,,"1,0
    ,0,0"
HKLM, "SOFTWARE\Classes\CLSID\%ClassId%\InProcServer32", "TrustLi
    b",,"%49000%"
```

The "{2CDCA141-0029-A32B-CC6B-00528E3624D0}" is a unique identifier, which can be generated with the program guidgen.exe that comes with Visual J++. The "1,0,0,0" is a version string, and represents version 1.0.0.0 of this CAB file.

Now, in the work directory, create a CAB file with the cabarc utility, which is available from Microsoft's site.

```
cabarc n -s 6144 -p OurCABFile.cab *.*
```

This is an unsigned CAB file. However, the "-s 6144" option specifies that 6K of space should be reserved in the compressed CAB file for a digital signature. To sign the CAB file, you need to use the signcode.exe program in the Authenticode package, available from Microsoft's site. You will also need an IE-compatible digital certificate and key pair. Microsoft provides programs for creating a key pair and a CSR, so you can request a signing certificate from a CA. Once you have a signing certificate, you can sign the CAB file with the command

```
signcode -prog OurCABFile.cab -spc OurCredentials.spc -pvk
  our_privkey.pvk
```

The OurCredentials.spc file is a file containing your digital certificate, obtained from the CA, and the our_privkey.pvk file is a file containing your private signing key.

The resulting signed CAB file will permanently install itself on the IE client machine when downloaded. You use an object tag to cause this CAB file to be installed on clients. For example,

```
<OBJECT CLASSID="clsid:2CDCA141-0029-A32B-CC6B-00528E3624D0"
  CODEBASE="OurCABFile.cab#Version=1.0.0.0">
</OBJECT>
```

Furthermore, when the HTML is changed and a new version number is inserted, the CAB file will automatically be downloaded again and installed.

JRE

The Java Runtime Environment (JRE) represents two things: (1) a native executable for running a standalone Java program; and (2) a Java environment which can be used by *any* native program to run a Java program. Thus, the JRE executable is an example of the kind of native program described in (2). To avoid confusion, I will distinguish the two by calling (1) the "JRE executable" and (2) the "JRE environment" when it is not clear which is meant.

The purpose of the JRE is to provide a Java execution environment and command for end users. While the JDK is for developers, the JRE allows users to run Java programs without having to install all of the Java development tools included in the JDK. The JRE is also packaged like any end-user application: it comes in a self-installing program, which the user merely has to download and click on. (The JDK comes in that form as well nowadays, although, as a developer, I wish it did not. I prefer development tools which require me to configure them, because that is the only way to really know what needs to be configured!)

When you distribute an application that uses the JRE, the JRE's existence can be either transparent to the end user or explicit. You can make it transparent by bundling the JRE with the delivered application, but doing so adds the JRE's size to the application. Alternatively, you can ask the user to install the JRE separately and give them the URL of Sun's web site, where the JRE is located (http://java.sun.com/products/jdk/1.1/jre). All they need to do is download the JRE to a file, and then double-click on it. (They can then also download the Performance Pack, which includes the JIT compiler, and double-click on that—that is all that is necessary to install these.)

The default CLASSPATH used by the JRE is

```
%JRE_TOP%\lib\rt.jar;%JRE_TOP%\lib\i18n.jar;%JRE_TOP%\lib\
  classes.jar;
    %JRE_TOP%\lib\classes.zip;%JRE_TOP%\classes
```

"%JRE_TOP%" translates to where the JRE is installed and running from ; it has a bin and a lib directory under it.

On 95/NT, your DLLs should be placed in the%JRE_TOP%\bin directory. On Solaris, place the .so file in the $(JRE_TOP)/lib/$(ARCH)/$(THREADS_TYPE) subdirectory, where $(ARCH) denotes the target architecture (e.g., "sparc"), and $(THREADS_TYPE) is the type of threads the Solaris VM is using (at the time of this writing, this must be "green_threads"). (Note: Make sure that you do not name any of your libraries identical to any JRE libraries!) Your Java program can then load any of your libraries with a Runtime.loadLibrary() call. Otherwise, you will have to use the Runtime.load() method.

To invoke a Java program, use either jre.exe or jrew.exe with your Java main class as a parameter. The latter brings up a shell window, and the former executes without a window.

It is possible to create a C program that invokes the JRE. I do not recommend this, however, because it results in a system-dependent executable, which must invoke the Java interpreter or JRE anyway, so there is no advantage. Nevertheless, if you must, there are examples of how to do this in the JRE documentation.

Performance Extensions

How to Install the JIT.

The Symantec JIT is included with a VM performance pack for the NT/95 platform. This JIT may ship as a standard component in a future release. If your release does not include the JIT and performance extensions and you would like to install them, first make sure that the JRE is installed, and then simply download the Performance Pack from http://java.sun.com/products/jdk/1.1/jre (or similar location for jre 1.2) and double-click on the downloaded executable.

This installation will only affect your JRE. If you are running programs with the JDK and want to test their performance using the JIT, you can do so by setting the JAVA_COMPILER environment variable, or alternatively the java.compiler system property, to "symcjit." For example, to run the java command with the JIT,

```
java -Djava.compiler=symcjit MyMainClass
```

If you are running the jre program and do not want the JIT to be used, you can specify the -nojit option.

```
jre -nojit MyMainClass
```

You might try disabling the JIT if a program seems to be unstable. JITs are fairly new, and not all the bugs have been worked out of them.

HotSpot

Sometime in 1998 JavaSoft will be releasing an improved JIT called HotSpot™, which will have even greater performance than the current JIT, by about a factor of between two and three according to JavaSoft's own tests. HotSpot derives its speed from advanced dynamic bytecode compilation and other techniques including

- Aggressive inlining
- Only the sections of code that most affect performance are compiled
- Analyzes the behavior of the program as it runs, and uses that information to perform optimizations
- Greatly improved implementation of monitor synchronization
- Improved garbage collection technique

In order to make the most use of HotSpot's capabilities, you should keep your methods small, since small methods are easier to analyze for inlining.

Creating an Installable Java Application

If you don't want to deal with browser or deployment issues, but want the platform independence or other advantages of Java, such as high programmer productivity, you can create an installable Java program which end users can install to operate like a native program—except that it runs under a Java interpreter or JIT.

You might wonder, if you are going to install a program on a user's machine, why not just create a native executable for that machine? Well, you can. Most Java IDEs today allow you to generate a native binary executable. Java then runs on a par with C++, with all the performance of a native program, except that the Java program is many times easier to develop because of the streamlined nature of the language and also the elegantly simple but incredibly powerful API. If you generate a native executable, however, you lose the advantages of platform independence for deployment, and you reintroduce the possibility of viruses and subversive programs.

There are many products on the market that let you create a self-installing Java program. Here is an example of how an end user installs a self-installing Java application, packaged using Install Shield Java Edition (which I will refer to as "jshield" for brevity, since that is the name of the Install Shield Java Edition main program):

```
jre -cp . OurInstallerClass
```

I am, of course, assuming that you have the JRE installed on your system. You can also use the JDK. This command will invoke the specified class of your install program, and add the current directory to the JRE's classpath (for this process).

From then on, the process is as automatic as if you were installing a native binary program. However, unlike a binary install, this installation will work on any machine that has a Java VM. It is a platform-independent installation!

A word about using the JDK: if you invoke jshield with the JDK's java program instead of the JRE, jshield will assume you are telling it that you want to use the JDK's Java classes for running jshield in the future. This may not be desirable because as a developer, you probably move your JDK around sometimes, or use multiple JDKs, for different releases of Java. When you install a program, however, you are playing the role of an end user, and you should specify a stable and infrequently moved Java installation such as the JRE. This is up to you, however. (I had a long argument about this with one of my developers, who insists that it makes more sense to install with the JDK—to each their own!).

On Windows platforms, most installers let you have the installation program place a shortcut in the user's system Start menu—as a separate item, or in the Program or Startup folder on the desktop, or in the Send To right-click menu. Here is a typical command that you ultimately want to be run to start an installed Java program:

```
jre -cp myjarfile.jar -Dmyproperty="my property value"
  MyMainClass
```

This is what needs to occur when the user selects the program in the Start menu. In this example, the JAR file "myjarfile.jar" is appended to the classpath of the JRE process, and the value for a Java property called "myproperty" is passed to the JRE. To accomplish this in a self-installed program, you may run into two difficulties: if your program uses native libraries, you will need to tell your Java program where to look so that it can find them; and setting the Java program's classpath. The problem is that many installers, including jshield, do not provide a convenient way to set the PATH for the Java process. In addition, the installer may not let you pass parameters, such as -D parameters, *to the JRE* (as opposed to the Java program). These requirements can usually be accomplished by writing installer plugins or special install scripts, but there is an easier way.

Installing Native Libraries

If your program uses native libraries, use the Runtime.load() method instead of Runtime.loadLibrary(). The former takes an absolute path instead of looking in the system PATH. You can pass the absolute path of where the library is installed (usually the installation directory) to the program using a program command line argument.

Appending to the Classpath

Simply set the property system.class.path in your program. Pass the classpath in as a program command line argument. Do *not* set or append to a system's classpath (or path, for that matter) as part of installation.

Which VM?

When you create an installation program, jshield presents you with a list of Java virtual machines it knows about. As the developer, you have the opportunity to specify a subset of these as compatible with your application. If the end user does not have one of those you specify, the installation will terminate. You can also select "all"; this will normally be your selection, unless you are deliberately writing platform-specific code. (Applications which include native libraries, are of course, platform-specific.)

Builds

jshield lets you initiate an install program build from the command line. For example,

```
"Program Files\JShield\bin\jshield" MyProject.isj
```

The "isj" extension is used by jshield to identify MyProject.isj as a project, containing all the settings you have entered. You may want to add a line like this to your product's makefile, for doing full system builds from a script. This is a valuable feature since builds are generated repeatedly and the process of creating a build needs to be reliable.

One word of caution about making platform-independent builds: be careful about case. When you specify files, use the exact case of the file. UNIX systems are case–sensitive, but NT and Windows systems are not. Java is case–sensitive on all systems. When specifying file extensions to include or ignore from a build, specify both upper and lower, (e.g., .txt and .TXT).

Other Alternatives

There are also programs, such as NET-Install (20/20 Software Inc.), which allow you to publish installable software on a web site so that users can install software in one step by clicking. Well, sort of: the user has to first install the plugin that does this. Netscape and IE also have their own persistent applet technology (Smart Update and CAB files, respectively), which permanently add an applet's class files to the browser. This has the disadvantage that the procedure is different for each browser; also, these procedures are notoriously complex and hard to get working in practice, especially if you have to create a setup that is sensitive to which browser the end user has. (I know experienced Java developers who spent weeks on these issues alone before having success, only to have their scripts broken by IE 4, which now recognizes the archive tag.) Until the browser issues stabilize, it may be prudent to have a browser-independent solution. Besides, if you install a program using one of the browser-based techniques, the program is going to end up using the browser's VM, with all the associated problems there.

Finally, you will probably want to provide instructions to users on how to obtain the JRE, for those users who choose to install using that VM. This should include a link to Javasoft's site, and an explanation of what the JRE is and why they need it. For an intranet application this is a minor issue, since the system administrator can perform the JRE installation.

The Java Activator (aka Java Plugin)

The Java Activator, recently renamed the Java Plugin (I will use the term "Activator" here, since "Java Plugin" sounds confusingly generic), is a browser plugin, written by Sun, that executes Java programs. The purpose of the Activator is to eliminate the issue of browser dependence for Java software, since all software executing within the Activator will (in theory) execute the same, regardless of browser. All that is needed is a version of the Activator for that browser.

The end user does not have to know to install the Activator, as it is self-installing. This is accomplished with the use of the embed tag in Navigator, and the object tag in IE, and with self-installing JAR and CAB files, respectively. Eventually it may use the object tag in both.

The embed and object tags run (and install if necessary) the Activator plugin, within the viewing area defined for it in the embed or object tag. Here are examples of the required HTML.

For Navigator:

```
<EMBED
   type="application/x-java-vm/java-applet"
   width="600" height="300" align="baseline"
   code="MyAppletClass.class"
   codebase="classes/"
   MyJavaAppletParam="Some parameter value"
   AnotherJavaAppletParam="123"

 pluginspage="http://java.sun.com/products/activator/ea2/plugin
   -install.html">
   <NOEMBED>
      You need Netscape Navigator to view MyAppletClass
   </NOEMBED>
</EMBED>
```

For IE:

```
<OBJECT
   classid="clsid:8AD9C840-044E-11D1-B3E9-00805F499D93"
   width="600" height="400" align="baseline"
   codebase="http://java.sun.com/activator/Jinstall_ea2.cab#
      Version=1,0,2,0">
   <PARAM NAME="code" VALUE="MyAppletClass.class">
   <PARAM NAME="codebase" VALUE="classes/">
   <PARAM NAME="type" VALUE="application/x-java-vm/java-applet">
   <PARAM NAME="MyJavaAppletParam" VALUE="Some parameter value">
   <PARAM NAME="AnotherJavaAppletParam" VALUE="123">
      You need Internet Explorer to view MyAppletClass
</OBJECT>
```

Thus, the end user does not actually have to know to previously install the Activator. Of course, if they are accessing a web page that uses the Activator for the first time, they will be asked to download it and then experience a long delay while it is retrieved from Sun's site and then installed. In addition, Navigator requires you to restart it after a plugin (such as Activator) has been installed in order to use it. Once installed, however, the Activator is permanent and does not have to be downloaded again.

There are two versions of the Activator: one for Navigator 3.0 or later, and one for IE 3.02 or later. At this time it basically supports NT 4.0 and later, 95 and later, and Solaris 2.4 and later. For other platforms use the applet tag. You can write very complicated HTML and Javascript to create web pages that automatically determine if the Activator should be run, and which. Sun provides templates for this, and even a conversion program that will parse HTML and regenerate it with applet tags converted into the appropriate Javascript to do this automatic determination. However, if you have a standard browsing platform within your organization, and your applets are going to be used only on that browser, you should consider writing the HTML by hand, and tying it to the browser of choice. For example, on Navigator the Javascript calls the LiveConnect interface, which starts Netscape's Java VM—just to make the determination of what platform the browser is running on—only to then start the Activator's VM; so in the case of Navigator, two different VMs will have to load in succession to view the applet. This prospect makes chills go down my spine, and the machine had better have lots of memory! The Javascript generated is also quite complex, and may present maintenance problems as new browser versions, operating systems, and versions of HTML are released.

In my opinion, therefore, Activator is more appropriate for internal and extranet applications, rather than the web. The Activator is a brilliant stroke on Sun's part to remove the browser issue as an obstacle to implementing Java applets within organizations. Due to browser incompatibilities at the HTML level, however, it may be challenging for webmasters to use it reliably and robustly for Internet applets. That is not to say it cannot be done, however.

If you target a specific browser, and design the HTML to call the Activator in the way required by that browser, then why use the Activator at all? Why not just use the browser's built-in Java capability? The reason is that the Activator loads a pure Java VM. It is much less trouble to reengineer HTML pages to specify a new browser than to reengineer all your Java programs. It is extremely important that a large organization use open standards and be consistent about which standards it uses. Using a particular browser's implementation of Java is inviting maintenance problems down the line. The Activator is a bridge to avoid having to write browser-specific code until the Java standardization issue is worked out.

Self-Updating Deployment

Castanet: Creating a Self-Updating Channel

Castanet is an application deployment technology developed by Marimba, Inc., a company founded by four people who were key players in the development and evaluation of Java: Kim Polese, Arthur van Hoff, Sami Shaio, and Jonathan Payne. Castanet, which is often described as a "push" technology, allows software to be treated as an appliance, by completely standardizing and automating the distribution, installation, updating, and uninstallation (when desired) of applications. Castanet may be the most robust and practical Java platform available today. The benefits of the technology are almost too numerous to mention.

- Automatic deployment and update of content

- Centralized administration of applications

- *Makes software into an appliance*—users just point and click to get an application they want, and everything is automatic from that point on; installation is completely automatic, as is uninstallation

- One of the purest Java platforms available (uses the JRE)

- Robust—extremely reliable platform; does not leave extraneous files on your system when an application is uninstalled

- Extremely efficient content transfer—extremely small granularity

- Unlike with a browser, applications that can run off-line

- Just as secure—a security manager with configurable security (signing); SSL for content transfer

- Fast—uses Symantec's JIT

- Highly scalable (repeaters and proxies)

- Built for business: can traverse firewalls; allows you to create secure channels

The basic way Castanet works is as follows. A client component called the Castanet Tuner allows users to subscribe to collections of content—which may include programs, web pages, and other kinds of content (see below)—from one or more servers. The server is called a Castanet Transmitter. An administrator uses the Castanet Publish tool to add to the set of content made available by a transmitter. A client-side tuner periodically (based on channel configuration parameters set during publishing, and also on user preferences) attempts to contact the transmitter associated with each channel to which it is subscribed, and requests an update. When a transmitter receives an update request, it compares what the tuner has with what the latest content is for the channel, and sends the changes.

Note that the interaction between the client (the tuner) and the server (the transmitter) is only for the purpose of updating content; if the content consists of a program, there is generally no reason the program should need to contact the transmitter, unless the operation of that particular program involves frequent updating (e.g., a stock market ticker program). Most channel programs can, therefore, operate independently of the transmitter, which mainly serves the purpose of keeping content up to date.

A channel's content can be one of these primary types:

- A Castanet "application"

- An applet

- A Marimba Bongo presentation

- An HTML website

A Castanet application is a Java class which implements the marimba.channel.Application interface. This interface specifies the methods required for a tuner to instantiate, start, and stop a channel application, as well as enable the channel to request services from the tuner, such as inquiring about other channels and initiating updates.

A channel can be an applet as well. In this case, the tuner automatically wraps the applet in a Castanet application so that it can run it. From the developer's point of view, however, it is merely an applet. For applet methods that require a browser, such as showDocument(), the tuner dynamically invokes the platform's browser.

A Bongo presentation is a top-level container component in Marimba's Bongo GUI development toolkit, which can be used to develop interactive applications. The Castanet tools are themselves written using Bongo.

One can also publish a web site using Castanet. When this is done, and someone subscribes to it, the entire contents of the web site is copied to the subscriber's local machine, and is maintained in sync with the central transmitter. When the user starts such a channel, the user's browser is launched. The user must configure their browser to use the tuner as a proxy, and all URL requests go through the tuner, which decides if requests can be satisfied from channel content or it must access the web. Thus, one can browse the web site without having Internet access, which is ideal for online documentation that must be available instantly at all times, but maintained up to date.

The only administration "work" required on the client side is the initial installation of the Castanet tuner program, which, once installed, is self-updating as well. The tuner is the client software that implements the protocol with Castanet transmitters, and provides a user interface for the user to manage channels to which he or she subscribes.

The core of the technology is a replication protocol for updating remote objects. Anyone who is familiar with a Palm Pilot™ organizer understands the value of this concept: an automated system for keeping two distinct software systems in sync. The task of a tuner is to periodically contact the transmitter associated with each subscribed channel, and ask for updates. With Castanet, updates are sent as difference files, and only for those files which have changed since the last update. If only a small section of a single file has changed, the update could actually consist of just a few bytes, with a small amount of additional overhead to implement the protocol handshaking. The handshaking protocol itself is extremely optimized, and a transmitter can usually know immediately what files a tuner needs based solely on a composite checksum of the channel's contents sent by the tuner.

To publish a channel, a channel administrator merely needs to place the latest channel content in a working directory, and use the Castanet Publish tool to copy that content into the transmitter's set of published channels. This is an easy process that is completely GUI-driven.

An important feature of channels is that each channel has a special work area on a client machine, called the channel *data directory*, which the channel program can read and write persistent data to. This work area is associated uniquely with the channel, which results in a very tidy configuration: the tuner knows where all the code and data files associated with every application are. For applications which must go outside of this somewhat restricted model, channel signing allows you to create channels that can read and write any files on a client system.

Another feature is that each time a tuner requests an update for a channel, the tuner sends with the request a special piece of data called the channel's profile. The profile is a persistent byte array associated with the channel that is written and maintained by the channel application. What the channel writes to the profile is completely up to the needs of the application, but it is normally user preferences for the channel. Thus, for example, if a user customizes a channel to specify which features are desired, these settings can be saved in the profile and later sent to the transmitter, which can use the profile to customize what it sends to the client with the update request.

A Castanet transmitter can therefore respond in more complex ways than simply delivering identical content to all subscribers of a channel. A channel can have a plugin, which is a transmitter-based Java module that executes each time a tuner requests an update to a particular channel, in order to make decisions about content uniquely for the requesting tuner. It uses the profile sent with each request to help it decide what content to send to the client. Thus, content can be customized on a per-user basis.

An important additional feature is logging: interaction logs can be written by client channel applications, and these entries are automatically timestamped and sent to the transmitter with each update request.

The Application Interface and the ApplicationFrame

A channel must implement the interface marimba.channel.Application, which has these methods:

```
void setContext(marimba.channel.ApplicationContext)
void start()
void stop()
boolean handleEvent(java.awt.Event)
```

In practice, you do not need to implement all of these. You can simply extend marimba.channel.ApplicationFrame, which provides a default implementation for all of these methods, and also provides a GUI frame for the application to run in (a channel does not have to have a visual component). The implementation of handleEvent() provided by ApplicationFrame retrieves configuration properties for the channel, which were set by the administrator when the channel was published last, and uses those properties to determine the default update policies for the channel. Policies include updating at frequent intervals, or only when the user requests it.

Normally you would override the start() method in order to provide behavior for the application. This method is only called once during the lifetime of a channel object instance, and when stop() is called the instance is destroyed. This is in contrast to the start() and stop() methods in an applet, which can be called multiple times, and are intended to have the effect of pausing and resuming an applet.

The ApplicationFrame class has a getContext() method, which returns the ApplicationContext object passed into setContext(ApplicationContext), which is called automatically by the tuner when it starts a channel. The ApplicationContext object is the channel's gateway to the tuner and indirectly to the channel's transmitter. Some of the methods available to a channel via the ApplicationContext object are

> URL **getBase()**—Return a URL representing the root location of the channel's content on the tuner.

> URL **getDataBase()**—Return a URL representing the root location of the channel's data directory on the tuner.

> String **getDataDirectory()**—Return a host-dependent file path for the channel's data directory on the tuner.

`Updates` **`getPendingUpdates()`**—Return a list of the files affected by the most recent update request; these updates have not yet been installed, and will not be unless the channel calls the installData() method.

`void` **`installData`**`(String dir)`—Incorporates the pending updates into the channel's content as a unit.

`boolean` **`appendLog`**`(byte data[])`—Appends arbitrary data, with an automatic timestamp, to a log, which is sent to the transmitter and then cleared when the next update is performed.

`boolean` **`appendLog`**`(String data)`—Same as above, but for string data.

`byte[]` **`getProfile()`**—Return the profile byte array for this channel on the tuner; the profile is a persistent channel-modifiable object that is sent to the transmitter with each update request, and is normally used to save customization settings to be read by a transmitter plugin.

`boolean` **`setProfile`**`(byte data[])`—Set the profile.

`void` **`restart`**`()`—Destroy the channel object, and reinstantiate and start it.

`void` **`update`**`()`—Request an update from the channel's transmitter.

`String[]` **`listChannels`**`()`—Return a list of the URLs of the channels this tuner is subscribed to currently.

The additional ApplicationContext methods, which are self-explanatory, are

```
URL getCodeBase()
boolean channelFileExists(String path)
String[] listChannelDirectory(String directory)
String getServerName()
String getChannelName()
String getParameter(String nm)
long publishTime()
long updateTime()
void stop()
void startChannel(String serverName, String channelName)
void subscribeChannel(String serverName, String channelName)
void unsubscribeChannel(String channelName)
void removeChannel(String channelName)
String getChannelStatus(String channelName)
AudioClip getAudioClip(URL ur)
Image getImage(URL url)
void showDocument(URL url)
```

```
void showDocument(URL url, String frame)

void showDocument(String url)

void showDocument(String url, String frame)

void showStatus(String msg)
```

Signing the Channel

Signing a channel allows the channel to go outside of the security sandbox on the client and read and write arbitrary files, open network connections, and in general do anything a standalone application can do.

To sign a channel, you must obtain a signing certificate first. A signing certificate is just a certificate which has the signing capability flag enabled within itself. To obtain a signing certificate, you can use the Castanet Publish tool's Security tab: just click "Request Certificate." Make sure you are connected to the Internet before you do, because it will eventually launch your browser and take you to Verisign's web site to submit your certificate request. It will also enter an unsigned certificate and key pair in your Transmitter's certificate and key database.

When you receive the signing certificate from Verisign (probably in an e-mail), you will need to replace your unsigned certificate with the new one. Select the unsigned certificate you had created during the request process, click on "Install Certificate," and follow the instructions.

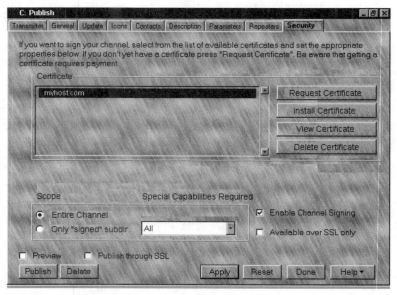

Figure 3–1 The Castanet Publish Tool's Security Tab

Signed channels have the full capabilities of a standalone Java application, and can read and write files, open network connections, and load native libraries. To sign the channel, click on "Enable Channel Signing" before you publish. You must also select the channel capabilities. Currently the choices are "All" and "None." Eventually this will be more granular (see the "Security" chapter, for more about the JDK 1.2 Protection Domain model).

You can also elect to sign only a special "signed" subdirectory. In this case, only the contents of a directory called "signed," immediately within your channel directory, is used to compute the channel's digital signature; so a plugin, for instance, is free to dynamically add dynamically generated unsigned content to the channel during client update requests without affecting the signature verification for the channel code.

In the section that follows the next one, I will demonstrate a complete Castanet application—an application which needs to be a signed channel in order to do its job. I will build an application which incorporates the ability to browse web servers.

Standardization Efforts: Distribution and Replication Protocol

In the summer of 1997 Marimba, Netscape, Sun, Novell, and At Home Corp. submitted a proposal to the World Wide Web Consortium to standardize the protocol used by Castanet as an extension to HTTP. The proposed standard is called Distribution and Replication Protocol (DRP). This work has spawned two companion IETF efforts as well: the Delta Encoding standard, for transporting objects using difference files; and the Instance Digests standard, for identifying an object based on a digest (i.e., a hash value). These are ongoing efforts at this writing, and their completion and ratification will result in an open standard for incremental software updating and distribution. It is an immense accomplishment for Marimba, a company only two years old, to have created a standard of such significance.

An Application That Can Browse: An Example of Castanet

Most corporations now use internal web sites to publish information used by employees to perform their jobs; and most companies now also have external web sites that provide information to the public about the company's business. As a result, it is increasingly a requirement that business applications have a web component, to allow users of the application to view data needed to complete the mission of the application. This situation is partly an outgrowth of the use of CGI to implement applications, but is also simply a result of the ease and versatility of web publishing. A consequence has been that browsers are now viewed as an application deployment platform, because of the convenience of this way of accessing company data, and because it is perceived that the same versatility browsers and the web provide for data publishing will apply to application deployment.

The last assumption is not true. Applications are more complex to develop and maintain than static web data. Furthermore, browsers, while good data publishing platforms, are not good application deployment platforms. A browser is a suitable deployment platform when the end user is not expected to know ahead of time what applications he or she might want to access. This would apply to the general public, but would not apply to many corporate users. For mission critical applications, it can usually be assumed that an application has gone through a lifecycle process of procurement or construction and installation, and that users have a predetermined need for an application. They therefore do not need to "browse" to find it. The flexibility of a browser is therefore of less value, and application stability and readiness are far more important. A persistent deployment technology such as Castanet is then a preferred choice.

Yet for most business applications today, the need to access web data while using the application is still a requirement. It would therefore be desirable if the application itself could access the web, without the overhead and user interface imposed by a full-blown browser. What we need is a browsing "component" that can be instantiated into any application to perform the browsing function as an adjunct to the application, instead of as its main activity. The HotJava Bean is just such a component.

The HotJava Bean is a full HTML 3.2-compatible renderer, with support for frames, tables, and even applets! It is in fact the very component used in the HotJava browser to give it its functionality. Therefore, anything the HotJava browser can do, the HotJava Bean can do.

The HotJava Bean is a Java bean which would normally be used within an IDE tool, to build an application. You would import the bean into the tool, then drop it into your application, and hook up its event sources and listeners. You would size the component to provide it with just the application area it needs for its purpose. In your application, you would control or monitor the activities of the component, which might include causing it to retrieve and display content from specific URLs known by your application.

We will not use an IDE here, because it may not be the IDE you are using, and thus would not be very useful. We will instead instantiate the bean as you would any other Java object: we will create an instance of it, add it to a container, and then call its methods directly. Our application is called "BigCorporateApp," and it merely instantiates the HotJava Bean and then allows the user to choose from one of three URLs hard-wired into the program. We will implement the application as a Castanet channel. The appearance of the program is shown below.

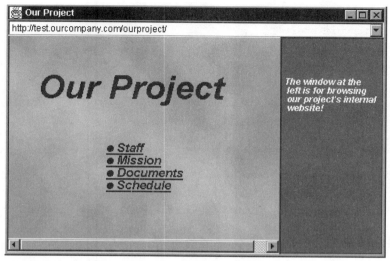

Figure 3–2 An application with an embedded browser

The largest panel in Figure 3–2 is the HTML renderer (the HotJava Bean). Above it is a choice list which displays a set of URLs for the user to select from. When a URL is chosen, the application calls the renderer's setDocumentString() method, which causes it to retrieve the URL and display it.

To the right of the renderer a label with a message is instantiated. In a real application there would likely be other application components and information displayed, such as information retrieved from a database. We conceive that the main purpose of the application would be to retrieve other data and perform business functions, and that the browsing function on the left is merely a supportive function; it might even be present merely to display help files (in that case, the renderer could perhaps be displayed in its own frame).

This application has a hard-wired list of URLs that the user can display. An alternative would be to publish the URL list as part of the channel, but I have hardcoded them for simplicity.

```
public class BigCorporateApp
extends marimba.channel.ApplicationFrame
{
   public static final String[] allowedURLs =
   {
     "http://test.ourcompany.com/OurProject/",
     "http://internal.ourcompany.com/GrandeProject",
     "http://internal.ourcompany.com/SkunkworksProject"
   };
```

```java
public void start()
{
  super.start();

  // Give the frame the ability to be closed

  addWindowListener
  (
    new java.awt.event.WindowAdapter()
    {
      public void windowClosing(java.awt.event.WindowEvent e)
      {
        dispose();
        getContext().stop();
      }
    }
  );

  setSize(600, 400);

  // Identify the file where user selections are saved between
  //     sessions

  String sep = "\\";
  try { sep = System.getProperty("file.separator"); } catch
    (Exception ex) {}
  selectionFileName = getContext().getDataDirectory() + sep +
    "selection.txt";

  // Create a set of URL's for the user to choose from

  java.awt.Choice choice = new java.awt.Choice();
  for (int i = 0; i < allowedURLs.length; i++)
  {
    choice.addItem(allowedURLs[i]);
  }
```

The start() method of this application defines an ItemListener event adapter for the choice control. Whenever the user selects a URL from the choice list, the adapter calls setDocumentString() for the renderer component.

```
choice.addItemListener
(
   new java.awt.event.ItemListener()
   {
      public void itemStateChanged(java.awt.event.ItemEvent e)
      {
         String selection = allowedURLs
            [choice.getSelectedIndex()];
         try
         {
            java.io.File f = new java.io.File
               (selectionFileName);
            java.io.DataOutputStream dos =
               new java.io.DataInputStream(f);
            urlString = dos.writeUTF(selection);
            dos.close();
         }
         catch (Exception ex)
         {
            // Could not save the selection!
            ex.printStackTrace();
         }

         // Fetch and display the selected URL content
         littleBrowserWindow.setDocumentString(urlString);
      }
   }
);
```

We also must not forget to instantiate the renderer and load it with a default document. The document we use initially is the one that was last viewed in the previous session. This is saved by the application in the channel's data area.

```
add("North", choice);

   // Instantiate the browser bean
```

```java
        littleBrowserWindow = new
          sunw.hotjava.bean.HotJavaBrowserBean();
      add("Center", littleBrowserWindow);

      validate();

      // Display what choice user selected last time

      try
      {
         java.io.File f = new java.io.File(selectionFileName);
         java.io.DataInputStream dis = new
           java.io.DataInputStream(f);
         urlString = dis.readUTF();
         dis.close();
      }
      catch (Exception ex)
      {
         // File not found - display the first URL as a default
         urlString = allowedURLs[0];
      }

      littleBrowserWindow.setDocumentString(urlString);
   }

   public void stop()
   {
      dispose();
      littleBrowserWindow = null;
      super.stop();
   }

   private sunw.hotjava.bean.HotJavaBrowserBean
      littleBrowserWindow;
   private String urlString;
   private String selectionFileName;
}
```

Netcaster: Creating a Netcaster Channel

A channel developed with Castanet will run in a Castanet tuner or in Netscape Communicator's Netcaster component. A channel therefore can be used by Communicator clients without having to install the tuner. This may be an advantage in an environment in which Castanet deployment is the best solution, but system administration policies preclude installing additional client software or require that Java software run in a browser.

Netcaster or Castanet channels may be addressed in a Netcaster-enabled browser by a URL of the form

```
castanet://transmitterhost[:transmitterport]/channelname[?command]
```

This URL will be processed by Netcaster to start the specified channel on the user's machine. Web access is not required to do this. Here is an example of a URL to start the channel "My Channel" on the transmitter "trans.mycompany.com":

```
<A HREF="castanet://trans.mycompany.com/My_Channel">My
  Channel</A>
```

Note that spaces in the channel name must be replaced with underscores when constructing the channel URL. In fact, any characters other than a through z, A through Z, or 0 through 9 must be represented by an underscore.

The command may be one of the following:

> **subscribe**—Subscribe to the channel (and download it).
>
> **start**—Launch the channel; subscribe to it first if not already subscribed.
>
> **stop**—Stop the channel if it is running; this has no effect on HTML channels.
>
> **update**—Attempt to contact the transmitter host and perform an update of the channel.
>
> **log=[tag,]URL**—Add the URL, or if specified the optional tag value, to the channel's log file. This log file is transmitted to the transmitter host for processing every time an update occurs.

For example, the URL

```
<A
 HREF="castanet://trans.mycompany.com/My_Channel?start">Launch
 My Channel</A>
```

launches the channel "My Channel" on the user's machine. If the user does not have this channel on their machine (i.e. they are not yet subscribed to it), the host "trans.mycompany.com" is contacted, and the channel is subscribed to and downloaded, and then started.

If the channel is an HTML channel, its HTML pages will contain links and images, as would any web page. You can add a "?log=" parameter to these links and image references. This will cause the containing channel's log to have the specified information appended to it, thereby maintaining a record of HTML content the user looks at. For example, if an HTML page in the channel contains

```
<A HREF="?log=http://www.somewhere.com">Click here for a million
   dollars!</A>
```

the URL "http://www.somewhere.com" will be appended to the log file when (or if) the user clicks on it. Similarly, the URL of the image reference,

```
<IMG SRC="?log=BeachScene.jpeg">
```

will be appended to the log file whenever the image is loaded by the browser. If you want information other than the URL to be logged, you can use the "tag" form of the log parameter. For example,

```
<IMG SRC="?log=User wants to go to the beach,BeachScene.jpeg">
```

will cause the text "User wants to go to the beach" to be logged instead of "Beach-Scene.jpeg."

Netcaster and Castanet share the same underlying technology. In fact, I have been assured by Marimba that the code is one and the same. However, in a practical sense, if you are developing a channel to be used primarily in Netcaster on the web, you will probably want to develop a Netcaster preview page. A preview page allows the user, who is unfamiliar with a channel, to view an introductory description of the channel prior to subscribing to it. This is important because the act of subscribing is significant: the channel's entire content is downloaded and installed. The user therefore needs to know what they are getting into before they click "Subscribe"; the preview provides this. Developing a preview boils down to developing a web page, and providing a castanet: link on it.

For mission critical business applications the preview is less important, since in such applications users are less likely to be "browsing" and will have a business need to subscribe to a channel.

Netscape's SmartUpdate

Netscape provides a technology similar to Microsoft CAB files for creating persistent and self-updating Java (and Javascript) programs. This feature is called Smart Update, and is based on JAR files. Netscape also has a product called "Mission Control," which is used to centrally manage and update applications deployed via Smart Update. Thus, the system administrator can use Mission Control, in concert with a network of Netscape browser clients, to remotely install and update applications on clients.

Smart Update is superficially similar to Castanet. However, the level of granularity of a Smart Update transfer is an entire JAR file. I will not go into the details of Smart Update here, but if you need a simple update mechanism and your client platform is Netscape's browser, you might consider using Smart Update.

NC Deployment

Network computers, often referred to as "NCs," are diskless workstations which replace personal computers in many applications for the same reasons that voice mail has replaced answering machines: a user can get to their data from anywhere within a network. This is, at least, from the user's perspective; there are other perspectives, however.

The real justification of NCs is their lower total cost of ownership. Many studies have indicated that over the lifetime of a typical NC and a typical personal computer, the total cost of depreciating and maintaining a personal computer is double the cost of an NC. The reason is that the cost of PC (or NC) hardware is only a small fraction of the cost of maintaining software and peripherals on such systems. This includes the per-system cost of system administrators, who must typically go around and troubleshoot user software configurations, and set up all these machines constantly with new applications, fix networking problems, address security concerns, and install upgrades. Given the current complexities of PC operating systems, it is a nightmarish task. NCs attempt to say "no" to all this, and return to the concept of centralized administration, as in the days of mainframes, but still allow users to keep personalized workspaces and use advanced interfaces.

An NC retrieves three kinds of data from the server machine to which it is connected: common data, user personalization data, and user application data. The user personalization data is configuration information that represents the user's ID, application preferences, and so on. The common data is made available to the NC by a web server on the server machine. In addition, an NC may have access to the rest of the network or Internet via HTTP and other protocols. User application data is an NFS mounted directory for the user's application data files. This last category is optional, and may not be configured in some installations.

Castanet

The primary use of Castanet in an NC environment is for centralized maintenance of a large number of NCs, deployed across multiple NC servers in a wide area network. While NCs solve the end-user software deployment problem, there is still the problem of maintaining software versions on the server machines to which the NCs are connected. For example, a network might have 1000 NCs connected to 45 NC servers. Thus, while the scope of the software deployment problem is reduced by two orders of magnitude, the problem is still present.

NCs obtain their application software from a local web site published on the server machine to which they are attached. The software deployment problem can therefore be solved by publishing this local web site from a central location using a Castanet transmitter. Each local web server then has a tuner, and subscribes to this channel. The NCs attached to the local server are configured to use their server's tuner as their HTTP proxy; thus, any HTTP channels to which the server is subscribed are available to the NCs. The NCs must also be configured to obtain their web applications from the channel's URL. The content is therefore local to the NC server, but always up to date.

Thus, distribution is achieved by breaking the problem into tiers, with web servers running on the NC server machines providing applications to the NCs, and one or more transmitters on a central server providing application updates to all of the web servers. This is a highly scalable arrangement, because updates received from the transmitter are incremental, and also because transmitters can be tiered as well (this is called a *proxy transmitter*).

WAN Configurations

NCs are best used in a configuration in which the server is local to the NC. In fact, for most NC brands this is a requirement. Thus, in a typical scenario there might be a server situated in a branch office, with a cluster of NCs attached. The server might be connected via a 56K frame relay line to a larger WAN. All applications running on the NCs obtain their code from the local server, and the WAN connection is only used to access the Internet or remote corporate data. This topology is shown in Figure 3–3.

In another scenario, the WAN is local and accessible by a high-speed line or the NCs may even be on the same LAN as other NC clusters. This opens up some possibilities for application design, as will be discussed next.

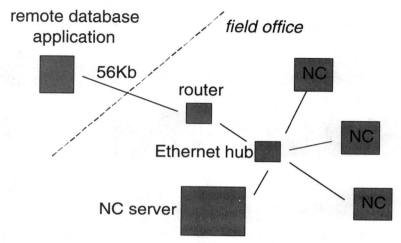

Figure 3–3 A field office NC cluster with a slow connection to the corporate WAN.

Suppose the primary software application is designed as a heavy Java client? In this case, all code executes on the NC machines. If it is a database application, there is likely to be a substantial amount of code, possibly including schema tables if a persistence layer is implemented. All of this will have to be transferred to the client upon application connection or user logon. If the application is located on a remote machine outside of the local NC cluster, all this traffic will be external to the cluster. If the connection between the cluster LAN and the wider corporate network is a slow connection, a heavy client application will require a multitiered deployment approach, for example, using Castanet as described above (see Figure 3–4). If the WAN connection is fast, this is not a consideration. If the connection is slow, and Castanet is not an option, a heavy client design may be ruled out, and much effort will have to be spent making sure the application is as lightweight as possible. This may mandate the use of servlets, or distributed objects.

Some NCs have local disk storage which is used for virtual memory. NC's which have user-accessible local storage lose the primary benefit of an NC: centralized backup of all data, and remote administration of local systems. Once you allow users to store data locally, you might as well give them PCs.

Some NCs also come with a version of Java built in. For example, IBM's Network Station 1000 comes with Java 1.1 installed natively as part of the machine.

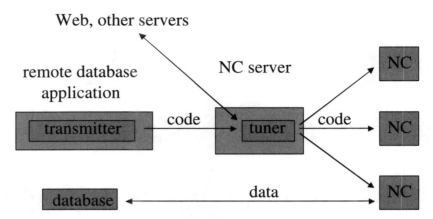

Figure 3–4 Using a transmitter to solve the slow field office connection problem.

Locale-Specific Publishing with Castanet Repeaters

You can use replication gateways called "repeaters" to implement locale-specific channels. The Castanet Publish tool allows you to specify a list of remote transmitters that act as repeaters. It not only publishes the content to these, but instructs the main transmitter to redirect each new request to this channel to one of these repeaters. How it chooses is based either on a round-robin policy or a time-zone proximity policy. The latter can be used as a criterion for selecting content which is locale-specific.

It should be noted that if a channel has a plugin, the plugin runs in the repeater. You can program it, however, to contact the original transmitter (or any) host for any services. Normally, it would directly contact any database services it needs. Thus, multiprocessing of requests is achieved by having the plugins run in the repeater hosts, allowing for greater scalability.

When a Repeater Goes Down

When a repeater goes down, a client remembers the original transmitter location and returns to that. If the plugin is internationalized/localized, it will have to detect its time zone or some other criteria (e.g., the name of the host it is running on) in order to choose a locale. If the repeater later goes down, requests will return to the original transmitter host, which will have a different hostname than the repeater, so the above localization determination will fail. This can be addressed by having the repeater store on each client a repeater or locale flag (which perhaps the user can change if desired). If the repeater goes down and an update is forwarded back to the main transmitter, the plugin can read the profile to determine the client's locale.

Propagation of Log Files

Since the plugin runs on the repeater, the log files are processed and saved on the repeater. It is possible to design the plugin to periodically or synchronously forward log entries to a central location for aggregation or data analysis. This can also be done by an additional program that runs outside the context of the plugin, although this is not recommended since the transmitter synchronizes access to the log, and an external program would not participate in this synchronization.

Centralized Administration of Repeaters.

The Publish tool provides for centralized publishing and determination of redirection to repeaters. It does not provide any repeater management or monitoring at this time. Features which may be added are centralized aggregation of log files, and correlation of log files between repeaters and primary transmitters after repeater failures.

Servlets

A servlet is a Java-based web server extension program. It is the Java equivalent of native web server extension technologies, such as Microsoft's ISAPI and ASP and Netscape's NSAPI. The main differences are that:

- The servlet API is a standard Java extension, and therefore portable and platform-neutral.

- Servlets are secure, since they operate within the context of a security manager, similar to applets.

- The servlet API is vastly easier to use than comparable proprietary native APIs.

Server extension APIs have been used mostly in high-performance applications, in which the overhead of a CGI-based solution was unacceptable. The reason is that conventional extension APIs are so difficult to learn and get working reliably that they have only been used when the justification was very strong. Since a native extension API operates within the process context of the web server, a failure of the extension module can bring the server down. Server extensions are extremely hard to test and debug.

On the other hand, CGI has its own very substantial shortcomings. Conventional CGI programs operate as a separate process which must be allocated anew with each request. Thus, there is a great deal of overhead in servicing a CGI request.

Furthermore, since the process terminates when the request has completed, it is difficult to implement a service that maintains persistent connections to other services; for example, each request may require the newly started CGI process to open a connection to a database, retrieve data, close the connection, return the data, and then exit. Opening a database connection may require several hundred milliseconds; add this to the CGI process creation time, and it is clear that there is quite a bit which has to occur before the CGI program can return even the smallest amount of data. CGI programs also tend to have a large footprint, and this combined with the initialization overhead makes CGI not very scalable.

Server extension APIs, including the Java servlet API, and CGI share the request/response model of HTTP, since they operate within the context of an HTTP request. In this model, an incoming request has an input stream associated with it, as well as an environment context and an output stream for results. It is up to the application to perform parsing of the input stream and formatting of the output stream. Most APIs provide methods for retrieving HTTP header and other data from the environment context. The Java servlet standardizes this API, greatly reducing the maintenance problems for which both CGI and server extension programs are notorious.

The Java servlet API provides a highly scalable model for adding functionality to web servers. A servlet runs as a thread within the context of the web server's Java virtual machine. Since all exceptions in Java can be trapped by the VM, it would take a bug in the virtual machine itself to crash the web server. It also means that servlets can handle a very large volume of requests, since the footprint of the VM process is shared by all servlets—in fact, even the servlet object instance itself is shared between multiple invocations of the same servlet, and the implication of this is that servlets can provide persistence between invocations for maintaining database and other connections. Servlets therefore have significant advantages over alternatives, in the areas of

- Stability
- Scalability and Performance
- Persistence

Security

Security is no small consideration with any kind of server extension or dynamically invoked program through a web server. CGI is an enormous security hole for administrators, especially ISPs, so much so that many ISPs prohibit CGI programs. Native server extensions are not allowed by ISPs and are only appropriate for internal applications. Servlets change these rules, however, and an administrator could allow servlets to be used with substantial confidence—more so than most CGI programs.

Many ISPs implement a sandbox for CGI processes to run in. UUNet is an example of this: any CGI program invoked by a UUNet web server runs in an "R-box" with a restricted set of resources and privileges. The Java servlet model provides a similar kind of sandbox, but in a standard and portable manner. An administrator familiar with the servlet model as it applies to an Apache web server running on Solaris can directly apply that experience to a servlet running under IIS on NT. The existence of a standard and portable security model is an enormous advantage for both administrators and developers, who can solve the security problem once for their application, instead of once for each platform. Administrators of corporate networks can rest easier, knowing that no servlet can do what it is not specifically configured to do, and further that if one should fail, it will not bring the server down.

Invoking a Servlet

There are three ways to invoke a servlet.

1. *url*—The URL of the servlet is specified directly. For example,

```
http://myhost/servlet/mypackage.myservlet?parm1=abc&parm2=def
```

would invoke the servlet *myservlet* in package *mypackage*, in the *servlets* directory on host *myhost*. (The "/servlet/" in the URL is not missing an "s"—this tells the server the URL is a servlet.) Note that parameters are specified using the HTTP GET query syntax. They may also be specified as input tags in an HTML form.

2. *HTML-embedded*—The name of the servlet is embedded in an HTML page, similar to the way one embeds an applet in an HTML page. However, in the manner of a server-side include, the <servlet> tag in the HTML is processed by the server, and output from the servlet is substituted in its place. For example,

```
<html>
Customer Status...<br>
<servlet name=CustomerStatus code=customer.CustomerStatusImpl>
<param name=firstname value=abe>
<param name=lastname value=lincoln>
</servlet>
<br>
</html>
```

The HTML file must have a .shtml extension. A codebase parameter may be specified as well. However, some servers at present require a servlet deployed in this way to reside in the server's *servlets* directory, even if a codebase parameter is specified.

3. *chaining*—This is configured by the web server administrator. Chaining allows servlets to be invoked automatically based on the MIME type of a data stream. The technique of chaining can be used to automatically filter or process data of certain types.

The Servlet Programming Interface

You can either extend the abstract class HttpServlet, or implement the Servlet interface directly. You might choose to do the latter if your servlet needs to extend some other class for some reason. The Servlet interface methods are:

init(ServerConfig)—This initializes the servlet. The web server instantiates and initializes a servlet the first time it is needed. Once the servlet is initialized, the servlet instance continues to exist until the web server is stopped, or it is explicitly destroyed by an administrator. In the init() method you would normally open database or other server connections required to service requests. In addition, you must save the ServletConfig parameter that is passed in, because the server may ask for it back by calling the getServletConfig() method on the servlet (described next).

getServletConfig()—Returns the ServletConfig object reference that the servlet saved in its init(ServletConfig) method.

getServletInfo()—Returns author, version, and copyright info.

service(ServletRequest, ServletResponse)—This is the method called by the web server whenever an HTTP request invokes the servlet. Each request is serviced in a separate thread, in the virtual machine of the servlet object. The implementation of this method should therefore be thread-safe, since the servlet object instance may be servicing several HTTP requests at the same time, each in a different thread. The HTTP request input stream can be obtained from the ServletRequest argument, and the HTTP output stream from the ServletResponse argument.

destroy()—In this method you should release all servlet object resources, (close database connections, etc.). This is also your last chance to write or commit persistent data, or make final log entries.

Example: The CustomerManager Servlet

I will demonstrate writing a servlet with a complete example, a small application which has two personalities: a servlet personality, and an RMI server personality. The servlet serves the function of letting web-based users query for information on a customer, and the RMI service allows an administrator to obtain more complete information and update the database. The administrator's user interface is shown in Figure 3–5

An administrator would use the above applet to maintain the database of customers. The admin applet accesses the servlet object, which is also an RMI server object, using the RMI protocol. The servlet also provides a servlet interface for nonadministrative web users who want to query the database for information on a customer. In this simple example, the query simply returns the customer's name and age, based on a query string containing the name..

Figure 3–6 shows what happens if you invoke this servlet by entering its URL directly into a browser. The servlet requires two query parameters: *firstname* and *lastname*, and it returns the customer data in a stream to the browser. How it does so will be explained later.

Since in this case the servlet is also an RMI server object, it needs a remote interface to export its services. The Java interface for the servlet is shown in the code below.

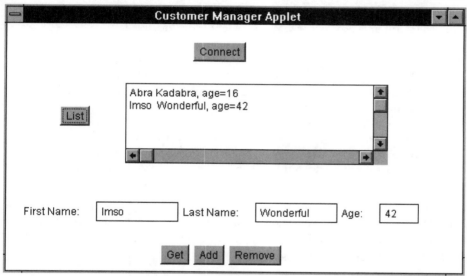

Figure 3–5 User interface for accessing the Customer Manager servlet's RMI-functions

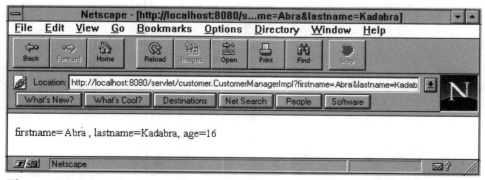

Figure 3–6 Accessing the servlet using a URL

```
package customer;
import java.rmi.*;

/**
 * Interface for CustomerManager servlet, which has dual-
 * personalities: http and RMI.
 *
 * Allows one to write services that can be accessed from any
  * browser, and across a firewall without tunneling.
 */

public interface CustomerManager extends Remote
{
    public Customer getCustomer(String firstname, String
        lastname) throws RemoteException, Exception;
    public Customer[] getCustomers() throws RemoteException,
        Exception;
    public void addCustomer(String firstname, String lastname,
        int age) throws RemoteException, Exception;
    public void remCustomer(String firstname, String lastname)
        throws RemoteException, Exception;
}
```

Our servlet, as an RMI server object, maintains a persistent database of customer data. For simplicity, I have implemented this database simply as a serialized object file. The Customer class is

```
package customer;

public class Customer implements java.io.Serializable
{
    private String lastname;
    private String firstname;
    private int age;

    public Customer(String firstname, String lastname, int age)
    {
        this.firstname = firstname;
        this.lastname = lastname;
        this.age = age;
    }
```

```
public String toString() { return "firstname=" + firstname +
   ", lastname=" + lastname + ", age=" + age; }

public String getFirstname() { return firstname; }

public String getLastname() { return lastname; }

public int getAge() { return age; }
}
```

Let's now look at the implementation of the servlet. The init(ServletConfig) method first saves the ServletConfig parameter and then calls the internal method init(), which does the bulk of the initialization, including registering the object as an RMI service, and loading the customer data; in a real application, this would be a database connection. The code for load() and save() is shown at the end of this example.

```
package customer;
import java.io.*;
import javax.servlet.*;

/**
 * Implementation of the CustomerManager.
 */

public class CustomerManagerImpl
   extends java.rmi.server.UnicastRemoteObject
   implements CustomerManager, Servlet
{
   private ServletConfig servletConfig;
   private java.util.Vector customers;
   private boolean bound = false;

   public CustomerManagerImpl() throws java.rmi.RemoteException
      { super(); }

   //
   // Servlet methods...
   //
```

```java
public void init(ServletConfig c) throws ServletException
{
  servletConfig = c;
  init();
}

protected void init() throws ServletException
{
  try
  {
    java.rmi.registry.Registry registry =
      java.rmi.registry.LocateRegistry.getRegistry();
    registry.rebind("CustomerManager", this);
    bound = true;
    System.out.println("Server bound to CustomerManager");
  }
  catch (Exception ex)
  {
    System.out.println("Could not bind:");
    ex.printStackTrace();
  }

  // Load file
  try
  {
    load();
  }
  catch (Exception ex)
  {
    System.out.println("Error reading customer file:");
    ex.printStackTrace();
    throw new ServletException("Terminating due to prior
      error");
  }
}

public ServletConfig getServletConfig()
{
  return servletConfig;
}
```

```
public String getServletInfo()
{
   return "CustomerStatus Servlet";
}

public void destroy()
{
   // Save file
   save();
}
```

The service() method is the method called by the web server to satisfy servlet invocation requests. In my implementation, I first obtain the two query parameters "firstname" and "lastname." Based on these, I look the customer up in the database and obtain a Customer object for that customer. I then return a stream of data about that customer to the output stream of the current HTTP connection, which can be obtained from the ServletResponse argument:

```
public void service(ServletRequest request,
      ServletResponse response)
   throws ServletException, IOException
{
   System.out.println("Service...");

   if (! bound)
   {
      response.getOutputStream().println("Not bound");
      return;
   }

   // Identify customer
   String firstname = request.getParameter("firstname");
   String lastname = request.getParameter("lastname");
   if ((lastname == null) || (firstname == null))
   {
      response.getOutputStream().println(
         "Both last name and first name must be specified");
      return;
   }
```

```
   // Retrieve information on the customer
   System.out.println("firstname=" + firstname);
   System.out.println("lastname=" + lastname);
   Customer customer = null;
   try
   {
      customer = getCustomer(firstname, lastname);
   }
   catch (Exception ex)
   {
      throw new ServletException("Error looking up customer.");
   }

   // Return information on the customer
   if (customer == null)
   {
      response.getOutputStream().println("Customer could not be
         found.");
      return;
   }
   response.getOutputStream().println(customer.toString());
}
```

The remote services this object exports involve searching for a customer based on a name, getting a list of all customers, adding a customer to the database, and removing a customer. Note that these method implementations are synchronized to protect the customer's object from simultaneous access by multiple servlet request threads; in a real application using a database, this synchronization would probably not be necessary because it would be provided by the synchronization inherent in the database's transaction mechanism.

```
   //
   // CustomerStatus methods...
   // The remote entry point implementations are synchronized,
   // because they may be called my multiple server threads,
   // either as an RMI service, or as a servlet service.
   //
```

```
public synchronized Customer getCustomer(String firstname,
   String lastname) throws java.rmi.RemoteException, Exception
{
   return findCustomer(firstname, lastname);
}

public synchronized Customer[] getCustomers() throws
   java.rmi.RemoteException, Exception
{
   Customer[] ca = new Customer[customers.size()];
   for (int i = 0; i < customers.size(); i++)
   {
      Customer c = (Customer)(customers.elementAt(i));
      ca[i] = c;
   }
   return ca;
}

public synchronized void addCustomer(String firstname, String
   lastname, int age) throws java.rmi.RemoteException,
   Exception
{
   Customer c = new Customer(firstname, lastname, age);
   customers.addElement(c);
   save();
}

public synchronized void remCustomer(String firstname, String
   lastname) throws java.rmi.RemoteException, Exception
{
   Customer c = findCustomer(firstname, lastname);
   if (c == null) throw new Exception("Not found");
   customers.removeElement(c);
   save();
}

protected Customer findCustomer(String firstname, String
   lastname)
{
   for (int i = 0; i < customers.size(); i++)
   {
```

```
      Customer c = (Customer)(customers.elementAt(i));
      if (c.getFirstname().equals(firstname) &&
        c.getLastname().equals(lastname))
      {
        return c;
      }
    }
    return null;
  }
```

The load() and save() methods are as follows, although again, in a real application, these would perform database accesses.

```
protected synchronized void load() throws Exception
{
  // synchronized to protect access to customers object

  System.out.println("Loading CustomerFile...");
  File file = new File("CustomerFile");
  FileInputStream fis = null;
  try { fis = new FileInputStream(file); } catch
    (FileNotFoundException ex) {}
  if (fis == null)
  {
    customers = new java.util.Vector();
  }
  else
  {
    ObjectInputStream ois = new ObjectInputStream(new
      FileInputStream(file));
    customers = (java.util.Vector)(ois.readObject());
    ois.close();
  }
  System.out.println("...done loading.");
}

protected synchronized void save()
{
  // synchronized to protect access to customers object

  System.out.println("Saving CustomerFile...");
```

```
File file = new File("CustomerFile");
try
{
  ObjectOutputStream oos = new ObjectOutputStream(
    new FileOutputStream(file));
  oos.writeObject(customers);
  oos.close();
}
catch (IOException ex)
{
  System.out.println("Error writing customer file:");
  ex.printStackTrace();
}
System.out.println("...done saving.");
}
```

Finally, for testing purposes it helps to have a main method, which is included here for completeness.

```
public static void main(String[] args) throws Exception
  // for testing only
{
  System.setSecurityManager(new
  java.rmi.RMISecurityManager());
  CustomerManagerImpl m = new CustomerManagerImpl();
  m.init();
}
}
```

The code for the administration applet, which accesses the servlet object via RMI, is not included here because it is not important to understand servlets, but it is provided on the CD included with this book.

This servlet must be invoked as a servlet prior to being accessed via the administrative tool. The reason is that the init() method is the method which registers the object as an RMI service, and init() is not called until the servlet is invoked for the first time (after a web server restart).

Testing and Deployment

Javasoft provides a development kit for servlets, called the Java Servlet Development Kit (JSDK), available free from their web site. It contains a servlet test bench server called the Servlet Runner. The Servlet Runner is a trivial web server which supports servlets invoked by URL, but not as HTML-embedded servlets. For final testing, you can test your servlets on the Java Web Server, which is JavaSoft's full-featured web server written in Java. You can also use the Tengah web and application server, included for evaluation on this book's CD.

A servlet may either be installed either locally on a web server, or remotely, in which case the servlet actually resides on another server. Servlets locally installed on a web server should be placed in the *servlets* directory (or, if the servlet is in a package, its package should be in the *servlets* directory), and then identified to the server using its administration tool for security configuration. Servlets installed in this way will have either full or configurable privileges, depending on the server's policy. The Java Web Server, for example, gives full privilege to a locally installed server. Remotely installed servlets are considered untrusted by default, and must be in a signed JAR file. An administrator identifies a remote servlet to a server by specifying a URL that ends with the name of the signed JAR file. A remote servlet's privileges are configured by the server's administrator.

Some web servers require a patch to be installed to enable servlet support. Eventually, given the growing importance of Java, most servers will likely include support for Java CGI and Java servlets. In the meantime, installing a patch or plugin is a small price to pay given the tremendous benefits of a standard and robust security model, scalability, maintainability, and single-language development. It must also be contrasted with the comparatively greater difficulty of developing reliable applications using native server extension technologies; for example, it is far easier to create a servlet than to write IIS parse maps and deal with extension control blocks, or NSAPI pblocks and Request data structures.

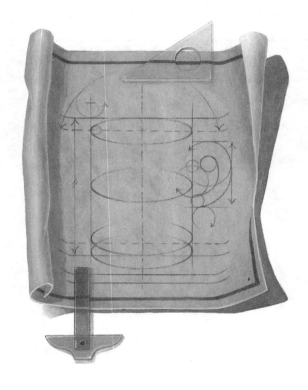

CHAPTER

4

- Introduction
- Data Encryption, Keys, and Certificates
- Secure Communication Protocols
- The Java Security Model: Protecting the Local System
- JCC

Java Security and Electronic Commerce

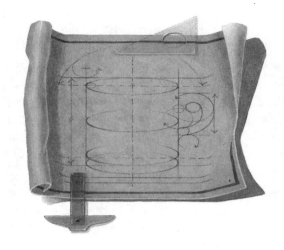

Introduction

Security is the first concern of any serious large-scale application. Business applications invariably convey sensitive information, to which access must be authorized. Mission-critical systems must further be protected against the destruction or theft of information. Single-user systems must also be protected, because in the aggregate they constitute a large part of the business computing environment.

Security concerns for business applications generally fall into these domains:

- *Security of content*—The protection of *information at its point of origin*, prior to transmission or retrieval

- *Security of communications*—The protection of *transmitted information* against theft or modification while in transit or being retrieved

- *Security of the corporate computing infrastructure*—The protection of *the local environment* from the actions of newly installed content after transmission and acceptance into the local environment

Within *each* of these three domains, there is a need to:

- *Establish proof of identify*: The source and destination of the information are who they say they are.

- *Establish proof of information integrity:* The information has not been altered since the originator created it.
- *Ensure privacy:* The information cannot be read by an unauthorized party.

The specific needs and emphasis on each of the above depend on the application and the environment. Java provides an extremely secure base infrastructure from which applications that have all of the above requirements can be met. This security derives from the fundamental design of the Java virtual machine, and from the extensive security features of the standard and extended APIs.

The subject of security is very complex; however, it should not be necessary for a developer to read several books on encryption and security before being able to grasp what is important, and how the APIs fit together. The goal of this chapter is therefore to make sense of these different Java APIs and aspects of Java security to the extent necessary in order to evaluate and apply them. To accomplish that, it is necessary to provide a background on many security fundamentals—some very new, and some long-established.

Before proceeding, I should stress that the term "secure" means different things to different people. To the average person—who thinks nothing of signing a credit card imprint in a restaurant and leaving it behind in the hands of restaurant staff—the definition of "secure" is far different than what the National Security Agency means when it uses the term "secure." In this book, which focuses on Java applications that use security, the term "secure" is relative to the levels of security that are commonly expected and tolerated in business and commercial applications.

Data Encryption, Keys, and Certificates

Encryption is the process of converting data from a readable form to an unreadable form, such that only the intended recipient knows how to reconvert it back into a readable form. This is usually accomplished by inputting the readable information into an algorithm for encryption. The information is then transported to the recipient, by any means, and the recipient then inputs the received encrypted information into an algorithm that reverses—*decrypts*—the encrypted information, thereby retrieving the original text.

Encryption is the primary means used to transmit data securely over the Internet. The reason is that since the Internet is a public network, it is not possible to rely on exclusive use of network equipment or lines to separate one's data from the outside world; one has little control over which routers a message will pass through before reaching its destination, and who might be capturing or analyzing messages which pass through that equipment. Therefore, it is necessary to make sensitive data unintelligible to all but the sender and the receiver, and this is the role encryption plays.

In addition to encrypting the data, it is necessary to make sure that the data is being received from or sent to the right party, not an impostor; it may also be necessary in some circumstances to prove after the fact that a particular party *did* take part in a communication or transaction. It is therefore often important, for a variety of reasons, to authenticate one or both parties when communicating. The primary mechanisms used for authentication are passwords, digital certificates, and physical identification tokens.

A digital certificate is an electronic document, conforming to a well-defined standard, which contains verifiably correct information. I will discuss the kinds of certificates that are important for Java applications, including what is inside of a certificate and what they are used for.

Encryption algorithms fall into two main categories: symmetric and asymmetric key encryption, and I will start by discussing these. I will explain the techniques used for exchanging cryptographic keys, and the practical legal restrictions that exist for using cryptographic keys and cryptography. I will then explain some of the implementations that use these techniques, including SSL, CORBA, and various Java deployment platforms.

Symmetric Key Encryption

Symmetric key encryption algorithms are used to achieve efficient high-throughput encryption of information. For example, a symmetric key algorithm would be used to implement encryption for a secure socket stream connection to transmit arbitrarily large amounts of data securely. A symmetric key algorithm uses a single key for both encryption and decryption, and therefore both parties—the sender and the recipient—must have privately exchanged this key ahead of time, by some other means. This kind of key is usually referred to as a "secret key." Figure 4–1 depicts encryption and decryption using a secret key.

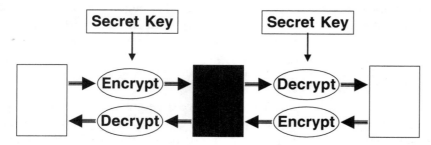

Figure 4–1 Encrypted communication with a symmetric key: You and another party both use a single shared secret key to encrypt and decrypt messages; you must have previously exchanged this key secretly.

Symmetric Key Algorithms

Symmetric encryption algorithms generally fall into the categories of block ciphers and stream ciphers. A block cipher takes as input a block of information at a time, whereas a stream cipher operates on a stream of input data a byte at a time. Here is a list of some of the more prevalent symmetric encryption algorithms.

DES—"Data Encryption Standard"; U.S. government standard. It is a block cipher, normally used with a 56-bit key. Some people suspect that the U.S. government may have the ability to break it, although there is no direct evidence of this. "**Triple-DES**" (**3DES**), which is currently the algorithm of choice in banking and secure Internet Mail (S/MIME), applies the algorithm three times, resulting in an encryption that is approximately twice as hard to break. DES is defined by the NIST in FIPS 46-1 and 46-2. DES has been broken with brute force attacks, but the computing resources required were extremely large and therefore do not result in the algorithm being considered less secure than previously thought (i.e., it was known that it could be broken in this manner). Recently 3DES has also been shown to be no stronger than DES under certain conditions.

RC2—A block cipher that was a trade secret of RSA Data Security until very recently (they published it finally in 1997; however, the algorithm had been anonymously published prior to that).

RC4—A stream cipher. This was a trade secret of RSA Data Security; however, it was also anonymously published. RSA still considers it proprietary.

RC5—A block cipher, published and patented by RSA.

IDEA—The "International Data Encryption Algorithm" (IDEA) from ASCOM Systec, Switzerland; used by the Pretty Good Privacy (PGP) system; patented.

In addition, the U.S. government (through NIST) has begun the process of developing a new algorithm, to be an open and nonproprietary standard, called Advanced Encryption Standard (AES), to replace DES. Submissions of proposed algorithms by the public ends in June 1998.

Public Key Encryption

A public key encryption algorithm requires two different keys. One key is typically designated the "private key," the other the "public key." The public key can be revealed to parties other than one of the communicating parties, without compromising the security of the communication. Algorithms which have two keys are often referred to as "asymmetric" algorithms, and the public and private key pair are referred to as "asymmetric keys."

The important characteristic of public key encryption algorithms is that if data is encrypted using one of these two keys, it can only be decrypted with the other. Thus, for example, if you have a pair of asymmetric encryption keys, you can give one of them to other people to encrypt messages to be sent to you, and then only you will be able to decrypt them by using the other key, which you have not given out.

The advantage of asymmetric encryption is therefore that you can send the encryption key using unsecure means, knowing that the party who receives it will be able to send secret messages to you that only you can decipher. This does not prevent someone else, however, from receiving the key and forging messages, pretending to be the other party. If you exchange keys via an unsecure means, it is therefore necessary to *authenticate* the messages subsequently sent to you (i.e., prove that they are all from the intended party).

Asymmetric keys are usually used in such a way that each party has a separate pair of public and private keys, and exchange public keys using any (unsecure) means. In practice, however, this technique is used only to transmit small amounts of data, since it is computationally inefficient compared to symmetric algorithms. For example, the Secure Socket Layer (SSL) protocol first allows both parties to exchange a secret (symmetric) key by transmitting it securely using asymmetric encryption or a secret key exchange algorithm. Once the parties both know what the symmetric secret key is, they use it for all subsequent communication during that session; the symmetric secret key is referred to as a "session key." (Note: the details are more complex; SSL actually uses multiple keys, but that is not important for this discussion.) Figure 4–2 illustrates encryption and decryption using a public key algorithm.

In addition to asymmetric encryption algorithms, there are other kinds of asymmetric key algorithms, including signature algorithms and key exchange algorithms.

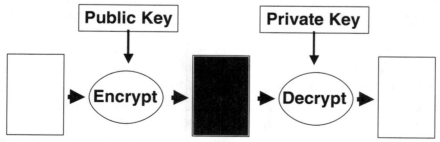

Figure 4–2 Encrypted communication with public and private keys: you use their public key to encrypt a message, they use their private key to decrypt it; they use your public key to encrypt a message, you use your private key to decrypt it.

A signature algorithm is a one-way encryption algorithm which allows you to create and verify a digital signature. One key (the private key) is used for signing, and the other (the public key) is used for verifying. A key exchange algorithm is an algorithm which allows two parties to cooperatively compute a common symmetric key, without directly exchanging that key. Examples of these techniques will be discussed under "Asymmetric Key Algorithms" below.

Asymmetric Keys for Authentication

In addition to encrypted transport of symmetric keys and other small amounts of information, asymmetric encryption can be used for authentication. The concept is as follows: if one of your asymmetric keys is known only to you (i.e., is private), only you will be able to generate messages that can be decrypted with the other key. The other key can be made public, and given to others for the purpose of authenticating your messages.

All you need to do is send a short message encrypted with your private key, and the mere fact that others can decrypt it proves that the message originated from you. (This assumes that no one has stolen your private key!) In this situation, the authentication message is something that you want others to be able to decrypt— it is not private—so you use your private key to encrypt it so that others can use your public key to decrypt it. If you wanted to send encrypted information, you would instead use the recipient's public key to encrypt it so that only they could decrypt it. The authentication process is shown in Figure 4–3.

There is still the risk that someone could intercept your authentication message and then use it later to pretend to be you. Recipients would receive a message purporting to be from you, encrypted with your private key—the very same message you sent some time before. They may believe it, or instead this "replay" attack can be protected against by challenging you, issuing you the command: "if you are who you say you are, then encrypt this for me," followed by a random[1] message for you to encrypt. If you can encrypt a message randomly constructed by the other party on demand, and they can decrypt it using your public key, then indeed you must be the holder of the private key. ([1]Ordinarily you would add some data of your own to their random message, in effect saying "this is a test," otherwise, they could dupe you by asking you to sign something that they can then pass off as authenticated by you.)

In the scenario just described, we used authentication to prove the identity of a party in a communication. Suppose instead you want to prove that an item of data is authentic, regardless of who is sending it? A piece of data which has the ability to authenticate itself could be sent around within a network, and even posted for general use. Users of the data could use the data without fear that it had been altered. Data can be authenticated by attaching to it a verifiable

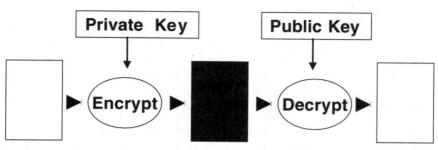

Figure 4–3 Authentication (proof of identity): they use your public key to decrypt a signature.

encrypted signature of the data. A signature is an encrypted hash value that is a function of the data itself, and if it is encrypted using the private key of the data's creator, users who have the public key can decrypt it and compare the signature with a recomputed hash of the data. Thus, users need to know the public key and the hash algorithm.

Message Digests

The hash functions used in signatures are often called "message digests," or simply "digests" for short. They are algorithms which take a message of arbitrary length as input, and produce a (usually fixed-length) numeric value. Properties of good hash algorithms include irreversibility: the practical impossibility of finding one or more input messages that produces a given hash value; apparent randomness, such that the input acts like a random number seed, and even the tiniest change in the input results in an output with no similarity to the previous value; and the near impossibility of finding *collisions*, or two messages that have the same hash value. These properties are important for applications where a hash value is used to represent or identify a piece of data, but should not reveal anything about the data; and to be able to prove message validity.

Some of the more important message digest algorithms include:

Secure Hash Algorithm-1 (SHA-1)—Developed by the U.S. government, it takes as input a message of arbitrary length and produces as output a 160-bit "hash" of the input. SHA-1 is fully described in FIPS 180-1. IETF has selected SHA-1 as the preferred one-way hash function for the Internet Public Key Infrastructure (PKI).

Message Digest 2 (MD2)—This is used by privacy enhanced mail (PEM) for certificates [RFC 1422] [RFC 1423] [RFC 1319]; now considered obsolete for new uses.

Message Digest 5 (MD5)—Used in many existing applications (including Marimba's Castanet), it was developed by Ron Rivest in 1991. It takes an input message of arbitrary length and produces a 128-bit hash result, specified in RFC 1321. At this time, the algorithm appears to have potential weaknesses, so new uses are not recommended.

Asymmetric Key Algorithms

The most widely used asymmetric key algorithms in use today are the DSA, RSA, and Diffie-Hellman algorithms. These are used for two primary purposes: implementing symmetric key exchange or negotiation; or as a digital signature.

Digital Signature Standard (DSS) and Digital Signature Algorithm (DSA)

The terms "DSS" and "DSA" are often used interchangeably. The DSA algorithm is defined in Digital Signature Standard, NIST FIPS 186, and was developed by the U.S. government. It is a digital signature algorithm that uses the RawDSA asymmetric transformation (also described in FIPS 186) along with the SHA-1 message digest algorithm.

When signing, the DSA algorithm generates two values. These values are commonly referred to as "r" and "s." X.509 v3 certificates represent these as a sequence of two integers, and together they represent the signature. The s value is a function of the private key used, which is a random number, and of a 160-bit SHA digest of the message being signed; and the r value is a function of a random number and prime modulus and divisor. The signature can later be proved to be valid by checking that it satisfies certain equations involving the public key, which is itself a function of the private key. The verification algorithm also needs to know the values of three public parameters, known as "p," "q," and "g," used when signing.

One aspect of this algorithm is that it is designed specifically for signing. Unlike the RSA algorithm, you cannot use DSA for encrypting data, only for verifying it. Nor can you use a private key as a public key, and vice versa—a DSA private key can only be used as a private key, and a DSA public key can only play the role of a public key. For this reason, DSA is often described as a "one-way" or "irreversible" algorithm.

The U.S. government holds patent 5,231,668 on the Digital Signature Algorithm (DSA), which has been incorporated into Federal Information Processing Standard (FIPS) 186. The patent was issued on July 27, 1993. However, NIST has stated publicly that DSA is available "royalty-free to users worldwide."

RSA (Rivest, Shamir, and Adleman)

The RSA asymmetric key encryption algorithm is the predominant public key algorithm used worldwide. Unlike DSA, the RSA algorithm can be used for either signing or encryption. Furthermore, it is bidirectional, in that a public key can decrypt messages encrypted with the private key, and vice versa, so in effect either key in a pair can play the public or private role. A key is composed of a set of two numbers, known as the "modulus" and the "exponent." Thus, a private key consists of a modulus and a "private" exponent, and a public key consists of the same modulus and a "public" exponent. No other parameters need be known to decrypt messages or perform verification.

The RSA algorithm, which is described in RSA Laboratory (http://www.rsa.com) Technical Note PKCS#1, is typically used in combination with either the MD2, MD5, or SHA-1 message digest algorithms for computing digital signatures.

The patent for the RSA algorithm is actually owned by the Massachusetts Institute of Technology, which has granted RSA Data Security, Inc., exclusive sublicensing rights. The patent (U.S. patent no. 4,405,829) expires on September 20, 2000. This patent is not recognized in Europe, which has led to widespread use of the algorithm there.

The Internet Engineering Task Force (IETF) has specified RSA as an algorithm for digital signatures in its PKIX standard. Therefore, those who implement products using the PKIX standard may be required to obtain a license from RSA. RSA has stated a policy of granting nonexclusive licenses to users of the patent, with royalties currently computed at 2% of the selling price of a product that makes use of the patent (of course, subject to change). Normally, of course, you would obtain a cryptographic package that includes an RSA license. RSA itself markets such a package for Java applications, called "JSafe."

Diffie-Hellman (DH) Key Agreement

The Diffie-Hellman key agreement protocol is different from RSA and DSA in that it is not intended for encryption or verification; its purpose is to allow two parties to exchange a symmetric key without actually transmitting the value of the key.

The algorithm works as follows. Consider a function $f(g, x)$, known to two parties, A and B, wishing to exchange a secret, and assume that the value of g is a nonsecret algorithm parameter known to both parties. Suppose also that A has a secret key, a, known only to A, and that similarly B has a secret key, b, known only to B. Both parties now apply the known (and public) formula $f(g, x)$, supplying their secret key for x, and they exchange their results.

```
A computes ka = f(g,a), and sends this to B.
B computes kb = f(g,b), and sends this to A.
```

Both parties now apply the formula again, but this time substituting the value they were sent for the parameter g:

```
A now computes Ka = f(kb, a) = f(f(g,b), a)

B now computes Kb = f(ka, b) = f(f(g,a), b)
```

If $f(g,x)$ has the property that $f(f(g,a), b) = f(f(g,b), a)$, for any a and b, then both recipients have in fact computed the same value (i.e., $Ka = Kb$)—this is their *shared* secret key—but no one else can know the value, because no one else knows either secret key (a or b), and the information publicly exchanged cannot be used to reverse-compute a or b.

A function that has the property specified above is exponentiation: $((g \exp a) \exp b)$ has the same result as $((g \exp b) \exp a)$, for any a and b; these are equivalent to $(g \exp (a * b))$. Exponentiation is therefore used as the function; and in order to bound the value to a certain size, the computation is done modulus a large number, which is chosen as a prime.

The algorithmic parameters that need to be specified are therefore the modulus and g, which for various mathematical reasons is required to be a primitive root of the modulus. The values for a and b can be chosen at random. This is an important fact, because it means that they can be unique for each session, and do not need to be stored. In other words, the Diffie-Hellman key agreement algorithm does not require that a private key of any kind be maintained, so there is no risk that a private key might be discovered over time. This is one reason that it is increasingly becoming an algorithm of choice in new Internet standards.

A variation of the technique, called "ephemeral Diffie-Hellman," is used when the public parameters (the modulus and the value of g) are not known ahead of time. In this case, one party can specify the values to be used for the parameters, and sign the specification. As long as the other party can authenticate the signed parameter specification, these parameters can then be trusted as originating from the communicating party, and used to perform the key agreement algorithm. Any signing algorithm, such as DSA or RSA, can be used to sign the parameter specification. (The reason for being so careful about making sure the parameters originate from a trusted party is that you do not want to take a chance that someone might give you a unique set of parameters which have a mathematical property that can be exploited in order to more easily guess your session key.)

The Diffie-Hellman key agreement algorithm is covered by patent no. 4,200,770, which expired on August 19, 1997.

Elliptic Curves

Elliptic curve algorithms are a class of algorithms that are just starting to come into use. At present, few products use elliptic curve algorithms, but this may change. Two new standards under development related to elliptic curves are ANSI X9.62 and ANSI X9.63; see http://www.certicom.ca.

Import and Export Laws

Applications and software that are deployed via the Internet can reach any location in the world. It is therefore important to have a basic understanding of the restrictions that exist regarding the transport of encryption software, since encryption is a major component of most software that provides security features.

The United States

The export of cryptographic software from the United States is regulated by the U. S. Department of Commerce, Bureau of Export Administration. Posting or distributing cryptographic software on the Internet is considered to be exporting, unless you have a means of preventing foreigners from accessing it (e.g., by verifying that their host is located within the United States). This includes any software that bundles cryptographic packages.

The policy for exporting authentication-related algorithms is more lenient than for exporting encryption, and the BEA is willing to review applications on a case-by-case basis. The current guidelines limit asymmetric keys to 512 bits. The restriction for symmetric keys is 56 bits, with certain conditions: from Sec. 734.2, *Important EAR terms and principles*, of 15 CFR dated December 30, 1996, "if an exporter makes satisfactory commitments to build and/or market recoverable encryption items and to help build the supporting international infrastructure." This relaxation holds until January 1, 1999.

For "mass-market" software, a relaxed set of criteria is applied: "The data encryption algorithm must be RC4 and/or RC2 with a key space no longer than 40 bits.... The key exchange used in data encryption must be: (A) A public key algorithm with a key space less than or equal to a 512 bit modulus and/or; (B) A symmetrical algorithm with a key space less than or equal to 64 bits."

Financial institutions and foreign subsidiaries of U.S. companies can apply for higher strengths using 128-bit DES, without having to meet key recovery requirements, as long as the software can only be used in a financial application. It should be pointed out that regardless of whether a product fits any of these criteria, even the 40-bit mass-market criteria, an exporter must still apply for a license, unless the encryption product is already licensed for export.

These restrictions are quite ineffective. Encryption algorithms and products are widely available worldwide; a foreign entity does not need to obtain them from the United States. The export restrictions merely serve to hinder the widespread use of secure electronic communication. Many people think that the export control restrictions are being used, in reality, to slow the use of encryption in domestic applications, because the government knows that U.S. companies need to operate multinationally nowadays, and so will use a level of encryption that can be deployed uniformly for all their locations. What the government is really worried about is that if everything starts to be encrypted, they will not know where to invest their decryption efforts.

There has also been a recent court case in which the Export Administration Regulations restricting the export of encryption were declared to violate the First Amendment and are therefore unconstitutional. It is not clear at this point how the regulations will adapt to meet these new legal challenges.

Only a lawyer can truly evaluate the legal obligations you have with regard to these issues, so the information presented here is for general informational purposes only; you should consult an attorney before importing or exporting any technologies that you think might be restricted, especially since the situation changes almost monthly.

International

Import and export rules for encryption technology vary from country to country. Two important multinational treaties that relate to the export of encryption software are the "Coordinating Committee for Multilateral Export Controls" (COCOM), and the "Wassenaar Arrangement on Export Controls for Conventional Arms and Dual-Use Goods and Technologies," usually referred to as the Wassenaar Arrangement. COCOM allowed the export of encryption software except to certain countries deemed "dangerous." COCOM was dissolved in 1994, but some countries still follow its provisions. The Wassenaar Arrangement was formed in 1996 as a successor to COCOM. It has very similar provisions to COCOM, but does not appear to address the export of encryption software via the Internet.

Here is a survey of the current rules that exist in some countries. Remember, again, that only a lawyer can truly evaluate the legal obligations you have with regard to these issues, so this list is for general informational purposes only, and to give you a feel for the kinds of restrictions that exist; you should consult an attorney before importing or exporting any technologies that you think might be restricted. These rules, and their interpretation, also change frequently.

Canada—Unrestricted export between the United States and Canada, but if originally exported from the United States, re-exportation from Canada is subject to U.S. rules. For export to countries other than the United States, Canada adheres to COCOM.

United Kingdom—Export over the Internet is unrestricted.

Sweden—Adheres to Wassenaar Arrangement.

Spain—No restrictions.

Singapore—Must apply to import or send encrypted data over telecom lines.

Japan—Adheres to Wassenaar Arrangement.

Germany—Export outside the European Union (EU) is restricted by license.

France—Export of authentication is permitted, but you must file; export of encryption requires a license. Some restrictions on the use of encryption, especially when the use is anonymous. There is also a key-escrow scheme, which allows unrestricted use.

Java Security Providers

The Java security architecture allows security algorithms to be plugged in using the Provider interface. A security provider is a package that implements a set of security algorithms, which may include digest algorithms, signing algorithms, and encryption algorithms. A provider package must also have a class which extends java.security.Provider; it is the job of the constructor of this Provider class to actually install the different algorithms. It does this by setting certain (undocumented!) properties in itself (the Provider class extends java.utl.Properties, which extends Hashtable), which identify the algorithms it supports. These properties basically take the form

```
<engine_type>.<algorithm_name>
```

where <engine_type> is one of

- AlgorithmParameterGenerator

- AlgorithmParameters

- KeyFactory

- KeyPairGenerator

- MessageDigest

- Signature

For each of these there is an abstract class in package java.security with the name <engine_type>Spi, and also a class <engine_type>, which extends <engine_type>Spi. A provider must extend the engine classes in order to provide security algorithms. For example, if a provider wishes to implement a Signature algorithm, it must extend java.security.Signature and implement the abstract methods defined in SignatureSpi.

In order to make the engine class (and therefore the algorithm) available, the provider class adds it to its list of properties.

Unless you are developing security algorithms, you will not need to worry too much about this. If you are using the algorithms implemented by a security provider, you will merely need to install and possibly specify the provider. Once a provider is installed, the Security class knows how to examine the properties of each installed provider and find the ones that implement specified algorithms.

Adding a Security Provider

To statically add a provider to your Java installation, you must make an entry for the provider in the java.security file in the lib/security directory of your JDK, of the form

```
security.provider.n=<provider-master-class-name>
```

where *n* is a sequential number consistent with the other providers defined in the file (i.e., no gaps), beginning with 1. The provider master class name will be specified in the documentation that comes with the provider implementation. It is the class that extends the Provider base class.

To add a provider programmatically, you can use the Security.addProvider() method. The Security class has additional methods for managing providers. The changes you make in this way are not permanent, however, since they are not reflected in your java.security file.

The JDK default provider is named "SUN." There is also an additional provider, "SunJCE," which comes as part of the Java Cryptography Extensions (JCE) packages. These are in a separate package, because they implement encryption algorithms that are not exportable without a license and so cannot be freely distributed as the rest of the JDK can be.

Encryption Algorithms Included with the Java APIs

The Java Cryptography Extensions (JCE) comprise a set of additions to package java.security that implement cryptographic streams. JCE adds to the SUN provider implementations for Data Encryption Standard (DES) and Triple DES (3DES-EDE with 168-bit key) (i.e., encryption). These features, while part of package java, are distributed separately from the JDK because of the restrictions on the export of encryption technology imposed by the U. S. Department of Commerce Export Administration Regulations.

Application developers would not typically use this directly for an application, because it is only part of the problem. This API is intended to be a component of an SSL or other end-to-end implementation. It has the cryptographic components necessary to implement SSL.

There is the temptation to create "cheap" encryption by implementing an encrypted stream without authentication. However, this is foolhardy, because authentication is a large part of the problem, and an encryption solution must address it. Providing stream encryption for Internet tunneling, without authentication, is like sending a securely locked package to someone and not having it signed for at the receiving end.

There are situations, however, in which simple encryption is appropriate. For example, a colleague of mine markets a program called BackOnline, which provides web-based backup for data. This product encrypts the data when it is transferred to the server, but never decrypts it until it returns to the client. Authentication is therefore less of an issue, because no one reads the data except the originator. On the CD that accompanies this book, I provide an example of password-based encryption using the JCE.

The following list specifies the algorithms recognized by the Java API. Included algorithms are marked with an asterisk, or two asterisks if they are part of the JCE. These are the "standard" names by which the Java API knows these algorithms.

Standard names defined by JDK 1.1 and 1.2:
> *Included with SUN provider for JDK1.1, 1.2
> **Included with SunJCE Provider for JCE1.2/JDK1.2

Digest algorithms:
- **SHA-1*** (also **SHA***)
- **MD5** *
- **MD2**

Asymmetric key encryption algorithms:
- **RawDSA**
- **RSA**

Digest/asymmetric key signing algorithms:
- **SHA-1/RSA**—Signature created by encrypting an SHA-1 digest with an RSA cipher

- **MD5/RSA**—Signature created by encrypting an MD5 digest with an RSA cipher

- **MD2/RSA**—Signature created by encrypting an MD2 digest with an RSA cipher

- **DSA***—Signature created by applying RawDSA to an SHA-1 digest

Symmetric key encryption algorithms:
- **DES****

- **IDEA**

- **RC2**

- **RC4**

Standard names defined by JCE (all these are included in the SunJCE provider):
- **DESede**—DES-EDE.

  Related (to handle block ciphers such as DES):

    ECB—Electronic Codebook Mode, as defined in the National Institute of Standards and Technology (NIST) Federal Information Processing Standard (FIPS) 81

    CBC—Cipher-Chaining Mode, as defined in NIST FIPS 81

    CFB—Cipher-Feedback Mode, as defined in NIST FIPS 81

    OFB—Output-Feedback Mode, as defined in NIST FIPS 81

- **DH**—Diffie-Hellman key agreement

- **PBEWithMD5AndDES**—Password-based encryption, as per PKCS#5

  Related:

    PKCS5Padding, NoPadding—Specifies to use PKCS#5 padding, or not

Overview of X.509 Certificates

A digital certificate is an digitally signed document which serves the purpose of providing a specific set of authenticated information. The information is authenticated because the signature is verifiable proof that the document has not been altered, and because the signature can be proved to have been created by a trusted party. Generally, the signed content includes the identity of the originator of the certificate and their public key. A certificate is therefore a reliable way to distribute one's public key.

Let us consider an example. Suppose you have a public key and want to send it to someone. You could create a certificate that includes your name and your public key, and then have a trusted third party sign the certificate. Anyone who receives the certificate can verify the contents of the certificate simply by verifying the signature. Basically, they prove that the name and public key were used to create the signature, and therefore have not been modified since the signature was created.

The signature is created using the private signing key of the trusted third party. To perform the verification, you need the trusted third party's public key. It seems that to get this, you need their certificate—and so we have kind of a catch-22, since to verify a certificate we need another certificate, and so on. Where does it end? The assumption is that at some point you obtain the certificate of a trusted party through some physical means that you trust, such as by obtaining it from someone on a diskette; or perhaps the certificate was included with a product such as a browser. Such "trusted certificates" are usually issued by entities called "certificate authorities" (CAs), whose main business is to issue these certificates. A CA provides a strong guarantee that their certificate keys are kept in a safe place, just as a bank guarantees that your money is kept in a safe place.

Practically the only kind of certificate you are likely to encounter nowadays on the Internet is an X.509 certificate. The X.509 certificate standard was first published in 1988 as part of X.500, revised as version 2 in 1993, and again as version 3 in 1996.

Version 3 has a loophole: using the "extensions" provision, it is possible to create X.509 v.3 certificates of different kinds particular to an application. Thus, just because your certificate is X.509 v.3-compliant does not give you any indication whether it will work in your application, because your application may need certain extension fields to be filled in. This means that the providers of certificates are in a position of being the providers of unique certificates for potentially each user, and for potentially every application that user uses. What a nice position to be in!

This is what is contained in an X.509 certificate, in exactly this sequence:

```
version (i.e., version 1, 2, or 3)
serial no.
signature algorithm id
issuer distinguished name
validity period
subject distinguished name
subject public key info (algorithm, key)

Version 2 extensions (IETF recommends against using of these):
  issuer unique id
  subject unique id

Version 3 extensions:
  triplets, {extension name, criticality, extension value}

  digital signature
```

Here is an example. This is a human-readable dump of the CA certificate for RSA Data Security, included with Netscape Communicator 4.0. It is a self-signed certificate—hence the subject and issuer are the same. As you can see, it is a version 1 certificate. The actual certificate is encoded in a format called "DER-encoding."

```
Version: 1 (0x0)
Serial Number:
    02:41:00:00:16
Signature Algorithm: md2WithRSAEncryption
Issuer: C=US, O=RSA Data Security, Inc., OU=Commercial
  Certification Authority
Validity:
    Not Before: Nov  4 18:58:34 1994 GMT
    Not After : Nov  3 18:58:34 1999 GMT
Subject: C=US, O=RSA Data Security, Inc., OU=Commercial
Certification Authority
Subject Public Key Info:
    Public Key Algorithm: rsaEncryption
    Public Key (RSA): (1000 bit)
        Modulus (1000 bit):
            00:a4:fb:81:62:7b:ce:10:27:dd:e8:f7:be:6c:6e:
            c6:70:99:db:b8:d5:05:03:69:28:82:9c:72:7f:96:
            3f:8e:ec:ac:29:92:3f:8a:14:f8:42:76:be:bd:5d:
            03:b9:90:d4:d0:bc:06:b2:51:33:5f:c4:c2:bf:b6:
            8b:8f:99:b6:62:22:60:dd:db:df:20:82:b4:ca:a2:
            2f:2d:50:ed:94:32:de:e0:55:8d:d4:68:e2:e0:4c:
            d2:cd:05:16:2e:95:66:5c:61:52:38:1e:51:a8:82:
            a1:c4:ef:25:e9:0a:e6:8b:2b:8e:31:66:d9:f8:d9:
            fd:bd:3b:69:d9:eb
        Exponent: 65537 (0x10001)
Signature:
    76:b5:b6:10:fe:23:f7:f7:59:62:4b:b0:5f:9c:c1:68:bc:49:
    bb:b3:49:6f:21:47:5d:2b:9d:54:c4:00:28:3f:98:b9:f2:8a:
    83:9b:60:7f:eb:50:c7:ab:05:10:2d:3d:ed:38:02:c1:a5:48:
    d2:fe:65:a0:c0:bc:ea:a6:23:16:66:6c:1b:24:a9:f3:ec:79:
    35:18:4f:26:c8:e3:af:50:4a:c7:a7:31:6b:d0:7c:18:9d:50:
    bf:a9:26:fa:26:2b:46:9c:14:a9:bb:5b:30:98:42:28:b5:4b:
    53:bb:43:09:92:40:ba:a8:aa:5a:a4:c6:b6:8b:57:4d:c5
```

Note that the signature algorithm may be different from the subject public key algorithm. The signature algorithm is what the CA uses to sign the certificate; the subject public key algorithm specifies the type of key the subject has generated. Very frequently these are the same algorithm, but there is no strict reason why they have to be. (Some protocols may require that they be the same.) As a practical matter, if the algorithms are different, the probability is higher that software using the certificate will not have one of the algorithms.

Different kinds of keys have different value components, as explained earlier when asymmetric algorithms were discussed. Also, a Diffie-Hellman certificate will have DH parameters. Still, a DH certificate will be signed with some signature algorithm, such as DSA or RSA.

Version 3 Extensions

The X.509 version 3 extensions are:

> Authority key identifier—Identifies a particular issuer public key in cases when the issuer has more than one signing key

> Subject key identifier—Identifies the subject's public key; may be a hash-code of the key

> Private key usage period—Specified if the private key has a different validity period than the certificate

> Policy information—Identifies CA policies that apply to the certificate; may specify a notice to be displayed for users, and identify a Certification Practice Statement

> Policy mappings—Only used in CA certificates; correlates end-usage policies with CA policies

> Subject alternative names—Provide additional identities for the subject in addition to the distinguished name, such as e-mail address, DNS name, IP address, and a URI

> Issuer alternative names—Provides additional identities for the issuer

> Subject directory attributes—Not usually used

> Basic constraints—Indicates whether the subject of the certificate is a CA and how deep a certification chain may be through that CA

> Name constraints—Identifies a name space in a certification chain which must contain all subjects in subsequent certificates

> Policy constraints—Specifies that each certificate in a chain contains a policy identifier, or excludes policy mapping

> CRL distribution points—Identifies how CRL information is obtained

> Key usage—Defines the CA's intended purpose of the key contained in the certificate (e.g., encryption, signing)

> Extended key usage—Identifies additional purposes for usage, typically specific to the enduser's (as opposed to the CA's) domain

> IETF extension—The only IETF extension: identifies an online validation service supporting the CA

Key Usage and Extended Key Usage

As shown above, X.509 version 3 defines a "key usage" extension and an "extended key usage" extension. The key usage extension specifies the intended purpose of the public key contained in the certificate. The usages (which may be combined in certain ways) defined for the key are:

> digitalSignature—Authentication
>
> nonRepudiation—Nonrepudiation service which protects against the signing entity falsely denying some action
>
> keyEncipherment—For enciphering keys for transport
>
> dataEncipherment—For enciphering user data
>
> keyAgreement—Key agreement, for example, when a Diffie-Hellman key is to be used for key management
>
> keyCertSign—Verifying a signature on certificates (for CA certificates only)
>
> cRLSign—Verifying a signature on CRLs
>
> encipherOnly—Enciphering data while performing key agreement
>
> decipherOnly—Deciphering data while performing key agreement

The extended key usages proposed by the IETF at the time of this writing are:

> serverAuth—Web server authentication
>
> clientAuth—Web client authentication
>
> codeSigning—Signing of downloadable executable code
>
> emailProtection—E-mail protection
>
> ipsecEndSystem—IP security end system (host or router)
>
> ipsecTunnel—IP security tunnel termination
>
> ipsecUser—IP security user
>
> timeStamping—Binding the hash of an object to a time from an agreed-upon time

These must be consistent with the key usage indicators, according to a set of consistency rules. These extended uses are not at present used by the JDK, however.

The most common kinds of certificates a user or system administrator will encounter are client certificates, server certificates, signing certificates, and CA certificates. Client certificates are used by end users to authenticate themselves to a server. A client certificate would have its clientAuth flag set, as well as its digitalSignature flag and perhaps its nonRepudiation flag. A server certificate is used to authenticate a server to clients, and provide a key for encrypting session keys that are exchanged, which may then be used for encryption. A server certificate would have its serverAuth flag set, its digitalSignature and nonRepudiation flags set, and perhaps others. A signing certificate is for signing data (e.g., applets or other content distributable to clients), and would have its codeSigning flag set. A CA certificate is usually self-signed, and serves the purpose of a top-level trusted item used to verify other certificates. Assuming a CA certificate has been obtained by a satisfactorily secure means (e.g., bundled with a product in a physically sealed software product package), or is posted somewhere against which it can be compared, the CA certificate's public key can be used by clients to verify a server's certificate.

You will not normally have to know what key usage modes are in effect for a certificate unless your certificate is not working, and you cannot get support from your certificate vendor or certificate server vendor, and you need to diagnose what is wrong yourself. This could occur if you have your own certificate server, and the certificates you are creating do not seem to work.

Different Kinds of Certificates (sigh...): My Soapbox

Sometimes things go so far awry that one just has to stand up and say something about it.

A certificate should contain one assertion: I AM <a-specified-entity>; and it should provide the capability to sign things, and/or seal (encrypt) things. It should be that simple. A certificate should *not* be used to transfer information (messages) other than what is required to accomplish its main purpose: authentication of identity. Messages should be defined in protocols, and encrypted or signed if necessary for authentication and privacy. Certificates should *not* contain things like "Vendor no. XXX," "Point-of-origin," "Address," "Host-name," and so on. Would you want your current address in your birth certificate? Of course not, because if you move, you would need to update your birth certificate and have it reprinted—kind of silly, right? And imagine if each time you had to make such a change, it cost you $400!

A certificate is merely a digitally signed document. However, it should be a special kind of document. As long as an entity's identity can be verified, using a certificate signed by a trusted party, that entity can use their certificate to sign, and therefore verify, any other information that needs to be exchanged by an application or protocol. There is no need to go back to a certificate authority to sign protocol-specific information. That signing can be delegated.

The obstacle to this is that server vendors are using the X.509 v.3 extensions feature to add application-specific information to the certificates required by their servers, and then requiring you—the user—to go to the CA to obtain a certificate just for their server. The result is that you need to get separate server certificates for your Netscape server, your Microsoft server, your Castanet server, and so on. In fact, you need to get a separate certificate for *each machine* on which these servers run; and if you move a server from one host to another, you usually have to go back to the CA and pay another fee (around $400 at the time of this writing)! (Embedding the hostname protects the administrator against stolen keys, but there are better ways to do this.) It does not have to be this way. (Complain to your server vendor!)

What SET Uses

"SET" is the Secure Electronic Transaction standard, developed by Visa, Master-card, and others. It is the standard that will be used for consumer credit card pur-chases over the Internet. While SET is a closed system, and SET certificates can only be used for SET applications, the world is watching SET to see how certifi-cates measure up in volume use, where the stakes are high. Lessons learned from SET will surely be applied elsewhere. SET is supported by the Java Electronic Commerce Framework, as will be discussed later in this chapter.

SET uses X.509 v3 certificates with these standard extensions:

- Authority key identifier

- Key usage

- Private key usage period

- Certificate policies (several extensions related to this)

- Subject alternative names

- Basic constraints

- Issuer alternative names

SET has also added these "private extensions," which are unique to SET:

- HashedRootKey

- CertificateType (SET defines these types: Cardholder, Merchant, Payment-Gateway, GeoPoliticalCertificateAuthority, BrandCertificateAuthority, Root-CertificateAuthority, CardholderCertificateAuthority, MerchantCertificateAuthority, PaymentCertificateAuthority, and various combinations of some of these)

- MerchantData

- CardCertRequired

- Tunneling

- SETExtensions

What Java Uses

As you can see, all of the different kinds of certificates we have looked at claim to be X.509 v3 compatible. However, they all have extensions of various kinds—extensions not recognized by each other. Again, this is because these certificates are being used as customized signed documents, to carry information. In some cases, as with SET, there is good reason to define a closed system, since these uses are new, and the participants want to maintain control to ensure success. Hopefully the tendency to create closed systems will not continue, however.

The Java security APIs can handle any X.509 certificate that uses algorithms for which there is a provider installed. The tools which generate certificates, however, generate a X.509 v.1 certificate. Javasoft will likely maintain compliance with any modifications to the standard defined by the IETF. The actual X.509 implementation is specified by the cert.provider.x509 property in the security properties file (java.security in the lib/security directory), with a default value of sun.security.x509.X509CertImpl.

Obtaining a Server Certificate

Obtaining a server certificate (e.g., for a secure web server or a secure CORBA ORB), is normally done through a user interface included with the server product itself. The server knows what X.509 v.3 extension attributes to write into the certificate request, usually including the hostname or IP address of the machine the server is running on (which must be the same machine on which you create the request).

The server will guide you through the process of key pair generation, storing the private key in the server (encrypted with a user-supplied password), generation of a blank certificate with the new public key to send to the CA, wrapping it in a Certificate Signing Request (CSR; usually as defined in RSA PKCS#10), and sending it out for signing; at this point, you may have to prove your identity to the CA. This is usually a particular CA with whom the server vendor has a relationship.

The CA will then add information to the certificate such as expiration date and CA information. The CA encrypts a hash of the information in your certificate using their private key (i.e., signs it) and stores the result in your certificate. They then send the certificate back to you.

You then go back to the server's certificate request user interface, and tell it the file name where the returned certificate resides. (The CA may have sent it to you via e-mail.) The server will then install the certificate into its certificate database, replacing the self-signed certificate it created earlier with the one signed by the CA.

Smart Cards and Embedded Keys

A smart card is a credit-card-sized device which has an embedded microprocessor and nonvolatile memory. Metal contacts on the surface of the card allow it to connect to a communication bus when inserted into a smart card reader. A smart card can serve many functions, ranging from holding medical information to storing electronic cash ("E-cash"); or it may simply provide a tamper-proof token for authenticating a user.

Since a physical token can be made tamper-proof, it can itself serve as a kind of certificate. This is what currency is: tamper-proof documentation of a debt. However, just as with currency, techniques evolve over time to defeat tamper-proofness or to duplicate tokens. Relying on physical tamper-proofness alone is not sufficient if there is a lot at stake. That is why many smart cards also require a password (i.e., a PIN number), which the user must enter each time the card is used, just as with a bank card. The user must therefore be in possession of the card and also know the password.

Since smart cards contain computers, their function is only limited by the ingenuity of smart card designers. Some smart card APIs have built-in support for encryption and even certificate management. The smart card can therefore be used to store certificates and encrypted private keys. This obviates the need to keep private keys on a user's machine, making it possible for users to roam from computer to computer, and carry their certificate and key database with them.

Javasoft has developed a version of the Java VM for smart cards. The JavaCard API, now in version 2, is supported by a range of smart card manufacturers. Some of them are listed below.

- Gemplus (http://www.gemplus.com/)

- Bull/CP8 (http://www.cp8.bull.net/)

- Dallas Semiconductor (http://www.dalsemi.com/)

- De La Rue (http://www.delarue.com/)

- Geisecke & Devrient (http://www.gdm.de)

- Schlumberger (http://www.cyberflex.austin.et.slb.com/)

- Toshiba (http://www.toshiba.co.jp)

(Note: Netscape supports smart cards. Unfortunately, the brands supported do not, at this time, intersect with those that support the JavaCard API! Netscape's supported smart card brands are Litronic, Netsign, and Datakey's SignaSURE. Hopefully, over time, all brands will support the JavaCard API.)

The JavaCard 2.0 API has built-in support for DES and 3DES encryption, and SHA-1 message digests. It also directly supports RSA signing. Interestingly, it does not provide the DSA algorithm; possibly it was felt that one public key algorithm was sufficient, in the interest of conserving space and keeping ROM usage low. There is no built-in certificate management, but certificates can, of course, be stored as a DER byte array.

Interestingly, the JavaCard Java VM fits in 16K of memory. Yes—that is "K," not "M." (This takes me back 20 years!) This was achieved by eliminating most of the APIs that it was felt were not relevant for smart card applications, which do not have user interfaces and don't need to connect with any device except for a smart card reader. JavaCard programs also do not have automatic garbage collection, so if your program creates an object, the object never goes away. Since JavaCard programs run for the life of the card, the strategy is to create all the objects you need at initialization and reuse them.

Smart cards—Java or otherwise—require support on the computer in which they are used. In the case of a Java application, the smart card needs to have a security provider class (most likely with a native interface to the card reader) that makes the security features (such as encryption or signing) available to the Java application. Java applications then see the card simply as another security provider.

Key Management

An application that wants to provide user authentication must have a way to manage client and CA certificates and keys. For this purpose, the application needs to have, or have access to, a key and certificate database. For example, Netscape Communicator has one for each user, located in files called key3.db and cert7.db. Castanet also allows you to view/manage certificates accepted from a transmitter. Castanet does not maintain a client-side certificate database of its own, however (at this time).

Currently, the key databases in these products are not accessible to you programmatically. This may change when these and similar products incorporate Java 1.2, since Java 1.2 includes a key database facility called a KeyStore. The key store is by default stored in a file named .keystore in the user's home directory, as determined by the "user.home" system property.

Creating a Key Manager

A key management tool allows users to manage their keys and certificates—both the certificates that pertain to them, and the certificates they receive from others. Such a tool would allow users to:

- List certificates

- Import/remove certificates

- View certificates (before and after installation)

- Verify certificates

To implement this, you can use an existing key store implementation, or write your own. In either case, we are still dealing with a key store, so the rest of the code is the same. We will use Sun's default KeyStore, sun.security.tools.JavaKeyStore.

First we must instantiate the keystore manager. We do this as follows:

```
KeyStore ks = KeyStore.getInstance();
```

This will create an instance of the class specified by the keystore property (with default value of "sun.security.tools.JavaKeyStore") in the file java.security in the java.home/lib/security directory.

All this does is create an empty keystore. To load a keystore database:

```
// Specify where the key database is - this can be anywhere
String fname = System.getProperty("user.home") +
  System.getProperty("file.separator") + ".keystore";
// Load the key database; skip this if keystore is new
FileInputStream is = new FileInputStream(fname);
ks.load(is, "myCertDBPassword");
is.close();
```

Our application, however, could allow the user to select a key store manager class, and a key store database as well.

Next, we can list the certificates in the key store:

```
TextArea list = new TextArea(5, 30);
add(list);
Enumeration entries = ks.aliases();
for (; entries.hasMoreElements();)
{
   String alias = entries.nextElement();
   if (ks.isKeyEntry(alias)) list.append("Key: ");
   else if (ks.isCertificateEntry(alias)) list.append("Cert: ");
   list.append(alias + "\n");
}
```

To select and instantiate a client certificate,

```
Certificate[] certChain = ks.getCertificateChain(alias);
```

The first certificate in the array is the certificate associated with the alias; the rest are the certificates of CAs which signed the first certificate, and then each other, ending with the root CA's certificate.

(If you store server certificates in your database, you will need to use the getCertificateAlias(Certificate cert) method to match them.)

This would be done to view a certificate. It would also be done by SSL code that wanted to use a certificate from this database, either to verify a trusted server certificate, or to provide a client certificate for user authentication.

The user will want to view a selected certificate. These methods can be used for x.509 certificates:

getPublicKey()—Return the public key of the certificate.

getIssuerDN()—Return the issuer distinguished name value from the certificate.

getIssuerUniqueID()—Return the issuerUniqueID value from the certificate.

getKeyUsage()—Return the BitSet for the KeyUsage extension, (OID = 2.5.29.15).

getNotAfter()—Return the notAfter date from the validity period of the certificate.

getNotBefore()—Return the notBefore date from the validity period of the certificate.

getSerialNumber()—Return the serialNumber value from the certificate.

getSigAlgName()—Return the signature algorithm name for the certificate signature algorithm.

getSigAlgOID()—Return the signature algorithm OID string from the certificate.

getSigAlgParams()—Return the DER-encoded signature algorithm parameters from this certificate's signature algorithm.

getSignature()—Return the signature value (the raw signature bits) from the certificate.

getSubjectDN()—Return the subject (subject distinguished name) value from the certificate.

getSubjectUniqueID()—Return the subjectUniqueID value from the certificate.

getTBSCertificate()—Return the DER-encoded certificate information, the tbsCertificate from this certificate.

getVersion()—Return the version number value of the certificate.

For example, we might want to display the certificate owner's distinguished name, the issuer's distinguished name, the key usage (what the certificate can be used for), the validity period, the serial number, the signing algorithm, the version number, and the actual public key of each certificate in the chain:

```
Panel p = new Panel();
p.setLayout(new GridLayout(7, 1));
for (int i = 0; i < certChain.length; i++)
{
   Certificate cert = certChain[i];
   p.add(new Label("Owner: " + cert.getSubjectDN().getName()));
   p.add(new Label("Issuer: " + cert.getIssuerDN().getName()));
   BitSet usage = cert.getKeyUsage();
   p.add(new Label("Key Usage: "
      + "Authentication: " + (usage.set(0) ? "yes" : "no") + "   "
      + "Encryption: " + (usage.set(3) ? "yes" : "no") ));
   p.add(new Label("Valid from " +
cert.getNotBefore().toString()
      + " to " + cert.getNotAfter().toString()));
   p.add(new Label("Serial No.: " +
cert.getSerialNumber().toString()));
   p.add(new Label("Sig. Alg.: " + cert.getSigAlgName()));
   p.add(new Label("Version: " + cert.getVersion()));
}
add(p);
validate();
```

Key usage bits are:

Bit	Usage
0	digitalSignature
1	nonRepudiation
2	keyEncipherment
3	dataEncipherment
4	keyAgreement
5	keyCertSign (CA's)
6	cRLSign
7	encipherOnly
8	decipherOnly

Surprise, this is just what is defined in the evolving IETF standard!

To import a new certificate, you must construct a Certificate object from the bytes that compose the certificate. The java.security.cert.X509Certificate class has a get-Instance() method for constructing a certificate from serial input:

```
File f = new File("MyCertFile");
InputStream is = new FileInputStream(f);
byte[] bytes = new byte[f.length()];
is.read(bytes);
X509Certificate cert = X509Certificate.getInstance(bytes);
```

When a certificate is added, a key pair may also be added. To add the certificate and a private key to your certificate database,

```
ks.setKeyEntry(alias, key /*byte array - the key you obtained*/,
  password, new Certificate[] { cert })
FileOutputStream os = new FileOutputStream(fname);
ks.store(os, "myCertDBPassword");
os.close();
```

A common way of obtaining a certificate is from a web site. The application/x-x509-ca-cert and application/x-x509-user-cert MIME types are used by both Netscape and Internet Explorer for transferring certificates. Unfortunately, a certificate transferred in this way will be automatically installed into your browser's certificate database, or in the case of Internet Explorer in the registry, which is not what we want in this case (because here we are merely using the browser to obtain the certificate; we are not assuming our application is browser-based): we want to put it into our own application database. Specifying Save-To-Disk does not seem to work either with most CAs, since the CAs certificate transfer process is usually written in JavaScript and transfers the certificate directly to the client JavaScript application. Communicator now has the ability to import and export certificates, however. Thus, once the certificate is installed into your browser, you can export it to a file, and then load it into you own keystore using the above routines. In addition, Netscape has announced that it plans to expose its keystore API.

Certificate verification involves decrypting the signature stored in the certificate, using the signer's (usually a CA) public key. Applying the signer's public key to the certificate's encrypted signature should yield a decrypted message that contains a reproducible hash of the identity of the signer. If this is successful, it proves that the signer's private key was used to produce the encrypted signature. To verify a certificate, you can use the verify() method:

```
try
{
   cert.verify(cert.getPublicKey());//public key should also
                                    //be compared with its
                                    //known value
}
catch (java.security.GeneralSecurityException)
{
   System.out.println("Whoooaaaa—certificate does not verify!");
}
```

To implement all this as an application (or as a channel), all we have to do is create a user interface framework for managing all this.

Secure Communication Protocols

The Secure Socket Layer (SSL) Protocol

The Secure Socket Layer (SSL) protocol is a protocol for creating secure connections between a client and a server across a network. Netscape developed the SSL protocol in order to create a way for their browser to be used with their server products to conduct electronic commerce, securely, and with the confidence that consumer financial data—in particular, credit card data—transmitted over the Internet could not be compromised. Ironically, the mere fact that they developed this mechanism may have heightened fears about Internet commerce rather than quelled them (just as the fact that Java has built-in security protections has raised consciousness about Java security issues). A consumer's actual financial liability with any credit card purchase is usually quite limited in practice, so Internet credit card fraud may have received more attention than it deserves—at least from the consumer's point of view. Nevertheless, the need for secure transmission of information via the Internet is a real one for many applications, financial and otherwise. The SSL protocol was a breakthrough in making this possible.

SSL attempts to solve the full end-to-end secure transmission problem: it provides for identity authentication of both the client and server (although client authentication is optional in many server products that use SSL); and it encrypts the data that is transmitted. The protocol is flexible, and allows for dynamic specification of cipher algorithms. It is also largely automatic from the user's point of view. The only complication is that one or both ends of the communication link must have a digital certificate or private/public key pair, which must be installed in some way by the administrator or user.

It should be noted that SSL is a secure connection protocol and does not address the issue of logging. If an application needs to record who did what, and when, the application needs to provide for this. While SSL can authenticate users, it does not automatically record sessions, much less what takes place in them. If you need to provide logging of any kind, your application generally must add this.

The protocol can be used in many ways. However, the basic operation of the SSL protocol commonly uses this sequence:

1. Exchange digital certificates (usually server certificate, sometimes client certificate as well).

2. Verify the certificate(s) and authenticate identity.

3. Securely (via asymmetric key encryption or negotiation) exchange symmetric encryption keys to use for subsequent data transmission.

4. Begin data transmission.

This exchange is depicted in Figure 4–4.

The actual protocol has many additional features. For example, either communicating party can request at any time that the cipher be changed. (It is a common technique in secure communication systems to change keys at frequent intervals during a session.) Authentication of the client (the originator of the connection) is optional in most uses, but SSL APIs do not mandate authentication of either party.

The protocol actually is layered into multiple protocols. The two primary layers are the SSL Handshake Protocol and the SSL Record Protocol. The Handshake Protocol defines the session establishment messages that travel between the client and server at the start of a session. The Record Protocol defines a lower-level messaging band in which the Handshake Protocol and all application data is wrapped. Error conditions that generate alerts travel in this band.

The Record Protocol message types are:

- change_cipher_spec
- alert
- handshake
- application_data

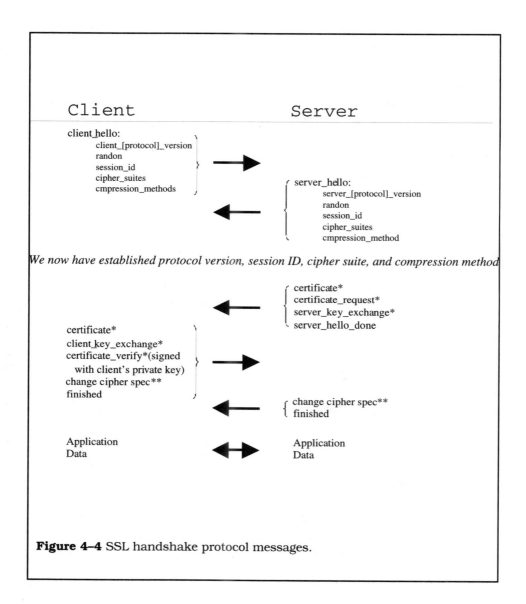

Figure 4–4 SSL handshake protocol messages.

The SSL Handshake protocol message types are:

- hello_request
- client_hello
- server_hello
- certificate
- server_key_exchange
- certificate_request
- server_hello_done
- certificate_verify
- client_key_exchange
- finished

Session key exchange can be by any of the following techniques:

- Diffie-Hellman
- RSA encryption
- Fortezza Key Exchange Algorithm (similar to Diffie-Hellman; uses a hardware token)

Netscape has a patent on SSL, but allows royalty-free implementation, providing that those implementations do not claim their own patent rights that infringe on Netscape's patent.

Transport Layer Security (TLS)

Transport Layer Security is an IETF effort aimed at standardizing the SSL protocol. It is anticipated that most future implementations of SSL will move to TLS, and support SSL only for the sake of backward compatibility. This is not hard to do, however, since TLS is extremely similar to SSL 3.0.

The supported key exchange algorithms recommended by the IETF, as of this writing, are:

- Diffie-Hellman
- RSA
- Kerberos

Unless a particular usage requires otherwise, the following cipher suite is always included in a TLS implementation. See the next section for an interpretation of this name.

```
TLS_DHE_DSS_WITH_3DES_EDE_CBC_SHA
```

Interpreting Cipher Suite Names

The SSL and TLS Hello handshake involve the negotiation of a cipher suite to be used between the client and server, among other things. A cipher suite is a set of algorithms, including the key exchange protocol, the symmetric cipher algorithm to be used, and the hashing algorithm to be used. The identification of the cipher suite is numerically encoded, but the specifications define a set of names for recognized cipher suites.

Consider the cipher suite name

```
TLS_RSA_WITH_RC4_128_MD5
```

The basic sequence for deciphering these (no pun intended) is

```
<protocol>_<key-exchange-algorithm>_<cipher-algorithm>_<hash-
   algorithm>
```

Therefore, "TLS_RSA_WITH_RC4_128_MD5" uses RSA encryption for exchanging secret keys; those keys are 128-bit RC4 keys, and the hashing algorithm for computing digests is MD5.

Now let's consider

```
TLS_DHE_DSS_WITH_3DES_EDE_CBC_SHA
```

This suite specifies DHE_DSS for key exchange. The "DHE" part stands for ephemeral Diffie-Hellman, and DSS specifies that the DSS algorithm should be used for signing the Diffie-Hellman parameters so they can be authenticated by the other side. Moving down to the cipher algorithm, "3DES_EDE_CBC" specifies triple-DES with Cipher Block Chaining, a technique applicable to block ciphers such as DES. "SHA," of course, specifies SHA as the hashing algorithm to use.

What about this:

```
TLS_DH_DSS_EXPORT_WITH_DES40_CBC_SHA
```

This suite specifies Diffie-Hellman key exchange, using DSS for authentication. The session encryption algorithm will be DES, with a 40-bit key (i.e., exportable, for mass-market software), and so on.

Use of HTTPS (HTTP/SSL or HTTP/TLS) URLs

Java platforms such as browsers and the Castanet tuner provide their own URL stream handler factory to allow URLs for recognized protocols to be handled. For example, Communicator does something like the following when it initializes a virtual machine:

```
java.net.URL.setURLStreamHandlerFactory(new
   netscape.net.URLStreamHandlerFactory());
```

In a Communicator applet or a Castanet application, you can therefore use an SSL URL to access a location that uses SSL, and cause the browser's or tuner's built-in SSL stream handler to be used. For example, you could do something like the following:

```
URL url = new
  URL("https://securehost.mycompany.com/privatestuff.cgi");
URLConnection uc = url.openConnection();
uc.connect();
OutputStream os = uc.getOutputStream();
...write posted output (securely)...
InputStream is = uc.getInputStream();
...get response (securely)...
```

In the above example, a port is not specified in the URL, so in all likelihood the stream handler will use port 443, which is the default port for HTTPS connections (for either SSL or TLS).

Of course, you can only use the connection in a manner supported by that type of connection, as defined by the stream handler created for you by the stream handler factory. In particular, an HTTP or HTTPS connection will probably have restrictions on when and how you can read and write from the stream, and it will also depend on the object (URL) to which you are connecting (i.e., whether or not it is a program or a static object). See the chapter on Internet protocols for more information.

Implementing Secure ORB Connections

The OMG has defined a security service for CORBA, and in addition has defined an implementation of IIOP, called SECIOP, which uses that service to provide secure connections between CORBA clients and servers. The ink is barely dry on this very complex standard, and many CORBA vendors have already created SSL implementations that serve the same purpose as SECIOP. Until SECIOP is more widely adopted, it is probably more useful to look at an SSL CORBA implementation.

The first issue you will have to resolve is whether you need client-side authentication. Generally, intranet applications do not need this unless the server application needs to access a user database of some sort, and perform activities based on who the user is. For example, a call center application might access a sales agent database, and add transactions that affect the agent's commissions. In such an application, client authentication is probably desirable.

If you need client authentication, you will need to decide where you will keep the client certificates and private keys. Will they be in the form of smart cards, carried by users? Or will they be stored on users' machines with the keys password-encrypted? Let's assume that you have implemented a client certificate database, as demonstrated earlier. You therefore have the capability to retrieve a user's certificate. Here is an example of how you might access a Java 1.2 key store to obtain a server certificate for servicing an SSL CORBA server connection, using Visigenic's SSL implementation:

```java
import org.omg.CORBA.ORBPackage.*;
import com.visigenic.vbroker.ssl.*;
import java.security.*;

public class MyClient
{
    public static void main(String[] args)
    {
        // Specify the Visigenic SSL/IIOP provider
        java.util.Properties p = new java.util.Properties();
        p.put("ORBServices", "com.visigenic.vbroker.ssl");

        // Initialize the ORB
        org.omg.CORBA.ORB orb = org.omg.CORBA.ORB.init(args, p);

        // Get the user's certificate alias
        String alias = ...prompt for alias...

        // Load our client certificate chain
        KeyStore ks = KeyStore.getInstance();
        String fname = System.getProperty("user.home")
            + System.getProperty("file.separator") + ".keystore";
        InputStream is = new File(fname);
        ks.load(InputStream stream, String password);
        Certificate[] certChain = ks.getCertificateChain(alias);

        // Instantiate a Visigenic "certificate manager"
        CertificateManager cm = CertificateManagerHelper.narrow(
            orb.resolve_initial_references
            ("SSLCertificateManager"));
```

```
// Provide client certificate chain to the certificate
// manager, which
// will provide it to the server when requested
byte[][] cchain = new byte[certChain.length][];
for (int i = 0; i < cchain.length; i++)
{
   // This is a critical statement: it is how we will pass a
   // certificate,
   // loaded from a Java 1.2 keystore, to a Visigenic SSL
   // cert manager
   cchain[i] = certChain[i].getEncoded();
}
cm.setCertificateChain(cchain);

// Get private key password from user
String password = ...prompt...

// Obtain client private key from our database
PrivateKey epk = getPrivateKey(alias, password);

// Provide private key, so that client can answer
// challenges; note that
// it was stored in encrypted form, so the
// CertificateManager will have
// to decrypt it
byte[] encrPK = cm.decodeBase64(epk.getEncoded());
cm.setEncryptedPrivateKey(cncrPK, password);

// Find our server object
OurServer ourServer = OurServerHelper.bind(
   orb, "OurServer");

// Get the "Current" object - this is a proxy for the server
// SSL context
Current c = CurrentHelper.narrow
   (orb.resolve_initial_references("SSLCurrent"));

// Verify the server object's certificate
X509CertificateChain cc =
 current.getPeerCertificateChain(ourServer);
checkCertChain(cc);
```

```
        // Get some other server object, by method call
        SomeOtherServer sos = ourServer.someMethod();

        // Now check that server object's certificate as well
        current.getPeerCertificateChain(sos);
        checkCertChain(cc);

        ...do other stuff...
    }
    static void checkCertChain(X509CertificateChain cc)
    {
        byte[] cbytes = cc.berEncoding();
        Certificate cert = X509Certificate.getInstance(cbytes);
        PublicKey pk = cert.getPublicKey();
        try { cert.verify(pk); }
        catch (java.security.GeneralSecurityException ex)
        { System.out.println("Server certificate not valid!");
          System.exit(0); }
    }
}
```

(Note: To use Visibroker's SSL feature with the Netscape browser, you must add some runtime components to the browser. You must add Visigenic's native SSL library (which includes the RSA BSafe cryptographic algorithms) to your Netscape bin directory, and you must add Visigenic's SSL classes (in a JAR file) to your system's classpath. A similar modification is needed for Internet Explorer.)

Implementing Secure RMI

I will now demonstrate how to create a secure RMI server and client using SSL sockets. For this demonstration, I will use the Phaos SSL socket library from Phaos Technologies. (Note that at the time of this writing, Phaos has two versions of their product: a trial version and a commercial version. The trial version uses an older Phaos API which is very different and is not based on Java 1.1 sockets, so it will not work. For this example, you need the newer commercial version. A null-encryption version of the newer 1.1-compatible version is included on this book's CD-ROM.)

First define a socket factory class by extending RMISocketFactory. This class has two methods you must implement: createSocket() and createServerSocket(). Note that in this example the CA's certificate is in a file called "CACert.der," the server certificate we are using is in a file called "MyServerCertificate.der," and the user's (client's) certificate is in a file called "MyCertificate.der." Also, the server's private key is in a file called "MyServerPrivateKey.der," and the user's private key is in a file called "MyPrivateKey.der." In a real application we would obtain all these from a certificate database, or use a user interface to allow the user and/or server administrator to identify them, instead of hard-coding filenames as is done here.

```
import java.rmi.server.*;
import crysec.SSL.*;// This is the Phaos package
public class SSLRMISocketFactory extends RMISocketFactory
{
```

First we need to implement the createSocket() method for creating client sockets.

```
public  Socket createSocket(String host, int port) throws
  IOException
{
    X509 acceptedCACert = new X509(new File("CACert.der"));
    SSLParams params = new SSLParams();
```

If your application requires client authentication, it needs to do something like the following:

```
    // If using client-side authentication:
    SSLCertificate cert = new SSLCertificate();
    cert.certificateList = new Vector();
    // Now load the client certificate and the CA's certificate
    // in DER format.
    // These are the files obtained from the CA.
    // You could replace this with an access to a certificate
    // manager.
    cert.certificateList.addElement(new X509(new
     File("MyCertificate.der")));
    cert.certificateList.addElement(acceptedCACert);
    cert.privateKey = new RSAPrivateKeyPKCS8(
       "password", new File("MyPrivateKey.der"));
    params.setClientCert(cert);
    // End client authentication code
```

Now specify what cipher suites the client prefers. The selection of cipher suite is up to the server, but the client has to say what it has.

```
short[] cipherSuites = new short[1];
cipherSuites[0] =
    SSLParams.SSL_RSA_WITH_3DES_EDE_CBC_SHA;
params.setClientCipherSuites(cipherSuites);
SSLSocket s =  new SSLSocket(host, port, params);
```

We have now constructed an SSL client socket. We need to get the server's certificate and validate it. Then I also do some other checks, which you don't have to do, but this is just to illustrate. When these checks are done, return the socket.

```
SSLCertificate scert = s.getServerCert();
if (scert == null) throw new IOException("No server
 certificate");
if (! scert.rootCAvalid()) throw new IOException("CA's
 certificate not valid");

// Check the CA's distinguished name
X509 cacert = scert.rootCA();
if (! cacert.getIssuer().equals
   (acceptedCACert.getIssuer()))
      throw new IOException("Hey - this is not our CA!");

// Check the CA's public key
if (! cacert.getPublicKey().equals
   (acceptedCACert.getPublicKey()))
      throw new IOException("Hey - this cert doesn't really
        belong to our CA!");

// Report that we have accepted the CA
X509 cacert = scert.rootCA();
System.out.println("We have accepted a certificate signed by "
   + cacert.getIssuer().toString());

return s;
}
```

Now we have to implement the createServerSocket() method for creating server sockets. This is very similar, so I will only point out the differences.

```
public  ServerSocket createServerSocket(int port) throws
    IOException
{
    SSLParams params = new SSLParams();

    // Get server certificate chain
    SSLCertificate cert = new SSLCertificate();
    cert.certificateList = new Vector();
    // Now load the server certificate and the CA's certificate
    // in DER format.
    // These are the files obtained from the CA.
    // You could replace this with an access to a certificate
    // manager.
    cert.certificateList.addElement(
        new X509(new File("MyServerCertificate.der")));
    cert.certificateList.addElement(new X509(new
        File("CACert.der")));
    cert.privateKey = new RSAPrivateKeyPKCS8(
        "password", new File("MyServerPrivateKey.der"));
    params.setServerCert(cert);
```

```
    SSLServerSocket ss =  new SSLServerSocket(port, params);
```

We have now constructed an SSL server socket. If we are requiring client-side authentication, we need to check the client's identity. If the client passes, return the socket.

```
    // If you are using client-side authentication:
    if (ss.getClientCert() == null)
      throw new IOException("No client certificate");
    if (! ss.getClientCert().rootCAvalid())
      throw new IOException("CA's certificate not valid");
    // End client-side authentication
    return ss;
  }

}
```

We can use the socket factory we have created in our RMI application. All we need to do is create an instance of the factory, and call RMISocketFactory.setSocketFactory().

```java
import java.rmi.server.*;
public class MyClientClass
{
  static
  {
    SSLRMISocketFactory sf = new SSLRMISocketFactory();
    RMISocketFactory.setSocketFactory(sf);
  }

  public static void main(String[] args)
  {
    ...now we can use RMI as we would before...
  }
}

import java.rmi.server.*;
public class MyServerClass
{
  static
  {
    SSLRMISocketFactory sf = new SSLRMISocketFactory();
    RMISocketFactory.setSocketFactory(sf);
  }

  public static void main(String[] args)
  {
    ...now we can use RMI as we would before...
  }
}
```

JDK 1.2 introduces some new methods in the RMISocketFactory that you may implement if you are using JDK 1.2.

```java
public abstract Socket createSocket(String host, int port,
  SocketType type) throws IOException;
```

```
public abstract ServerSocket createServerSocket(int port,
  SocketType type) throws IOException;
```

The SocketType constructor's prototype is defined as follows:

```
public SocketType
(
   String protocol, // string identifying socket protocol
   byte refData[], // optional array of bytes with additional
   // protocol data
   Object serverData // server-specific protocol data
);
```

At the time of this writing, the specific information that must be provided to construct this object is not well defined. The intent is to allow the construction of different socket types (e.g., for different kinds of encryption) to implement dynamic cipher changes. Therefore, you can either implement your own socket type parameters, or simply ignore them.

You also need to create an SSL socket factory for the RMI registry, since your RMI clients will be using SSL sockets, and they will be contacting the registry. Here is an example of an SSL registry implementation:

```
public class SSLRegistryImpl extends RegistryImpl implements
  Registry
{
   public SSLRegistryImpl(int p) throws RemoteException
     { super(p); }

   public static void main(String[] args)
   {
     System.setSecurityManager(new RMISecurityManager());
     RMISocketFactory.setSocketFactory(new
       SSLRMISocketFactory();
     SSLRegistryImpl = new
       SSLRegistryImpl(Integer.parseInt(args[0]));
     synchronized(new Object()) { wait(); }// block this thread
       forever
   }
}
```

Passing Through a Firewall

One of the greatest technical challenges today for implementing Internet and extranet applications is firewalls. Most firewalls only permit certain protocols to pass, including HTTP access via port 80 and FTP access via port 21 (with special provisions for the FTP data connection), so endusers behind such firewalls—which includes users in most corporations—cannot access many important protocols from hosts external to the firewall. Many middleware vendors have "tunneling" components, which allow their protocol to be wrapped inside of an HTTP connection, to overcome this problem.

A widely used technique to allow a protocol to pass through a firewall is to wrap the protocol in a protocol that is permitted by the firewall, such as HTTP, and have a special gateway program at the other end remove the wrapper and pass the actual data to the intended application. For example, Javasoft makes available a program called the RMI CGI Gateway (actually, its filename is "java-rmi.cgi"), for allowing RMI connections to pass through firewalls. You need to use this program if the firewall will not allow requests to the RMI server object's assigned port number to pass. This CGI program receives RMI invocation requests and passes them to the appropriate RMI server object; responses are returned to the client in the output stream of the CGI program. Connections are transient; but the CGI gateway takes care of maintaining or reestablishing the connection to the server object when requests are received.

Let's look at an example. On the server, run the server program with the -D option specifying the name of the host it is running on, for example,

```
java -Djava.rmi.server.hostname=<this-host>
  YourServerImplClassName
```

Use the domain name of the host—not its IP address.

The RMI Gateway program is located in the JDK bin directory. Install a web server on the server machine if there is not one running there already. Place the java-rmi.cgi program in the web server's cgi-bin directory (you must have a directory called "cgi-bin" under your web root). Set an environment variable for CGI processes (or for your system), called "java.home," to point to where the JDK is installed; this will enable the CGI program to find the Java interpreter.

This is only part of the problem. We have provided a way to receive RMI requests wrapped in HTTP and unwrap them. We still need to provide a way for clients to redirect their requests to their proxy. We need the equivalent of the proxy setting in a browser. Java actually provides an undocumented way to do this. For example, the following will direct your VM to use the specified proxy and port for all socket requests.

```
System.getProperties().put ( "proxySet", "true" );
System.getProperties().put ( "proxyHost", "MyCompanyProxyHost" );
System.getProperties().put ( "proxyPort", "8000" );
```

There are limitations with HTTP-based RMI tunneling, however. A firewall will prevent RMI clients from being able to receive callbacks from the server, and performance will also be significantly degraded due to the need to repackage and forward requests.

Proxy Tunneling

A far superior technique is to create a persistent passthrough connection between a firewall to a well-known port number outside the firewall. This can either be done with authentication of the destination server, or without authentication. A simple extension to the HTTP protocol, known as "proxy tunneling," provides the capability to create such a pass-through connection.

Proxy tunneling began as a means to pass SSL-encrypted sessions through a firewall proxy, and was called "SSL tunneling." Since the session is encrypted and opaque, the proxy cannot perform its normal protocol and content filtering functions, and therefore SSL traffic cannot be filtered by a proxy except on the basis of destination host and port number. If the endpoint is trusted, however, or if at least the destination is a well-known port, there is a corresponding level of assurance that the traffic is trustworthy, and can be allowed. This is an administrative decision.

In order to support the pass through of opaque sessions through a proxy, the HTTP CONNECT method was devised. Unlike with the HTTP GET or POST method, which create a transient connection to send a request or data and get a response, the CONNECT method establishes a persistent bidirectional pass-through, creating a socket connection to the destination host and port and forwarding the SSL or other protcol as is.

In order to use proxy tunneling, the client application as well as the proxy must support the proxy tunneling extension to HTTP. In the case of a Java client, there are normally two ways to approach this. If the Java client is running in a browser, it can use the browser's built-in SSL and tunneling capability in order to establish the tunneling session. This is achieved by using an HTTPS URL as previously discussed. The browser's SSL implementation is tunnel-aware. If, however, the client is not running in a browser, then this is not an option, and the SSL package (or whatever application protocol you are using, e.g. HTTP5) must support tunneling. These two scenarios are shown in Figure 4–5.

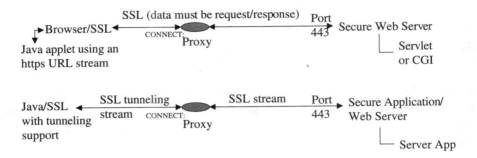

Figure 4–5 Two forms of SSL firewall tunneling.

Now let's discuss the server side of things. If the server is a web server, and the server application is implemented by a servlet or CGI program, data will have to be request/response, as is required by web-based content transfer. If, however, the server is an application server that supports SSL, it will have to pretend to be an HTTP server and listen on an allowed port (such as the HTTPS 443 port), but in fact it is free to set up full-duplex connections between clients and server applications.

In the first case above, a Java applet uses the browser's HTTPS protocol in order to access the browser's built-in SSL capability. In this case, the destination server will need to use a protocol supported by the browser— i.e. HTTPS. The Java client merely accesses the HTTP stream for sending and receiving data, as discussed earlier.

In the second case, a Java client—probably one written using an application server's client development toolkit—establishes a proxy tunneling connection through the firewall, to the destination application server. The application server routes the data to the requested application.

If two proxies are involved, which would be the case if the server itself is behind a firewall, the client proxy would establish a tunneling connection to the second proxy. In such a situation, however, communication is between two parties who trust each other (at least partially), and so those organizations may consider setting up a limited virtual private network (VPN), to link two of their subnets together.

Using a VPN

A VPN uses encryption and authentication to create a secure link across an open network, in such a way that parties participating in the VPN can share data as if it were within their own private network. The VPN software supplies the secure connection as its authentication method. For example, SOCKS 5 compliant VPNs allow the use of alternative authentication methods, and SSL is a popular one used by VPNs. A VPN connecting two networks using SSL authentication and encryption is depicted in Figure 4–6.

In a VPN scenario, the Java client and the server are not involved at all in the establishment or management of the secure connection—in fact, they are not even aware of it. Source and destination authentication is handled completely by the VPN. Most VPN software allows for single sign-on authentication at the user (client) end, so the user does not have to supply a password or smartcard each time a new connection is established, because the VPN operates at the network level and so this information is remembered in between applications. Note that at the server side, however, most secure servers do not interoperate with VPN software for SSL authentication, although this may change in future releases of SSL.

Figure 4–6 SSL supplied by a Virtual Private Network.

The Java Security Model: Protecting the Local System

So far I have discussed security as it relates mainly to the transmission of information. I will now shift to discussing the local environment, and what Java provides to protect it from invasion from attack by malicious software downloaded into the user's environment. This issue has become famous, in the context of "malicious applets," but it applies to any kind of software obtained from an untrusted source, whether the software is installed as an applet, a local application, a remotely installed Java servlet, or any other form. Luckily, Java has a security architecture to protect against such risks.

What could a malicious applet do without security management in place?

First of all, we should question if the risk is real: what can a malicious piece of software do, once installed in our system? Here are some hypothetical examples:

- It can peruse your internal network, and thereby discover your internal IP address structure.

- It can upload your Windows registry, or look for particular installed programs or data.

- It can steal your (or your company's) information.

- It can pretend to be you (placing orders, sending emails).

- It can mislead you, by masquerading as other applications.

- It can install other daemon programs, viruses, and backdoor patches which remain after you have removed the malicious program.

- It can overwrite your java.security file, so that the next time you start a VM, you are using a security provider with a trojan horse.

- It can replace classes in package java.

Because of the speed and automatic nature of computerized activities, it is conceivable that a suitably designed scheme could cheat a large number of people in a very short time, and the perpetrators be long gone before it is discovered. Money is not the only concern: large amounts of private information could be transferred in a very short interval of time—e.g. a company's entire customer database (imagine an applet that searched for *.ACT, uploaded it when it found it, and then erased all trace of this activity, and three days later the URL is "Not Found," and the perpetrators have by then stolen hundreds or thousands of customer databases and are now selling them overseas for cash!). It is not hard to think of other even scarier examples. Ideally, you would want the applet to have to ask permission to access a directory such as your ACT directory—which would surely tip you off!

The Sandbox Model

The Java sandbox is a metaphor for the concept that a piece of Java code obtained from an external source is untrusted, and therefore executes within a restricted environment. Within this environment, it is not permitted to access resources in the local system that are deemed sensitive from the point of view of security. The sandbox policy is implemented by a component called the SecurityManager, and all system code which provides access to sensitive capabilities requests permission from the security manager prior to each and every access.

Java 1.1 relaxes this model somewhat, and allows digitally signed applets to access the local system as if they were outside of the sandbox. In effect, if an applet is signed, the restrictions are disabled. Netscape modified this by adding its own supplementary model, much like the domain model to be discussed below. This "capabilities API" is discussed in the chapter on deployment and platforms. Castanet allows locally installed channels that are signed to run as local code. Internet Explorer allows signed applets to run as local code also.

Signing downloaded code is not sufficient, however. I recall a Dilbert cartoon in which Dilbert installs a new program, and at the end the program prompts innocently, something to the effect, "Do you want to contact the program's manufacturer to register?". Dilbert pondered for a moment and then clicked "Yes," after which events proceeded beyond his control. At one point the program announces that it is removing files from his hard disk to make room for new software it is automatically ordering for him, using a credit card number that it has found on his machine.

The point is, if you obtain a program about which you do not have much information, you need to give it permission to do things in a step-by-step manner—not wholesale. Permission to access files should be limited to a user-specified directory or set of directories. Permission to access other hosts should be on a host-name-specific basis, and so on. It should not be all or nothing. Fine granularity of access permission is the direction in which Java is moving.

Logging—Does it Protect You?

Both Communicator and IE now provide logging for applets. However, if an applet is able to access any part of your hard disk, it can easily find the log and erase it after it has done its dirty work. It is therefore my humble opinion that the Java security manager should not allow an applet—even a signed one—to erase or modify the security log, replace any classes in package java, or change the security provider. JDK 1.2 will make it possible to distinguish between local applications and system classes, thereby allowing even local classes to be somewhat restricted.

Protection Domains

A *protection domain* is a logical entity which has associated with it a level of trust (permissions). Based on this trust, and a set of policies, an entity which regulates access to protected resources—an *access controller*—can decide if a domain should be allowed access to any specific resource.

JDK 1.2 implements a protection domain model, in which it identifies a collection of Java classes that came from the same source as belonging to a protection domain. Code from that domain may attempt to access protected resources, such as a hard disk. System code responsible for monitoring those resources has the responsibility to ask the system if the domain has permission to use the resource.

A *codesource* object identifies a codebase (where the code came from) and the set of public keys (if any) that signed the code. This represents the level of granularity in the current protection domain model. A smaller granularity may be implemented in the future, perhaps at the runtime (signed) object level.

In the JDK, a *policy* object implements the policy (including granularity) for assigning *permissions*. A set of permissions is associated with each protection domain (i.e., each codesource). There is only one policy object in effect at any one time. This policy object is consulted by an AccessController for making actual access right determinations whenever final system code that provides resource-level services requests it to by calling AccessController.checkAccess();.

The default JDK policy mechanism obtains permission specifications for the system from entries in a policy configuration file at <java.home>/lib/security/java.policy, and for users from <user.home>/.java.policy (these defaults are specified in the java.security file). It is not hard to imagine a runtime policy manager instead which allowed users to dynamically and interactively determine policy for specific codesources (i.e., URLs and certificates). A browser would likely implement such a policy manager.

In order to determine if a domain should be allowed to access a resource, the checkAccess() method must determine which domains are actually making the request. In other words, it must trace the thread of codesources that are currently active, and determine which domains are involved: it must walk back along the current thread's stack, checking permissions along the way.

There is a complication, though. Sometimes system code needs to access protected resources in a very specific way for a specific purpose, without giving the user application more general access to the same resource. For example, system code might need to access a property file; but this does not mean that the application which is calling the system routine should necessarily be given read access to the file system. The access to the property file occurs under the supervision of the system routine, and requires a temporary suspension of checking the permissions of the application's domain. This is accomplished by a mechanism that allows a system routine (or any routine for that matter) to say, in effect: "The buck stops here; I am going to do something, and assuming you let me do it, don't bother to check if my caller can do it, because I know what I'm doing." Such a section of code is called a *privileged section*, even though it is really a responsible section, rather than privileged, because even a privileged section is not exempt from its domain requiring permission in order to access a resource.

A section of code specifies that it is *privileged* (not really privileged, responsible) as follows:

```
public void somePublicService(...) // some service which
// requires no permission to use
{
  ...
  try
```

```
    {
       AccessController.beginPrivileged();
       ...code that attempts to access a resource that requires
          permission...
    }
    finally
    {
       AccessController.endPrivileged();
    }
    ...
  }
```

Lower-level system code that guards access to resources calls the AccessController.checkPermission() method when it needs to determine if the caller has the right to request the service. The checkPermission() method is normally used by final system code like this:

```
FilePermission p = new FilePermission("somedir/somefile",
  "write");
AccessController.checkPermission(p);// throws exception if we
  don't have permission
// If no exception occurred we are ok, and we can proceed
...access the protected resource...
```

The permission and action combinations that are defined in Java 1.2 are shown in the figure. You can compare this list with the Netscape capabilities list in the deployment platforms chapter.

Permission class name	Action
java.lang.RuntimePermission	"print.queueJob"
java.awt.AWTPermission	"systemClipboard"
java.awt.AWTPermission	"eventQueue"
java.awt.AWTPermission	"topLevelWindow"
java.io.FilePermission	" {name}", "delete"
java.lang.RuntimePermission	"fileDescriptor.read"
java.io.FilePermission	"{name}", "read"
java.lang.RuntimePermission	"fileDescriptor.write"
java.io.FilePermission	"{name}", "write"
java.io.SerializablePermission	"enableSubstitution"
java.io.FilePermission	"{name}", "read,write"
java.lang.RuntimePermission	"reflect.declared.{classname}"
java.lang.RuntimePermission	"Class.getProtectionDomain"

Figure 4–7 Java 1.2 Policy Permissions and Actions.

Permission class name	Action
java.lang.RuntimePermission	"Class.setProtectionDomain"
java.lang.RuntimePermission	"createClassLoader"
java.io.FilePermission	"{command}", "execute"
java.lang.RuntimePermission	"exit"
java.lang.RuntimePermission	"loadLibrary.{lib}"
java.util.PropertyPermission	"*", "read,write"
java.util.PropertyPermission	"{key}", "read"
java.lang.RuntimePermission	"setIO"
java.util.PropertyPermission	"{key}", "write"
java.lang.RuntimePermission	"thread"
java.lang.reflect.ReflectPermission	"access"
java.net.NetPermission	"Authenticator.requestPasswordAuthentication"
java.net.NetPermission	"Authenticator.setDefault"
java.net.NetPermission	"multicast"
java.net.SocketPermission	"{host}", "resolve"
java.net.SocketPermission	"localhost:{port}", "listen"
java.net.SocketPermission	"{host}:{port}", "accept"
java.lang.RuntimePermission	"setFactory"
java.net.SocketPermission	"{host}:{port}", "connect"
java.security.SecurityPermission	"Identity.addCertificate"
ava.security.SecurityPermission	"Identity.removeCertificate"
java.security.SecurityPermission	"Identity.setInfo"
java.security.SecurityPermission	"Identity.setPublicKey"
java.security.SecurityPermission	"IdentityScope.setSystemScope"
java.security.SecurityPermission	"Policy.getPolicy"
java.security.SecurityPermission	"Policy.setPolicy"
java.security.SecurityPermission	"Provider.clear.{name}"
java.security.SecurityPermission	"Provider.put.{name}"
java.security.SecurityPermission	"Provider.remove.{name}"
java.security.SecurityPermission	"Security.getProperty.{key}"
java.security.SecurityPermission	"Security.insertProvider.{name}"
java.security.SecurityPermission	"Security.removeProvider.{name}"
java.security.SecurityPermission	"Security.setProperty.{key}"
java.security.SecurityPermission	"Signer.getPrivateKey"
java.security.SecurityPermission	"Signer.setPrivateKeypair"
java.util.PropertyPermission	"user.language","write"

Figure 4–7 Java 1.2 Policy Permissions and Actions *(continued)*

The algorithm used by checkPermission() is as follows:

```
beginning with the current domain n, winding back through n
  domains on the stack,
domain = n;
while (domain > 0)
{
  if (domain does not have the specified permission)
    throw AccessControlException("request denied");
  else if (domain is privileged)
    return;// i.e. ok
  domain--;
}
return;
```

This is summarized in Figure 4–8.

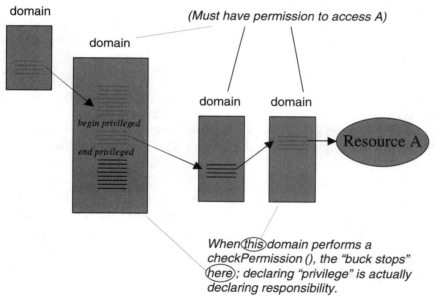

Figure 4–8 How a thread, which calls many domains, determines if it can access a resource.

Locally Installed Application Code

Java 1.0 and 1.1 divided Java code into two categories: code loaded from the local machine via the classpath (as specified by the property java.class.path or an environment variable), and code obtained via a class loader. Code resident on the local system is always completely trusted in Java 1.0 and 1.1. Unfortunately, this simplification does not lend itself to Java platforms that allow for self-installing downloadable software, such as Castanet or Netscape's UpdateNow. It is necessary to be able to distinguish between local system code and locally installed applications.

For this reason, Java 1.2 redefines the Java classpath. In Java 1.2, the property java.class.path, set by the CLASSPATH environment variable, no longer includes the Java system classes, which are assumed to reside in the installation's lib/classes.zip file, unless the command-line flag -Xsysclasspath specifies a different path. Classes in the classpath, which no longer include system classes, are now loaded with a special class loader. This allows the controlled installation of system extensions, and classes on the classpath must conform to policies specified in the policy file, even if they come from the local disk.

The Policy File

The purpose of a policy file or a policy database is to prevent users from "clicking away security." What good does it do the user if the browser asks the user if an applet can open a socket to a remote host, if the user does not understand the ramifications of that? Or if the user is so tired of being asked such things that he or she automatically clicks "yes" to each request?

A policy file or database allows the administrator of a system to configure the system's security policy to allow certain operations, so that the user does not have to be asked dynamically. In fact, a browser such as Netscape Navigator which supports its own capabilities API (discussed in the deployment chapter) has its own policy database, which gets updated automatically whenever the user clicks "yes" or "no" on such a permission dialog. An organization that needs to deploy Java software in a secure way needs a way to preconfigure policies, based on a list of trusted hosts. Applications which are trusted can even be given the right to update this database, for example through a trusted host's list control panel.

There can be more than one policy file. The default policy implementation (implemented by java.security.PolicyFile), uses the property values policy.url.* to find policy files. These property values are specified in your java.security file. The default values are:

```
policy.url.1=file:${java.home}/lib/security/java.policy
policy.url.2=file:${user.home}/.java.policy
```

where the values in ${} get expanded to their Java system property values. For example, the property user.home, on an NT computer that belongs to a network domain, will normally expand to C:\WINNT\Profiles\<your-domain-logon-id>. The URL is relative to the policy file location, or may be an absolute URL.

The default therefore is to have a single system-wide policy file, and a policy file in the user's home directory. Since policy files are loaded in the order specified by the policy.url.* trailing number, the default is to have the system policy file load first, followed by the user's policy file. If no policy file is specified, the built-in sandbox policy is used. In assigning policy URL property names, do not skip a number, because if you do those following the skipped number will not be seen. You can specify an additional or different policy file when you run an application by using the "-usepolicy" command argment.

Policy File Syntax

The policy file has entries that grant privileges. Each entry consists of a "grant" statement, which contains a set of permission declarations. The grant may be unconditional, or may be conditional based on a codebase and/or a signing alias. For example,

```
grant signeBy "marketing", codebase "http://sales.theircompany.com"
{
    permission java.io.FilePermission "C:\\orderlogs\\*", "read,
        write";
    permission java.net.SocketPermission
        "orders.ourcompany.com:6000", "connect";
};
```

grants file read and write permission to the C:\orderlogs\ directory on a Windows system. The "*" indicates that the permission is to be applied recursively, to all subdirectories; if it were not present, the permission would only apply to the specified file or directory. The signedby clause is optional, as is the codebase clause. If neither appears, the permission is granted unconditionally. If one or both appear, the permission is granted based on whether the code is signed and comes from the specified codebase, respectively.

Note that URLs always use forward slashes, even on a Windows system, whereas a file specification should use the syntax appropriate for the host on which the policy file resides. You can use the syntax ${/} instead of a slash or backslash pair if you want a file specification to be platform independent.

The syntax ${<property>} can be used to expand Java system properties. You could therefore have a permission in your policy file as follows:

```
permission java.io.FilePermission "${user.home}\\*", "read, write";
```

This would grant read and write permission to all files under the user's home directory.

Implementing a Customized Policy

You can replace the policy file with your own, or even implement a policy database. You might do this if, for example, you are writing a server that you want to be extensible, such that users can add their own "plugins" to the runtime without threatening the stability of the server. Basically, for each plugin you would assign a URL, and keep a database of URL (codesource) v. permissions. When a plugin is installed, you would update the permission database. You would need to extend java.security.Policy, and implement the evaluate() method.

```java
public class PluginPolicy extends java.security.Policy
{
   public PluginPolicy() {}

   public void init()
   {
      // Load default policy configuration, in case database
        cannot be opened
      super.init();
      ...open your policy database...
   }

   public PublicKey[] getPublicKeys(Object signers[])
   {
      return super.getPublicKeys(signers);
   }

   public Permissions evaluate(CodeSource codesource)
   {
      ...check the database...
   }

   public void addPermission(String permissionClassName, String
      targetResource, String action,
         String codebase, String signerAlias)
   throws GeneralSecurityException
   {
      ...add the permission to your database...
   }
```

```
public void revokePermission(String permissionClassName,
    String targetResource, String action,
      String codebase, String signerAlias)
{
    ...remove the permission from your database...
}
}
```

To enable this new policy class, just edit the policy.provider entry in your java.security file:

```
policy.provider=PluginPolicy
```

Using Thread Groups to Segregate Rights within a VM

Sometimes you need to restrict access to resources based on criteria other than where the code originates from. For example, you might have a server program which creates threads to satisfy user requests. Depending on the user, you might want to associate a different policy for each thread for the thread's lifetime.

You can accomplish this by writing your own security manager for the server application. The server manager can create different thread groups for different classes of user requests, and associate policies on a thread-group basis. Since it is possible to restrict a thread's ability to access or modify its thread group, there is no way the thread can "escape" from the thread group sandbox. This is shown in Figure 4–8.

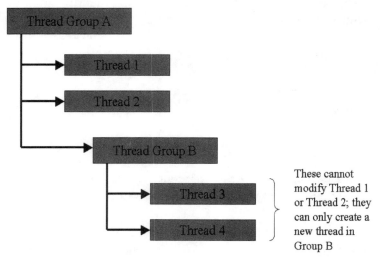

Figure 4–9 Our thread access policy.

Let's consider an example in which we want to restrict our service threads such that they can only write files in a specified directory; furthermore, if a filename has the suffix ".private," the service thread cannot modify it. I will assume that the service threads are implemented by a class called "Gremlin," which implements Runnable. Here is an outline of the security manager class:

```
class GremlinWatcher extends SecurityManager
{
    private ThreadGroup seniorThreadGroup;
    private String gremlinDirectory;
    public GremlinWatcher(ThreadGroup seniorThreadGroup, String
gremlinDirectory)
        {
```

Note that in the constructor we specify the thread group that will own the gremlin thread group. We also specify the directory in which gremlin threads can write.

```
        super();
        this.seniorThreadGroup = seniorThreadGroup;
        this.gremlinDirectory = gremlinDirectory;
    }
```

We need to protect against gremlins trying to modify their thread group, to defeat our thread-group based security restrictions:

```
    public void checkAccess(Thread t)
    {
        ThreadGroup g = t.getThreadGroup();
        checkAccess(g);
    }
    public void checkAccess(ThreadGroup g)
    {
        ThreadGroup tg = Thread.currentThread().getThreadGroup();
        if (! tg.parentOf(g)) throw new SecurityException();
    }
```

Next we need to implement our file write restriction policy: a gremlin can write files within its gremlin directory, but not if the filename ends in ".private."

```
public void checkWrite(String file)
{
   ThreadGroup tg = Thread.currentThread().getThreadGroup();
   if (tg != seniorThreadGroup)
   {
      // Perform checks; if checks fail, throw exception

      java.io.File f = new java.io.File(file);
      String path = f.getAbsolutePath();
      if (! path.regionMatches(
         true, 0, gremlinDirectory, 0,
          gremlinDirectory.length()))
         throw new SecurityException(
         "Cannot write file outside of Gremlin Directory");

      if (f.getName().regionMatches(true, f.getName().length()
       - 8, ".private", 0, 8))
         throw new SecurityException(
         "Cannot write private file");
   }

   // return ok
   System.out.println("File " + file + " may be written");
}
```

The remaining methods in the security manager should throw an exception, unless we want to allow gremlins to perform those accesses.

Here is a program which instantiates the gremlin security manager:

```
public final class GremlinWorrier
{
   private static ThreadGroup gremlins;

   private GremlinWorrier() {}
  // private - we don't want any gremlins instantiating it

   public static void main(String[] args)
   {
```

Create the gremlin security manager, and a thread group for any gremlins to run it.

```
SecurityManager sm = new GremlinWatcher(
    Thread.currentThread().getThreadGroup(), args[0]);
System.setSecurityManager(sm);
gremlins = new ThreadGroup("Gremlins");
try
{
```

Now let's create a gremlin, and run it in the gremlin thread group.

```
Runnable gremlin  = (Runnable)(new Gremlin());

// Create a new thread for gremlin, in the gremlin's
  thread group.
// Within that thread group, they can do whatever they
    want!
Thread t = new Thread(gremlins, gremlin);
t.start();
}
catch (Exception e)
{
    e.printStackTrace();
}
}
}
```

JCC

Overview

Java Commerce Client (JCC) is a component framework for building a consumer interface to an electronic ordering and payment system. JCC addresses the problem of payment, and interfacing to the range of commerce servers and electronic commerce protocols. It also addresses how the user maintains a set of electronic payment instruments locally so that they do not have to constantly reenter credit card or other information. Payment instruments can include credit cards, e-cash cards, debit cards, and so on. A database of the information about the user's instruments is maintained on the user's system. JCC does not provide specific support for constructing merchandise catalogs or browsing facilities, or for electronic shopping baskets, and assumes that facilities such as these can be constructed through standard APIs or other toolkits.

When an application that incorporates the JCC is used, the user does not normally see any JCC features until it is time to make a payment for merchandise. At that time, the application invokes the JCC runtime, and a "wallet" application appears, either in a separate frame (for an application) or in a browser window.

The JCC has a default wallet user interface (UI) built into it, which actually looks like a leather wallet. However, the entire UI is customizable, so it can be made to look completely different. Regardless of its appearance, the wallet UI has three visual areas: the *function selector area*, the *instrument selector area*, and the *client area*.

The function selector area is where a consumer selects from a list of built-in and installed operations. Built-in operations may include obtaining a log of all transactions made with the wallet, and listing or changing preferences. Installed operations are those operations which have been installed by the user, typically as a result of accessing a web site and clicking on a Java Commerce Message (JCM) URL (described below), which contains instructions in it for downloading a new function.

The instrument selector area displays a list of the credit cards, debit cards, frequent flier cards, and any other financial instruments the user has entered into the wallet. The wallet has user interface controls for adding instruments, and the JCC API has components for defining new kinds of instruments.

The client area is the area that is used by whatever function the user selects in the function selector area, in order for it to display and obtain information from the user to perform that function. A purchase function, for example, will normally display an invoice of selected merchandise, and allow the user to examine it and either proceed with the purchase or cancel it. Later in this chapter, I will demonstrate how to write such a function for performing an online purchase.

The JCC's primary means of communication with a commerce application is through the JCM it receives. The JCM is a formatted message that contains all or most of the information a JCC operation needs to perform its function; all that is needed typically is user approval. Sometimes a JCC operation may add additional information to a JCM to complete it, such as information about the purchaser. Once the JCM has been made complete, it is acted upon by sending it to a protocol object, which then performs a financial transaction in cooperation with a remote commerce server, using a server URL identified in the JCM. When this completes, the transaction has been performed. Figure 4–9 illustrates this interaction.

For example, suppose the user is using a shopping application which contains an online catalog and an electronic shopping basket that allows the user to add to a list of items selected from the catalog. After the user has selected all the merchandise they want to buy, the application tallies all the selected merchandise (again, how that merchandise is selected and kept track of is outside the scope of the

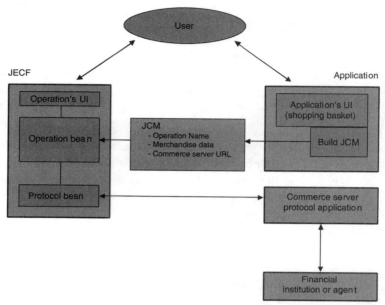

Figure 4–10 Flow of a JCM from a commerce application to the JCC.

JCC), and constructs a JCM that lists the merchandise and all purchase information, such as price, quantity, and tax rates. The application then sends the JCM message to the JCC, which brings up a wallet UI in response and allows the user to complete the transaction. As you might guess, to do this the message must have information in it identifying a remote commerce server and application to communicate with for conducting the financial transaction protocol. When the transaction is completed, the JCC generates a TransactionEvent signaling to the application that the transaction has either succeeded or was aborted.

There are two common scenarios for transporting the JCM from the commerce application to the JCC: the application may be integrated with the JCC and pass the JCM by making direct method calls into the JCC; or the application may run on a server and send the JCM via HTTP. To support the latter scenario, Javasoft has defined a MIME type for JCM messages. A web server can be configured to recognize files ending with a ".jcm" extension and send a JCM to a browser as type "application/x-java-commerce." A JCC-aware browser—one that has been configured to start the JCC as an application when a JCM MIME object has been received—will automatically pass the JCM to the JCC, allowing the user to view details of the pending financial transaction and pick a financial instrument to use to complete it.

Cassettes and Commerce Beans

A "commerce cassette" is a plugin component that extends the JCC. Cassettes are implemented as JAR files. A cassette is primarily a collection of classes and resources assembled together for a purpose and distributed as a unit. The contents are usually interdependent. A cassette is usually signed.

A cassette contains "commerce beans." It is important to distinguish between a commerce cassette and a commerce bean. A cassette may have multiple beans, intended to work together and support each other; or a cassette may simply have a new instrument, protocol, or UI for the user to install into their JCC for other cassettes to use. Cassettes are therefore containers for distributing new capabilities and associating them as from the same origin, whereas beans provide functionality. The JCC also looks for specific items in a cassette, such as a CassetteControl class (explained later), to help it figure out what is contained in the cassette and how to register its contents in the JCC's database of operations, protocols, and instruments, and in general how to install the contents of the cassette into the JCC.

These are the currently defined categories of commerce beans:

Operation—Operations are developed by vendors who want to enable you to conduct a commerce transaction with them, in a manner that utilizes their special services. An operation normally implements an operation UI that is displayed in the client area within the overall JCC UI.

Service—An arbitrary commerce GUI application. Services are operations that do not use financial instruments.

UI—The containing UI for the JCC. You can develop your own, to be displayed when your cassette is used.

Instrument—A financial instrument, such as a credit card, smart card, or other device or component supplied by a financial institution to enable a user to perform a transaction against an account. Instrument beans are normally developed by financial institutions.

Protocol—Implements one of the recognized financial transaction protocols, such as SET or Mondex. Protocol beans are developed by Javasoft or third parties that specialize in commerce protocols.

Preference—For setting any user preferences.

Gate—For registering security gates. This is not implemented at the time of this writing.

An operation bean provides the JCC with a new function it can perform, such as making a purchase, transferring money—or even making a bid in an online auction! The client area of the JCC application allows the operation to display any media that is needed for its style of interaction—one can imagine an auctioneer graphically displayed, and audibly rattling off bids. More typically, operations consist of simple purchases or modifications to accounts. Operations are therefore the services that get invoked to perform an end-to-end commerce activity, such as buying some merchandise. In contrast, UIs, instruments and protocols get invoked to support operations.

When the JCC receives a JCM that has an operation attribute, it looks in its database to see if there is an operation with that name registered and, if so, which cassette it is in. It then loads the operation. The JCC then looks at attributes in the JCM to see which instruments and protocols are specified as valid for this transaction. It checks its registration database to see which instruments and protocols it has, and forms a subset that is the intersection of what is required and what it has. At this point, the operation is able to ask the JCC for this list of instrument and protocol combinations, and present it to the user to choose from. The operation will normally supply a UI to enable the user to make this selection; this UI displays in the client area of the JCC, along with a rendering of an invoice. The invoice is constructed using information also obtained from the JCM; item descriptions, quantities, and prices. Once the user has selected a payment instrument and protocol, and approved the invoice, the operation can invoke the specified protocol with the instrument, and the protocol takes it from there, contacting the commerce server specified in the JCM.

JCC operation beans are usually very visual, since the user interacts directly with the operation to select payment instruments and examine invoices or accounts, or whatever is required by that kind of operation. There may even be sound files associated with the operation. The resources needed to perform the operation are normally packaged in the cassette in which the operation is distributed. When an operation begins, therefore, the JCC provides a context object that can be used by the operation classes to retrieve the resources packaged with the operation. The context object is an instance of the class CommerceContext, and is somewhat analogous to an applet context. It provides convenience methods such as getImage(), getAudio(), and showDocument().

The precise workings of this framework is very complex, and there are lots of variations that are possible. I will therefore use an example to illustrate what happens; but first we need to look at the security framework and JCM message format a little more closely.

Gateway Security Model

The Java 1.2 security model supports associating predefined capabilities with "codesources"—authenticated code that comes from the same source. The JCC requires these additional features:

- Ability to define new capabilities—defined by writers of protocols and services.

- Ability to dynamically install components and give them permanent permission to access capabilities—without prompting the user. A protocol is required for allowing a cassette to prove that it has been given the right (by a trusted third party) to access a specified capability.

The standard Java 1.2 security model does not support either of these.

Java 1.2 introduces the concept of privileged sections. A section of code is designated by a programmer as privileged when the author of the code is certain that the code can be safely used by other applications, without compromising resources used by the privileged section. It effect, the privileged section is taking responsibility for security, and exporting an API that uses a resource in a safe guaranteed manner.

This approach assumes that users of the API are from other, untrusted sources. What if the underlying privileged code needs to be extended later? Short of updating the code, there is no built-in mechanism for adding new features in a modular way, and allowing them to verify each other as legitimate. In other words, there is no safe and automatic plug-in capability built into the security model.

This is what the Gateway Security Model of the JCC adds. It allows producers of cassettes to make new cassettes available that work with other cassettes they have written, in an automated way. The cassettes know how, with the help of the JCC, to authenticate each other (without prompting the user), and make their services available—to each other. Cassettes can *define new capabilities*, and export those capabilities to other cassettes that they can authenticate as being from a source they trust. An arbitrator of which capabilities to export and to whom is called a "gate."

Unfortunately, this kind of sophisticated capability is not implemented yet in the current JCC release, so I cannot give you an example of it. The current implementation uses a fixed set of capabilities, and cassettes cannot export their features to each other; they can only be invoked by the JCC itself.

The gateway model defines the concept of a role, which is the right to use a specified capability. The JCC roles are defined in the JCC Role Table. These are the role definitions, as specified in the current JCC specification. Use these role names for any JCC methods that require a role name, such as when creating a Ticket instance (see below):

CASSETTE—Gives the cassette the capability to install

PROTOCOL—Gives the cassette the capability to register protocols

INSTRUMENT—Gives the cassette the capability to register instruments

OPERATION—Gives the cassette the capability to register operations

UI—Gives the cassette the capability to register user interfaces

NATIVE—Gives the cassette the capability to register native code. One can use this role to install classes in the system classpath to work around the native code binding bug in JDK 1.1.X for classes loaded from custom class loaders. It is recommended that this feature be used minimally since it will be unavailable after the release of JDK 1.2

SERVICE—Gives the cassette the capability to register Service cassettes

W_USER—Gives the cassette the capability to use the WalletUserPermit (read wallet database)

W_OWNER—Gives the cassette the capability to use the WalletOwner-Permit (modify wallet database)

C_USER—Gives the cassette the capability to use the CassetteUserPermit (modify cassette registry)

Even in the current implementation, a gate must be used to obtain permission to use features of installed cassettes. The only gate available is a built-in "wallet-gate," which is given to an operation automatically when the JCC calls an operation's setWalletGate() method at the start of an operation. The wallet gate is called to obtain a "permit" object, which serves as a facade object for accessing the features of other cassettes. For example,

```
walletPermit = walletGate.getWalletUserPermit(new
    Ticket("W_USER"));
```

returns a permit object, which can then be used to access the methods that pertain to the wallet USER role. These include getting valid instruments and protocols that are valid for a JCM, and registering listeners for changes to instruments. A wallet gate is therefore an intermediary that provides a permit object, based on the program's request for a role that is known to the wallet gate, and the permit is used to actually access services—the services are never called directly.

A future release of the JCC will allow cassette developers to write interoperable cassettes, and take on the responsibility of deciding to which cassettes to grant access to their capabilities. That is, they will define their own gates, with associated custom roles, and these gates will manage their own roles.

Java Commerce Messages (JCM)

A JCM is merely a file or message containing attributes in name-value pairs. However, the JCM class has methods for filtering a JCM to produce JCM subtrees. A JCM therefore logically contains a hierarchy, with hierarchical levels separated by a period. For example,

```
abc.def=Hi there!
```

defines a hierarchy, with "abc" containing "def," and the leaf node "def" within "abc" having the value "Hi there!"

There are six sections defined for a JCM message. Let's look at each.

Header Information—*Includes the JCM version and authentication information. For example,*

```
jcm.version=0.8
```

A future release will have attributes for digital signatures.

Operation Specifier—*Specifies an operation to perform. For example,*

```
Operation=MyPurchaseOperation
```

Operation-Specific Parameters—*Includes a list of compatible instruments and protocols. The information in this section is specific to the operation. For example,*

```
valid.instruments = Visa, Mastercard
valid.protocols = Mondex
offer.currency=USD
offer.expires=2/1/1999
offer.lineItem.1.description=Cure For Insanity
offer.lineItem.1.quantity=1 EA
offer.lineItem.1.shipWeight=0.1 LBS
offer.lineItem.1.unitPrice=0.50 USD
offer.orderID=00001
offer.shipWeightUnit=LBS
offer.shipping=1.0 USD
offer.taxRate=0.085
seller.image=./drdan.gif
seller.name=Dr. Dan
seller.url=http://www.drdan.com/cfi.html
successURL=http://www.drdan/cgi-bin/paid.cgi?00001
failureURL=http://www.drdan.com/cgi-bin/failedpayment.cgi?00001
```

Protocol-Specific Parameters—*The information in this section is specific to the protocols supported by the operation, and there is a section for each protocol listed in the valid.protocols attribute. For example,*

```
protocol.Mondex.merchantAccount=0886553997886
protocol.Mondex.merchantID=8574679475454
protocol.Mondex.valueAcquirer=http://abc.com/
```

Requirements—*This section indicates which instruments, protocols, cassettes, and so on are required. For example,*

```
requires.cassette = MyPurchaseOperation_1.0
requires.protocol = Mondex
```

Location URLs for requirements Listed Above—*This section tells where to find other cassettes, or JCMs that in turn tell where to find cassettes. The JCC will attempt to download these from the Internet. For example,*

```
locator.cassette.purchase_1.1[1] =
  http://foo.bar.com/purchase/purchase.jar
locator.cassette.purchase_1.1[2] =
  http://www.cassette_cache.com/purchase/purchase.jcm
locator.protocol.SET = http://url1/setinstaller.jcm,
  http://url2/setprotocol.jar
```

Javasoft is defining a set of JCM protocols useful for most E-commerce applications, including a purchase protocol. You can create your own, however, and define JCM messages to support it.

Building an Operation Bean

I will now explain how to build an operation bean. I could explain a different kind of bean, but operation beans are the type most analogous to an "application," from a programmer's point of view. It is the operation bean that "does something" for the user. Other beans exist primarily so that operation beans can function.

To create an operation bean, you must implement the Operation interface. This is the only required interface. These are the methods:

setJCM(JCM message)—Called by the JCC to pass to this operation instance the commerce message to process. You will normally extract information from the message and use that information to initialize objects needed for processing the message, then return. The JCM contents should not be changed by the operation, except by calling setJCM().

JCM **getJCM**()—Accessor; return the JCM that was passed in via setJCM().

setCommerceContext(CommerceContext ccntxt)—Called by the JCC to pass to the operation a commerce context to use. You must save this. The context can be used to obtain resources from the codebase associated with the operation.

CommerceContext **getCommerceContext**()—Accessor. Return the commerce context set via the setCommerceContext() method.

setID(RowID abID)—A set accessor, used by the JCC to find the entry it creates in the database for this operation instance. Just save the value passed in, and return it in getID().

RowID **getID**()—Just return the value you saved when setID() was called.

String[] **getJCMDescription**()—Return an array of human-readable descriptions of each JCM property used by this operation. Each description should be in the form "name=description."

setWalletGate(WalletGate wgt)—Save the wallet gate. Also, obtain from the gate any permits that this operation will need, for example, by calling Wallet-Gate.getWalletUserPermit(). You can then, at this time or later, use the permits to perform actions that require the permit, such as WalletUser-Permit.getID(). Note that if the getXXXPermit() operation fails, the current API will throw an Error (this will change in a future release), so you need to catch Error or Throwable.

WalletGate **getWalletGate**()—Accessor. Return the wallet gate set via setWallet-Gate().

boolean **canUseProtocol**(Protocol prot)—All JCM messages are required to have an Operation= field. If the operation uses one or more protocols, it must have a valid.protocols= field, and probably a valid.instruments= field, to specify the protocols allowed and the instruments that can be used with those protocols. The protocols specified must be registered with the JCC. The canUseProtocol() method should return true if the protocol parameter is a class or interface corresponding to or extending from one of the protocols this operation can use. In general, do not simply compare the parameter with a general interface type such as PurchaseProtocol; check for compatibility with the protocols that must be specified in the JCM. Examples of protocols are SET, SSL, and Mondex; compare the protocol parameter with the classes or interfaces corresponding to these.

String **execute**() throws Exception—Called by the JCC after wallet gate and protocol operations have been performed, and after the commerce context has been set, and the JCC is ready to actually process the transaction. The JCC will normally call getClientContainer() if this object implements ServiceUI, and add the returned container object to the JCC UI to display the operation. In general, you should do the following: add the operation as a listener to the permit for any instrument-related events that may occur, and then block until the operation is done. When the operation is done, you should notify all transaction listeners by calling their transactionPerformed() method, and sending them a TransactionEvent with either a TRANSACTION_COMPLETED or TRANSACTION_CANCELLED status.

String **getStatus**()—If an exception occurred during processing, this returns a string describing the cause of the error. Otherwise, it returns null.

String **getName**()—Return the name of the operation, as specified during registration when the CassetteControl.install() method calls registerOperation().

refreshDependencies()—In this method you should refresh all data that is dependent on the JCC database, instruments, or instrument protocols. This is often implemented in a separate thread, because it may be time-consuming and should not tie up the initiating thread.

addTransactionListener(TransactionListener listener)—Allows TransactionListeners to register to receive a TransactionEvent when the operation completes or aborts.

removeTransactionListener(TransactionListener listener)—Remove a TransactionListener.

Displaying the Operation

To enable your operation to display itself, the operation class must implement the ServiceUI interface. If your operation implements this interface, the JCC will use it to display the operation when the operation is performed (when it calls the operation's execute() method). The UI displayed via these methods appears in the client area of the wallet.

getClientContainer(CommerceContext, Dimension)—Return the Container object to be used to display the operation visually in the JCC client area. This method is called by the JCC prior to calling execute(), so this is your last chance to construct the UI object for the operation.

getSelectedImage(CommerceContext, Dimension)—Return an image, sized to Dimension, to display as an icon for the operation when it is selected in the JCC's operation list.

getUnselectedImage(CommerceContext, Dimension)—Return an image, sized to Dimension, to display as an icon for the operation when it is not selected in the JCC's operation list.

getSelectorText()—Returns the text the JCC UI will display in the operation list under the operation's icon.

setWalletGate(WalletGate)—Same as for the Operation interface.

Our operation (or an adapter in it) may implement InstrumentListener. This allows the operation to track changes to available instruments. The source of such events is the wallet permit. The InstrumentListener methods are:

instrumentAdded(RowID)—An instrument was added by the JCC

instrumentChanged(RowID)—An instrument has changed

instrumentRemoved(RowID)—An instrument was removed from the JCC

instrumentTypeAdded(RowID)—An instrument type was added to the JCC

instrumentTypeChanged(RowID)—An instrument type has changed

instrumentTypeRemoved(RowID)—An instrument type was removed from the JCC

In general, you should call refreshDependencies() in each of these methods.

Let us look at an example. Be forewarned that the JCC API will likely have changed somewhat by the time you read this. Therefore, expect to have to make some changes.

This example illustrates how you can write an operation commerce bean, which can be used to perform transactions, in this case purchases. The main class, MyOperation, implements both the Operation and ServiceUI interfaces. The operation interface specifies the methods required for an object to play the role of an operation, and the ServiceUI interface specifies the methods needed for an operation UI to be displayed within the operation area of the JCC UI.

```
import javax.commerce.base.*;
import javax.commerce.database.RowID;
import javax.commerce.cassette.*;
import javax.commerce.gui.image.URLImage;
import javax.commerce.util.*;
import java.net.URL;
import java.awt.*;
import java.awt.event.*;
import java.util.Vector;
import java.util.Date;


public class MyOperation
implements Operation, ServiceUI
{
  //
  // Operation methods
  //
```

```
public void setJCM(JCM message) { jcm = message; }

public JCM getJCM() { return jcm; }

public void setCommerceContext(CommerceContext ccntxt)
   { ctxt = ccntxt; }

public CommerceContext getCommerceContext() { return ctxt; }

public void setID(RowID abID) { rowID = abID; }

public RowID getID() { return rowID; }

public String[] getJCMDescription() { return jcmDescription; }

public void setWalletGate(WalletGate wgt)
{
   walletGate = wgt;
   walletPermit = wgt.getWalletUserPermit
      (new Ticket("W_USER"));
```

The JCC calls the setWalletGate() method at the start of an operation. In the method's implementation, we obtain from the wallet gate a permit object, for the W_USER role. This object then allows us to add a listener to react to changes in the set of instruments in the wallet.

```
walletPermit.addInstrumentListener
(
   new InstrumentListener()
   {
      public void instrumentAdded(RowID id)
      { refreshDependencies(); }
      public void instrumentChanged(RowID id)
      { refreshDependencies(); }
      public void instrumentRemoved(RowID id)
      { refreshDependencies(); }
      public void instrumentTypeAdded(RowID id)
      { refreshDependencies(); }
      public void instrumentTypeChanged(RowID id)
      { refreshDependencies(); }
```

```
            public void instrumentTypeRemoved(RowID id)
            { refreshDependencies(); }
       }
    );
}

public WalletGate getWalletGate() { return walletGate; }

public boolean canUseProtocol(Protocol prot)
{
   return (prot instanceof PurchaseProtocol);
}

public String execute() throws Exception
{
   // Wait until the UI messages us that the user is done
   executeSemaphore.block();
```

The execute() method is called after the JCC has performed all initialization
related to loading the operation and is ready to turn control over to the operation itself. All we do here is block, and wait to be notified by our UI code that
the operation is completed. Our UI conducts the process of obtaining a choice of
payment instrument and protocol from the user, and approval of an invoice
which the UI displays.

```
   // Done
   ui = null;

   // Send all transaction listeners a Transaction event
   TransactionEvent te = new TransactionEvent(this,
     txnStatus);

   return (txnStatus == TransactionEvent.TRANSACTION_COMPLETED ?
     "Success" : "Not completed");
}

public String getStatus()
{
   return (txnStatus == TransactionEvent.TRANSACTION_COMPLETED ?
     null : "Not completed");
```

```
    }

    public String getName()
    {
        return getClass().getName();
    }

    public void refreshDependencies()
    {
        buyerID = walletPermit.getID();

        try { currentIPSet =
         walletPermit.getInstrumentProtocols(jcm, this); }
        catch(java.io.IOException e) { throw new Error("Unable to
         get instrument protocol"); }

        ui.refreshDependencies(jcm);// refresh the operation's UI
    }
```

The refreshDependencies() method is the entry point for updating the state of the operation in response to any changes that might affect the operation. For example, the user may remove a payment instrument from the wallet while the operation is underway; in that case, the operation's state must be recalculated, and its UI must be refreshed as well.

An important action performed here is the call to getInstrumentProtocols(). This returns an array with elements of type InstrumentProtocols. An InstrumentProtocols object lists the protocols available in the user's JCC that are compatible with a particular instrument: the array of these objects is the set of instruments available and their available protocols. This will be used later in the operation's UI when we provide the user with a list of instruments and protocols from which to choose. See the refreshDependencies() method in the MyOperationUI class below. Note that the getInstrumentProtocols() method takes a JCM as a parameter; it is at this time that the JCM is parsed for protocol information, including the location of the commerce server to contact to transact the protocol.

```
    public void addTransactionListener(TransactionListener
    listener)
    {
        txnListeners = TransactionMulticaster.add(txnListeners,
        listener);
    }
```

```java
public void removeTransactionListener(TransactionListener
listener)
{
   txnListeners = TransactionMulticaster.remove(txnListeners,
   listener);
}


//
// ServiceUI methods
//

public Container getClientContainer(CommerceContext ctxt,
Dimension dim)
{
   ui = new MyOperationUI(this, ctxt, buyerID, walletGate,
   walletPermit, dim, jcm);
   refreshDependencies();
   ui.addActionListener// for the ui to signal us when it is
                        done
   (
      new ActionListener()
      {
         public void actionPerformed(ActionEvent e)
         {
                executeSemaphore.resume();
         }
      }
   );
   return ui;
}
```

The getClientContainer() method is called by the JCC to obtain a reference to a
Container object that can be instantiated into the wallet's client area. This may be
called prior to the execute() method, so you do not have a chance to set the container up in that method; you must create it here. Note that this implementation
installs an ActionListener—which we will notify later from the UI when the transaction is completed—and the listener in turn unblocks the execute() method's
thread, allowing the execute() method to complete and return. This signals the
completion of the operation to the JCC.

```java
/**
 * Return an icon-like image, that represents the operation,
 * in its "selected" state. Size it to dim.
 */

public Image getSelectedImage(CommerceContext ctxt, Dimension
dim)
{
   Image image = null;
   try
   {
     image = ctxt.getImage(this,
     "OpDownImage.jpeg").getScaledInstance(
        dim.width, dim.height, Image.SCALE_SMOOTH);
   }
   catch (java.io.IOException ex) { ex.printStackTrace(); }
   return image;
}

/**
 * Return an icon-like image, that represents the operation, in
 * its "unselected" state. Size it to dim.
 */

public Image getUnselectedImage(CommerceContext ctxt,
Dimension dim)
{
   Image image = null;
   try
   {
     image = ctxt.getImage(this,
     "OpUpImage.jpeg").getScaledInstance(
        dim.width, dim.height, Image.SCALE_SMOOTH);
   }
   catch (java.io.IOException ex) { ex.printStackTrace(); }
   return image;
}

public String getSelectorText() { return "My Operation"; }

void setTxnStatus(int st) { txnStatus = st; }
```

```
    //
    // Private objects and data
    //

    private WalletUserPermit walletPermit;
    private String buyerID;
    private JCM jcm;
    private InstrumentProtocols[] currentIPSet;
    private CommerceContext ctxt;
    private RowID rowID;
    private WalletGate walletGate;
    private int txnStatus;
    private TransactionListener txnListeners;
    private Semaphore executeSemaphore = new Semaphore();
    private MyOperationUI ui;
    private String[] jcmDescription =
    {
       // Describe each required JCM attribute
    };
}


/**
 * A user interface for allowing the user to interact with the
 * operation.
 */

class MyOperationUI extends CWPanel
{
   public MyOperationUI(MyOperation op, CommerceContext ctxt,
      String buyerID, WalletGate wg,
      WalletUserPermit wp, Dimension dim, JCM jcm)
   {
      this.op = op;
      this.ctxt = ctxt;
      this.buyerID = buyerID;
      this.walletGate = wg;
      this.walletPermit = wp;
      this.dim = dim;

      // Build all UI components
      setSize(dim);
```

```
// ...we assume the user is already looking at the
// merchandise in the main
// application. We just display an invoice form, with a "BUY
// NOW" button

validate();

// Fill any contents that depend on the operation state
refreshDependencies(jcm);
}


public void refreshDependencies(JCM jcm)
{
// ...refresh the UI; only update fields which have contents
   that are obsolete
// ...i.e. do not write over user-entered fields

// Allow user to pick an instrument and protocol, from the
// list of instrument/protocol combinations
selectedIP = ...get the current selected instrument from
the user
```

This operation UI implementation uses a method called refreshDependencies() to initialize or refresh the UI state.

A crucial action that this method performs is obtaining the selected payment instrument and protocol from the user. The details of this are not shown here, because they involve a lot of UI code. The JCC API provides a suite of UI classes tailored to assist with this—in fact, at this time you must use these components, since they are designed to work with the JCC container objects. These components are very analogous to Swing components, and, in fact, may change to be compatible with Swing (another reason not to go into detail on this). However, regardless how the UI controls are implemented, you will need to list the available instruments, and can do so using InstrumentProtocols.instrument.getDescription() and getVisualRepresentation(). You can get the list of available protocols for each instrument using the InstrumentProtocols.protocols[] attribute. (One would assume that the instrument and protocols attributes will evolve into accessor methods in a future release of JCC.)

```
// Get the selected instrument
Instrument instrument = selectedIP.instrument;
```

```
Protocol p = selectedIP.protocols
[selectedIP.selectedProtocol];
PurchaseProtocol protocol = (PurchaseProtocol)p;

// Set the protocol information from the JCM
JCM j = null;
try
{
   j = jcm.getJCM(JCM.PROT + "." + protocol.getName());
}
catch (Exception ex)
{
   ...the JCM did not specify the protocols
}
protocol.setProtocolJCM(j);

// Set the commerce context
protocol.setCommerceContext(ctxt);

// Set the wallet gate
protocol.setWalletGate(walletGate);

//
// Now extract operation parameters from the JCM, for this
// purchase operation
//

// Instantiate the parser utility for extracting purchase
// info from the JCM
PurchaseJCMParser parser = new PurchaseJCMParser(jcm);
```

The PurchaseJCMParser class is a class written by Javasoft to provide convenient extraction of attributes from JCM's intended for purchase operations.

```
// Construmct a merchant, from the JCM
String sellerName = parser.getString("seller.name",
"Warning");
URL sellerURL = parser.getURL ( "seller.url", "Warning" );
URL sellerImageURL = parser.getURL ( "seller.image",
"Warning" );
URLImage sellerURLImage = null;
```

```
if (sellerImageURL != null) sellerURLImage = new
URLImage(sellerImageURL);
Merchant merchant = new Merchant(sellerName,
sellerURLImage, sellerURL);


// Construct a buyer
// Note that this requires the JCM to be dynamically
// constructed, since
// it contains buyer information.
```

Below it is assumed that the JCM contains bill-to information (i.e., information about the buyer). This would require that this information has been added to the JCM at some point dynamically, perhaps after merchandise had been selected. It could have been done on the server, in the shopping application; or it could have been done by the operation class. In this example I am assuming it was done on the server before the JCM was received by this operation.

```
String line1 = parser.getString("buyer.billto.address1",
"Warning");
String line2 = parser.getString("buyer.billto.address2",
"Warning");
String line3 = parser.getString("buyer.billto.address3",
"Warning");
AddressRecord billToAddress = new AddressRecord(line1,
line2, line3);
Buyer buyer = new Buyer(buyerID, billToAddress);


// Construct a total, for all goods selected
Vector itemVector = parser.getLineItems("offer.lineItem",
"Error");
```

The getLineItems() method of the PurchaseJCMParser() convenience class returns a set of PurchaseLineItem objects. This is another convenience class developed by Javasoft to support the processing of purchase operations. The PurchaseLineItem object contains information about each invoice line item, including the merchant's unique identifier for the item, the merchant's textual description of the item, the quantity specified for purchase, the price per unit, the weight per unit, the discount per item, and the tax rate for the item. All this information is extracted from the JCM for each invoice line item by the PurchaseJCMParser getLineItems() method.

```
...now compute the total for all line items, including
taxes, etc....
...One would think that this would be included in the JCM,
but at the present time it does not appear to be...
Money total = Money.Make(...a parsable string representing
a currency amount...);
     (should be able to get from the JCM)


// Get the human-readable summary of the transaction
String summary = parser.getString("offer.briefdescription",
"Warning");


// Construct an invoice
class MyInvoice extends Invoice
{
   public MyInvoice(String s, Money t)
   {
     summary = s; total = t;
   }


   public String getSummary() { return summary; }
   public Money getTotal() { return total; }
   private String summary;
   private Money total;
}
Invoice invoice = new MyInvoice(summary, total);
     ...note that Javasoft has defined a PurchaseInvoice
     class, but it is not included in the JECF API at this time
```

In the above, I create an instance of a final summary invoice to be used to construct the PurchaseParams object below. The latter is what is finally passed to the instrument protocol selected earlier by the user.

```
class MyPurchaseParams implements PurchaseParams
{
   public MyPurchaseParams(Merchant m, Buyer b, Invoice i)
   {
     merchant = m; buyer = b; invoice = i;
   }


   public Buyer getBuyer() { return buyer; }
```

```
        public CommerceContext getCommerceContext() { return
        ctxt; }
        public InstrumentProtocols getInstrument() { return
        selectedIP; }
        public Invoice getInvoice() { return invoice; }
        public Merchant getMerchant() { return merchant; }

        private Merchant merchant;
        private Buyer buyer;
        private Invoice invoice;
    }
    PurchaseParams purchaseParams =
        new MyPurchaseParams(merchant, buyer, invoice);
}


/**
    * Call this in response to a UI event that confirms the
    * purchase.
 */

public void performPurchase(PurchaseProtocol protocol,
    PurchaseParams purchaseParams)
{
    try
    {
        protocol.actUpon(
            purchaseParams.getInstrument().instrument,
            purchaseParams);
    }
    catch (TransactionException ex)
    {
        //...display an error dialog
        op.setTxnStatus(TransactionEvent.TRANSACTION_FAILED);
        signalCompletion();
        return;
    }
```

At last! The Protocol.actUpon() method passes final purchase parameters to the protocol, and the protocol takes it from there. The protocol will contact the commerce server that is identified in the JCM for transacting the purchase. Next we need to log the transaction.

```
try
{
  walletPermit.logTransaction
  (
    new Date(),
    op.getName(),
    protocol.getName(),
    purchaseParams.getInstrument().instrument.getName(),
    purchaseParams.getMerchant().getName(),
    purchaseParams.getInvoice().getTotal(),
    purchaseParams.getInvoice().getSummary()
  );
}
catch (Exception ex) { ex.printStackTrace(); }

op.setTxnStatus(TransactionEvent.TRANSACTION_COMPLETED);
signalCompletion();
}
```

My signalCompletion() method merely notifies all ActionListener—recall that the operation class's getClientContainer() method added an adapter to this class to listen for ActionEvents—and that adapter signals the execute() method to unblock, allowing the operation to complete.

```
public void addActionListener(ActionListener l)
{
  actionListener = AWTEventMulticaster.add(actionListener, l);
}

public void removeActionListener(ActionListener l)
{
  actionListener = AWTEventMulticaster.remove
  (actionListener, l);
}

protected void signalCompletion()
{
  // Send event to all action listeners that we are done
  if (actionListener != null)
```

```
      {
         actionListener.actionPerformed(new ActionEvent(
            this, ActionEvent.ACTION_PERFORMED, null));
      }
   }


   private InstrumentProtocols selectedIP;
   private MyOperation op;
   private CommerceContext ctxt;
   private String buyerID;
   private Dimension dim;
   private WalletGate walletGate;
   private WalletUserPermit walletPermit;
   private ActionListener actionListener = null;
}


/**
 * A semaphore for controlled blocking and unblocking. Objects
 * that instantiate this class can block
 * a thread by calling block(); another thread can then unblock
 * that thread by calling resume() on the
 * semaphore instance.
 */

class Semaphore
{
   public synchronized void block()
   {
      try { wait(); } catch (InterruptedException ex) { notify();
      }
   }


   public synchronized void resume()
   {
      notify();
   }
}
```

JCC Threads

In this example I do not create any threads explicitly. If your commerce bean needs to create a thread, you should use the JECF.makeThread() method. This will create a thread in the thread group for the operation. Doing this allows the operation's threads to be managed collectively, and possibly terminated as a group if the operation needs to be terminated for some reason. You should never create a thread by simply creating an instance of Thread—always use the makeThread() method.

CassetteControl

To create a cassette, you must always create a class called "CassetteControl," which extends javax.commerce.cassette.Cassette. In the CassetteControl class, override install(), and call one or more of the following methods, depending on the kind of cassette and what commerce beans it contains. Register a wallet UI after you register any operations, because wallet UI registration examines the list of registered operations.

registerOperation (String operationName, String classname)—This results in the operation being listed as an available operation in the operations panel, which is on the right side of the default JCC wallet UI. When you call this in install(), you pass it the class name of an Operation class.

registerInstrumentType (String instrumentType, String classname)—This results in the instrument being listed in the available instruments panel in the middle of the default JCC wallet UI. Specify an Instrument class.

registerProtocol (String protocolName, String classname)—This registers a new protocol with the JCC.

registerWalletUI (String uiName, String description, String classname)—This registers a new wallet UI, which is the overall container for the JCC display. The newly-registered wallet UI becomes the "preferred" wallet UI for the cassette that registers it.

registerService (String serviceName, String classname)—This registers a Service UI class.

registerPreference (String preferenceName, String classname, String unselIcon, String selIcon)—This registers a Preference UI class.

The CassetteControl class can be anywhere (in any package) in your jar file. The CassetteClassLoader will find it and use it when the cassette is installed.

Invoking the Operation

To invoke an operation, you must give it a completed commerce message. There are two approaches to constructing a commerce message: construct it on a server, and provide it to the client; or construct it on the client.

JavaSoft has defined a MIME type for commerce messages. A JCC-aware browser that receives such a MIME type will start the JCC, provide it with the message so that it can parse the message for an operation, and then start the identified operation.

Alternatively, you can start the JCC programmatically on the client, which may be an application or an applet. Use the following static method in class JECF:

```
public static String startOperation(JCM jcm, AppletContext
context, TransactionListener l)
```

For example,

```
String jcmString = ...create a complete JCM message for a
 purchase operation, based on the set of items in a client
 program shopping basket...
String result;
try
{
   result = JECF.startOperation(new JCM(jcmString),
   getAppletContext(), this);
}
catch (Exception ex)
{
   System.out.println("Too bad - you can't buy it! Ha-ha-ha! - "
 + result " + "; " + ex.getMessage());
}
```

This will, of course, only work in a browser that is JCC-aware. For an application, the applet context parameter should be null.

Creating the Cassette

To create the cassette, package up all the classes into a JAR file, using the standard JDK jar tool as you would with any JAR file. At the time of this writing, the cassette signing tool was not available, so I will not discuss how to sign the cassette. However, it is possible to bypass signing for testing and sign it when you are all done. Here is how.

To test the operation, you will have to write an install JCM. Here is an example:

```
Operation=install
install.cassette=MyOperation_1.1
```

```
locator.cassette.MyOperation_1.1=file:/yourdirectory/MyOperatio
  n.jar
```

To disable security for testing purposes, add the line "jecf.security=false" to the jecf.properties file found in your ~/.jecf directory, or on NT or 95 in the "\Program Files\JavaSoft\jecf\.jecf" directory. *Make sure you turn security back on before you use the JCC for any commerce applications.*

To test the cassette, launch the JCC with this JCM. If you are using Windows95 or NT and have installed the JCC, you can double-click on the JCM in the file manager; or you can start the JCC commerce browser application, and click on the install JCM in that application (which is actually a browser).

CHAPTER
5

Java Database Connectivity

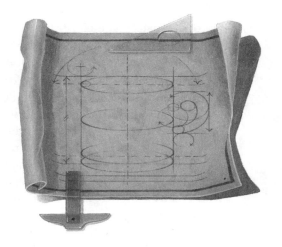

Most multiuser computing applications center around access to data. At the core of any large application there is a database of some kind, which stores the state of the system. Business applications usually use relational databases today, which provide multiuser concurrency and transaction control, high throughput, and advanced features for data recovery in the event of system failure. These are necessary features for a mission-critical system.

Standards such as SQL have provided programmers with tools to define data in powerful and universal ways so that the data model can be developed independent of the decision of which database to use. The relational model, which was controversial in the mid-'80s, is now a universally accepted standard. The Java JDBC (Java Data Base Connectivity) API defines a standard way of accessing a relational database from a Java application, regardless of where the application is running and where the database is (i.e., it supports remote clients in a transparent way).

This location independence is a powerful feature. It means that database programs can be written which can easily be deployed as an application or as a Web applet. Web-deployed applets can be inserted into Web pages, providing instant access to realtime data as easily as if the database were running on the user's machine. While it is possible to provide access to databases using CGI programs, Java programs are orders of magnitude more maintainable, more robust, easier to develop, and more secure than equivalent CGI-based solutions. Furthermore, the decision of how to deploy the program—as an applet, a stand-alone application, or a "push" channel (see the "Platforms" chapter), and as either a thin-client design or a heavy client—can be deferred, and a change in decision does not require a significant new investment in staff or training.

Having a universal and portable implementation language—Java—also makes it possible to develop platform-independent object models directly in the implementation language: the resulting object models are then portable. This has opened up the field of object-oriented databases, which were niche products prior to Java but are now rapidly gaining acceptance. These products, which are quickly maturing, are beginning to provide the same fail-safe features and scalability, and nearly the performance of relational systems. In addition, they come in many varieties, from small-footprint systems to high-performance distributed database engines. The developer has a great deal of choice in selecting a database system suited to the application. Object-oriented databases, by their very nature, provide many benefits that relational systems do not, which I will discuss. In terms of acceptance, object-oriented databases are now where relational databases were in the mid-'80s: at the threshold of their time. The challenge to the providers of these products is to prove that they are scalable and reliable.

In this chapter I will first provide a foundation for the JDBC API. I will then explain object-oriented databases, and discuss their unique characteristics. With these established, I will then give an overview of transaction and concurrency concepts, and provide a framework of transaction models that are applicable to persistent objects and databases. Throughout this, I will use as many examples as possible, to make the discussion concrete and show actual implementations. I will wind up by addressing synchronization issues that pertain to database client deployment.

Using JDBC

The JDBC API is a "thin" API, which wraps SQL and query responses in an object layer. The API is contained in package java.sql. In this section I will examine the features of JDBC, and how to use it.

Most JDBC programs do these things:

- Load a JDBC driver.
- Establish a connection to a database by specifying the database's URL.
- Optionally interrogate the database for what capability subset it has.
- Optionally retrieve schema metainformation.
- Construct an SQL or callable statement object, and send queries.
- Process query results; the transaction completes when the results have all been retrieved.
- Close the connection.

JDBC is based on ODBC, so there is a great deal of conformance between the two. In fact, Sun supplies a bridge between them so that you can access any data source that has an ODBC driver (this is a large set of applications) using the JDBC API.

An important component of a JDBC implementation is the JDBC driver. The driver establishes the connection to the database, and implements any protocol required to move queries and data between the client and the server. From an API perspective, the driver does this by manufacturing an object that implements the java.sql.Connection interface for the client to apply JDBC calls against. From a protocol perspective, the Connection object created by the driver must either convert query transport requests into DBMS native API calls (for a type 1 or 2 driver), or marshall the requests into a stream and send them to a remote middleware component (which may have its own driver, for connecting to the database on the server side; this middleware driver has nothing to do with JDBC).

In addition, the driver must therefore perform data type mapping between JDBC and database types, and interpret SQL escape sequences. The JDBC specification permits data type extensions, so the driver can map vendor-specific database types to a vendor-specific package of Java types.

Two-Tier vs. Three-Tier

Products like Oracle's SQL*Net allow database clients to access a database remotely, so distributed clients are nothing new. SQL*Net is a multiprotocol proxy which forwards database requests from the current host to the host that has the data, in a way which is largely transparent to the application, even to the extent of allowing transactions to overlap between hosts. This proxy component can be thought of as a middle tier, sitting between the application and the databases the application uses. The component is a generic utility that is largely transparent to the application, so it is sometimes viewed as merely a communication layer rather than a tier in its own right—it depends on your perspective.

Protocols like SQL*Net are proprietary, however. You cannot use SQL*Net, for example, to access a Sybase database. JDBC does not define a standard wire protocol for database access—not even a default one—but it does define a standard programmatic way of accessing databases, independent of where they are located and what brand they are. It is up to the JDBC driver manager to locate the driver for that database, and it is up to the driver to make the connection and transport the data.

Building two-tier and three-tier applications with JDBC is therefore easy, because the developer can focus mostly on the application rather than where the database is or what kind it is. The developer further has the choice of programming their own middle tier, using a generic technology like CORBA, or obtaining a multitier driver product like Symantec's dbANYWHERE or WebLogic's Tengah/JDBC product. Regardless, the client-side application which actually makes the queries is the same, and need not know if the database is installed locally or remotely. Since Java clients are web-deployable, this means that the client can be used from anywhere in a local or wide area network, and access multiple databases any-where—potentially around the world.

What Is a "Thin Client"?

A heavy client architecture is one in which a program resident on each client machine interacts with a server. This is called "heavy" because the client application is usually large, and makes substantial use of client-side services for its operation. A great deal of application logic usually resides on the client in such a system.

By contrast, a thin client architecture is one in which the client is a general-pur-pose component, such as a web browser (or other deployment component), and most application logic resides on a server. Unfortunately, as discussed in the Distributed Computing Protocols chapter, the term "thin client" has come to be somewhat muddled, and now can also mean a heavy client written in a trans-portable language like Java, and which uses a "thin" server driver. For example, a large Java client program which uses an all-Java JDBC driver is often referred to as a thin client design, when in fact the client is anything but thin. In this book I will use the term "thin client" to mean either server-generated HTML, or a lightweight program, with a small footprint, which makes limited use of cli-ent-side services; and I will use the term "thin driver" to refer to a lightweight server protocol component, which has a small footprint and makes limited use of services for the system in which it executes (the client).

JDBC Driver Types

Selecting the right driver is an extremely critical decision for a project. Do not assume "all drivers are alike"; and do not treat a driver as a commodity item. Driv-ers add significant value to a system, and their features vary tremendously. Further-more, there is significant risk that you may take certain features for granted, only to find the driver you have selected does not support those features. You should create a checklist of the features you need and desire, and verify that the driver you select has those features. This chapter will help you to prepare such a list.

Ultimately, the database drivers have the burden of providing the flexibility and features allowed by JDBC. Javasoft has defined these numbered driver categories:

>Type 1: JDBC/ODBC
>Type 2: Native-API
>Type 3: Open Protocol-Net
>Type 4: Proprietary-Protocol-Net

I will now discuss each one.

Type 1: JDBC/ODBC

Type 1 drivers do not have any host redirection capability, and require that an ODBC driver for the database be installed. A type 1 driver merely translates queries obtained by the driver into equivalent ODBC queries and forwards them, typically via native API calls, directly to the ODBC driver. Since native API calls are involved to access to ODBC driver, a type 1 JDBC driver usually needs to load a native library component and access it with native methods. The JDBC/ODBC bridge driver (sun.jdbc.odbc.JdbcOdbcDriver) provided by Sun with the JDK is an example of a type 1 driver.

It is noted that a type 1 driver does not itself provide any host redirection capability. However, if the ODBC driver is itself a network driver, it does not preclude it.

The basic usage configuration for a type 1 driver is shown in Figure 5–1.

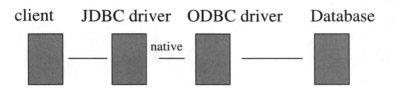

Figure 5–1 Type 1 JDBC driver

Type 2: Native-API

Like a type 1 driver, a type 2 driver provides no host redirection for database queries; however, it does not use ODBC, but instead directly interfaces to a vendor-specific driver or database API, such as Oracle's OCI ("Oracle Call Interface").

The basic usage configuration for a type 2 driver is shown in Figure 5–2.

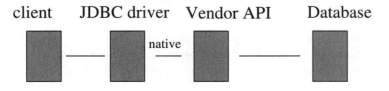

Figure 5–2 Type 2 JDBC driver

Type 3: Open-Protocol-Net

A type 3 driver is one that has the capability to forward database requests to a remote data source. Furthermore, type 3 drivers can interface to multiple database types, and are not vendor-specific. This is, or course, a matter of degree, as such drivers usually have a set of database types to which they can connect.

In this configuration, all native code is relegated to a net server gateway component, which may run on a remote machine. The net server component may or may not use ODBC in order to actually access the database; this is transparent to the client. To make matters confusing, this net server component often requires a driver of its own. From the point of view of the JDBC client, however, the client driver, which is written completely in Java, communicates with the net server using a database-independent protocol, and the net server translates this protocol into database commands for whatever type of database it is connected to.

The basic usage configuration for a type 3 driver is shown in Figure 5–3.

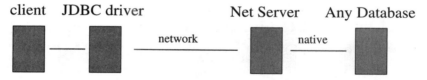

Figure 5–3 Type 3 JDBC Driver

An interesting type 3 driver in the public domain is the RmiJdbc driver, developed by the INRIA/France Mediation Project (http://dyade.inrialpes.fr/mediation/download/). It is based on RMI as a wire protocol, and one can even obtain the remote interface definition to make RMI calls to it directly.

Type 4: Proprietary-Protocol-Net

A type 4 driver has the same configuration as a type 3 driver; however, it uses a wire protocol specific to a particular vendor, and is intended for accessing only that vendor's brand of database. Client-side code is unaffected, and it should be possible to substitute a type 4 driver for a type 3 (or a different type 4) if database brands change.

JDBC does not define a standard wire protocol for database access, which is a good thing, because it opens the door for type 4 drivers that provide optimized access to specific databases without any change to the client code.

The basic usage configuration for a type 4 driver is shown in Figure 5–4.

Figure 5–4 Type 4 JDBC Driver

While type 4 drivers have the greatest opportunity to have good performance compared with the more generic type 3 drivers, they tend to be the most problematic in terms of implementing the JDBC functionality, because they are usually implemented on top of the DBMS's native stream protocol, which was most likely developed before JDBC existed. For example, one widely used type 4 driver we tested, from a major vendor, did not allow us to retrieve column names, presumably because this information is not available via the native protocol used by the driver.

Often type 3 and 4 drivers do not implement concurrency models supported by their type 1 and 2 counterparts. This may be because middleware implementations associate a transaction with a thread, so the stream protocol must know how to reconnect to the same thread in order to retain transaction context across JDBC calls. (ORB products such as Visigenic's Visibroker allow a single-thread-per-connection model as an optional connection mode, which is compatible with the JDBC model of one transaction per connection.) Given these considerations, there seems to be an inclination for driver vendors to take a shortcut and not support certain isolation modes. Often it is the drivers from the database vendors themselves that have such limitations, while drivers from "driver companies" are more fully developed.

Driver Comparisons

Internally we have done extensive testing of drivers provided by different manufacturers, and have been amazed at the variety of performance characteristics. Drivers change continually, so I will not attempt to compare them by vendor here, and the list below leaves the providers anonymous. This list is a sampling of results for the driver products of a few vendors. The list shows the divergence—in some cases not as one would expect—in driver performance from different providers.

Time to Retrieve 5000 Bytes*
(*Result set retrieval and data transport to close transaction)

>   *Type 1*
>   JDBC/ODBC bridge: **0.65**
>
>   *Type 2*
>   Vendor A: **0.96**
>
>   *Type 3*
>   Vendor A: **2.3**
>   Vendor B: **0.97**
>
>   *Type 4*
>   Vendor C: **1.28**

This indicates that it is worthwhile to compare drivers and select the best one, since it can change the performance of your application by a factor of two or even more. Note also that comparing type 1 or 2 drivers with type 3 or 4 is like comparing apples and oranges. When selecting a driver brand, one should only compare a type 1 or 2 with another type 1 or 2; or a type 3 or 4 with another type 3 or 4. Drivers of type 1 or 2 can only be compared with drivers of type 3 or 4 for the purpose of evaluating an overall system design. Also, there is more to drivers than raw performance; driver features are discussed in the next section.

High-Performance Driver Features

Drivers vary enormously in their features. Some features may be important to you, and others may not. I will now discuss the major categories of features.

Thread/Connection Model

JDBC requires that a driver support multiple connections per client. This implies that the client application can open several connections and perform a separate transaction on each of these concurrently in a separate thread.

How the driver implements this is not specified. The driver may open a separate socket connection for each connection, or it may multiplex JDBC connections on a single socket. This has performance implications with regard to scalability for large numbers of clients. It is impossible to anticipate beforehand which approach will yield better performance for the application, since it depends on the details of how connections are demultiplexed in both the server-side driver component and the network software as well, and the latter may be operating-system-dependent. The only way to know is to run tests simulating the loading factor the application is expected to encounter, and compare drivers by running tests under load.

Firewall Traversal and Security

Some drivers have the ability to tunnel through a proxy firewall, by embedding their protocol inside of the HTTP protocol. The driver may require the application to configure it by setting a property (a proxy address). (The Driver.getProperty-Info() method can be used to obtain the properties a driver requires to be set.) This issue is discussed in more depth later in this section.

Some drivers use IIOP as their wire protocol. In this case, if the firewall is configured to allow IIOP to pass (usually by mapping all IIOP requests to a single port, and filtering out non-IIOP traffic on that port), the driver will be able to operate without tunneling. This is a very open approach, and is being used by more and more driver vendors. Similarly, if the firewall is configured to allow RMI to pass through, RMI-based drivers will be able to operate without tunneling.

Some drivers also provide secure connections using SSL. If your connection will be traversing the Internet and you are concerned about privacy, you should investigate using a driver that provides SSL connections.

An example of a driver that has all of these capabilities is WebLogic's Tengah JDBC driver. This product provides HTTP tunneling, and can use IIOP as its wire protocol. It uses SSL to provide a secure connection between the client and the Tengah component, which is the link that is exposed to the network in most cases. Another example is Sybase's JConnect, which provides both HTTP tunneling for penetrating a firewall, and SSL for secure connections between the client and the Sybase database server.

Caching

Drivers can perform caching of various kinds to speed up queries. Some of these are:

- *Row prefetching*: When you retrieve a result set, the rows are not actually transferred until you request them one by one. Some drivers perform row prefetching in anticipation that you will ask for the next row before you actually do.

- *Row caching* ("array fetch"): This is related to row prefetching; the driver retrieves a block of rows at a time.

- *Connection caching:* A driver may maintain a set of reusable database connections for a given user; clients that connect as this user transparently reuse this persistent connection, thereby avoiding database connection time and reducing the overall server-side footprint per client.

- *Schema caching:* Drivers have the job of translating SQL from generic SQL into a vendor's specific SQL. To do this, they often need to consult the database schema. A driver may perform schema caching in order to speed this up.

Early Binding of Stored Procedures

A driver may instruct the database to locate and load stored procedures (in JDBC, "callable statements") while the SQL is being processed by the driver so that the procedures are ready to execute as soon as the database engine needs them.

Support for "Hints"

Hints are constructs that appear in an SQL construct to tell the database engine what strategy to use for implementing a query. A driver will ordinarily pass hints on through to the database. A general-purpose thin type 3 driver might strip hints out, since hints are DBMS specific—this is something to evaluate when choosing a driver.

Support for DDL

Some drivers allow you to perform DDL operations, and some do not. If your application needs to do things like "DROP TABLE," you should check whether your driver allows this operation. Note that SQL92 assumes that any DDL operations constitute a new transaction.

Database Feature Support

Your database may have specific features that you want to use, and you should test your driver to make sure it supports these. For example, outer joins may be supported by the database but not the driver. There are methods defined in the java.sql.DatabaseMetaData class which you can call to determine if a particular feature is supported by the database or driver servicing that connection.

JDBC Compliance

The method java.sql.Driver.jdbcCompliant() can be used to determine if a driver has passed Sun's JDBC compliance test. If this method returns false, it does not necessarily mean the driver is not JDBC-compliant; however, if it returns true, it *is* compliant. Compliant drivers support the full JDBC API and have full support for SQL 92 Entry Level. A compliant driver will return true when tested for these features:

- **nullPlusNonNullIsNull** (concatenation between a null and nonnull value is null)

- **ANSI92EntryLevelSQL** (supported)

- **CorrelatedSubqueries** (supported)

- **LikeEscapeClause** ("{escape 'escape-char'}" is supported)

- **MinimumSQLGrammar** (the ODBC Minimum SQL grammar is supported)

- **MixedCaseQuotedIdentifiers** (mixed-case quoted identifiers are case sensitive)

- **NoNullableColumns** (columns can be defined as nonnullable)

- **SubqueriesInComparisons** (subqueries in comparison expressions are supported)

- **SubqueriesInExists** (subqueries in "exists" expressions are supported)

- **SubqueriesInIns** (subqueries in "in" statements are supported)

- **SubqueriesInQuantifieds** (subqueries in quantified expressions are supported)

- **TableCorrelationNames** (table correlation names are supported)

and false for:

- **MixedCaseIdentifiers** (mixed-case unquoted identifiers are case sensitive)

Loading a Driver

The driver manager (java.sql.DriverManager) uses the Java property "sql.drivers" to identify the classes that contain JDBC drivers. The driver manager will register the drivers in this list. Any application can set this property, but in practice drivers are usually registered automatically by causing their class to be loaded: a driver is required to automatically register itself by executing code in a static block in the driver's class. Thus, all you have to do is either instantiate the driver, for example,

```
MyVendorsDriver driver = new MyVendorsDriver();
```

or explicitly load its class, for example,

```
Class.forName("MyVendorsDriver");
```

When a driver is subsequently needed to complete a database connection, specified by a URL, the driver manager will try each registered driver until a driver reports that it can handle the URL's protocol (returns true to the acceptsURL() method).

JDBC from an Application

A Java application which uses JDBC can identify the driver to use by listing the driver's class in the sql.drivers property, or by explicitly loading the driver class. In either case, the driver class must be in the virtual machine's java.class.path property (i.e., the classpath).

Once the driver is loaded, a type 1 or 2 driver should be able to connect to a database identified by a local URL (i.e., on the same machine), or any database reachable by any native driver that the JDBC driver supports. For example, if you are using Javasoft's ODBC bridge driver, you would be able to connect to any database on that machine which has an ODBC driver installed. This is shown in Figure 5–5.

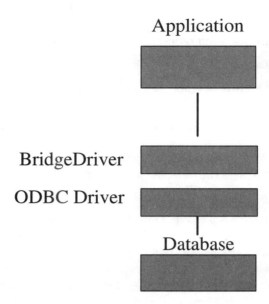

Figure 5–5 Type 1 JDBC on the same machine as the Database.

As another example, if your driver is Oracle's OCI driver, which is a native driver that uses Oracle native call interface, you would be able to connect to any Oracle instance on that machine, or any Oracle database reachable from your machine, via SQL*Net.

Using a type 3 or 4 driver, an application should be able to connect to a database identified by a local or remote URL. In the latter case, a middleware daemon running on the database machine would process streamed requests and convert them into native driver calls. An example of a type 3 remote driver is Symantec's dBANYWHERE product.

JDBC from an Applet

Connecting from an applet presents some special problems that do not exist for an application. These include:

- Driver in the codebase
- Middleware
- Firewall issues
- Security of transmitted data
- Authentication

The last three items are related to security, and I will discuss them later in this chapter and in the chapter on security. For now, let me address the first two, which are architectural issues.

In order for the driver manager to locate the driver, it must be able to find the class, as specified either in the java.sql property or if you explicitly load the class. In either case, a class loader must physically locate the class, from either the user's local disk or the codebase from which the applet was obtained. When deploying a JDBC applet, therefore, you will need to make sure that the driver's classes are in the codebase for the applet. Assuming the driver is packaged in a JAR file, this can be achieved by adding that JAR file to the HTML ARCHIVE tag for the applet.

The next consideration is the configuration of the server middleware component that intermediates between the communication connections to its drivers and the database. Consider the following scenario.

The driver in Figure 5–6 is an applet-deployed JDBC driver. This kind of driver is often referred to as a "thin" driver, because it is written purely in Java and does not make use of any native or client-based services other than those provided by Java. It is merely a communication manager for connecting to the server-side middleware.

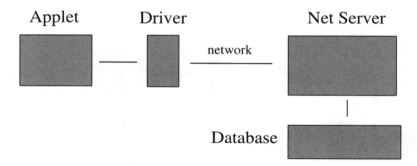

Figure 5–6 Applet-deployed JDBC driver, and server-side Proxy Middleware.

The middleware has the task of managing multiple sessions with all of the JDBC applets connecting to the database, and proxying requests and results between the client-side driver and the database.

Database connection establishment overhead can be mitigated by using a middle tier that maintains a connection pool. However, you still have the delay of connecting to the middle tier.

Connecting to a Database

To open a connection to a database, you call the driver manager's static getConnection() method and provide it with a URL to locate the database:

```
Connection con = DriverManager.getConnection(
    "jdbc:my_vendors_driver://host:port/datasourcename", userid,
        password);
```

If the database is not actually on the same machine as the middleware, but is being accessed from there by the middleware using a proprietary network database protocol such as SQL*Net, the middleware will need to know the ultimate location of the database so it can provide this to the network software. Thus, the URL can be somewhat more complex, and actually requires two hostnames in it. The exact format is specified by the driver manufacturer.

If the client is an applet running in a browser outside of your firewall, and the client's network has its own firewall, the driver may have to wind its way through two proxies. In addition, if your organization's policy does not permit running applications (such as middleware) other than a web server on the applet host, you will need to redirect the driver's connection yet again to the ultimate middleware host. Often this web server redirection program is implemented as a Java servlet so that it can be run on a web server. If you put all of this together, you obtain a picture something like the one in Figure 5–7.

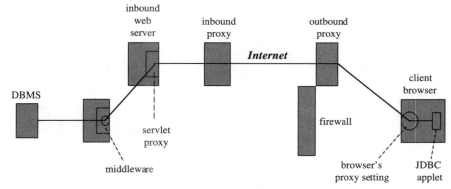

Proxy settings for a client JDBC driver:
- **The client network HTTP proxy (because the driver may not recognize the browser's proxy setting)**
- **The servlet gateway**

Figure 5–7 Using a servlet to redirect DBMS requests.

As you can see, there are many opportunities for a bottleneck to occur in a scenario such as this. In particular, several routing components are effectively application-level routers (proxies or middleware), rather than packet routers optimized for the task. If there are a large number of clients, some percentage of them will have open database connections, each of which increases the resources required by the driver as well as network resources. In some cases it may be desirable to locate an authenticated application server outside of the organization's inner firewall as a front end to requests from extranet clients.

The driver may also require your applet to set a Java property to specify the parameters required by a Java servlet redirection gateway. The applet may even have to obtain the location of the user's own network proxy from the user and set this as a property so that the driver can communicate out through the user's firewall. This depends on how the driver is written, and whether it uses the browser's socket facility or a pure Java one.

The bottom line is, design and test your planned configuration early. I have seen many projects progress to an advanced point, only to find that the driver did not support a critical capability.

Displaying Database MetaData

The JDBC DatabaseMetaData class allows your application to obtain information about the database and DBMS, including its catalog (if any), tables, and features. Here is an example of getting a database's metadata object, and then requesting a list of all of the tables in the database.

```
DatabaseMetaData dmd = con.getMetaData();
ResultSet tables = dmd.getTables(null, null, null, null);
```

The parameters on the getTables() statement are selection criteria, including name matching. Null values cause "any" to match. The return type is a result set, which can be scrolled through to obtain information about the selected tables, such as the column names and data types.

Result Sets: Making a Simple Query

To perform a query, you need to first construct a Statement object. You can reuse this object for multiple queries. Using the statement object, you can call the executeQuery() method to transport SQL to the database:

```
Statement statement = con.createStatement();
ResultSet   rs = statement.executeQuery("SELECT *
      from PRODUCTS");
```

The object returned is a ResultSet. A ResultSet is a table of rows. The rows are accessed in sequence; you can't go back and reread a row once you have read it, though JDBC2 will relax this. (Thus, repeatable reads are not an issue within a result set; this is discussed later.) In order to access the first and each successive row, you must call the ResultSet's next() method.

The row you are currently on represents a logical cursor into a result table returned from the query. To retrieve column values by name or position from the current row, you can specify a column by either name or ordinal position. For example, both of these retrieve int values from the current row:

```
rs.getInt("COL1");    // gets int value from column COL1 of
                          //current row
rs.getInt(2);     // gets int-value from the second column of the
                     //current row
```

To retrieve a column value as an object, use the Object-type accessor.

```
rs.getObject("COL1");      // returns a java object, depending
                              // on type of COL1
rs.getObject(2);       // returns a java object, depending on
                          // type of column 2
```

ResultSet is an interface, so you can implement your own ResultSet object from any base class. Thus, there is no reason why, for example, you could not in theory create a serializable ResultSet or other exotic types of ResultSet.

Cursors

A result set has an implied cursor. You can get the cursor name using the getCursorName() method. If the database supports operations using cursors, you can use this cursor name in subsequent statements. Use the supportsPositionedUpdate() and supportsPositionedDelete() methods to determine if the database (and driver) support these operations. Even if the database supports them, the driver may not, especially for some type 3 and 4 drivers.

Joins and Outer Joins

There are many different ways to specify an outer join, and there is a way preferred by JDBC. First, however, we must understand what a join and an outer join are.

A "join" is a query made against two or more tables, in which columns from each table are selected based on a criterion that "joins" the tables (e.g., that a value in one table must equal a value in another table).

Consider these two tables.

Table 5-1 Employee

EMPNO	ENAME	DEPTNO
7521	WARD	30
7782	CLARK	10
7839	KING	10
7844	TURNER	30
7900	JAMES	30
7934	MILLER	10

Table 5-2 Department

DEPTNO	DNAME	LOC
10	ACCOUNTING	NEW YORK
30	SALES	CHICAGO
40	OPERATIONS	BOSTON

Here is a join:

```
rs = stmt.executeQuery("SELECT D.DNAME, E.ENAME FROM DEPT D, EMP
  E WHERE D.DEPTNO = E.DEPTNO");
```

Table 5-3 Join

DNAME	ENAME
SALES	WARD
ACCOUNTING	CLARK
ACCOUNTING	KING
SALES	TURNER
SALES	JAMES
ACCOUNTING	MILLER

An ambiguity occurs if some of the values in one table do not appear at all in another table being joined. For example, in the above tables department 40 is not represented at all in the EMP table. Perhaps it is a new department. We still might want it included in the join, however, so we do not forget about it. In other words, if we are trying merely to create a cross-reference of department name to employee, do we want departments without employees to be left out of the list? If the answer is no, we need to tell the query engine to do an "outer join." Here is an outer join, using Oracle's syntax.

```
rs = stmt.executeQuery("SELECT D.DNAME, E.ENAME FROM DEPT D,
    EMP E WHERE D.DEPTNO = E.DEPTNO (+)");
```

Table 5-4 Outer Join

DNAME	ENAME
ACCOUNTING	CLARK
ACCOUNTING	KING
ACCOUNTING	MILLER
SALES	JAMES
SALES	TURNER
SALES	WARD
OPERATIONS	**null**

Here is an outer join, using JDBC standard escape syntax.

```
rs = stmt.executeQuery("{oj DEPT D LEFT OUTER JOIN EMP E ON
    D.DEPTNO = E.DEPTNO}");
```

Not all drivers support this syntax. For example, on Oracle 7.3 with Oracle's thin JDBC driver, this results in the error "Nonsupported SQL92 token: oj."

With these DatabaseMetaData methods, you can find out if outer joins are supported:

```
supportsOuterJoins()
supportsFullOuterJoins()
supportsLimitedOuterJoins()
```

Statements that Don't Return a ResultSet

SQL INSERT, UPDATE, and DELETE operations do not return a result set. For these kinds of statements, use the Statement's executeUpdate() method instead of the executeQuery() method. For example,

```
stmt.executeUpdate("INSERT...");  // for INSERT, UPDATE, and
   DELETE operations
```

Some JDBC drivers allow you to execute DDL statements, and some do not. In general, use the metadata interface to determine the capabilities of the database; for example, the rather long-winded method

```
supportsDataDefinitionAndDataManipulationTransactions()
```

returns true if DDL operations are allowed.

Prepared Statements

A prepared statement is one which is precompiled and potentially preoptimized, with placeholders for parameter substitutions. In theory, the DBMS can create a query plan ahead of time for a prepared statement, and have it ready to run each time the query is invoked. Prepared statements are useful in loops, which execute the same SQL repeatedly with minor variations. While it is true that most data-bases keep query caches so that they do not need to create query plan all over again if an SQL statement is repeated, in theory a prepared statement could save a lot of overhead, or the DBMS having to determine if the query is similar to one executed previously.

Here is an example of a JDBC prepared statement:

```
java.sql.PreparedStatemet ps = con.prepareStatement("SELECT *
   FROM TAB1 WHERE COLA=?");
```

This creates a prepared statement that is ready to be executed. To execute the statement, you must supply values for the positional parameters placemarked by "?" symbols. You use the set<type>() method to do this, where the <type> depends on the data type of the column. For example,

```
ps.setInt(1, 1000);   // sets the first "?" parameter to
   "1000"
```

sets the value of the first positional parameter (the first position is indicated by the "1") to the value 1000. Having supplied values for all positional parameters for the statement object, you can then execute a query with

```
ResultSet rs = ps.executeQuery();
```

For some databases prepared statements execute as ordinary statements, because the database caches them regardless, and handles them in that manner.

For Large (BLOB and CLOB) Parameters

Binary Large Objects (BLOBs) are often used to store media data and documents in a database. To pass a BLOB value in JDBC, construct a prepared statement, create an input stream to read the BLOB data, and pass the input stream to the prepared statement as follows:

```
PreparedStatement ps = con.prepareStatement("INSERT INTO TAB1
    VALUES (?, ?)");
ps.setString(1, "Anatoli Knapsackovitch");
java.io.File f = new java.io.File("mug.jpeg");
ps.setBinaryStream(2, new java.io.FileInputStream (f),
    f.length());
```

The PreparedStatement.setBytes() method can be used to pass a Java byte array to a BINARY, VARBINARY, or LONGVARBINARY column value instead of passing the bytes via a stream.

For reading binary values as a stream from a result set column, you can use the getBinaryStream(), getAsciiStream(), and getUnicodeStream() methods; or you can use the getBytes() method to obtain the value as a byte array.

You can request a conversion of a binary stream to character format by using the getAsciiStream() and getUnicodeStream() methods. The PreparedStatement setAsciiStream() and setUnicodeStream() methods will send an ASCII and Unicode stream data (CLOBs) to the database, respectively, performing any conversion required by the database to store the data in the database's internal format.

Similarly, Character Large Objects (CLOBs) can be passed as streams using the setUnicodeStream() and setAsciiStream() methods. You can retrieve CLOBs from a result set as a stream, using the getAsciiStream() and getUnicodeStream() methods, or as a string using the getString() method.

When retrieving a BLOB or CLOB as a stream, you must read the stream before performing any more getXXX() operations on the result set, because the stream is automatically closed on the next getXXX() call.

Dates and Times

To represent dates and times, use the JDBC "escape" syntax, which consists of curly braces with a command/parameter pair inside. For a date value, the command is "d." For example, to represent a date, use

```
{d 'yyyy-mm-dd'}
```

To represent a time, use

```
{t 'hh:mm:ss'}
```

To represent a timestamp, use

```
{ts 'yyyy-mm-dd hh:mm:ss.f . . .'}
```

Note that some systems have restrictions on timestamps. For example, some databases (such as MS SQL Server) do not allow more than one timestamp column per table.

Data Type Mappings

In order to write a portable application, you should avoid using database data types that are specific to a brand of database. This is often easier said than done, because some databases do not provide needed types or combine the use of types. For example, Oracle uses DATE for time and timestamp values. In contrast, SQLServer has DATE, TIME, DATE&TIME, and TIMESTAMP.

JDBC defines the types mappings from SQL types to corresponding Java types; and also from the Java types to SQL types. The mapping of SQL types to and from Java types is listed in Table 5–5.

Table 5-5 Type mappings between SQL and Java

CHAR	→ String		→	VARCHAR or LONGVARCHAR
VARCHAR	→ String			
LONGVARCHAR	→ String			
		converts to ⇨	(any)	

Table 5-5 Type mappings between SQL and Java(Continued)

NUMERIC	→ java.math.BigDecimal		→	NUMERIC
DECIMAL	→ java.math.BigDecimal			
		converts to ⇨		TINYINT, SMALLINT, INTEGER, BIGINT, REAL, FLOAT, DOUBLE, DECIMAL, (NUMERIC), BIT, CHAR, VARCHAR, LONGVARCHAR
BIT	→ Boolean		→	BIT
		converts to ⇨		(same as BigDecimal)
TINYINT	→ Integer		→	INTEGER
SMALLINT	→ Integer			
INTEGER	→ Integer			
		converts to ⇨		(same as BigDecimal)
BIGINT	→ Long		→	BIGINT
		converts to ⇨		(same as BigDecimal)
REAL	→	Float	→	REAL
		converts to ⇨		(same as BigDecimal)
FLOAT	→ Double		→	DOUBLE
DOUBLE	→ Double			
		converts to ⇨		(same as BigDecimal)

Table 5-5 Type mappings between SQL and Java(Continued)

BINARY	→	byte []		→	VARBINARY or LONGVARBINARY
VARBINARY	→	byte []			
LONGVARBINARY	→	byte []			
			converts to	⇨	BINARY
DATE	→	java.sql.Date		→	DATE
			converts to	⇨	CHAR, VARCHAR, LONGVARCHAR, TIMESTAMP
TIME	→	java.sql.Time		→	TIME
			converts t	⇨	CHAR, VARCHAR, LONGVARCHAR
TIMESTAMP	→	java.sql.Timestamp		→	TIMESTAMP
			converts to	⇨	CHAR, VARCHAR, LONGVARCHAR, DATE, TIME

While many drivers will automatically convert Java values into the type of the corresponding table column, even if the column is a proprietary type, it is a good idea—if possible—to define the schema in terms of the standard types common to most systems, and for which a Java-to-SQL mapping is defined.

Functions

Most databases provide a set of scalar functions for constructing expressions. JDBC does not require that a particular set of functions be supported, but rather defines a list of functions which can be supported, and, if they are, should have the specified profile (or be convertible to that profile by the driver).

To call a function, use the escape syntax with the "fn" keyword, as shown in this example:

```
ResultSet rs = statement.executeQuery("{fn ABS(" + alpha + ")}");
```

It is the responsibility of the driver to map these functions to functions actually provided by the database where possible. These DatabaseMetaData methods can be used to obtain a comma-separated String list of which of the functions are supported:

getNumericFunctions()

getStringFunctions()

getTimeDateFunctions()

getSystemFunctions()

The numeric functions defined are:

ABS(number)	LOG10(float)
ACOS(float)	MOD(integer1, integer2)
ASIN(float)	PI()
ATAN(float)	POWER(number, power)
ATAN2(float1, float2)	RADIANS(number)
CEILING(number)	RAND(integer)
COS(float)	ROUND(number, places)
COT(float)	SIGN(number)
DEGREES(number)	SIN(float)
EXP(float)	SQRT(float)
FLOOR(number)	TAN(float)
LOG(float)	TRUNCATE(number, places)

The string functions are:

ASCII(string)	LTRIM(string)
CHAR(code)	REPEAT(string,count)
CONCAT(string1, string2)	REPLACE(string1, string2, string3)
DIFFERENCE(string1, string2)	RIGHT(string, count)
INSERT(string1, start, length, string2)	RTRIM(string)
LCASE(string)	SOUN-DEX(string)
LEFT(string,count)	SPACE(count)
LENGTH(string)	SUBSTRING(string, start, length)
LOCATE(string1, string2, start)	UCASE(string)

The time and date functions are:

CURDATE()	MONTH(time)
CURTIME()	MONTHNAME(date)

DAYNAME(date)	NOW()
DAYOF-MONTH(date)	QUARTER(date)
DAYHOFWEEK(date)	SECOND(time)
DAYOFYEAR(date)	TIMESTAMPADD (interval, count, timestamp)
HOUR(time)	TIMESTAMPDIFF(interval, timestamp1,timpestamp2)
MINUTE(time)	WEEK(date), and YEAR(date)

The system functions are:

DATABASE()

IFNULL(expression, value)

USER()

A data type conversion function is also specified:

CONVERT(value, SQLtype)

where SQL type may be BIGINT, BINARY, BIT, CHAR, DATE, DECIMAL, DOU-BLE, FLOAT, INTEGER, LONGVARBINARY, LONGVARCHAR, REAL, SMALL-INT, TIME, TIMESTAMP, TINYINT, VARBINARY, or VARCHAR.

Callable Statements

Most DBMSs provide stored procedures, also referred to as *persistent stored modules* (PSMs). These are program routines, stored in a database, which are invoked by SQL. JDBC supports this model with the CallableStatement object. To call a stored procedure, you first construct a CallableStatement, using positional parameter notation as for a prepared statement. For example,

```
CallableStatement cs = con.prepareCall("{ call DAILY (?, ?) }");
```

creates a callable statement, with two parameters.

You must register each parameter that can return a value (i.e., each OUT or INOUT parameter). You do this with one of the registerOutParameter() methods. For example,

```
cs.registerOutParameter(2, java.sql.VARCHAR);
```

You must set the values of input parameters the same way you set positional parameters in a prepared statement. In fact, CallableStatement extends from PreparedStatement. Once you set parameter values, you can execute a callable statement the same way you execute a prepared statement.

To retrieve the values of returned parameters, you can use the get<type>() methods. For example,

```
cs.getInt(2);
```

retrieves the value of the second parameter, which must be an OUT parameter. Before retrieving any OUT parameter values, however, you must retrieve all statement result sets. Many stored procedures return one or more result sets; you must scroll through all of these before OUT parameters are accessible. For example,

```
if (cs.execute())
{ // there is a result set...
    ResultSet rs = cs.getResultSet();
    // get rows
    for (; rs.next(); ) { ...get any row values... }
}
String s = cs.getString(2);   // get the OUT parameter value
```

If there is the possibility that the statement might return more than one result set, you can use the getMoreResults() method to check if there is another result set.

Stored procedures can also return values. If a stored procedure returns a value, define the callable statement as such:

```
CallableStatement cs = con.prepareCall("{ ? = call SUMMARY(?) }");
```

Note that the result is identified as an OUT parameter by the first "?" symbol. A return value is treated as the first OUT parameter, and it must be registered as any OUT parameter.

```
cs.registerOutParameter(1, java.sql.INTEGER);
cs.registerOutParameter(2, java.sql.REAL);
```

Transactions

A database transaction is a discrete set of database operations with a well-defined begin point and a well-defined end point, such that the entire set of operations can be treated as a unit for controlling change to the database. The end point of a transaction is when the transaction is committed and made permanent, or aborted ("rolled back") and the changes discarded. JDBC specifies these policies related to transactions:

- One transaction exists at a time per connection: the concept of multiple nested transactions is not supported. However, implementations can allow clients to create multiple connections.

- Drivers are required to allow concurrent requests from different threads on the same connection; if the driver cannot multiplex them, they are performed in series.

- You can cancel a statement asynchronously by calling the statement's cancel() method from another thread.

- Each statement is a transaction by default (auto-commit mode). In auto-commit mode, commit() is called automatically when the statement completes (all ResultSet rows have been retrieved). Use setAutoCommit(false) to turn auto-commit off.

- Deadlock (a situation in which two transactions are waiting for each other, with no means of resolving the wait) detection behavior is not specified. Most implementations throw an exception, but it could be an SQLException or a RuntimeException, or even an Error.

If autocommit is disabled and you perform a transaction that obtains locks (such as when using SELECT ... FOR UPDATE with Oracle), your locks will remain in effect until either you explicitly call commit() or abort(), you close the connection, or the statement is otherwise closed. (A statement is closed automatically when the statement object is garbage collected, but you can also call close() explicitly.)

Isolation Levels Defined by JDBC

An important issue with transactions is to what degree other transactions can observe or participate in the effects of changes your transaction has made, prior to when those changes are committed: this is known as the "isolation" policy. JDBC does not impose transaction isolation requirements on an implementation. It does, however, define these isolation modes in the java.sql.Connection class. (See the section on Database Locking and Isolation later in this book for more explanation of isolation and locking modes and the terms used below.)

TRANSACTION_NONE: Transactions are not supported. (This would be applicable, for example, if one were using JDBC to access a nontransactional data source, such as a file or spreadsheet.)

TRANSACTION_READ_UNCOMMITTED: Dirty reads, nonrepeatable reads, and phantom reads can occur. (SQL Isolation Level 0)

TRANSACTION_READ_COMMITTED: Dirty reads are prevented; nonrepeatable reads and phantom reads can occur. (SQL Isolation Level 1)

TRANSACTION_REPEATABLE_READ: Dirty reads and nonrepeatable reads are prevented; phantom reads can occur. (SQL Isolation Level 2)

TRANSACTION_SERIALIZABLE: Dirty reads, nonrepeatable reads, and phantom reads are prevented. (SQL Isolation Level 3)

You can call the DatabaseMetaData.supportsTransactionIsolationLevel() method to see if the driver and database support a given isolation level, and if so attempt to set it with the Connection.setTransactionIsolation() method.

Deadlock Detection and Response

Given the same application, it is possible that deadlocks can occur on some systems and not others, because it is affected by locking granularity (table vs. row or page) and policies (e.g., lock escalation) of the DBMS. For example, Oracle never escalates locks within the same granularity, but it does escalate lock modes within a level of granularity, whereas Sybase escalates locks from the page to the table level. Also, the application can unwittingly cause lock escalation by requesting objects for update, or simply by making additional read requests. Again, different databases have different policies.

In general, your application must be prepared to catch deadlock errors. Unfortunately, the JDBC specification does not define how a driver should respond to a deadlock (i.e., what kind of exception is generated). Most likely the driver will generate an SQLException, but you cannot be sure without checking.

Asynchronous Execution

JDBC does not support multiple transactions per connection. However, a client application may create multiple connections, and perform a separate concurrent transaction on each connection, by executing them in separate threads. A JDBC driver is supposed to allow this mode of operation. As will be discussed later, some object database products do not allow this. Surprisingly, there are mainstream relational database products that do not even allow multiple connections per client process using the DBMS's own drivers. Multithread concurrency is an important capability, and you should not take for granted that a given JDBC driver in combination with a given DBMS provides it.

In addition, operations on java.sql objects is multithread-safe. Thus, multiple client threads can access result sets and other JDBC objects without fear of corrupting those objects.

Multithreading is important in applications that support the workstation paradigm, as opposed to the transaction terminal paradigm: a user can have several things going on at once, in different windows. An example from our own work is a bank loan system's "minimize" feature, which allowed the user (a loan officer) to handle impromptu telephone inquiries from customers without interrupting other loan applications being worked on at that moment.

Handling Connection Loss

It is a common occurrence that a client application may lose its connection to the database unexpectedly. This may be a result of loss of a communication link, an administrative shutdown, or an unrecoverable protocol error detected by the driver. Since connection loss is asynchronous, but the database connection belongs to the thread that established it, an error will be thrown during the next or current attempt to access the connection. This kind of error should not be treated as an unrecoverable error, but handled gracefully.

The error is easily trapped by wrapping each database access in a throws clause. If all database accesses are encapsulated in access routines, the throws clause can be in the access routine to avoid cluttering code. Some database drivers will attempt to reconnect transparently when a connection is lost, and, if a connection is reestablished, determine if the original transaction's thread can still be connected to; and if not, throw an exception. Regardless, if the connection is ultimately lost and an exception thrown, it is up to the application to either try to reestablish the connection and replay the transaction (if possible), or inform the user of any changes that were lost.

Dealing with the Time Delay of Connecting to a Database

Connecting to a database can require from tens of milliseconds to several seconds. More typical is a delay of a hundred milliseconds or more. When combined with network traffic, application load, and the overhead of middle-tier software, the actual delay to create a connection can be protracted. While the connection is being established, the user is free to click about on the user interface and try to use the connection before it actually exists. The application design must take this possibility into account.

Three states which are important are the states of "have not attempted connection yet," "in process of connecting," and "have completed a connection." Rather than setting a synchronized flag to indicate these states, it is usually sufficient to synchronize access to the connection handle. This will force threads trying to use the handle to block until the handle is available.

Premature clicking will not happen if the connection was initiated by user action and the GUI system employs a single thread to handle user events, such as the AWT does, but this behavior should not be relied on. Alternatively, connection establishment and long-running transactions may be implemented in separate threads. Performing queries in the GUI's event thread (which handles button clicks) is not generally a good idea, because the time delay of a database operation is indeterminate, and menus and other GUI elements will be inaccessible in the meantime. If separate threads are used to initiate connections and perform queries, the connection object—and any objects affected by queries—need to be protected.

The Problems with "Active" Controls

Many database component libraries provide control components such as scrollable lists and tables that maintain an active connection to the database and are self-updating. This approach works best for small databases used by a few people or a single user. If the system is a multiuser system, the isolation level impacts the manner in which the component is updated, and in some situations the user may think they are seeing current data when in fact they are seeing a snapshot. JDBC also does not require that a result set be backward scrollable (although JDBC 2 will add this feature), so JDBC does not provide a standard way for JDBC component vendors to implement this, although most do. Reverse scrolling may be implemented by the driver or the control. If this feature is used, the precise semantics of the mechanism should be examined to determine if it is desirable for the application.

Unicode Support

Most databases have no problem storing multibyte character strings. For example, if you store the Java string value "W\u00e4hrung" ("Währung," which means "currency" in German) in Oracle with the following statement:

```
stmt.executeUpdate("INSERT INTO DEPT VALUES (60,
    'W\u00e4hrung', 'Berlin')");
```

and then retrieve it with a query, you will get back the same identical string value. In general, if you plan to internationalize your application, you should make sure that the database and driver can handle Unicode strings.

Sorting and Comparing Unicode Using the Collator and CollationKey Classes

Java has two classes for performing locale-sensitive comparisons and sorting of Internationalized string values. These are the Collator and CollationKey classes. For comparing individual strings, use the Collator class. For performing multiple comparisons using a single string, use the CollationKey class. Here is an example of using the Collator class:

```
Collator c = Collator.getInstance(Locale.US);
c.setStrength(Collator.IDENTICAL);
c.setDecomposition(Collator.FULL_DECOMPOSITION);
int r = c.compare(string1, string 2);
if (r < 0)
    System.out.println("string1 < string2");
else if (r == 0)
    System.out.println("strings are equals");
else
    System.out.println("string1 > string2");
```

In the above, the "IDENTICAL" strength setting specifies that the strings must be identical to match, and that, for example, the comparison is case sensitive. The possible strengths are:

IDENTICAL—This is the strongest (most "picky") form of comparison. Only lexically equivalent strings are considered identical. Unicode has multiple ways of representing many characters, including a single-character representation, and a compound "base" and "nonspacing" representation; and also, sometimes a pair of characters are considered equivalent to a different single character, such as "ll" and "l" followed by "l." The comparison result depends on the locale.

TERTIARY—Very small differences result in the characters being considered distinct, including case.

SECONDARY—A middle ground, usually representing case insensitivity.

PRIMARY—The least strong (least picky) form. If the two characters cannot be considered equivalent in any way for the specified locale, they have a primary difference. For example, "a" and "b" have a primary difference because they are completely different characters, whereas "a" and "ã" would probably be considered the same in most locales; case insensitive as well.

The decomposition level specifies the Unicode compatibility mode for multicharacter forms and variations that are considered lexically equivalent. There are three possible settings for this:

NO_DECOMPOSITION—Accents will not be taken into account, leading to incorrect sorting order for languages that have accents.

CANONICAL_DECOMPOSITION—Accents are taken into account.

FULL_DECOMPOSITION—Multicharacter forms are sorted correctly. This is important for some Asian languages.

Use the CollationKey class to repetitively compare a string value with other strings. For example,

```
CollationKey ck1 = c.getCollationKey(string1);
for (int i = 0; i < strings2.length; i++)
{
    CollationKey ck2 = c.getCollationKey(strings2[i]);
    if (ck1.equals(ck2)) { return; }
}
// not found
throw new Exception();
```

Searching with LIKE

Some drivers we have tested support the LIKE clause, and some do not. LIKE expressions are used to match strings based on wildcard expression rules, rather than exact character-by-character matching. This can be used to implement very powerful searching for person and place names, and other strings for which a record must be identified but the complete spelling is not known.

In a LIKE expression, "%" matches zero or more characters, and "_" matches exactly one character. You can override this and cause these characters to be treated literally by escaping them with an escape character. The escape character may be different on different systems, however. JDBC lets you use the "{escape 'escape-character'}" syntax to specify an escape character in LIKE expressions. For example, in this example we are saying "treat any character immediately following '$' literally, rather than as a wildcard":

```
stmt.executeQuery(
"SELECT FNAME FROM DOCFILES WHERE FNAME LIKE '%$_%' {escape '$'}");
```

Unicode may also not be directly supported by the DBMS, so characters may get converted internally to Ascii for searching and queries. If you are storing Unicode, in particular character sets for languages other than English, make sure that queries perform as you expect when searching based on a Unicode string. Again, most databases can handle this. For example, Oracle in combination with its "thin" all-Java driver has no trouble finding "Währung." However, you should run a test to make sure.

The Name Ordering Problem

A problem with international applications is that different cultures order name components differently. For example, while most Western cultures list the family name last, most Eastern cultures list the family name first. For example, the English name John W. Smith identifies John W. as belonging to the Smith family; while the Chinese name Tan Sai Cheong identifies Sai Cheong as belonging to the Tan family. Some cultures do not even recognize the concept of a family name. For example, it used to be a practice in Scotland to use the father's first name as the last name for a child (e.g. William, of Jonathan); if William then has a son, he might name him Stephen, of William. This practice is rare nowadays, however.

A solution for name searching is to be agnostic with regard to the ordering of name components, and search every possible combination. Also, international applications should not force a cultural bias on users. A field for family name should be labeled as such, not as "last name."

Representing Decimal and Monetary Data Types

Representing monetary types is problematic for two reasons: precision and locale-specific representation. In choosing a representation, one must be sure that it can handle the range of values which will be represented, and that precision, rounding, and arithmetic and conversion rules specific to the application are adhered to. For example, for monetary types, a given legal jurisdiction or accounting practice may require rounding up according to a certain formula or alternating up/down technique. In parsing and displaying values, locale-specific rules require displaying the correct currency symbols in the right positions, and radix and point separators following the correct number of digits. What would seem to be a simple problem turns out to be extremely complex.

Using Long

The advantage of using long to represent monetary values is that it is a built-in type, and thus efficient. The disadvantages are that the range may not be enough for some applications.

A long is a 64-bit signed quantity. This yields a numeric range of 2^{63}, or 8×10^{18}; so, to represent a monetary value to 3 decimal places (i.e., thousandths of a currency unit), we have a range of 8×10^{15} currency units, or 8 million billion. If your application might be computing account totals larger than this, using long may require special provisions for your largest accounts.

You may also want control over rounding behavior. This is only an issue with percentage, fractional multiplication, and division calculations, and for those you can write special routines that implement the rounding rules you prefer; but you would probably need to do this regardless of the representation used.

Using BigDecimal

The BigDecimal type is a Java class, defined in package java.math. This means that all of its operations are defined as methods, and simple operations such as addition will need to be expressed as a method call. Java, unlike C++, does not support operator overloading, so there is no way to get around this.

In practice, using the BigDecimal type is not as inconvenient as you might think. Arithmetic routines are usually encapsulated into other higher-level routines that perform specific calculations for an application; it would be extremely poor design not to encapsulate such code into a well-defined "business rules" package that performs these calculations. Therefore, the actual impact on your code, from an aesthetic and programming convenience point of view, should be minimal. The main drawback is speed. Calculations using the BigDecimal type will be thousands of times slower than calculations using the long type. Depending on how often these calculations are done, this may or may not be a problem.

It may be possible to use a hybrid approach in some applications. Account balances, for example, could be represented by long values and converted to BigDecimal values whenever division and multiplication are required. Again, this conversion should be encapsulated within the calculation routines and hidden from the rest of the code.

Here are some examples of using BigDecimal:

```
BigDecimal oneThousandPointOhSevenFive = new
  BigDecimal("1000.075");
    the scale is 3
    the intValue() is 1000
```

To round a value and specify that rounding should use the "half-even" method, in which the calculation rounds up if the digit to the right of the discarded fraction is >= .5 and the digit to the left is odd, and otherwise round down:

```
BigDecimal dollarsAndCents =
    oneThousandPointOhSevenFive.setScale(2,
    BigDecimal.ROUND_HALF_EVEN);
      the scale is 2
      the intValue() is 1000
      the full value is 1000.08 - we have rounded, and lost
        precision
```

To perform arithmetic operations, use the add(), subtract, multiply(), and divide() methods, such as in

```
BigDecimal difference =
    dollarsAndCents.subtract(oneThousandPointOhSevenFive);
      the scale is
      MAX(dollarsAndCents.scale(),
          oneThousandPointOhSevenFive.scale()) = 3
      the intValue() is 0
      the full value is 0.005
```

To convert BigDecimal values to other types, there are conversion methods—one for each Java intrinsic numeric type. Of course, depending on the value being converted, a loss of data may result.

Is Java Year-2000-Compliant?

The Date type is internally represented as a long, with the value zero set to January 1, 1970. This does not mean dates prior to 1970 cannot be represented; they are simply negative numbers (internally). Nor does it mean you have to subtract 1970 from all your years: this is taken care of for you by the Date and Calendar class methods. In fact, when you retrieve the year value using the Calendar class, the number you get is simply the year (e.g., for the year 2000, you get 2000).

Year values are also continuous across the year 2000 threshold. Thus, if you add one (1) day to December 31, 1999, you end up with January 1, 2000.

One way in which the year 2000 is kind of unique is that it is divisible by 400, and also by 100. The rule for leap years is that a leap year occurs if a year is divisible by 4 but *not* divisible by 100—unless it is divisible by 400, in which case it is still a leap year. The year 2000 is therefore a leap year, because it is divisible by 400. The JDK correctly reports that the year 2000 is a leap year, and that there are 29 days in February 2000. Here is the output of a test:

```
calendar with year set to 1999: Thu Dec 30 22:23:30 EST 1999
one day later...Fri Dec 31 22:23:30 EST 1999
another day later...Sat Jan 01 22:23:30 EST 2000
Add 58 days:Mon Feb 28 22:23:30 EST 2000
another day later...Tue Feb 29 22:23:30 EST 2000
```

The Date type can represent a time range of 2^{64} milliseconds, which corresponds approximately to 500,000,000 years. This clearly encompasses the year 2000, as well as any conceivable long-term mortgages!

What about java.sql.Timestamp? That is a date/time class as well. The Timestamp object is a composite of a Date and a separate nanosecond value. It therefore can handle any range that Date can handle.

Thus, the JDK is year-2000-compliant. In fact, Javasoft claims to even have accounted for leap seconds.

Note also that some DBMS implementations of SQL dates run out in the year 2036! This is a while from now, so you might think we don't have to worry about this just yet; but what about a banking loan application? A 40-year mortgage created in 1998 would mature in the year 2038. Make sure that the data range handled by the database—not just Java—supports the range you need and beyond!

My Soapbox: When to (and not to) Store Serialized Data

The term "impedance mismatch" is often used to identify the inefficiencies that result from using a relational database with an object-oriented language. The fact that a term from electrical engineering has been appropriated to describe a computer science problem is indicative of the fact that these inefficiencies are hard to summarize. In fact, relational databases can be used quite effectively with object-oriented languages. The JDBC API is an object-oriented API for accessing relational systems. JDBC queries return objects—ResultSet objects—which are objects just like any other in Java. Using JDBC, a relational system can be accessed with no less inherent efficiency than if it were accessed by query from any other language.

The real impedance mismatch comes into play when systems are not used correctly. For example, a relational database should not be used to store objects. This is a different situation from products which implement an object model using a relational database engine. Those products take account of caching and data integrity requirements, and allow an object model to be efficiently implemented directly on legacy relational systems. A different, and sad, scenario is when objects are stuffed into a relational database, and the resulting system is described as object oriented.

This may sound so absurd that no one would do this, but in fact I have seen it done many times. The justification is usually that the data is being stored in the form of the objects that will later be needed, so there will be a single query to obtain the object. This is rarely the case once the system starts to be used, however. As more queries are added, a situation soon results where in order to obtain a small piece of data, one has to retrieve and reconstitute an entire large-grain object, only to throw most of it away. What usually happens is that the application starts to evolve bizarre caching strategies in order to implement an incremental query capability, which should be performed by the DBMS.

It is almost never advisable to store serialized objects in a database, unless it can be guaranteed that those objects have nothing to do with the database's application domain. Such a situation is exemplified by a user interface, in which it is desirable to restore the client's GUI appearance, based on the user's identity, from any client machine. In this case, storing the GUI state as a serialized object for later retrieval makes a roaming client possible. Of course, the system must know what to do if the same user is logged on in more than one location.

A final caution about storing serialized objects in a database is that doing so embeds in the database assumptions about the structure of the serialized objects. If a later release of the software changes the implementation of the serialized object classes, all of the serialized objects in the database will become unreadable. If the changes satisfy compatibility rules, this can be solved by implementing a readObject() method[a] in the new version of the class, unloading all of these objects, and reloading them. Otherwise, an unload, convert, and reload program will have to be written; or, if the objects are not critical data (e.g., they might simply be the visual GUI state), they may be simply be deleted.

[a]*If a class has a readObject() method with the signature void readObject(ObjectInputStream), this method is used instead of the default method for reconstituting the object. See the explanation in the javadocs for the Serializable interface.*

JDBC 2

A large set of new features are added to JDBC in JDBC version 2, which is scheduled for release in the summer of 1998. These new features are optional for an implementation, and therefore the task of selecting a database driver is now even more complex than before, as driver providers are free to implement features as appropriate for the intended use of their product.

The enhancements are divided into two groups: core features enhancements and extended feature enhancements. The core enhancements take the form of new methods and capabilities added to the existing java.sql classes, and new classes added to package java.sql. The extended enhancements are provided by a new package: javax.sql. I will first explain the enhancements to the core java.sql package, and then discuss the extended enhancements.

Result Sets

So far the ResultSet type we have discussed in this chapter is an object type that has the ability to scroll forward through a query result. Depending on the implementation, rows in the result set may be obtained dynamically as it is scrolled, or the result set may be built statically all at once when the query statement is executed. Regardless, there is no mechanism defined for a result set to scroll backwards, and in this way, the issue of repeatability of data read by a result set is avoided. Many vendors have nevertheless provided their own backward scrolling capability, with semantics particular to their implementation.

To address this, JDBC 2 defines three types of result set:

> *forward-only*—same as before: the JDBC ResultSet type. Exact behavior depends on the implementation: may be computed at creation, or as it is scrolled.

> *scroll-insensitive*—Filled when created. Static. Does not even reflect changes made in the current transaction.

> *scroll-sensitive*—dynamic. Reflects current state of the transaction's data. Exact behavior depends on the isolation policy of the database and transaction.

A scroll-insensitive result set is a fully constructed object, which is filled with data when the query is performed. Scrolling through the result set does not perform any database operations, as they have all been completed. The result set is a snapshot of the way the data was when the query was performed.

A scroll-sensitive result set is dynamic, and may—may—reflect changes made to the database during the course of the user's transaction. Whether it does or not depends on the isolation mode in effect for the transaction. I will not get into the details of this now, as these issues are discussed in details later in this chapter. Suffice it to say that a scroll-sensitive result set has the ability to reflect database changes, whereas a scroll-insensitive result set does not.

In addition, a result set may now be declared to be of one of these types:

> *read-only*—the contents have at most read locks

> *updatable*—the contents have write locks or an automatic optimistic mechanism, and the result set may be modified by the transaction. (Provides a platform-independent way of saying "SELECT ... FOR UPDATE".)

These modes determine whether a transaction can use a set of new updateXXX() methods on the result set, to change the values of its rows. A read-only result set may not be so modified, whereas an updatable result set can. In addition, an implementation will likely map these settings to multi-transaction concurrency control policies, which affect the ability of others to obtain access to the data represented by the result set, at the same time that our transaction is in progress. A read-only result set allows all other transactions read access to the data, whereas an updatable result set may place write locks on the affected data, thereby preventing others from accessing the data until the transaction is complete. Again, exactly what the system will do depends on the concurrency control policies and techniques used by the database and the driver. Database concurrency control and locking is discussed later in this chapter.

Here is an example of creating a statement that is both scroll-sensitive (dynamic) and updatable:

```
Statement s = connection.createStatement(
   ResultSet.TYPE_SCROLL_SENSITIVE,
   ResultSet.CONCUR_UPDATABLE);
ResultSet resultSet = s.executeQuery("SELECT N FROM TALLIES");
```

Since the statement is updatable, we can use the ResultSet updateXXX() methods on it:

```
resultSet.next();
resultSet.getInt("N");
resultSet.updateInt("N", 45);
```

Since the result set is scroll-sensitive, we should see the change we made if we re-read the current row:

```
int newN = resultSet.getInt("N");      // should return 45
```

In addition, we can be confident that the database will prevent others from reading or modifying this data until our transaction commits, since the result set data is locked for update. The semantic details of this and how it is implemented depends on the concurrency control and locking mechanisms of the database, and the driver implementation.

The possible values for the result set type parameter of a statement are TYPE_FORWARD_ONLY, TYPE_SCROLL_INSENSITIVE, and TYPE_SCROLL_SENSITIVE. The possible values for the concurrency parameter are CONCUR_READ_ONLY and CONCUR_UPDATABLE. You can test how the database and driver handle updates with the following new DatabaseMetaData methods:

```
supportsResultSetType(int type)
supportsResultSetConcurrency(int type, int concurrency)
ownUpdatesAreVisible(int type)
ownDeletesAreVisible(int type)
ownInsertsAreVisible(int type)
othersUpdatesAreVisible(int type)
othersDeletesAreVisible(int type)
othersInsertsAreVisible(int type)
updatesAreDetected(int type)
deletesAreDetected(int type)
insertsAreDetected(int type)
```

It is not clear from the current specifications what will happen to an updatable result set if the result set is computed, for example as a result of a join, and there are no drivers to test for this at the time of this writing. However, it is likely that result sets that cannot meet the updatable requirement will throw an exception when created by a query, or when an update is attempted (the former would be preferable; this is another thing to add to your list of driver evaluation criteria!).

You can also add a row to a result set. To do this, you must temporarily move to the virtual "insert row", using the moveToInsertRow() method, perform updateXXX() calls to add column values to the new row, and then finally call the insertRow() method. For example, to insert a *new* row in the result set that has one int-valued column,

```
resultSet.moveToInsertRow();
resultSet.updateInt(1, 60);
resultSet.insertRow();
```

In addition to the standard ResultSet next() method, scroll-insensitive and scroll-sensitive result sets can use these new ResultSet methods for effecting positional control:

first()—Set the position to the first row in the result set.

last()—Set the position to the last row.

previous()—Set the position to the previous row.

afterLast()—Prepare to decrement backward from the end, using the previous() method.

beforeFirst()—Prepare to increment forward from the first row using the next() method.

`relative()`—Increment or decrement the current row position. (There must be a current row—can't be before first or after last)

    `absolute()`—Set the position to a specified row.

    `isAfterLast()`—Return true if the position is after the last row. (False if there are no rows)

    `isBeforeFirst()`—Return true if before the first row. (False if there are no rows)

New methods are also added to provide hints to the driver to allow it to optimize its operations when fetching and scrolling. These are the setFetchSize() and set-FetchDirection() methods. For example,

```
resultSet.setFetchDirection(ResultSet.FETCH_FORWARD);
```

tells the driver that we will be scrolling primarily forward, and that it can optimize its operations for that. The possible values for the setFetchDirection parameter are FETCH_FORWARD, FETCH_REVERSE, and FETCH_UNKNOWN. To help the driver perform array fetching optimizations (discussed earlier), the set-FetchSize() method can be used to recommend to the driver how many rows it should fetch at once. For example,

```
resultSet.setFetchSize(20);
```

tells the driver it should retrieve twenty rows at a time, in anticipation of all of those rows being read by the current transaction. You can also set fetch direction and size hints for the statement object.

The new ResultSet methods are summarized in Table 5-6.

Table 5-6 New ResultSet methods

Object getObject(String columnName)
int findColumn(String columnName)
java.io.Reader getCharacterStream(int columnIndex)
java.io.Reader getCharacterStream(String columnName)
BigDecimal getBigDecimal(int columnIndex)
BigDecimal getBigDecimal(String columnName)
boolean isBeforeFirst()
boolean isAfterLast()
boolean isFirst()
boolean isLast()
void beforeFirst()
void afterLast()
boolean first()
boolean last()
int getRow()

Table 5-6 New ResultSet methods(Continued)

boolean absolute(int row)

boolean relative(int rows)

boolean previous()

void setFetchDirection(int direction)

int getFetchDirection()

void setFetchSize(int rows)

int getFetchSize()

int getType()

int getConcurrency()

boolean rowUpdated()

boolean rowInserted()

boolean rowDeleted()

void updateNull(int columnIndex)

void updateBoolean(int columnIndex, boolean x)

void updateByte(int columnIndex, byte x)

void updateShort(int columnIndex, short x)

void updateInt(int columnIndex, int x)

void updateLong(int columnIndex, long x)

void updateFloat(int columnIndex, float x)

void updateDouble(int columnIndex, double x)

void updateBigDecimal(int columnIndex, BigDecimal x)

void updateString(int columnIndex, String x)

void updateBytes(int columnIndex, byte x[])

void updateDate(int columnIndex, Date x)

void updateTime(int columnIndex, Time x)

void updateTimestamp(int columnIndex, Timestamp x)

void updateAsciiStream(int columnIndex, java.io.InputStream x, int length)

void updateBinaryStream(int columnIndex, java.io.InputStream x, int length)

void updateCharacterStream(int columnIndex, java.io.Reader reader, int length)

void updateObject(int columnIndex, Object x, int scale)

void updateObject(int columnIndex, Object x)

void updateNull(String columnName)

void updateBoolean(String columnName, boolean x)

void updateByte(String columnName, byte x)

void updateShort(String columnName, short x)

void updateInt(String columnName, int x)

void updateLong(String columnName, long x)

void updateFloat(String columnName, float x)

void updateDouble(String columnName, double x)

Table 5-6 New ResultSet methods(Continued)

void updateBigDecimal(String columnName, BigDecimal x)

void updateString(String columnName, String x)

void updateBytes(String columnName, byte x[])

void updateDate(String columnName, Date x)

void updateTime(String columnName, Time x)

void updateTimestamp(String columnName, Timestamp x)

void updateAsciiStream(String columnName, java.io.InputStream x, int length)

void updateBinaryStream(String columnName, java.io.InputStream x, int length)

void updateCharacterStream(String columnName, java.io.Reader reader, int length)

void updateObject(String columnName, Object x, int scale)

void updateObject(String columnName, Object x)

void insertRow()

void updateRow()

void deleteRow()

void refreshRow()

void moveToInsertRow()

void moveToCurrentRow()

Statement getStatement()

Object getObject(int i, java.util.Map map)

Ref getRef(int i)

Blob getBlob(int i)

Clob getClob(int i)

Array getArray(int i)

Object getObject(String colName, java.util.Map map)

Ref getRef(String colName)

Blob getBlob(String colName)

Clob getClob(String colName)

Array getArray(String colName)

Date getDate(int columnIndex, Calendar cal)

Date getDate(String columnName, Calendar cal)

Time getTime(int columnIndex, Calendar cal)

Time getTime(String columnName, Calendar cal)

Timestamp getTimestamp(int columnIndex, Calendar cal)

Timestamp getTimestamp(String columnName, Calendar cal)

Batch Updates

A "batch update" mechanism has been added to support a more efficient execution of updates, allowing several updates to be processed by a DBMS with a single DBMS call. For example, the following creates a statement and adds two

batched INSERT operations to it, to be performed in series. It then executes the
batched statement and commits the results. Note that an exception can occur as a
result of any portion of a batched update, so we should disable auto-commit so
that we can treat the entire batched operation atomically as a single transaction:

```java
connection.setAutoCommit(false);
try
{
   Statement s = connection.createStatement();
   s.addBatch("INSERT ...");
   s.addBatch("INSERT ...");
   s.executeBatch();
   connection.commit();
}
catch (SQLException ex)
{
   try { connection.rollback(); } catch (Exception ex2) {}
}
```

Prepared and callable statements can participate in batch updates as well. The following example creates a prepared statement, and batches two executions of the
statement, each using different parameters:

```java
connection.setAutoCommit(false);
try
{
   PreparedStatement ps = connection.prepareStatement(
      "INSERT INTO TABA VALUES (?, ?)");
   ps.setString("ID", "A-210-003");
   ps.setString("Name", "Ima Lemmon");
   ps.addBatch();

   ps.setString("ID", "C-101-001");
   ps.setString("Name", "Rob R. Barron");
   ps.addBatch();

   ps.executeBatch();
   connection.commit();
}
catch (SQLException ex)
{
   try { connection.rollback(); } catch (Exception ex2) {}
}
```

A batched callable statement works the same way. However, a batch update callable statement may not have OUT or INOUT parameters.

You can test if the database and driver support batch updates with the new DatabaseMetaData supportsBatchUpdates() method.

New Types

In order to accommodate SQL3, and in addition the storage of persistified Java objects in a standard RDBMS-supported way, JDBC 2 add new column types to the java.sql.Types class. The additions are:

> JAVA_OBJECT—A persistified Java object. Objects of this type can be retrieved directly using the ResultSet's getObject() method, and stored using the updateObject() method.

> DISTINCT—Analogous to an IDL typedef. Effectively aliases for type specifications. For example, "CREATE TYPE NAME VARCHAR(10)". The standard Java-to-SQL type mappings apply, based on the underlying actual type of the data.

> STRUCT—Analogous to an IDL struct. Manifest by the new java.sql type Struct. The contents of a Struct are retrieved when the Struct is retrieved, and have normal Java object lifetime semantics. The Struct method getAttributes() can be used to retrieve the Struct's contents. Use the ResultSet getObject() methods to retrieve a Struct. Use the PreparedStatement setObject() method to store a Struct.

> ARRAY—An array of values of a specified type. Manifest by the new java.sql type Array. Only valid for the duration of the transaction that created it.

> BLOB—Binary large object. Manifest by the new java.sql type Blob. The contents of the object is not transferred to the client unless explicitly requested, via the Blob's getBytes() or getBinaryStream() methods. A Blob object is only valid for the duration of the transaction that created it.

> CLOB—Character large object. Manifest by the new java.sql type Clob. Similar to BLOB, value is not actually transferred unless explicitly requested via the getCharacterStream() or getAsciiStream() methods. Only valid for the duration of the transaction that created it.

> REF—For retrieving and passing (e.g. to an UPDATE) references to database data without actually retrieving the data. Manifest by the new java.sql type Ref. Valid for the duration of the connection. Useful for handling large data objects without having to transfer them to the client environment over a network.

The DatabaseMetaData class has the following new method to get information on the data types supported by the database:

```
ResultSet getUDTs(String catalog, String schemaPattern, String
  typeNamePattern, int[] types)
```

Each returned row contains:

> TYPE_CAT—String or null; the type catalog in which the type is defined, if any.
>
> TYPE_SCHEM—String or null; the type's schema, if any.
>
> TYPE_NAME—String; the type name.
>
> JAVA_CLASS—String; the fully-qualified name of the Java class that is constructed for values of this type.
>
> DATA_TYPE—short; the type code for this type (the value defined in java.sql.Types).
>
> REMARKS—Comment.

The JAVA_CLASS column identifies the Java class that maps to the database type, as discussed above. Actual instances used to update column values must be of this type or a subclass. The DATA_TYPE column specifies the typecode for uniquely identifying the JDBC database type.

Type Maps

Normally objects retrieved from columns of type DISTINCT or STRUCT result in a Java object of the mapped Java object type or a Java Struct object. However, a facility called "type maps" is provided to automatically encapsulate the conversion of database types to arbitrary client application types. All you have to do is implement the SQLData interface in your type, and register the type map with the database connection by calling its setTypeMap() method. For example, the following class encapsulates the construction of a user-defined type, Name, from a DISTINCT type which would otherwise map to a Java String:

public class Name implements SQLData

```
{
  public void readSQL(SQLInput is, String type)
  throws SQLException
  {
    sqlType = type;
    name = is.readString();
  }
```

```
    public void writeSQL(SQLOutput os)
    throws SQLException
    {
        os.writeString(name);
    }

    private String name;
    private String sqlType;
}
```

This code registers the type:

```
    java.util.Map map = connection.getTypeMap();
    map.put("NAME", Name.class);
```

Whenever a distinct type of type NAME is read from the database, an instance of Name will automatically be constructed, using the Name.readSQL() method. Similarly, Name objects inserted into the database will be converted to NAME column values using the Name class's writeSQL() method.

Java Objects

JDBC 2 supports database columns of type JAVA_OBJECT. Columns of this type represent persistified Java objects—perhaps objects which have been serialized, or stored as persistent objects in a database-supported manner. These can be objects such as Java documents or potentially large application objects of arbitrary types. The problem with doing this is that such objects are not accessed the way an RDBMS is designed to access its data. A serialized large object (SLOB) is not accessible to the database's normal mechanisms, and so it cannot be as efficient in a product designed for high performance relational access. All the code in the RDBMS designed to optimize table access is not applicable. The issue of code deployment, versioning and object obsolescence must also be addressed; these are not addressed by the current version of the JDBC 2 specification, and it will be interesting to see what support vendors provide for these requirements.

If one must store many Java objects, one might as well use an object database. However, admittedly there are cases in which objects need to be stored essentially for transfer or archival, and not accessed internally by the database. If used in this way, the object is just a BLOB. Providing special support for it in a relational database is of questionable value. These products are getting too big anyway.

In order to support Java object storage, the ResultSet getObject() method is extended to handle this new type. There is also an updateObject() method for updating rows containing Java objects.

Use of JNDI

JDBC 2 provides in package javax.sql a new type called DataSource, which allows JDBC databases to be located and connected to by using Java Naming and Directory Interface (JNDI). This provides an alternative to specifying a database URL, thereby freeing application code from having to know in advance the hostname on which a database is deployed, and even the name of the dataset. Once the data source is obtained, a client can log onto the database by using the data source's getConnection() method. For example,

```
Context context = new InitialContext();
DataSource ds = context.lookup("jdbc/MyDataset");
Connection connection = ds.getConnection("scott", "tiger");
```

establishes a database connection to a database dataset identified as MyDataset, regardless where the database resides, as long as it is registered with a directory service accessible by the JNDI interface.

Other Additions

JDBC 2 adds a new ResultSet type, called "RowSet". Rowsets are an extension feature (in package javax.sql) that implement the ResultSet interface but provide advanced concurrency control and cursor features, well-defined semantics, and component-like JavaBean encapsulation for use in assembling database applications. The RowSet specification is still young at the time of this writing.

JDBC 2 also adds support for distributed transactions using Java Transaction Service (JTS), and connection pooling for allowing implementations to implement database connection pools in an API-supported manner.

SQLJ (aka J/SQL)

In a joint effort, IBM, Oracle, Sybase, and Tandem have defined a standard for embedding SQL in Java programs. Analogous to embedded SQL for other languages such as C and C++, SQLJ leverages the host language and adds SQL features. SQLJ can be implemented either with a preprocessor that translates source into pure Java, or as a compiler which integrates SQLJ and Java source analysis into a single step.

A principal advantage of using SQLJ is that errors which would otherwise be detected at runtime can often be caught as type mismatch errors at compile time. For example, if the SQLJ compiler has access to the schema for the database the program is targeted for, it can check if query variables are matched to compatible Java types. By comparison, in a JDBC program such an error would only be detected when the actual query is run.

Basic Syntax

SQLJ is defined as a set of extensions to the Java language. Each SQLJ statement is preceded with a "#"; however, such a statement may continue onto any number of lines. As illustrative examples, the basic syntax of a select and insert is shown below, using SQLJ. Source and target Java variables are preceded by colons.

```
int age = 20;
#sql { SELECT NAME INTO :name FROM GREATVIOLINISTS
WHERE AGE < :age };
String attraction = "Tyrannosaur";
#sql { INSERT INTO THEMEPARK VALUES ( :attraction ) };
```

At present, only Java variables may appear following a colon. It is likely that an upcoming release of the SQLJ specification will permit Java expressions as well, such as

```
String[] team = { "Sculley", "Mulder" };
#sql { INSERT INTO XFILE VALUES ( :team[0], :team[1] ) };
```

Creating a Connection

To create a connection to a database at runtime, your SQLJ program must first declare a *context*. A context compiles into a class that contains information about a database connection. The generated class has four constructors which may be used to establish a live context instance. Parameters to these constructors include the URL of the database. There is also a static method generated which can be used to set a default context instance for the generated context class so that the context does not need to be specified in subsequent statements which would require a context.

An example follows. In this example, it is assumed that when the programmer invokes the SQLJ compiler, he or she specifies that class CarTable is the default context class; the default context instance of this class will then be used whenever a default context is determined

```
#sql context CarTable;// this generates a context class (but not
    // an instance)
public class MyClass
{
    public static void main (String argv[]) throws SQLException
    {
        // Now we create a context instance, and make it the default
        //   for the CarTable context class
        CarTable.setDefaultContext(new CarTable(argv[0]));
        double average;
        #sql { SELECT AVG(PRICE) INTO :average FROM CARDATA };
        // The above uses CarTable as the default context class,
        //   because the programmer
        // specified that when compiling, and obtains the default
        //   context instance by
        // calling CarTable's generated static method
        //   getDefaultContext()
    }
}
```

Note that in this example, the main method's argument, which presumably contains a database connect string, is passed to the constructor of the generated context class, CarTable. The CarTable context instance created as a result of the new operation is passed to CarTable's static setDefaultContext() method. The #sql statement that then follows executes in the default context of the CarTable class.

Improved Support for Cursors—Iterators

SQLJ expands on the Java result set and SQL cursors by defining *iterators*. An iterator automates the mapping of SQL query result columns to Java objects, thereby reducing potential runtime errors when trying to convert column values.

Iterators may be bound *by-position* or *by-name*. Positional iterators require you to use a FETCH ... INTO ... clause when retrieving a row in order to associate columns with Java variables that will hold the results. In contrast, by-name iterators generate Java-typed accessor methods uniquely for the result columns.

Here is an example of a positional iterator:

```
// Define an iterator - this generates an iterator class
#sql iterator Secrets (String, String, String);

Secrets i;// this is a reference to an iterator of the type we
    //defined
```

```
String org;
String secret;
String mole;
// Now perform a query that returns a result set with an
//iterator
#sql i = { SELECT ORG, TRADESECRETS, MOLE FROM COMPETITORS };
while (true)
{
  #sql { FETCH :i INTO :org, :secret, :mole };
  if (i.endFetch()) break;
  System.out.println(
  "Pssst - " + mole + " discovered " + org +
  " has this: " + secret);
}
```

Here is the same example, rewritten using a by-name iterator:

```
// Define an iterator - this generates an iterator class
#sql iterator Secrets (String org, String secret, String
  mole);

Secrets i;  // this is a reference to an iterator of the
            //type we defined
// Now perform a query that returns a result set with an
//iterator
#sql i = { SELECT ORG, TRADESECRETS, MOLE FROM COMPETITORS };
while (i.next())
{
  System.out.println(
  "Pssst - " + i.mole() + " discovered " + i.org() +
  " has this: " + i.secret());
}
```

Stored Procedures

SQLJ programs have neutrality of execution context, in that they are required to run the same whether they are run as a client program or a stored procedure. Many database vendors are currently readying products that implement a Java VM within their database engine for stored procedure execution, and SQLJ pre-processors will be a primary means of writing stored procedures for these platforms.

At present the SQLJ specification does not appear to preclude callable statements from returning any Java type—even general Java objects. After all, if the stored procedure is written in Java, and the calling program is a Java client, why not return any type? I raised this to the developers of the specification, and they replied that the intent for now was to limit return types to SQL types, thereby providing cross-compatibility with other kinds of stored procedures, and that the possibility of returning general Java types may be addressed in a future version.

Persistent Object Databases

A persistent object database provides a permanent storage mechanism for program objects. A Java persistent object database allows the programmer to define Java objects and save them in a database for later retrieval, possibly by a different virtual machine.

Why Use a Persistent Object Database?

JDBC defines an API for accessing a relational database (and many other data sources as well) using an SQL statement model. This approach suffers from some disadvantages, namely:

- The programmer must work with two very different languages: Java and SQL.

- SQL is primarily a runtime bound language, which makes testing difficult (this disadvantage can be addressed by using SQLJ, as discussed in this chapter).

- SQL is a very complex language, and understanding it thoroughly is a major career decision—it may be hard to find developers who understand both the implementation language and SQL sufficiently to develop effective and reliable applications.

An alternative approach is to use one language, and Java is a good choice for this. A persistent Java object database extends the Java semantic model to allow for persistent objects, using the reliable and easy-to-understand Java object model (or Object Design Language, ODL, model, which can be converted into Java), which retain their state between and across virtual machine instances. A significant performance advantage of this approach is that relationships between objects are maintained explicitly, rather than computed at runtime as is the case with a relational query. (Actually, relational performance is not so bad in this regard if foreign keys are used to define relationships between tables.)

(Another benefit is that some object databases make implementing optimistic locking easier, by allowing you to use object references outside of a transaction; then when you begin a new transaction, an exception is thrown if a reference is dirty. This will be discussed later.)

ODMG does not define a mechanism for how Java object persistence is implemented. Implementing a persistent object layer can be accomplished in a variety of ways. Some techniques used by current products are:

- Post-process Java class files (e.g., ODI's ObjectStore and PSE products; PSE is included on the CD that comes with this book); this is sometimes referred to as a "static" implementation.

- Post-process Java source code (some object/relational mapping products, such as O2's Java Relational Binding, worked this way when first introduced, but since then have been upgraded to use the above technique); this is also a "static" implementation.

- Provide a modified (persistent) virtual machine implementation (e.g., GemStone); this is sometimes referred to as an "active" implementation.

With static implementations, the basic idea is to replace normal Java object dereferencing operations in the code (bytecode or sourcecode, depending on the implementation) with calls to methods that operate on the database. Since this is done by a postprocessor, the persistence mechanism is transparent to the application, and the application only has to worry about concurrency issues, associated with multi-user access to the data. An active implementation is even more transparent, since the code is not modified at all; rather, the VM itself implements the persistence.

In addition, there are object-to-relational mapping products, often called "blend" products, which provide an object-oriented layer on top of a relational database. These will be discussed in a separate section.

How ODBMSs Work

Regardless of which implementation technique is used, a Java object database allows the programmer to deal strictly with Java objects of programmer-defined types. Predefined "database" types such as ResultSet are not used. This has the tremendous advantage that the business's object model can be defined explicitly in terms of a universal and well-defined language, making it portable and easy to understand across products, technologies, and methodologies.

To make a class persistent in a static implementation, all you do is run it through the persistent database product's persistence post-processor. Most implementations impose restrictions on what classes can be made persistent, however. For example, it is a common limitation that classes which are not user-defined cannot be made persistent. For example, java.awt.Applet or from somethirdparty.SomeClass could probably not be made persistent, because the persistence post-processor will not want to modify standard or prepackaged classes from external sources. Some persistence products also require that your own classes not extend from a base class which cannot be made persistent.

In practice this may not be as big a limitation as it sounds. Usually the classes you want to make persistent are of your own design, and are data containers of some sort—they constitute your database. Sometimes, however, you may want to make an AWT GUI component's state persistent, and to be able to do this, you will have to make sure the persistent database product has the capability to make classes that extend from package java (or other sources) persistent. Rather than making a user's GUI state persistent, a solution could be to serialize the GUI object's visual state using Java object serialization, and store that in the database or on the client machine. Of course, with this solution any database object references maintained by the GUI (as well as references to the GUI from database objects) would have to be transient, and rebuilt programmatically when the component is reinstantiated.

States of a Reference

Most ODBMSs use these concepts for references to persistent objects:

> Hollow/shadow—A reference to an object exists, but the object itself has not yet been loaded.
>
> Active—A valid reference, for an object that has been loaded.
>
> Stale—The object has not been reloaded since the last transaction (references do not necessarily remain valid between transactions—it depends on the ODBMS).

When you commit a transaction, some ODBMSs allow you to specify an option to keep references from becoming stale so that you can reaccess them in the next transaction. Otherwise, you would have to look up the root objects and traverse to the objects you need all over again.

Note that you can put a transaction "on hold" by calling leave(), and later calling join() to resume. (This is discussed below.) The object references will still be valid in the joined transaction. However, the transaction will hold all of its locks for the entire time period, which may not be desirable.

States of an Object

An object referenced in an ODBMS application may be in either a transient state or a persistent state. To be in a persistent state, the object must be persistent-capable as defined by the persistence mechanism of the ODBMS. The definitions for persistent and transient are:

> persistent—Stored in the database.
>
> transient—Not persistent at this instant (but may become persistent if later referenced by a persistent object). This is not to be confused with the Java *transient* keyword. An object referenced by an

object attribute that has a Java `transient` modifier may still be a nontransient (i.e., persistent) database object, if it is referenced by any other persistent object in the database.

The ODMG Object Model

The ODMG model attempts to unify the object database world by defining a standard model for object database products. The model has object-definition, query, and manipulation subsets. The object definition language (ODL) is based on the OMG IDL standard. The query subset (OQL) is based on SQL, but is greatly simplified. Object manipulation is normally accomplished with an API, and there is now a Java language binding.

The ODMG Java binding defines the following object classes:

- Database

- Transaction

- These collection classes:

    - SetOfObject—implements DSet, described below
    - BagOfObject—implements DBag, described below
    - ListOfObject—implements DList, described below

Unlike the Java binding for OMG (CORBA), which defines a set of org.omg packages, the ODMG Java binding does not define any predefined packages of its own; rather, vendors are free to put the ODMG classes into a package of their choosing.

The Database Class

The ODMG Java API standard does not define a method for creating a database, and leaves that up to the implementation (e.g., some implementations have a static create() method). Once created, however, the Database class has these methods for opening and operating on a database:

```
public static Database open(String name, int accessMode)
   throws ODMGException;
public void close() throws ODMGException;
public void bind(Object object, String name);
public Object lookup(String name) throws
   ObjectNameNotFoundException;
public void unbind(String name) throws
   ObjectNameNotFoundException;
```

Defining Root Objects

Before you can work with an existing database that you have opened with the open() method, you have to first get references to at least one object in the database. Once you have a reference to a persistent object, you can traverse through the object network using Java object references, just as you would in any Java program; however, you need a starting point.

Usually a starting point is some object that is a collection type. For example, you might want to find a particular employee, so you need to get a reference to an employee list. For this purpose, the employee list will need to have a name so that applications can find it. You can use the Database class's bind() method to give an object a name; for example,

```
myDatabase.bind(myEmployeeCollection, "EMPLOYEES");
```

From then on, you can always find this list—even from other processes and even after your program terminates—by calling lookup ("EMPLOYEES") after opening the database. Notice that you would not use the bind() method to give each employee a lookup name: it is not intended for that purpose. It is intended for identifying "root" entry points.

Some ODBMS products provide the ability to construct "extents." An extent is a collection of object instances which represent the total set of all objects in the database of a specific type. For example, you might construct an extent for class Employee, and thereby obtain a set of all employees. The ODMG specification does not specify support for extents at this time.

Collection Types

These collection interface types are defined by the ODMG Java binding:

- DCollection, extends java.util.Collection, and:

- DSet—extends DCollection, java.util.Set. An unordered DCollection, with no duplicates allowed.

- DBag—extends DCollection. An unordered DCollection, with duplicates allowed.

- DList—extends DCollection, java.util.List. An ordered DCollection, duplicates allowed.

- DArray—extends DCollection, java.util.List. A resizable array.

Notice that DCollection, and therefore all of the ODMG collection types, implement the java.util.Collection interface defined in Java 1.2. In addition, the DList and DArray types extend the Java 1.2 java.util.List type. Some of the methods in these types return they type java.util.Iterator, which is also a Java 1.2 type. The Iterator type is similar to the Java 1.0 Enumeration, but allows elements to be removed from it. Since an Iterator is not intended to be a persistent type, there is no corresponding DIterator interface defined by ODMG.

An implementation must provide concrete types that implement these, consisting of at least SetOfObject, ListOfObject, and BagOfObject. The only constraint on membership is that all members be Java Objects (i.e., there is effectively no type constraint). Other ODMG language bindings provide for other concrete collection types, of the general form SetOf<type>, and so on, but the Java binding only specifies those listed here. Thus, these collection types permit membership of mixed object types.

Collections are considered nonprimary containers: cloning a DCollection instance only clones the container, not the members; in other words, copies are shallow. The Java binding does not define the copy operation, however. It is up to the implementation or application to define such a shallow copy operation. These types are also mutable.

Notice that there is no hashtable object. Most implementations provide a persistent hashtable or dictionary class. You can also use the DCollection query() and selectElement() methods to find objects in any collection; these methods take a query predicate (i.e., the part of a WHERE clause that follows the "WHERE") as a parameter. However, beware that some "ODMG-compliant" products do not yet support this feature.

Of course, regular Java arrays are supported also.

The following table lists the methods defined in java.util.Collection, java.util.List, java.util.Iterator, and the ODMG collection interfaces.

Table 5-7 Collection types

java.util.Collection:

```
public int size();
public boolean isEmpty();
public boolean add(Object obj);
public boolean remove(Object obj);
public boolean contains(Object obj);
public java.util.Iterator iterator();
public boolean containsAll(Collection c);
public boolean addAll(Collection c);
public boolean removeAll(Collection c);
public boolean retainAll(Collection c);
public int size();
public boolean isEmpty();
public boolean add(Object obj);
public boolean remove(Object obj);
public boolean contains(Object obj);
public java.util.Iterator iterator();
public boolean containsAll(Collection c);
public boolean addAll(Collection c);
public boolean removeAll(Collection c);
public boolean retainAll(Collection c);
```

java.util.List (extends java.util.Collection):

```
pubic void add(int index, Object obj) throws ArrayIndexOutOfBoundsException;
public void set(int index, Object obj) throws ArrayIndexOutOfBoundsException;
public Object remove(int index) throws ArrayIndexOutOfBoundsException;
public Object get(int index) throws ArrayIndexOutOfBoundsException;
```

java.util.Iterator (An iterator over a Collection):

```
public boolean hasNext()
public Object next()
public void remove()
```

DCollection (extends java.util.Collection):

```
public Object selectElement(String predicate) throws QueryInvalidException;
public java.util.Iterator select(String predicate) throws QueryInvalidException;
public DCollection query(String predicate) throws QueryInvalidException;
public boolean existsElement(String predicate) throws QueryInvalidException;
```

Table 5-7 Collection types(Continued)

DSet (extends DCollection, java.util.Set):

> public DSet union(DSet otherSet);
> public DSet intersection(DSet otherSet);
> public DSet difference(DSet otherSet);
> public boolean subsetOf(DSet otherSet);
> public boolean properSubsetOf(DSet otherSet);
> public boolean supersetOf(DSet otherSet);
> public boolean properSupersetOf(DSet otherSet);

DBag (extends DCollection):

> public DBag union(DBag otherBag);
> public DBag intersection(DBag otherBag);
> public DBag difference(DBag otherBag);
> public int occurrences(Object obj);

DList (extends DCollection, java.util.List):

> public DList concat(DList other);

DArray (extends DCollection, java.util.List):

> public void resize(int newSize);

Persistence by Reachability

A class must be persistent-capable to be made persistent. It is not defined how classes are made persistent-capable. In practice, products use one of the techniques discussed earlier to make objects persistent-capable (i.e., using a postprocessor to insert database calls into class files, or providing a persistent VM).

Assuming an object is persistent-capable, the database will convert it from transient to persistent as needed. The ODMG specification says that when a persistent-capable object references other persistent-capable objects, those objects become persistent when the referencing object is saved. Thus, if you look up an object using the Database.lookup() method, and you attach other persistent-capable objects to that object by setting object references, all of those objects (and all persistent-capable objects they point to) will be saved when the transaction is committed, because they are all reachable from the root persistent object.

Object Locking

The ODMG object locking model is a simple one, which uses the concept of an "intention-write" lock (see the section on database locking). These three lock modes are defined:

READ: allows shared read access

WRITE: exclusive access; does not permit concurrent reads by other transactions

UPGRADE: an intention-write lock

Read locks are obtained automatically (implicitly) as objects are accessed. Write locks are obtained automatically (implicitly) as objects are modified. Use Transaction.lock(object, mode) to explicitly request or upgrade a lock.

The lock() method is used to explicitly request a lock on an object. Normally you will only call this method when you need to request an UPGRADE (intention-write) lock, since read and write locks are obtained implicitly as needed when you perform access and modify an object.

Request an UPGRADE lock for any object for which you intend to eventually implicitly or explicitly ask for a WRITE lock within the current transaction. Other concurrent transactions cannot get WRITE or UPGRADE locks for an object if there is an UPGRADE lock for that object. This allows other transactions to read the object until the moment you decide you are ready to request the WRITE lock, providing greater concurrency than if you requested the WRITE lock from the outset.

A transaction is terminated when you perform a commit() or abort(). At that time all locks are released, and object references become stale.

Transactions

ODMG supports Isolation Level 3 (serializability). (See the section on database locking.) This provides a complete guarantee of correctness of operation with regard to concurrent transactions.

The Transaction class has one constructor and these methods:

```
Transaction();// intended to be "public" - implementations
// make it public
public void begin();
public void join();
public void leave();
public static Transaction current();
public boolean isOpen();
public void commit();
public void abort();
public void checkpoint();
public void lock(Object obj, int mode);
```

It is important to distinguish between an instance of the Transaction class and a database transaction. Your program may perform several transactions over time using the same Transaction instance.

The join() operation connects the current thread to a Transaction instance. A thread cannot perform any database operations unless the thread is joined to some Transaction instance. This even includes connecting to a database. Thus, before you can open a database, you must create a Transaction instance first and join to it.

Instantiating a Transaction object implicitly joins the current thread to that instance, so you do not have to call join() unless you want to join the thread to a different Transaction instance. You might do the latter if you put that transaction on hold for a moment by calling leave(); the join() method lets you return to it.

To begin a database transaction, you call begin() on the thread's Transaction instance. To terminate a transaction, call either commit() or abort() to save changes or abandon them, respectively. In both cases, all locks held by the transaction are released. The checkpoint() method saves changes, but does not release the transaction's locks. The abort() method does not restore the prior program state of nonpersistent (i.e., transient) objects.

Thus, a Transaction object manages database transactions, and at any one instant may or may not have an actual transaction in progress. Your thread must be attached to a Transaction object in order to create objects in the context of that transaction. You cannot call begin(), commit(), abort(), checkpoint(), or leave() for a transaction to which you are not attached. Also, more than one thread can be joined to a transaction. In that case, the threads operate within the context of that transaction, and are responsible for synchronizing access to objects they share—even persistent objects. However, two threads that are *not* joined to a transaction should not share objects. In other words, do not allow one of your threads to read a persistent object reference obtained from a transaction to which your thread is not joined.

When you commit, references become stale. You can refresh them by refetching, starting from a root object. Some ODBMSs allow you to keep them from becoming stale, but then in your next transaction you may have to catch an exception for the object being dirty, since your commit released your lock on the object. Keeping references between transactions is a valuable feature, but is not specified in the ODMG standard, so use it with care, recognizing that it may make your program nonportable.

OQL (Object Query Language)

The OQLQuery class provides an SQL-like query capability for object databases, for retrieving objects and object collections based on a selection expression. To perform a query, you can either use one of the DCollection query methods, or create a OQLQuery object and execute its create() and execute() methods. The former is appropriate when you merely want to select some objects from an existing collection. For example,

```
DList mySalespersonList = (DList)(d.lookup("Salespeople"));
...
// Get the salespeople named 'Flint'
java.util.Iterator i = mySalespersonList.select("this.name
    like 'Flint'");
for (;;)
{
  try
  {
    Salesperson s = (Salesperson)(i.next());
    System.out.println(s.name);
  }
  catch (NoSuchElementException ex) { break; }
}
```

To perform a query, create an OQLQuery object, and initialize it with an OQL SELECT expression. Then call its execute() method. For example,

```
OQLQuery q = new OQLQuery(
  "select list.region from Salespeople where list.region.name
    like 'North America'");
DCollection regions = (DCollection)(q.execute());
```

Exceptions

The ODMG standard defines a list of Java exceptions, including the base type ODMGException. Again, these classes do not go into any particular package; that is up to the vendor. Nor is their inheritance defined; they may extend from a vendor's own exceptions.

One significant difference between an object database and a relational database is that with a relational database, an exception can only occur during a database operation. With an object database, since every object dereference is potentially a database operation, virtually any operation can result in a database exception. You must therefore treat database exceptions as a general kind of event that may occur in any statement. Note that an implementation may generate RuntimeExceptions or Errors as well for some database events (like deadlock), so do not simply catch ODMGException—this will probably not get them all.

As already mentioned, some ODBMS products allow a persistent object reference to span transactions. What if a subsequent transaction attempts to use a reference from an earlier transaction, and the referenced object is modified (i.e., has been modified by someone else)? If the database automatically reloads the object, it will probably invalidate other references; what if you try to use one of these? In general, if an object database allows references to span transactions, there must be a class of exceptions for dealing with dirty and stale references, and you will have to catch these in your code. Most likely, when you detect an object has changed, you will reload the object by going back to the object used to get to it, or even by reperforming a lookup() in the database and starting from scratch. You may then need to refresh all objects obtained from the invalid object.

An important class of exceptions that are generated by some products, but are not defined in the ODMG standard, are life-cycle exceptions, which indicate mismatches in database schema between the client and the server. This capability is very valuable for implementing replicated code architectures, as described in detail at the end of this chapter. If the database schema has been modified, applications should have a way to know, other than the system administrator taking the system down and sending everyone an e-mail. Look for exceptions with names like "DatabaseUpgradeException" or "SchemaEvolutionException."

Portability

ODMG compliance does not include binary compatibility. It is up to the DBMS vendor to decide what packages the ODMG classes go into, or what exception type ODMGException extends from. Therefore, even source code is not portable until you insert the appropriate import statements at the start of each source file, and then recompile. In addition, if your code creates databases, it must do so in a vendor-specific manner, since the ODMG standard does not define a Java API for creating a database. Finally, the form of the constructors for the SetOfObject, ListOfObject, and BagOfObject classes is not specified in the standard and thus is vendor-specific.

Since the ODMG exception types may derive from a vendor-specific type, it is not usually possible to combine two different implementations in the same program. If you do this, you cannot, for example, check if a returned exception was of a particular type, unless you fully qualify the package name.

Many ODMG-compliant DBMSs also have significant features that are not defined in the ODMG standard. For example, the ODMG standard does not require that object references remain valid from one transaction to the next, even if the transactions occur in the same thread. Thus, if your application does multiple commits, it has to refetch all data at the start of every transaction. The checkpoint() method, which allows you to combine what would have been two transactions into one, is not a solution when the first commit and the final commit are separated by a significant amount of time, during which all locks would have to be held. ObjectStore, however, allows you to keep your references from becoming stale after a commit; if you use their proprietary Transaction type and the following method:

```
myTransaction.commit
    (COM.odi.ObjectStoreConstants.RETAIN_READONLY);
```

A feature like this is very valuable; but, as with all extensions, you must evaluate the cost. In particular, does the requirement to use a proprietary type propagate, and preclude you from using other ODMG-compliant types? For example, if you use a proprietary transaction type, must you then use a proprietary database type, and so on, and so on? What starts out as an ODMG-compliant project may turn out to be completely noncompliant, merely as a result of a decision to use a single extension. Also, if the database is created using the vendor's proprietary API, can it later be accessed with the vendor's ODMG API, or do they create incompatible databases?

An Example: Creating a Persistent Database Application

I will now show an ODMG-compliant example, of a simple case of a program which updates a single field of a persistent object. The persistent class is Task, which contains merely a single field, called "name," which represents the name of a task. This persistent class has two accessor methods: getTask() and set-Task(String). The class must be processed in some way, by a persistence tool supplied by the vendor of the persistent database, in order to make it persistent-capable. Here is the Task class:

```
/**
 * Process this class with ODBMS's postprocessor to make it
 * persistent.
 */
public class Task extends Anything
    // some products require Anything to be a class you define,
    // and not
    // a third party or Java class; or, if they do, there are
    // restrictions
```

```
{
    public void setName(String n)
    {
    // Assume we are in a transaction
    name = n;
    }
    public String getName()
    {
    // Assume we are in a transaction
    return name;
    }

    private String name;
}
```

Below I define a program which attempts to open a database, find a persistent task list, find a particular task within the list, and then modify the name of that task.

```
/**
 * Transaction to rename a task. This class does not need to be
 * persistent, since it is not stored
 * in the database.
 */
public class RenameTask
{
    public static void main(String[] args)
    {
        String oldname = args[0];// the old name
        String newname = args[1];// the new name

        // Create a transaction object; this must be done before
        // you can open the database
        Transaction t = new Transaction();

        // Open the database
        Database d = null;
        try
        {
            d = Database.open("MyDatabase",
                Database.openReadWrite);
        }
        catch (Exception ex)
```

```
    {
        System.out.println("Unable to open database");
        System.exit(1);
    }
    // Start a transaction
    try
    {
        t.join();// Attach transaction t to the current
        // thread
        // The above is not necessary, since t's constructor
        // joins us automatically.
        // All database operations will now take place using
        // the transaction
        // of the current thread

        t.begin();// Start a transaction
    }
    catch (Exception ex)
    {
        System.out.println("Unable to start transaction...");
        ex.printStackTrace();
        System.exit(1);
    }
```

Below I use the Database lookup() method to find a persistent named object which I previously created. This object is a persistent collection type, in this case a DList. Note that the LockNotGrantedException can be thrown, indicating a sharing violation (i.e., the object is in use). Normally we might want to try again if that happens, but in this simple example, we just terminate.

```
    // Find the list of all tasks
    DList tasklist = null;
    try
    {
        tasklist = (DList)(d.lookup("OurTaskList"));
    }
    catch (LockNotGrantedException exa)
    {
        System.out.println("Unable to get task list; perhaps
            someone is modifying it");
        t.abort();
        System.exit(0);
    }
```

```
catch (Exception exb)
{
    System.out.println("Unable to locate task list!");
    exb.printStackTrace();
    t.abort();
    System.exit(1);
}
```

Once we have the persistent task DList object, we can use the collection selectElement() method to evaluate a query selection on that list. Here I tell it to select the element for which the "name" field is equal to the value of oldname.

```
// Find the task we are interested in
Task task = null;
try
{
    Object o = tasklist.selectElement("this.name=\"" +
        oldname + "\"");
    task = (Task)o;
    t.lock(task, Transaction.UPGRADE);
        // state our intention to modify it
}
catch (LockNotGrantedException exa)
{
    System.out.println("Unable to get task; perhaps
        someone is modifying it");
    t.abort();
    System.exit(0);
}
catch (Exception exb)
{
    System.out.println("Could not find task '" +
        oldname + "'");
    t.abort();
    System.exit(0);
}
```

Above, after we obtain the desired task, we attempt to promote the read lock we implicitly have on it to an UPGRADE lock. This tells the database that we *intend* to modify this object, and that it should prevent other transactions from obtaining an UPGRADE or UPDATE lock on it (i.e., prevent other transactions from modifying it).

```
// Attempt to set the task name, and commit the change
try
{
    task.setName(newname);// promotion to WRITE lock is
    // automatic
    t.commit();
    // At this point, any object references you have are
    // now stale

    // ObjectStore allows the following to keep your
    // references from becoming
    // stale; if you do this, you can still use the
    // reference to task in the next
    // transaction without re-fetching it:

    // t.commit(COM.odi.ObjectStoreConstants.
    // RETAIN_READONLY);

    // However, you would have to use ODI's
    // COM.odi.Transaction type, instead
    // of their ODMG-compliant COM.odi.odmg.Transaction
    // type. With any
    // ODMG-compliant product it is important to evaluate
    // if deviations like this
    // propagate, and cause you to have to use other
    // types that are also not
    // compliant.
}
catch (LockNotGrantedException exa)
{
    System.out.println(
        "Unable to get task for update; perhaps someone"
        + "is reading it");
    t.abort();
    System.exit(0);
}
```

```
catch (Exception exb)
{
    t.abort();
    exb.printStackTrace();
    System.exit(1);
}
System.out.println("Name updated");

// Get the task name, to see if our previous transaction worked
String s = null;
try
{
    // Start new transaction
    t.begin();

    // We have to refetch task
    ... do everything we did before to find task, but now
        we have to look for it by its new name...

    // With an ODBMS that allows us to retain active
    // references between
    // transactions, we can just do this instead:
    // s = task.getName();

    t.commit();
    d.close();
}
catch (LockNotGrantedException exa)
{
    System.out.println("Unable to get task; perhaps
        someone is modifying it.");
    System.out.println("Your change is being aborted");
    t.abort();
    System.exit(0);
}
catch (Exception exb)
{
    t.abort();
    exb.printStackTrace();
    System.exit(1);
}
```

```
        System.out.println("confirmed that task's new name=" + s);
    }
}
```

Serializing or Externalizing Database References; Interdatabase References

Maintaining references to objects between transactions is an important require-ment, and your application will probably need a strategy for doing that. The ref-erences can be either "lightweight," such that they actually only constitute an index of some kind for quickly looking up the object, or "heavyweight," repre-senting actual ODBMS references.

One valuable type of reference is an externalized object reference. Many products support reference externalization. An externalized reference is one the ODBMS can use to automatically locate the corresponding object and reconstruct a true persistent reference. Externalized references can be maintained outside of the transaction, and even outside of the process or application; they can even be writ-ten to disk.

As an example, ObjectStore allows you to do the following:

```
ExternalReference er = null;
try
{
    new ExternalReference(myPersistentObject);
}
catch (Exception ex)
{
    ...
}
transaction.commit();
...


...start new transaction...
try
{
    myPersistentObject = er.getObject();
}
catch (ObjectNotFoundException exa)
```

```
{
     ...(object is gone)
}
catch (Exception exb)
{
     ...
}
```

In this example, an external reference is created in one transaction, and later another transaction uses that value to recreate a true persistent object reference without having to look up the object all over again.

Building an Object Database Application Server

There are lots of reasons why you might choose to build an application server instead of implementing a heavy client and using a network driver for your object database application. One is that you might want to implement a custom security policy or facility for accesssing the database (e.g., with user identities stored and accessed via an LDAP server), and wrap all database accesses in a server-side object layer. Another is that your available network drivers have limitations, such as restricted support for full transaction isolation.

Some problems you will need to consider in implementing an object database tier include object serializability, transaction context loss across remote calls, and remote class deployment.

With some products, persistent objects cannot be made serializable, so the objects you send as remote query results cannot be persistent objects. Instead, you may need to define an equivalent serializable "message" version of the object, for transport to clients and back.

Regardless, before you serialize a persistent object or its message equivalent, you may need to perform a deep fetch operation on the object, to convert all of its references into active references, and their references, and so on, for all objects reachable from the object via nontransient references. You cannot rely on the serialization mechanism to do this, because it uses Java reflection, which will bypass the persistence mechanism entirely. In short, you should build your own serializable object by reading persistent objects first, and then use writeObject() to serialize it.

When performing remote transactions, you may want to invoke a remote method which initiates a transaction, does some work, and returns some partial results without committing the transaction yet. For example, the method may be for an incremental query. The difficulty is that, if you use RMI, you cannot know which thread will be used to perform the remote method call on the server. From the point of view of the ODBMS your transaction is on the server; if you disconnect from the transaction and the thread goes into a wait state (and most likely back into a thread pool), you will need to have a way of identifying the Transaction object on the next call, so you can call join() to reattach to it. Thus, your server application will need to maintain a look-up table that correlates clients with transactions. You will probably want to make this as transparent as possible, and pass a transaction handle of some sort (a lightweight index into your table) as a parameter on incremental query calls.

Another alternative is to use middleware that associates a thread or server object uniquely with a client session. For example, some CORBA products allow this as an option. Using this technique, all you need to do is have your server return incremental results. Then, on each successive call, the thread merely uses the same transaction object. In other words, each session keeps a transaction object to reuse. The disadvantage of this approach is that it is not scalable to large numbers of client connections.

Thus, there are three approaches to dealing with over-the-wire transactions:

(a) Retain transaction context, by coding server methods so that they leave() a transaction when they complete, and join() it when they start. To do this, there needs to be a look-up mechanism in the server implementation to identify the transaction. (Transaction is not serializable, so you cannot send it back and forth.)

(b) Use middleware which maintains an association between client connection and server transaction.

(c) Complete each remote call in a single transaction. In that case, each remote method implementation will have to start a transaction, look up whatever objects it needs, perform its work, and commit.

If you serialize true persistent objects and send them over the wire, you may have to provide for what happens when persistence facilities get called by those objects. Some products require you to deploy a "stub package" in your client classpath (or your archive tag if the client is deployed in a browser) to provide access to stub versions of classes that normally implement persistence facilities on the host and are referenced by persistent classes that you serialize. These stubs may either implement a remote protocol for interacting with the DBMS (i.e., as a network client); or they may merely be no-ops, specifically for serialized objects.

I will now present an example of an application that implements a middle-tier server to access a persistent object database using RMI. The example implements a remote object server, connected to clients via RMI, and illustrates some of the issues that you may encounter in building a distributed application that uses persistent object technology.

For simplicity, this example is coded as if it were a single-user application, and does not check for concurrency exceptions the way the earlier Task example does. In a multiuser application, you would have to do these checks, as in the Task example. Also, I use strategy (c) from above: implementing each remote call as a separate and self-contained transaction.

First I define interfaces: a remote interface for the task server, and a base-type interface for the task objects that will be sent back and forth as messages, and persistified:

```java
/**
 * These are the remote methods exported by the task server, which
 * the client may call. Each of these methods represents a remote
 * transaction.
 */
interface TaskServer extends java.rmi.Remote
{
    /**
     * Return a list of RemoteTask objects. We return RemoteTask
     * objects instead of SerializableTask objects, so that we can
     * reference the server's tasks when we manipulate the server's
     * task list (e.g. with the delTask() method).
     */
    public java.util.Vector getTasks() throws
        java.rmi.RemoteException;


    /**
     * Add a new task definition to the server's task list.
     */
    public RemoteTask addTask(SerializableTask task) throws
        java.rmi.RemoteException;


    /**
     * Remove the specified task from the server's task list.
     * Return false if the task was not found.
     */
    public boolean delTask(RemoteTask task) throws
        java.rmi.RemoteException;
}
```

```
/**
 * A Task is the object that the user defines and the system tracks.
 * This is the base type that defines what a Task does. In this
 * example, it is trivial: it merely sets and gets its name.
 */
interface Task
{
    /*
     * Accessor: set the name of this task.
     */
    public void setName(String name);
    /*
     * Accessor: get the name of this task.
     */
    public String getName();
}
```

Now I will define a remote task interface, to define the remote operations possible on a task. These operations occur on a remote proxy for a persistent task, which in turn operates on an actual persistent task. Note that this interface does not extend the Task interface. The reason is that a remote implementation may have to throw exceptions—in particular RemoteException—that are not appropriate for a local task implementation, and I do not want to be forced to add inappropriate throws clauses to Task; so I define a completely separate RemoteTask interface:

```
/**
 * Remote version of a Task.
 * Redefine the Task interface with the required remote
   exceptions.
 * RemoteTask objects are remote proxies for PersistentTask
 * objects.
 * Each of these methods represents a remote transaction.
 * We would like to extend this from Task; however note that
 * if we extended this from Task, each method of Task would have
 * to throw Exception, or an exception type that RemoteException
 * derives from.
 */
interface RemoteTask extends java.rmi.Remote
{
    public void setName(String name) throws
        java.rmi.RemoteException;
    public String getName() throws java.rmi.RemoteException;
}
```

Now let's look at the class implementations. (I will use Object Design's slightly variant version of their API, which allows me to use their RETAIN_UPDATE flag, for maintaining object references across transactions.) The task-server object has to implement the TaskServer remote interface, and extend the RMI Unicast-RemoteObject class, in order to obtain the desired remote behavior:

```
class TaskServerImpl extends java.rmi.server.UnicastRemoteObject
    implements TaskServer
{
    public TaskServerImpl() throws java.rmi.RemoteException
    {
        this.initThread = Thread.currentThread();

        // Open the database; create it if necessary

        COM.odi.ObjectStore.initialize(null, null);

        try
        {
            database = COM.odi.Database.open(
                "taskmaster.odb", COM.odi.Database.openUpdate);
            COM.odi.ObjectStore.initialize(getInitThread());
            COM.odi.Transaction tr =
                COM.odi.Transaction.begin
                (COM.odi.Transaction.update);
            persistentTasks =
                (COM.odi.util.OSVector)(database.getRoot
                ("PersistentTasks"));
```

I have now retrieved a collection object, called "PersistentTasks," which I stored at some previous time. I retain my reference to this object, even after I commit this transaction, by committing with the RETAIN_UPDATE flag. That way, I do not have to perform the potentially expensive look up on the "PersistentTasks" collection every time I make a query transaction that requires this collection.

Below I perform another optimization, which may be very inappropriate in some circumstances. For each persistent task, I construct a remote task proxy object, which can support remote calls of its own. I do this mainly for illustration, to show that we can create all kinds of server objects, standing in for persistent objects that have to remain on the database machine. If the list of tasks is long, you probably would not want to create all these remote objects ahead of time, and would only create them as needed.

```
System.out.println("There are " +
    persistentTasks.size()
        + " tasks in the database");
// Create remote proxies
for (int i = 0; i < persistentTasks.size(); i++)
{
    RemoteTask rt = new RemoteTaskImpl(
        this, (PersistentTask)
        (persistentTasks.elementAt(i)));
    remoteTasks.addElement(rt);
}
tr.commit(COM.odi.Transaction.RETAIN_UPDATE);
System.out.println("Database opened without error");
}
catch (COM.odi.DatabaseNotFoundException e)
{
    System.out.println("Database not found; creating...");
    database = COM.odi.Database.create(
        "taskmaster.odb", COM.odi.Database.ownerWrite);
    COM.odi.ObjectStore.initialize(getInitThread());
    COM.odi.Transaction tr =
        COM.odi.Transaction.begin
        (COM.odi.Transaction.update);
    persistentTasks = new COM.odi.util.OSVector();
    database.createRoot("PersistentTasks",
        persistentTasks);
    tr.commit(COM.odi.Transaction.RETAIN_UPDATE);
    System.out.println("Database created without error");
}
}
```

Having opened the database for this stateful object and initialized the Persistent-Tasks reference, our remote methods can be called to operate on the Persistent-Tasks collection. Here is the implementation of those remote server methods:

```
public java.util.Vector getTasks() throws
    java.rmi.RemoteException
{
    System.out.println("Returning task list (" +
        remoteTasks.size() + " tasks)");
    return remoteTasks;
}
public RemoteTask addTask(SerializableTask task) throws
    java.rmi.RemoteException
{
    System.out.println("Attempting to add task...");
    COM.odi.ObjectStore.initialize(getInitThread());
    COM.odi.Transaction tr =
        COM.odi.Transaction.begin
        (COM.odi.Transaction.update);

    PersistentTask pt = new PersistentTaskImpl(task);
    persistentTasks.addElement(pt);
```

Above I have constructed a new persistent task, using a serializable task message object sent by a client, as the sole constructor parameter. This message object contains enough information about the task to be created to create a persistent version of it. Then I have added the newly created persistent task object to the persistent list of tasks; and to keep things in sync, I also create a new remote task proxy object for the newly-created persistent task, and add it to the remote task list:

```
    RemoteTask rt = new RemoteTaskImpl(this, pt);
    remoteTasks.addElement(rt);

    tr.commit(COM.odi.Transaction.RETAIN_UPDATE);
    System.out.println("...Task added.");
    return rt;
}
```

Deleting a task is complicated by the fact that I am keeping separate but synchronized lists of persistent tasks and their corresponding remote task objects. Therefore, when I delete one, I must delete the other. Aside from this, it is straightforward.

```
public boolean delTask(RemoteTask task) throws
    java.rmi.RemoteException
```

```
{
    COM.odi.ObjectStore.initialize(getInitThread());
    COM.odi.Transaction tr =
        COM.odi.Transaction.begin
        (COM.odi.Transaction.update);

    // Remove the task from the remote task list,
    //     if it is in there;
    // if not, return false
    for (int i = 0; i < remoteTasks.size(); i++)
    {
        RemoteTaskImpl rt = (RemoteTaskImpl)
            (remoteTasks.elementAt(i));
        if (rt.equals(task))
        {
            try {remoteTasks.removeElementAt(i);}
            catch (ArrayIndexOutOfBoundsException ex)
            { throw new RuntimeException("Should not
                happen!"); }
            // the remote handle is now stale
            // Remove the task from the persistent task list
            persistentTasks.removeElement
                (rt.getPersistentTask());
            tr.commit(COM.odi.Transaction.RETAIN_UPDATE);
            return true;// success
        }
    }
    // did not find it - it must have already been deleted
    tr.commit(COM.odi.Transaction.RETAIN_UPDATE);
    return false;
}

/**
 * Accessor: return the thread that initialized the database.
 */
public Thread getInitThread() { return initThread; }
/**
 * The task server is a program, and needs a static entry point.
 */
public static void main(String[] args) throws
    java.rmi.RemoteException
```

```
        {
                // Create and install a security manager

                System.setSecurityManager(new
                        java.rmi.RMISecurityManager());
                // Publish the server
                TaskServer obj = null;
                try
                {
                        obj = new TaskServerImpl();
                        java.rmi.Naming.rebind(args[0], obj);
                        System.out.println(
                        "TaskServerImpl created and bound in the registry to
                                the name " + args[0]);
                }
                catch (Exception e)
                {
                        e.printStackTrace();
                }
        }
        private java.util.Vector remoteTasks = new java.util.Vector();
        private Thread initThread;
        private COM.odi.Database database;
        private COM.odi.util.OSVector persistentTasks;
}
```

The next class is the persistent task class. This class will be processed by the ODI post processor (or whatever persistence tools you might choose to use), to make it persistent. I would like to make this class serializable, so that it could be sent to clients by value, but some ODBMSs and blend products will not let me do this, because the postprocessor will add a base class that is not serializable. Check if the product you choose allows persistent objects to be serializable, and what the restrictions are, e.g., if your class extends from a serializable class in package Java.

Ideally, I would also like to make this class double as the remote version of a task, but I cannot because remote objects should extend UnicastRemoteObject, and I am assuming here that persistent objects must be postprocessed to extend an implementation-defined persistent base class (although as already explained, some products do not have that restriction); so, I create a separate remote object type to serve as a remote proxy for the persistent object. I could elect to not extend UnicastRemoteObject, but then I would be losing out on the encapsulation of remote behavior provided by this type.

```
/**
 * A persistent representation of a task.
 */
class PersistentTaskImpl implements Task
{
    public PersistentTaskImpl(SerializableTask serializableTask)
    {
        name = serializableTask.getName();
    }
    public void setName(String name) { this.name = name; }
    public String getName() { return name; }
    private String name;
}
```

Next I define the lightweight message object that describes a task. I define this separately because I am assuming that persistent tasks are not serializable. This is used to send new task definitions between the client and server.

```
class SerializableTaskImpl implements Task, java.io.Serializable
{
    public void setName(String name) { this.name = name; }
    public String getName() { return name; }
    private String name;
}
```

Here is the implementation of a remote task. This serves as a remote proxy for a persistent task. Every operation performed by a client on a remote task propagates to the corresponding persistent task. Note that each of its remote methods encapsulates a complete transaction.

```
class RemoteTaskImpl extends java.rmi.server.UnicastRemoteObject
    implements RemoteTask
{
    public RemoteTaskImpl(TaskServerImpl taskServer, PersistentTask
        persistentTask)
    throws java.rmi.RemoteException
```

```
    {
        this.taskServer = taskServer;
        this.persistentTask = persistentTask;
    }
    public void setName(String name) throws
        java.rmi.RemoteException
    {
        COM.odi.ObjectStore.initialize
            (taskServer.getInitThread());
        COM.odi.Transaction tr =
            COM.odi.Transaction.begin
            (COM.odi.Transaction.update);
        persistentTask.setName(name);
        tr.commit(COM.odi.Transaction.RETAIN_UPDATE);
    }


    public String getName() throws java.rmi.RemoteException
    {
        COM.odi.ObjectStore.initialize
            (taskServer.getInitThread());
        COM.odi.Transaction tr =
            COM.odi.Transaction.begin
            (COM.odi.Transaction.update);
        String s = persistentTask.getName();
        tr.commit(COM.odi.Transaction.RETAIN_UPDATE);
        return s;
    }


    /**
     * This method is not part of the remote interface.
     */
    public PersistentTask getPersistentTask()
        { return persistentTask; }


    private TaskServerImpl taskServer;
    private PersistentTask persistentTask;
}
```

An alternative architecture is one in which the middle tier is supplied by the object database product. In that case, the issue of serializing the persistent objects for transport goes away, because it is handled automatically by the persistent object layer. It is possible to design a heavy client, which accesses an object database on a remote server, while coding the application completely as if the database were local to the client. Most object database products provide remote access in this way.

The previous example does not address the issue of database object locking, for the sake of simplicity.

Evolution and Enterprise Integration

Once you have built an object database, you will have the problem of maintaining it, which may include any or all of the following:

- Changes to the schema

- Moving the database—to different architecture machines, and maybe to different brands of database

- Interconnecting the applications to other kinds of database

When schema changes occur, there is the possibility that you will have to unload and reload the database. Before choosing a database, you should ask:

- What kinds of schema changes require a reload?

- Is a partial reload possible, or do I always have to reload the entire database?

- What tools are provided for building the reload process?

If you should have to migrate the database to a new platform, you will need to consider if the new platform supports the ODBMS product; and even if it does, is the database format compatible across platforms? If you need to perform a cross-ODBMS load, the ODMG standard includes the specification of a standard format for unloading and storing object database data. This format can be used for unloading data from one database and loading it into another. You should make sure that your ODBMS has a tool for writing a database snapshot in this format, which is called Object Interchange Format (OIF). Also, what if the database becomes corrupted: do you have to reload the database from a snapshot, or is it possible to make spot repairs?

Even if your application is to be written in Java, what if you need to provide access to the database from other applications that are not written in Java? If this is a possibility, the ODBMS should support bindings for other languages. The primary issue is then compatibility between the database when accessed via multiple languages—i.e., can, e.g., a database written from Java, be read from a C++ application?

Application integration frequently involves event notification. If the ODBMS provides an event service, is it compatible with existing standards, such as the OMG Event Service?

Network Implementations

If your client application is to be deployed across a network, the application can either be designed as a two-tier or a three-tier configuration. A two-tier design will require that the ODBMS support a network implementation, in the same manner that a type 3 or 4 JDBC driver supports transparent remote access by clients.

Some ODBMS products use common protocols to implement the connection with the central database. For example, Poet uses IIOP as its wire protocol. Using a common protocol can help in establishing a pathway through a firewall. Also, you will want to check if the network client requires a native component, or if it is pure Java ("thin"). Is the network implementation secure, and can it tunnel through a firewall?

Concurrency and Performance

The ODMG specification does not specify anything about database physical lock granularity. From an API point of view, objects are locked. However, the ODBMS is free to implement this with segment or page locking. While it is often claimed that very granular locking reduces performance, this is only true in a system that is primarily readoriented. If the application involved updates during prime time, the highly granular locking can help improve concurrency. Some database systems claim to use very granular locking, but it turns out that when you implement serializable operation, the locking granularity has to become much larger; so evaluate this carefully, in terms of what type of locking is actually used in different situations.

If the ODBMS provides an administrator with the ability to organize data, e.g. grouping objects by type (extent) or by relationships, this can help to tune the application.

Some ODBMSs now provide multiversion concurrency control (MVCC), which is discussed later in this chapter. MVCC is a very sophisticated capability, which gives good benchmark results, and therefore makes the database vendor look good, but it is very hard to build reliable applications using this model and it should be used with care.

The quality of the database's OQL implementation will affect the speed with which OQL queries are processed. Also, the ODMG specification does not say anything about how queries are processed, such as whether they are atomic. The implication is that they are, since that would be consistent with the rest of the specification, but it is not explicitly stated. You should make sure that your implementation provides atomic query semantics. The specification also does not say if data retrieved in the process of performing a query is locked as a side effect.

Replication and Scalability

A system will often perform well for a small number of users, but perform poorly when lots of users are added. (This is discussed in the chapter on distributed applications.) A high performance ODBMS will probably have a multithreaded design, with full isolation between threads. Various limitations can still come into play, however, as the number of database connections is increased. For example, as locks increase, can the system still maintain a high level of concurrency? Does lock management overhead scale linearly? And what is the resource footprint of a single connection? What is the overhead of an application that has a lot of persistent objects loaded? Or of maintaining object references across transactions?

What if the system fails? Does the ODBMS product provide any mirroring features? Does it allow you to switch over to a mirror system, without loss of service?

Multiple Client Connections

Some object database products do not allow a single client process to open more than one database connection at a time. Further, some products I am aware of have this kind of limitation on some platforms, but not on others. (This problem also exists with some very popular relational databases.) The ability to open multiple database connections is often very valuable for work-process applications, in which users must juggle several tasks at the same time, so you should consider carefully if this is an important requirement, and check that the ODBMS can support it on your target platform.

Finding Objects

There are primarily two approaches to finding an object in an object database: obtaining an extent, and performing a query or search on the extent; or maintaining a collection object for aggregating objects to search on, and performing the query or search on that. While extents are not supported by the ODMG standard at this time, many products provide an extent capability. Usually people who have mostly worked with relational databases in their career prefer the extent approach, and people who have done object-oriented programming prefer the collection object approach.

Creating Incremental Queries

Both approaches suffer from a phenomenon: potentially highly variable result set sizes. For example, if one is searching for all objects for which a name attribute matches "Huckstable," there will probably only be a few. If one searches for

"Smith" in the United States or England, however, or for "Tan" in Singapore, there are likely to be a great many values in the result. This is problematic for an interactive application, since one does not want to have a huge result set, and suffer the delay associated, or having to scroll through them once they finally arrive.

The solution for cases in which this might occur is to design an incremental query capability. In order to allow the transaction to be completed with each iteration, so as not to keep the database locked, the application can construct an index, that allows it to figure out where it left off each time. For example, if the query returns the first 100 matches for "Smith," and they consist of Alan Smith through Barney Smith, the value "Barney Smith" could be passed the next time, to obtain matches from that point on. Of course, there is a uniqueness problem to deal with (there might be two Barney Smiths), and so you probably need to pass additional information, such as a number specifying the number of names which have been sent already which match the last name sent—i.e., how many Barney Smiths have been sent so far (usually the value of this will be one).

OQL versus Programmatic Traversal of Persistent Collections

To perform the search—again regardless of whether you use extents or collection objects—you can use OQL, or implement your own search using a hashtable object, for example. The ODMG standard does not specify any indexed persistent object types such as hashtable, but many products provide them. As already discussed, however, all ODMG DCollection types have a query() method, which can be used to perform a search. This may not help you find multinational names, however. (See the section under JDBC, on searching for Unicode using Collators).

Storing Persistent Object References Inside of Controls

Often the contents of user interface controls are obtained from a database. For example, your application might allow the user to select a brand of car, by picking from a drop-down list. The list of car brands available might be stored in the database, and if it is, a query will have to be performed to build the list. If the database has an object representing each car brand, you might want to store a persistent reference to that object in the list itself, so that when the user clicks on a selection, the associated object can be immediately identified.

This is not usually workable for a number of reasons. First, it means that your application will have to keep a transaction open for the duration of whatever the user is doing. An open transaction ties up resources. And what if you need to commit the transaction? When that happens, all of the references stored in the controls will immediately become stale, unless your ODBMS allows references to remain valid between transactions—and that has its own set of problems anyway.

There are other problems as well. For example, many controls which allow you to store general objects use the equals() method to determine which item was selected by the user. That means that you will have to implement the equals() method for your persistent objects.

In general, it is far better to store lightweight objects such as strings in controls, and have a mechanism for refreshing them when you receive an indication that they may be out of date.

Initial Instantiation of Control Objects

One disadvantage of the object/relational blending products is that they usually generate a substantial amount of code for mapping the object model to a relational model. While it is usually the case that mapping classes only need to be loaded as they are used, and so one does not have to load all this code at one time, this may be unacceptable if user interface elements need to display choice lists and other tabular kinds of displays of database data. For example, suppose the application needs to give users a choice of geographic regions. To do this, the application will have to obtain the available regions from the database. This data, and the associated object/relational mapping classes could be loaded as needed, but this would result in an unacceptable delay the first time the drop-down list is selected. Depending on the nature of the user interface, and what data will be needed up front with each visual interface component, a strategy may need to be devised for anticipating when classes will be needed and loading them "just in time"—before the user actually requests them.

The alternative is to load all persistence classes at application startup. This may take a long time, especially if the classes are located on a server, and the connection between workstations and the server is not a fast one. It may be acceptable if the application is usually left running, or if it is locally deployed, e.g., with Castanet, or installed as an application.

Even if the class loading problem is solved, there is still the delay of going to the database to fill the contents of a dropdown list. An alternative is to embed this kind of data into Java classes. Since the class loading delay has been solved, according to our assumption, it will be fast or done before actually needed. An example from my own work was the embedding of a medical terminology index into Java classes, which were then deployed via Castanet. Lookups to the dictionary were then avoided, and the data was kept current via the Castanet update protocol.

A different solution is to presume that the user will pause a little while to think before clicking on something on a user interface, and use this time to populate the controls in a separate thread. Care must be taken to ensure that the controls are thread safe.

All of this may not be implemented in the initial stages of the project, and a solution still must be found to allow the application to start quickly, so that programmers can test effectively. It will therefore be necessary to create a small test database, with a restricted subset of control data, so that dropdown lists that would ordinarily come up with a choice of 40 geographic regions instead come up with a choice of two—sufficient to demonstrate functionality and test against.

Object/Relational ("Blend") Persistence Mapping Products

Most organizations have relational databases. When a new object-oriented application is built, an important issue that comes up is whether or not to use that database or build a new one that is object based. If the relational database contains company data that is needed by the new application, then a link of some kind is needed to get data from the relational database to the object application. If, on the other hand, data generated by the object application will be used by other applications based on other technologies, then it may be necessary to provide a bridge from the object application to the others; often a relational database is used as such a bridge, although this is not a very effective way to implement such a bridge.

So called "blend" products are products which bridge the object-relational gap, either by mapping an object model to a relational database; or by generating an object model from a relational schema; or both. Some examples of such products are:

- O2's Java Relational Binding

- Poet SQL Object Factory

- Javasoft's JavaBlend

It generally makes sense to map a relational system to an object model, in order to allow relational data to be incorporated into object-oriented software without embedding SQL. From a purely technical point of view, however, it rarely makes sense, to map an object model to a relational database. Organizations which do this usually do it for nontechnical reasons, such as the desire to limit the number of kinds of database servers that must be administered. An organization which has a lot of expertise in maintaining an existing relational server may have confidence in its robustness or security features, and be justifiably reluctant to bring in another product when the existing one could be used instead. In such a situation, using an object-to-relational mapping may be a way to develop software using an object model, with the intention of eventually transitioning it to an object database. The mapping can be used as an interim solution to allow the relational server to be used. The object layer does not mitigate programming problems, however, in dealing with transactional issues and data consistency.

Some of these products do not allow you to access more than one kind of database, or multiple databases at the same time; so if you need to do this, you should check that the product supports it.

Object Transaction Models

Dealing with Java objects does not relieve the programmer from the need to consider transaction semantics. One must still define the boundaries of a transaction, when to commit, and potentially when to rollback. A model which omitted these features would fail to address the important requirement of defining isolation modes, and controlled commit of changes, which is extremely important in multiuser data applications. Persistent Java object databases therefore provide methods for defining transactions and their states. While most object databases define the granularity of a transaction as an object, the programmer must still consider the issue of what constitutes a logical transaction—which sets of object operations should be implemented as an atomic unit; and related to this, which sets of objects constitute pieces of a larger whole, and therefore should be changed together and kept consistent. It is therefore necessary to develop some concepts for defining the boundaries of a transaction that changes objects, rather than tables. For now, I will focus on transaction boundaries, and leave discussion of locking and isolation modes for a later section.

Transaction Boundaries

To successfully build a persistent object multiuser application, one must consider similar factors as when building a comparable relational application. Specifically, transaction boundaries, granularity, and correctness; and object locking and concurrent access policies. The considerations are the same—the implementation and specific techniques are different.

The basic rule of thumb in designing a transaction application for a relational database is: when a transaction completes, it leaves the database in a well-defined, self-describing state, so that any subsequent transactions by any other user can proceed based only on the content of the database. Sometimes a distinction is made between "logical" and "physical" transactions, in that the former represent a self-defining unit of work, and the latter represent actual and potentially incomplete physical updates to the data. When a physical transaction represents only a portion of a logical transaction, a mechanism must be designed into the application to ensure that other users do not use the results of the physical transaction until the entire logical transaction completes, which may be comprised of a series of physical transactions over time.

The reason that logical transactions may be divided into distinct physical transactions is because a logical transaction may require a long duration, and locking the relevant data for that period may have performance consequences for other database users. This distinction adds complexity to a design, but it is a valuable concept for large-scale applications.

An object-oriented database has the same considerations. Rather than designing tables, however, one designs an object model of the system under consideration. The object model is the same model that programmers write code against. The only difference between code that accesses the object model and the rest of the application code is that code that accesses persistent objects must occur within a transaction. Thus, one is still faced with the task of defining the logical transactions for the system.

Defining Objects by Composition

Transactions in an object-oriented database result in the creation or modification of objects and object trees—modification when history is not required, and creation when it is. Before explaining these distinctions, we must first understand an important concept: object composition. Consider the following:

```
class Book

{
    String title;
    int nPages;
    Date whenPublished;
}
```

Class Book contains references to two Java objects: one String and one Date. It also contains an embedded value: an int, containing the number of pages of the book. In Java objects may only be contained within other objects by reference, and so an instance of Book does not physically contain the corresponding title string, or the whenPublished date—it merely references them, as distinct objects. In the Book class, however, it is easy to see that the objects referenced by an instance of Book are logically part of that instance—they are unique to it, and inextricably linked. In such a case, one can imagine that if one were to make a copy of (clone) a Book, one would want to make a complete copy of all of its embedded objects as well, because we would then have two complete and distinct instances of book, rather than two Books which really point to the same internal data. In other words, if we make a copy of a Book, we want to be sure that we can modify that instance of book without affecting the original book. We can do this only if we clone all of its internal data when we copy it. (We will ignore the issue of immutable objects for the moment.)

Now consider the following modification to Book:

```
class AuthoredBook
{
     String title;
     int nPages;
     Date whenPublished;
     Author author;
}

class Author
{
     String name;
     String address;
     List otherBooks;
}
```

In this example, we have added an author reference. The question is: if we clone an AuthoredBook, do we want to clone the author as well? Probably not, because the author is distinct in its own right, and we really only want to maintain a reference to an independent Author object. In that way, if the author changes address, the new address will be reflected in all objects that references the author. In AuthoredBook, the piece of information that is *part of* (composes) the book is not the author, but the *reference* to an author. Defining which instance objects (i.e., class variables that are objects) logically belong to the containing class, and which are merely references to independent objects is called *defining the composition* of a class. Note that an instance object can belong to only one containing class; a composition therefore represents a hierarchy. Some nomenclatures refer to composition paths as "primary links."

In designing a persistent object system, it is very important to define the logical composition of objects. A transaction usually begins at the root level of some composition, and requires locks on contained objects down to some level along some path in the hierarchy for that composition. Depending on whether history is required for that composition, the transaction may result in an entirely new object subtree; or, if history is not required, some links or values may simply be modified.

A transaction is therefore viewed as the construction or modification of a complete composite object hierarchy. Object databases typically provide transaction isolation mechanisms to ensure the integrity of object modifications, but isolation is at the granularity of a Java class. An object database has no knowledge of object compositions. This is analogous to the distinction between logical and physical transactions in a relational database. The DBMS will ensure the integrity of a physical transaction, but it is up to the application to provide guarantees for logical transaction completeness and correctness (consistency). In other words, by explicitly defining transaction boundaries, the application design must not permit partial logical transactions to occur; and in the context of an object database, the application must make sure, through the design of its update processes, that the object composition model intended by the schema designers is adhered to. Using the example of the Book class above to illustrate, note that the whenPublished class variable is a Date object. It would be possible to go into the database and modify the Date object of any book, without locking the corresponding Book instance. Doing so, however, risks that at the same time, someone else is modifying the book, and setting the whenPublished reference to point to a different date object—and so, while we think we have reset the date, we have not succeeded, because someone else made the book point to a different date! The solution is to recognize that a Book object owns its whenPublished Date object, and we cannot allow any transaction to obtain the whenPublished Date without first obtaining (and locking) the book, i.e., we must obtain the composite subtree, from the root book down to the whenPublished object.

clone(), equals(), and deep versus shallow copy

The terms "deep" and "shallow" copy are used frequently to mean copying an object and all the things it points to (contains); and copying just the object's non-reference data, respectively. In Java, this distinction is not syntactically explicit because Java objects contain *all* their instance objects by reference. Further, as we have seen, it is important to distinguish between compositional and noncompositional links, and so a deep copy, if applied blindly, may copy too much.

C++ has the concept of a copy constructor, which serves the purpose of making a copy (clone) of an object. C++ confuses the issue, however, by allowing objects to physically contain other objects. It is often the case, in C++ and in Java, that an object logically contains another object, *regardless of whether it physically contains it* (e.g., several objects may share a single immutable copy of the contained object, by reference; this is often the case with string classes). The programmer is led to believe that if an object is included by reference, then a copy operation should not include the referenced object. This is not the case, however, and *the semantics of a copy operation require that contained or referenced objects are copied if they are logically owned by the containing object*. In C++ you would achieve this by writing the copy constructor with an initializer list that uses the members of the class to initialize the copy; if you don't do this, a shallow copy is effectively performed, since default constructors are then used for members. In Java, the equivalent decision comes into play in how you code the clone() method.

The Java Object class has a clone() method, which serves the purpose of a copy constructor. This method must be overridden, and implemented with compositional copy semantics, for any class which needs to provide a copy operation. Use the clone() method with care, since it is not an abstract method, and so every class inherits it—with incorrect default behavior. If your class needs a copy operation, you must redefine the clone() method as public, and provide a correct compositional implementation for it.

The Object class also defines a method called equals(), which can be used to compare the values of two objects. Comparing an object with its clone should return true. The default implementation of the equals() method is to simply compare the reference values of the target and parameter, which is not correct, because Java already has a built-in operator for comparing object references—the "==" operator. If your class needs to provide an equals() method, you must implement correct semantics for this method, and compare the class members one by one. If your class extends Object directly, do not include super.equals() as a required condition in your implementation.

Predefined Collection Types

A composite may consist of or contain a collection object of some kind. Most collection types do not implement clone() as a deep copy operation. However, many have a deep copy operation, and in fact must in order to be useful for defining object compositions. You may want to extend the type and implement clone() and equals() for the collection type, to make sure it has the semantics that are consistent with your application. In general, you will need collections that are "owning" collections, and collections that are "referencing" collections—i.e., not owning.

Thus, if you have a third party collection type called Collection, and it has deepCopy() and shallowCopy() methods, and you are satisfied that its equals() method implements the behavior you want, you might extend it as follows:

```
public class NonPrimaryCollection extends Collection
{
    public Object clone() { return shallowCopy(); }
}

public class PrimaryCollection extends Collection
{
    public Object clone() { return deepCopy(); }
}
```

Defining Mutability

Cloning entire composite objects is potentially very expensive. In practice, it is actually not very expensive, if care is taken to define object mutability. A *mutable* object is one which can be modified after it is constructed. Conversely, an *immutable* object cannot be modified once constructed.

The Java String class is an example of an immutable object. Once created, a String cannot be changed. Thus, in the previous Book class example, if one constructs an instance of Book, and sets the value of the title in the process, the String object pointed to by the title reference can never be changed. To change the book title, one must create a new String object, and set the title reference to point to it.

Immutable objects have an advantage in that they can be shared. If a single immutable object is shared by multiple other objects, those objects can rest assured that their shared copy will not be changed—because it is immutable. Thus, they have the perception that they have their own virtual private copy of the object, since its value will never change unless they change it—and in that case, they simply create a new immutable object (which might end up being shared).

Composite objects can use the immutable object concept to economize on object duplication during cloning. If a root object logically is composed of a tree of objects, then when the root object and its subtree is constructed, the subtree objects can be marked as immutable. A clone operation on the root would then know to copy immutable objects by reference, rather than by physical copy. Thus, when cloning an object tree, the only new storage required is for copying any objects that are not immutable.

A composite class may be treated as immutable, and then all child objects of the class should be treated as immutable—they should never be changed once constructed. Creating a new composite object would typically consist of cloning an existing object, as a starting point (or creating an empty object), and then setting its references to point to new instances of child objects, resulting in a new composite. The new composite might share immutable members with the cloned composite, but it has the appearance of having its own copy of everything.

You can enforce immutability by simply using discipline within your code; or, you can take advantage of the ability to define it explicitly. Java allows you to define objects which are final, but can be initialized explicitly. In other words, you can assign to them, but only once. Once they are given a value, the value cannot be changed. For example,

```
public class MyImmutableComposite
{
    public final String name;      // this is a "blank final" - it
                                   // becomes final once it is set
    public final int value;        // "      "     "     "     "

    public MyComposite(String n, int v)
    {
        name = n;// once set here, can never be changed
        value = v;//           "           "         "     "
    }
}
```

The above class defines an immutable type, because once an instance is created, its members can never be changed. This may be too restrictive an implementation, however, especially if the process of construction cannot be nicely encapsulated into a single routine, but rather is a long process involving user interaction. In that case, an immutable flag may be used, e.g.,

```
public class MyImmutablyFlaggedComposite
{
    private boolean mutable = true;
    private String name;

    public MyMutablyFlaggedComposite()
    {
        // This is initial incomplete construction only
    }

    public String getName() { return name; }
    public void setName(String n)
    {
        if (! mutable) throw new RuntimeException("Attempt to alter
            immutable object");
    }
```

```
public boolean getMutable() { return mutable; }
/**
  * Routine for setting this object's mutability. This is
  * package protected, so that only other
  * classes within this package can call this method. In
  * effect, we only want "friends" to call this.
  */
void setMutable(boolean m) { mutable = m; }
}
```

If a class that must be treated as immutable is from an external source, and you cannot modify its source code, then immutability will have to be handled as a policy implemented by the clients of the class; or, you could extend the class and add (im)mutability constraints.

The *Transient* Keyword

The keyword "transient" should not be interpreted to mean "nonprimary." Primary links are nontransient; but nontransient links may or may not be primary. If a link is marked as transient, it will not be made persistent—we want even nonprimary links to be persistent.

Unfortunately, serializing an object will collect all nontransient links (i.e., nonprimary links as well). Thus, to serialize a persistent object, you may need a method to construct a self-contained object for transport; but you would likely need this anyway, since it does not make sense to serialize persistent objects—you would likely construct a serializable "message" or "command" object.

Saving Change History

An important issue in most business applications is whether to save change history (which I will refer to as simply "history" for short) or not. Some transactions require history, and some do not. For example, a hospital application which records changes to a patient chart will likely require history, to show the complete picture of the patient's progress and treatment. On the other hand, a system which schedules the movement of materials in a manufacturing plant probably does not care where a certain item was last week—it only cares where it is right now—and so history is not needed.

Classes that do not need history should not be immutable. When we need to modify the object, we do it "in place"—simply modify it, without cloning. On the other hand, those classes that need history should be immutable. This especially applies to the root composite class of a transaction. When we need to change an immutable class instance, we are forced to clone the existing one and make a new copy. This ensures that the old copy is not modified (although, of course, we need to implement a change history retrieval mechanism to be able to find it).

To illustrate: If, for example, your application consisted of updates to flight reservations for passengers, the root object in a transaction would perhaps be an instance of an itinerary for a particular passenger. Since we would not care what changes had been made to the itinerary over time, prior to travel, and are only interested in the final flight bookings, we do not need change history. When making a change, we simply modify the reservation's references to existing flights. History is lost. If, on the other hand, we did care about history for some reason, then to make a change we would clone the existing complete itinerary for the passenger, and then make modifications as required.

It is important to realize that the clone operation does not necessarily physically copy all flight information. The only references that are traversed deeply by a clone operation are those that are not immutable, and those which are also owned by the current composite object (i.e., primary links). Thus, a clone operation may in fact be very economical, if the design allows for the designation of which links are primary, and which objects are immutable.

In summary, if we need to keep history, we must make the root transaction object immutable, so that when it must be changed, an entire new one must be created, preserving the old (which is presumably added to a history list of some sort).

For cloning, immutability means that copy-by-reference is feasible. It is purely an implementation consideration. Immutable or not, objects that are strict members of a composite object should not be changed, unless the root composite is obtained exclusively first. Since a clone operation assumes that an immutable object has immutable members, that means that no primary member of a subtree of an immutable object may be treated as mutable by any operation within the entire system. This guarantees that the clone operation can copy by reference, and be assured that members of the composite are correctly included in the copy. Further, mutability is a property that, once set to *immutable*, cannot be changed back, unless it can be guaranteed that all composite references to the object will be converted into new clones.

Views

Conceptually, views are noncomposite objects, which represent an alternative way of looking at a composite object, or some kind of cross section. A view does not own the objects that it is a view of. It may be a composite object in its own right, with attribute members, but it is not a view of those—it is the root composite. For example, a view may contain its own timestamp information, indicating an event, and indicating by reference which composite objects participated in that event. With regard to the timestamp information, the view object is a composite; but with regard to the references to other composites, the view object is merely a view.

As an example, a summary of all passengers on a specified flight would be a view. The view references the itinerary objects of various passengers, and associates them with a flight. The view does not own the itineraries—it merely references them—and cloning the view should at most result in copying references to itinerary components, and never actually copying the itinerary components, since the latter may change if the itinerary is updated. An exception is if a "snapshot" is taken, in that case, the view owns the snapshot—the snapshot is part of the view's composition—and the copy is therefore merely part of the process of constructing the view. From that point on, the snapshot is not related to the original itinerary—it is merely a snapshot of a historical itinerary.

Another type of view would be a proposed change to an object hierarchy. If the change is approved, the view can replace the actual object—the proposed view becomes the current approved version of the object.

Garbage Collection of Resources Assigned to Voided Objects

Just like Java, object databases have automatic garbage collection mechanisms that reclaim objects that are no longer referenced. As with Java, however, such mechanisms are not totally hands off: the programmer must still make sure that references to unused objects are set to null so that the mechanism will recognize an object as being unused. Dangling references to retired objects will prevent those objects from being reclaimed, and constitutes a memory leak.

An example of when this can occur is with nonprimary links. If an object is logically owned by another object, then the owning object has a primary link to the owned object. If the owning object is retired, then links to it will be programmatically set to null, freeing it to be collected—or so one would hope. Suppose, however, that the owned object still is pointed to by some other object that references it for some purpose. In that case, the object will never be reclaimed, because something points to it. Further, if the owned object has a pointer as well back to its parent, the parent will never be reclaimed, as a result of its child never being reclaimed. This cascading effect can tie up a lot of storage.

A concrete example may help. Consider the case of a banking application, in which a customer has obtained a loan, secured by securities. When the loan matures, it may be archived and deleted from the database. However, the securities used to secure the loan may still exist. The loan will surely reference the securing instruments, and those instruments will probably have pointers to all the loans they are currently being used to secure. If these "used-to-secure" pointers are not set to null when the loan is removed from the database, the loan objects may never get reclaimed, because the securities still point to them. This is a garbage collection issue, especially if the loan application cannot be sure who is making references to its objects. The solution is to have a database schema that is well documented and controlled by a database administrator; to have well-defined object composite hierarchies; and for each object type, to define the removal process for that object.

Database Locking and Isolation

Understanding Transaction Isolation

A database's transaction isolation level defines how it handles various situations involving simultaneous access to data by more than one transaction. Three important situations to consider are the cases of dirty reads, repeatable reads, and phantom reads.

Dirty read

A dirty read is when a transaction reads uncommitted changes made by another transaction. There is the risk that these changes may not be committed, and so the reading transaction will have read invalid data and not know it. From a transaction processing point of view, dirty reads are always undesirable. A collaborative groupware system, however, may permit dirty reads, although more likely it would use a versioning capability.

Repeatable read

Repeatable reads are guaranteed if the data read by a transaction is locked against changes from other transactions, until the current transaction is done. Thus, the transaction can presume that if it reads the same data twice, it will get the same result.

Some databases claim to have repeatable reads, by implementing a technique in which they present the user with a snapshot that remains static for the duration of the transaction—even though the data represented by the snapshot may be changed by another transaction. In effect, your snapshot represents an old version of the database. The usefulness of this way of achieving "virtual" repeatable reads is questionable. The right way to achieve repeatability is to lock data against being changed.

Phantom read

Phantoms are undetected items of data added to the database by another transaction while a transaction is in progress. The data that is added is undetected, because the current transaction is using the results of a query made when it started. In a system that is serializable, the entire set of data would be locked against updates, and so the phantom could not be created until the first transaction is done.

These isolation levels are recognized by the SQL2 standard:

0 ("Read Uncommitted"): Dirty reads, nonrepeatable reads and phantom reads can occur.

1 ("Read Committed"): Dirty reads are prevented; nonrepeatable reads and phantom reads can occur.

2 ("Repeatable Read"): Dirty reads and nonrepeatable reads are prevented; phantom reads can occur.

3 ("Serializable"): Dirty reads, nonrepeatable reads and phantom reads are prevented.

Locking

To address these phenomena, we have to distinguish between read locking and write locking, and various exclusivity modes of access. Read locking ensures that other transactions cannot obtain the data for update while one or more transactions that hold read locks on the same data are in progress.

Write locking, which can only be granted for an element of data if no other transaction holds a write lock on that data, obtains the data for update. Write locking can be exclusive (prevent other transactions from making dirty uncommitted reads of this transaction's changes) or not. If it is not exclusive, the isolation level determines the semantics of simultaneous reads while the update transaction is in progress.

The granularity for read locking may be a single row (ensures cursor stability), the portion of a result set read so far (repeatable reads), a full result set (ensures serializability), an object (for an object database), an arbitrary-sized block or page of records, or an entire table.

To be more precise, the most important locking modes we want for most applications are

- **read lock**—concurrent reads by other read-locking transactions are allowed, but writes by this or any other transaction is prevented. Prevents other transactions from obtaining an exclusive write lock.

- **write lock**—concurrent writes by other transactions are not allowed. Prevents other transactions from obtaining a write lock. Other transactions may read the data, but may not see your modifications until you commit them, depending on the isolation level. If you must escalate this lock to an exclusive write lock (see below) before making writes, then this lock is known as an **intention**

write lock. An intention write lock is useful for locking data ahead of time if you intend to update it, but want others to be able to read it in the meantime, until you are ready to actually do the update.

In addition, the following mode is useful to prevent other transactions from reading data that is going to change anyway

- **exclusive write lock**—concurrent writes *or reads* by other transactions are not allowed. Prevents other transactions from obtaining a read lock or any type of write lock.

A no-wait policy for lock conflicts is very useful. With such a policy, if a transaction tries to obtain a lock and cannot, due to a conflict, it would immediately throw an exception. This allows the application to possibly report to the user that the requested data is in use, or perhaps try the transaction again a few times. A system which automatically retries or waits will be dependent on the locking granularity of the particular DBMS for its design correctness.

Achieving Consistency

A database is "consistent" if its transactions do not make conflicting changes to the data.

Two approaches to providing true consistency across transactions are

Pessimistic Policy: Lock all data you use (write *or read*) in a transaction; or

Optimistic Policy: Before you commit your transaction, verify that nothing you have used (written *or read*) has been changed by another transaction—if so, raise an error condition and do not make any changes

A pessimistic approach can be implemented if all transactions obtain at least read locks on data they read, and write locks on data they write, and hold those locks until they commit. This approach is not the default update mode of many products, however. For example, Oracle has two kinds of isolation modes, which they call "Read Committed" and "Serializable." Neither mode guarantees correct and serializable transactions, unless queries occurring in update transactions use the "FOR UPDATE" construct, which enforces a write lock policy.

Unfortunately, different database products have different levels of locking granularity. Some databases lock at the record level, some at the page level, and some at the table level. Locking an entire table for every read is not practical in a high volume system. However, it may be the only way to guarantee correct and consistent results, unless your design ensures that you are never updating anything that is also being read, or if inconsistency is not a serious problem.

The Importance of Locking Data You Have Read

Consider the following example:

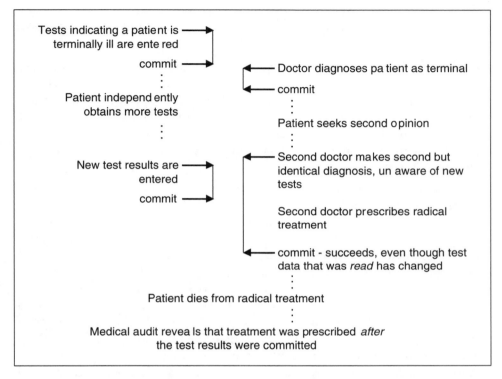

Figure 5–8 The possible consequences of not locking data that you have read

In the figure above, each vertical thread represents a thread of changes to a single type of data—a patient's set of test data on the left, and doctors' diagnoses on the right. Note that a policy that only locks data that is being changed will only lock data along a vertical line. Yet, the transaction on the right reads data created by the transactions on the left. That data is used by the second doctor to make a judgement. The fact that the data is always a "consistent" snapshot does nothing to prevent an incorrect decision from being made. Having consistent data is not useful if the data is out of date. Once something is out of date, it has become incorrect in the current time, as this example graphically shows.

The only way to ensure a correct decision process in the above scenario is to serialize the transactions. This goes beyond the "serializable" mode provided by Oracle. A truly serialized set of transactions would have the same effect as if they were performed in series. In the above scenario, performing them in series would have resulted in the second transaction on the left waiting for the one on the right to finish. This would be caused by, for example, placing a read lock on the patient's data, so that no one could update it until the transaction on the right finished. As a result, the first doctor, when updating the original diagnosis, would see the second doctor's diagnosis, and with much alarm, would cancel the radical treatment program.

A similar but slightly different scenario results if the second transaction on the left is initiated before the transaction on the right. If the second doctor performs the read before the transaction on the left commits, the data seen will be old, and the second diagnosis will be wrong. This again can be prevented by using a read lock on data that is read. In that case, the read lock will conflict with the write lock needed by the transaction on the left, and the two transactions will be forced to serialize.

It is important to understand that the phenomenon discussed here has to do with the consistency and validity of all data used—read or written—to compute a result or make a judgment. The data viewed by the doctor may or may not be consistent relative to any point in time—that is not the issue. The problem is that the data that the doctor read in order to make a diagnosis was allowed to change before the diagnosis transaction was completed. That data should have been locked against change; alternatively, it should have been checked for changes before the doctor committed. Further, using database triggers to enforce data consistency would not have prevented this problem, because the doctor's diagnosis cannot be implemented by an automatic trigger. The inconsistency is a logical one, that cannot be encoded, the result of which is the doctor's decisions and diagnosis. The doctor's eyes read data at the start of a transaction, the data changed, and the doctor entered and committed new information based on the old data.

Multi-Version Concurrency Control

Multi-Version Concurrency Control (MVCC) is a technique for achieving a form of virtual serializability, without paying the price of obtaining exclusive locks for data being read or in many cases even written. Each transaction is given a unique view of the database, representing a "snapshot" of the state of the data at the moment at which the transaction begins. This snapshot is computed, based on record modification timestamps.

Since the transaction has a snapshot computed at an instant in time, it is fully consistent within itself. For example, one can be sure that any relationship constraints between the data will hold, such as an account balance field being equal to the sum of account entries. MVCC is a way of putting blinders on, and saying, "I don't care what the rest of the world is doing—I'm operating on yesterday's assumptions, and results based on those assumptions are what you will get."

MVCC can be claimed to be serializable in the sense that it provides data update consistency, and so your transaction yields the same result whether someone else's transaction begins just after yours and proceeds in parallel, or waits until yours is almost done before it starts—your transaction behaves as an atomic unit. However, in many situations this is not good enough, as we saw above. It sometimes is vital to have the latest data, and know if someone has changed assumptions you have made. Sometimes MVCC is good enough, though. In applications that mainly provide data, and which do not need to be completely up to date, this tends to be adequate. MVCC systems are also vulnerable to the "Snapshot too old" message, indicating that the transaction has lasted too long and a snapshot can no longer be computed.

MVCC protects consistency within the isolated world of your snapshot, but does not guarantee correct operation in the context of the database as a whole. Global data integrity is therefore guaranteed relative to transaction start time, rather than transaction commit time. Data update integrity is measured relative to commit time.

In general, data consistency must be measured at commit time, not transaction start time, as is the case with MVCC. If measured in this way, MVCC without read or write locking of all data read and write locking of all data modified is not truly serializable.

Implementing Pessimistic Locking

Let's look at an example of using pessimistic locking. In the following program, I obtain data using Oracle's FOR UPDATE clause, which has the effect of obtaining an exclusive lock on the data. This ensures that locks are acquired on the data being read as well as written. Other transactions that read any of the same data *should also use* FOR UPDATE; otherwise, they may read obsolete data—this policy can be relaxed only if it is proven on a case by case basis that the results will still be correct.

```
Class.forName(drivername);
Connection con = DriverManager.getConnection(urlString, userid,
  password);
con.setAutoCommit(false);
```

```java
// Perform a query, and lock all rows that are involved
Statement s = con.createStatement();
ResultSet emps = null;
try
{
    emps = s.executeQuery
        ("SELECT * FROM EMP WHERE DEPTNO=30 FOR UPDATE");
    // The above is pessimistic, because we lock the required
    // records and don't release them
    // until we are completely done - see below.
}
catch (Exception ex)      // We catch Exception instead of
    SQLException,
                          // because we don't know if
                          // the driver will throw a RuntimeException
                          // if it detects deadlock
{
    // May be contention for this data, or even deadlock...notify
        user of potential contention
    con.rollback();
    return;
}


// Here we perform another query; locks are still in effect
Statement t = con.createStatement();
ResultSet nrs = null;
int n;
try
{
    nrs = t.executeQuery
        ("SELECT COUNT(*) FROM EMP WHERE DEPTNO=10"); nrs.next();
    n = nrs.getInt(1);
    System.out.println("There were " + n + " employees in Dept.
  10");
}
catch (Exception ex)
{
    // May be contention for this data, or even deadlock...notify
    // user of potential contention
    con.rollback();
    return;
}
```

```java
// Assign top-producing employees to dept 10, based on salary
try
{
    for (; emps.next();) // each employee
    {
        int eno = emps.getInt("EMPNO");
        int sal = emps.getInt("SAL");
        int deptno = emps.getInt("DEPTNO");
        if ((sal > 2000) && (deptno != 10)) s.executeUpdate(
            "UPDATE EMP SET DEPTNO=10 WHERE EMPNO=" + eno);
    }
}
catch (Exception ex)
{
    // May be contention for this data, or even deadlock...notify
    //    user of potential contention
    con.rollback();
    return;
}

try
{
    // Re-do the count; notice that we can see the effect of our
    // own update - others cannot
    // (Some databases have modes in which you cannot see your own
    // updates, until you commit)
    nrs = t.executeQuery
        ("SELECT COUNT(*) FROM EMP WHERE DEPTNO=10");
    nrs.next();
    n = nrs.getInt(1);
    System.out.println("There are now " + n +
        " employees in Dept. 10");

    // Now we commit, and free all rows that were locked.
    // According to a pessimistic policy,
    // we held all locks until our commit.
    con.commit();
}
```

```
catch (Exception ex)
{
    // May be contention for this data, or even deadlock...notify
    // user of potential contention
    con.rollback();
    return;
}
```

It is interesting that Oracle's own thin JDBC driver, as of this writing, throws the following exception if you attempt to set the isolation mode to SERIALIZABLE:

```
java.sql.SQLException: setTransactionIsolation: Only supports
TRANSACTION_READ_UNCOMMITTED
```

This is especially upsetting, given that Oracle itself only supports the READ_COMMITTED and SERIALIZABLE modes! (i.e., Oracle's driver claims it only supports an isolation mode that the Oracle server itself does not support!) Shop around for a driver from a third party that specializes in JDBC drivers.

Other drivers have other problems. The Sybase JConnect driver we tested, for example, as of this writing, does not allow you to call setAutoCommit() with a value of true—i.e., auto-commit is always off. As you can see, while the JDBC API is a generic API, the behavior of an actual application written with JDBC will vary from one database to another.

Using pessimistic locking for long durations—in "user time"—is generally a bad idea, for these reasons:

- A transaction will hold ALL its locks until it is committed, and some may have been converted to table locks (e.g., Oracle uses table locks when SELECT FOR UPDATE is used).

- Sequence numbers (such as Sybase's timestamp value) wrap eventually.

- The chance that the system will go down during the transaction is greatly increased.

- If the system uses MVCC, the chance that a "snapshot-too-old" or "rollback-segment-too-small" message is generated is greatly increased—system can no longer construct query results for a transaction that began a long time ago.

It may seen improbable that a user would take so long that some of these things could occur frequently. However, computers today are multiwindow, and if the work is process oriented rather than transaction oriented, it is very conceivable that users will often leave windows minimized or applications open for long periods—even weeks.

If user-time locks are needed, reexamine the design to see if they can be eliminated, and if not, consider a checkout model, as described later in this chapter.

Implementing Optimistic Locking

You can use a database's built-in optimistic mode to implement an optimistic policy, if it has one, or you can use granular and short-lived pessimistic locks and implement an overall optimistic policy yourself. The latter is necessary if the database does not have a truly serializable optimistic mechanism—one which prevents concurrent modification to data you have read—data which you have used to compute your own update.

Oracle maintains a "System Control Number" (SCN) to represent each database snapshot it uses. This is used by Oracle's SERIALIZABLE mode to implement an optimistic policy: When an Oracle "serializable" transaction commits, the SCN of the transaction is compared with the SCN of records it is trying to modify, and if their SCN is higher, the commit fails. Thus, the check is done at commit time, and so it is optimistic. However, this particular implementation does not prevent other transactions from updating data we have *read*, and therefore getting inconsistent data, as we have seen.

A true optimistic policy must check not only that data it wants to modify has not been changed by someone else, but in fact it must check that all data it has accessed in any way—has read, or wants to modify—has not been changed by someone else. With Oracle, to prevent that, a transaction modifying *anything* should, in general, use the FOR UPDATE clause for read queries, to lock the data that it reads, regardless of whether it updates that particular data or not. This, however, converts the policy from optimistic to pessimistic.

If this is done, the SERIALIZABLE mode is largely redundant, since it protects against data you are modifying from changing, but using FOR UPDATE will lock the data you read and thereby prevent it from changing—and usually you read data before you modify it.

To implement your own optimistic locking, you can either compare the actual values of data read and written to see if they have changed, or you can compare instead something else that tracks with the value of the data. An example of the latter is a hashcode of the data. Another example is a timestamp, of when the data was written. Some systems automatically timestamp or sequence records, and if that is the case and the sequence number or timestamp value is accessible, you can use it, or you can write your own timestamp.

Optimistic Locking Using Explicit Timestamps

Here is a simple example of using a manually written timestamp to verify that input data has not changed in the course of a transaction, and thereby implement an optimistic policy. (The TableArea class is not shown, but is assumed to be a TextArea which generates an ActionEvent when a row is clicked on, with the event's action command set to a string containing the row number that was clicked on by the user.)

```java
import java.awt.*;
import java.awt.event.*;
import java.sql.*;
import java.util.*;

public class DBDemo3 extends Panel
{
    static String drivername = "oracle.jdbc.driver.OracleDriver";
    static String urlString = "jdbc:oracle:thin:@a1:1521:ORCL";
    static String userid = "scott";
    static String password = "tiger";

    public static void main(String[] args)
    {
        Frame f = new Frame();
        f.setSize(600, 300);
        try
        {
            BDemo3 d = new DBDemo3();
            f.add("Center", d);
        }
        catch (Exception ex)
        {
            System.out.println("Could not complete query - try
                later");
            System.exit(0);
        }
        f.show();
    }
```

```
Connection con;
// Now display employees in a list, and allow user to select one...
Vector vn = new Vector();
Vector vi = new Vector();
Vector vt = new Vector();
TableArea textArea = new TableArea(5, 60);
TextField salField = new TextField(10);
public DBDemo3() throws Exception
{
    Class.forName(drivername);
    con = DriverManager.getConnection(urlString, userid,
        password);
    Statement s = con.createStatement();
    ResultSet emp = s.executeQuery(
        "SELECT * FROM EMP WHERE ENAME = 'JONES'");
    // We did not specify "FOR UPDATE", so locks will be
    // released as soon as
    // we are done reading the result set

    for (int r = 0;emp.next(); r++)
    {
        String name = emp.getString("ENAME");
        int id = emp.getInt("EMPNO");
        Timestamp ts = emp.getTimestamp("TS");
        vn.addElement(name);
        vi.addElement(new Integer(id));
        vt.addElement(ts);
    }
    textArea.set(vn);
    con.commit();// this guarantees we are freeing locks,
                // regardless of the autocommit state
```

```
textArea.addActionListener
(
    new ActionListener()
    {
        public void actionPerformed(ActionEvent e)
        {
            // Figure out which row was selected
            int row = Integer.parseInt
                (e.getActionCommand());
            // (we assume that the GUI component
            // triggering this
            // event has the ability to determine which
            // row the user selected)

            // Now correlate the row with the vector of
            // customers
            String name = (String)(vn.elementAt(row));
            int eid = ((Integer)(vi.elementAt(row))).
                intValue();
            int newsal = Integer.parseInt
                (salField.getText());
            Timestamp ts = (Timestamp)
                (vt.elementAt(row));
            try { updateSalary(eid, newsal, ts); }
                catch (Exception ex)
            {
                System.out.println(
                "Unable to update salary...stack trace
                    follows");
                ex.printStackTrace();
            }
            System.out.println("Update completed");
        }
    }
);
add(textArea);
add(salField);
}
```

```
/**
 * This action handler is called much later - in user time.
 */
public void updateSalary(int eid, int newsal, Timestamp ts)
    throws Exception
{
    // Look up the selected employee - lock records for the
    // time it takes to do this update only
    Statement s = con.createStatement();
    ResultSet rs = s.executeQuery(
        "SELECT ENAME, SAL, TS FROM EMP WHERE EMPNO = "
        + eid + " FOR UPDATE");

    // It is unlikely, although possible, that the person's
    // info has changed
    // since the earlier transaction - if it has changed, we
    // cannot be sure that we are using the right values
    rs.next();
    Timestamp newts = rs.getTimestamp("TS");
    if ((ts == null) || ts.equals(newts))
    {
        // ok - apply update
        String q = "UPDATE EMP SET TS=SYSDATE, SAL=" + newsal +
            " WHERE EMPNO=" + eid;
        System.out.println("Applying update: " + q);
        s.executeUpdate(q);
        con.commit();
        System.out.println("Salary modified: " + newsal);
    }
    else
    {
        // stuff has changed - all bets are off
        System.out.println("Salary not modified");
        con.rollback();
        throw new Exception("Must retry transaction - data is
            stale");
    }

    // Locks are now released
}
}
```

Optimistic Locking Using Object Comparison

Comparing timestamps has the disadvantage that a timestamp value has to be written to every record. Some databases (such as Sybase) write a timestamp automatically (actually, Sybase automatically writes a sequence number, called a timestamp, if a timestamp column is defined in a table), and in that case the trouble of writing a timestamp is not an issue. However, for other DBMS's, writing a timestamp to every record may be an impractical approach. In that case, an actual data comparison may be necessary.

A disadvantage of comparing data values directly, however, is that if new columns are added to a table, your code will have to be examined in many places, to make sure that the new columns are compared as well, if required by the application. Also, the entire set of data needed by the update transaction needs to be sent as well by the query transaction—i.e., it is sent twice.

If you are implementing your own multitier design, using an object streaming or application-specific protocol, you can put the above consistency checking logic into the middle tier. For example, the middle tier could perform a query, compute a digest of the query results and send it to the client, along with any data the client needs from the query, and then later during the update transaction it can redo the query and recompute the digest—an exception could be thrown if the digest value is different from last time. Consider the following example which uses an RMI-based middle tier database server object. Remember that, unless you are sure you can get away with not doing so, you must compare data you read as well as data you intend to update.

```
public class Digest implements java.io.Serializable
{
    public void equals(Object d)
    {
        if (! (d instanceof Digest)) throw new Error();
    }

    public String getValue() { return md5Value; }

    public Digest(byte[] data)
    {
        ...compute the MD5 digest value for the byte array...
    }

    private String md5Value;
}
```

```java
public class CustomerData implements java.io.Serializable
{
    public CustomerData(int id, String name, String address,
        String ssn, int age, String comments)
    {
        this.id = id; this.name = name;
        this.address = address;
        this.ssn = ssn; this.age = age;
        this.comments = comments;
        digest = computeDigest();
    }
    public int id;
    public String name;
    public String address;
    public String ssn;
    public int age;
    public String comments;

    protected Digest computeDigest()
    {
        // Concatenate all fields into a byte array, b
        ...

        // Construct a digest object
        return new Digest(b);
    }

    public Digest digest;
}

interface DBServer extends java.rmi.Remote
{
    public CustomerData getCustomerData(int id)
        throws java.rmi.RemoteException, Exception;
    public void updateCustomerData(CustomerData)
        throws java.rmi.RemoteException, Exception;
}
```

```java
public class DBServerImpl extends java.rmi.server.UnicastRemoteServer
implements DBServer
{
    public DBServerImpl(URL url)
    {
        // Create connection pool
        ...
        connection[i] = java.sql.DriverManager.getConnection(url);
        ...
    }

    public CustomerData getCustomerData(int id)
        throws java.rmi.RemoteException, Exception
    {
        // Get a connection
        java.sql.Connection con = ...get connection from pool

        CustomerData cd = null;
        try
        {
            CustomerData cd = getCustData(con, id);
            con.commit();
        }
        catch (Throwable t)
        {
            con.rollback();
            throw t;
        }
        finally
        {
            // Return the connection to the pool
            ...
        }

        // Return the customer data to the remote caller
        return cd;
    }

    protected CustomerData getCustData(java.sql.Connection con,
        int id) throws Exception
```

```java
    {
        java.sql.Statement s = con.createStatement();
        java.sql.ResultSet rs = s.executeQuery(
            "SELECT * FROM CUSTOMERS WHERE ID = " + id +
            " FOR UPDATE");
        // there should be only one row in the result set
        rs.next();
        String name = rs.getString("NAME");
        String address = rs.getString("ADDRESS");
        String ssn = rs.getString("SSN");
        int age = rs.getInt("AGE");
        String comments = rs.getString("COMMENTS");

        CustomerData cd = new CustomerData(id, name, address,
            ssn, age, comments);
        return cd;
    }

public void updateCustomerData(CustomerData cd)
    throws java.rmi.RemoteException, Exception
{
    // Get a connection
    java.sql.Connection con = ...get connection from pool

    try
    {
        CustomerData cdPrime =
            getCustData(java.sql.Connection con, cd.id);
    }
    catch (Throwable t)
    {
        con.rollback();
        ...return the connection to the pool
        throw t;
    }
```

```java
        try
        {
            if (cdPrime.digest.equals(cd.digest))
            {
                // ok - no change since last time; apply update
                Statement s = con.createStatement();
                s.executeUpdate(
                    "INSERT INTO CUSTOMERS VALUES (" +
                    cd.name + "," + cd.address + "," +
                    cd.ssn + "," + cd.age + ", " +
                    cd.comments + ")" + " WHERE ID = " +
                    id);
                con.commit();
            }
            else
            {
                // oops! - the checksum is not the same as
                // last time  - someone did an update!
                con.rollback();
                throw new Exception(
                "Data is stale!!! - retry transaction please");
            }
        }
        catch (Throwable t)
        {
            con.rollback();
            ...return connection to pool
            throw t;
        }
    }

    public static void main(String[] args)
    {
        try
        {
            // First try to establish database connection
            String driver = args[0];
            Class c = Class.forName(driver);// likely a type 1
                                            // or 2 driver
            String url = args[1];
```

```
            // Now publish this server object
            DBServerImpl s = new DBServerImpl(url);
            java.rmi.registry.Registry r =
                    java.rmi.registry.LocateRegistry.getRegistry();
            r.rebind("DBServer", s);
        }
        catch (Exception ex) ex.printStackTrace();
    }


    private java.sql.Connection[] connection;
}
```

The primary advantage of this scenario is that the application data does not have to traverse the network again just so the client can verify it has not changed—we have one round trip for the data, instead of a round trip and a one-way verification trip. However, note that this implementation has an update granularity equal to the size of the data retrieved, whereas the earlier examples allow the client to send back to the server only the changes desired. The choice of which strategy to use is actually part of the overall decision of which distributed architecture and protocols to use, and cannot therefore be made in isolation. There are also other variations on this technique, including implementing a customized object marshalling protocol; and calculating a digest as a side effect of transmission.

Checkout-based Locking (Application-based Write Locking)

The pessimistic and optimistic locking models owe their origin to transaction-based database applications, in which user operations are relatively short in duration—certainly less than the typical time between system restarts. As we have seen, the pessimistic model deals well with very discrete updates that are completed quickly—instantaneously to the user. The optimistic model allows for prolonged user access in the process of an update, but still assumes that such interaction is short compared to the expected time between accesses by other users, and also is shorter than the average time interval between system restarts. What about situations that do not fit either of these assumptions, for example when the user requires prolonged access, for days or more? Applications that fit this model include process-oriented applications that range from commercial loan preparation to engineering design. The salient feature is that work must be allowed to proceed in an uninterrupted and protected manner, for a long time, until the user is ready to submit it.

A checkout-based model assumes that

- The system can be expected to restart during the course of a user operation, making pessimistic locking impractical.

- Other users can be expected to try to access the data during the course of the user operation, making optimistic locking impractical. This may result either from usage patterns, or from the underlying DBMS failing to support the required lock granularity needed by the application.

It is further assumed that it would be unacceptable for other users to modify the data that the current user is working on. Still, they may either be granted read access to the work in progress, or to the last saved state of the data, depending on the requirements.

Checkout is generally designed into an application, although there are Java products that support it as a built-in feature. One such product is offered by Kinexis (http://www.kinexis.com), called Proposal Based Architecture. In this approach, a composite object is viewed as a "proposal," which is checked out for development. The object is a collection of information, together comprising a logical whole—a composite. While the object is being worked on, it is in the possession of a single party—perhaps even in a physical sense, e.g., in a mobile computer, separated completely from the primary database or server. When the proposal is completed, it is checked back in. Inherent in this approach is multiversioning, optimistic locking, and viewing a transaction as the construction of a composite object. The Proposal Based Architecture provides an infrastructure for implementing this functionality in a reusable way.

Implementing a checkout-based design requires careful designation of which objects represent composites. The target of a checkout operation is always the root of a composite. Often the object checked out is created as a side effect of the checkout operation; in this case the user process which checked out the object is viewed as performing a long-term construction of a new composite object—it is filling it in—and when it is done, it will check it in for the first time. Subsequent changes are either prohibited (if the object is immutable), or must be performed via a checkout.

Here I show a simple example of how one can implement checkout in a reusable class that can be incorporated into other classes that want to implement checkout. The basic idea is simple: you are merely giving each composition root object an owner attribute, and applications should attempt to become the owner before using the composition.

```java
public interface Checkable
{
    public final void checkout(User u) throws InUseException;
    public final void checkin(User u) throws
        TokenNotOwnedException;
}

public class CheckableDefault make this persistent
{
    public final void checkout(User u) throws InUseException
    {
        if (u == null) throw new RuntimeException("Null user");

        // Check validity of User object
        User.checkUser(u);

        // Perform a test-and-set on this object's token
        Transaction tr = new Transaction();
        tr.join();
        tr.begin();
        try
        {
            tr.lock(this, Transaction.WRITE);
            if (user != null)
            {
                if (user.equals(u))
                {
                    tr.abort();// we already have it
                    return;
                }
                else
                {
                    throw new InUseException();
                }
            }
            user = u;
            tr.commit();
        }
```

```
            catch (Exception ex)
            {
                // Object is locked by anther transaction; or it is
                // dirty
                tr.abort();
            }
    }
    public final void checkin(User u) throws TokenNotOwnedException
    {
            if (u == null) throw new RuntimeException("Null user");

            // Check validity of User object
            User.checkUser(u);

            Transaction tr = new Transaction();
            tr.join();
            tr.begin();
            try
            {
                tr.lock(this, Transaction.WRITE);
                if (user == null) throw new TokenNotOwnedException();
                if (! user.equals(u)) throw new
                    TokenNotOwnedException();
                token = null;
                tr.commit();
            }
            catch (Exception ex)
            {
                // Object is locked by another transaction; or it is
                // dirty
                tr.abort();
            }
    }
    private User user;
}
```

The User class can be declared final, with a private constructor, and a static dispenser method for dispensing instances of User under a security policy. Thus, one cannot create an instance of User without legitimately obtaining it, and further the system can check if a given User instance is still valid.

Here is an example of use:

```
public final class Task implements Checkable a persistent class
{
     private Task() {}
     public Task(String n) { name = n; }

     //
     // Checkable methods
     //

     public final void checkout(User u) throws InUseException
     {
         checkableDelegate.checkout(u);
     }
     public final void checkin(User u) throws TokenNotOwnedException
     {
         checkableDelegate.checkin(u);
     }
     final String name; // primary
     private Checkable checkableDelegate
         = new CheckableDefault();// primary
}
```

This example assumes that the ODBMS allows the object reference to remain valid outside the context of a transaction; otherwise, the transaction initiation and completion must be taken out of the checkout method and implemented by the caller. Alternatively, the checkout() and checkin() methods could be declared static and take an object external reference or an object key as a parameter, and fetch the object based on that.

Defining the Transaction Layer

In designing a middle tier, you need to decide at what level to start and commit transactions; that is, you need to define the transaction layer. It is not a good idea to distribute transaction control and database accesses throughout application code, for a number of reasons, including:

- A coordinated policy for starting and committing transactions should be encapsulated; examples of such policies may include choice of isolation mode, and choice of commit mode (e.g., keeping persistent object references alive)

- A coordinated policy for handling database errors should be encapsulated
- It would make it hard to identify code affected by persistent object model or data model changes
- A coordinated policy for notification of updates to specific persistent objects or data should be encapsulated (this will be discussed in more detail later)
- A coordinated policy for cleanup of retired persistent objects should be encapsulated

Instead, there should be a well-defined class of objects that implement a transaction layer. This layer represents the gateway to the database, and implements all policies for accessing that data. It is in this layer that one should coordinate transaction initiation and completion.

Sometimes a component in this layer needs to be able to handle two cases: one being that a transaction is already in progress, and the other that one is not. When this is necessary, most database products provide a method to test if a transaction is in progress for the current thread. Most object database products do not support nested transactions.

This means that complex operations that require several sub-transactions have no built-in protection against being aborted in the middle, after some transactions have been completed, but before the overall process has completed. The risk is that data may exist in the database in a logically incomplete state. A good design will explicitly define these intermediate states and transactions will be designed so that they recognize them.

Multidatabase Transactions

If an application needs to access more than one data repository or service to complete a request, it will need a mechanism for coordinating those accesses, and monitoring that all accesses complete. There are basically two approaches: a guaranteed delivery mechanism; and a transaction mechanism.

A guaranteed delivery mechanism is a fail-safe system, that promises that a message will reach the designated service, even if not right away. An example of such a product is IBM's MQ Series, which provides guaranteed delivery of messages via reliable message queues. There are MQ gateways to a great many applications and services, and so MQ is a powerful way to integrate back-end services into an application. Of course, there is a Java binding for MQ (as for many of IBM's products).

Using MQ, one could, for example, have a Java application which takes an order for a product, makes an entry in a local order database, and then dispatches an MQ message to an order fulfillment center's CICS system. The local application does not have to worry about coordinating a rollback of the local order if the communications link to the CICS system fails because it relies on the MQ system's guaranteed delivery promise that the message will get there and be processed.

Guaranteed delivery messaging systems usually do not provide real-time response. You can safely assume the message will get there—but you do not know when. Therefore, while a messaging approach simplifies system design, it is not practical in an application that must provide end-to-end acknowledgment of service completion in real time.

A different approach is to treat the entire operation as a transaction, with unreliable components. If any operation fails, the entire transaction must be rolled back. To implement this, you may need to rely on transaction services of multiple components. For example, if you need to make insertions into two different databases to complete a unit of work, you can consider these two insertions to constitute a single transaction. Neither database knows about the other transaction, however, and so the application must manage these two transactions, and roll them both back if either fails.

In practice, this is hard to implement, because it requires a two-phase commit process to be implemented by each database. Basically, each database must be told to make a tentative commit, and if all succeeds, they are told to go ahead and make the commit final. Systems that have software components called "transaction managers" are able to participate in such group transactions. Products that support the Enterprise JavaBeans framework take this a step further and greatly simplify the transactional aspect of application design, by defining a generic middle-tier architecture and delegating transaction control to a specific component. This is discussed in detail in the chapter on JavaBeans.

If the middle-tier services are of your own design (e.g., CORBA objects), and you are not using an Enterprise JavaBeans product, you can implement a two-phase commit mechanism using the Java Transaction Service, which is the Java implementation of the CORBA Transaction Service. The chapter on Distributed Computing Protocols discusses this issue in more detail.

Cleaning Up Partially Completed Logical Transaction Remnants

It is a misconception that database transaction technology prevents most applications from creating inconsistent results. It certainly helps, but in a high volume system, anything that can happen will, and if an inconsistent result only happens 0.01% of the time, that means that after ten million transactions there will be 1000 inconsistent results in the database. Depending on the nature of the application, this may be ignorable, or it may be absolutely unacceptable.

The reason that errors creep in is usually because complex logical transactions are broken up into multiple separate database transactions, and something goes wrong between one commit and the next. For example, suppose a demographic database has a transaction to set a customer's marital status, and another to set a customer's name. Suppose also that a female customer calls and says, "My boyfriend and I just got married, and my name is no longer Candace Walnoskipanovich (thank goodness!)—it is now Candace Kane." The operator enters and commits a transaction to set Candace's marital status, and then begins to enter another to set her new name, when suddenly the system goes down. There is now a person in the database, who is listed as married, with the last name of Walnoskipanovich. The woman on the phone has already hung up, thinking everything has been taken care of, and the operator is left with no way to correct the error, because in the confusion of the system failure, he has forgotten the caller's very hard-to-remember original last name.

This is a case in which a single logical transaction has been implemented with two independent physical transactions, most likely because the specific logical transaction of a simultaneous name and marital status change was not anticipated. In general, there can be consistency rules in a database that are not thought of at design time, but are discovered afterwards when the system is operational. Until these consistency rules can be added to the system's next release, there needs to be a set of processes for dealing with such inconsistencies, and "reaping remnants" of partially completed logical transactions. In our example, there could be a process for examining all female customers for which marital status was changed, but not the person's name, and producing a report of such instances for inspection and verification.

Inconsistent results can also occur as a result of failure of separate systems that participate in two-phase transactions. Most two-phase transactional systems are advertised as fully reliable, but in fact a system failure at just the right moment (after the second phase, but immediately before a write from a durable transaction log to the actual database). In such a case, partially complete results must be reconciled.

An Event Methodology for Database Applications

Traditional application design using relational technology uses relational table schemas combined with well-defined logical transactions to specify the object and temporal boundaries of operations on the database. Each transaction effects an atomic state change on the database, and each change of state constitutes an event. Regardless of the architecture of the application—single tier or multitier—the problem of notification of changes to interested clients must always be dealt with, i.e., the pessimistic versus optimistic locking issue. By treating updates to the database as events, it is possible to define an explicit framework for notification of clients whenever a change occurs that they have an interest in.

Object models do *not* obviate the concept of a unit of work. There is often the misconception that an object persistence layer makes persistence transparent, and that one does not have to worry about transactions—that consideration of transaction issues is a problem for relational database design only. Nothing could be further from the case. Current object databases (as well as the ODMG model) make transactions explicit. Further, the concept of a transaction is rooted in the requirements for atomicity, and for concurrent access by multiple users. The Java object model does not directly support the definition of object composites, and so there is no basis for deriving what an atomic or isolated operation should be. (Interestingly, the JavaCard API provides for the specification of transactional objects.)

An event model is an excellent framework for defining the transactional semantics of a system. The complete system model then consists of the schema, the transactions (transaction boundaries), the events signaled by each transaction, and the clients interested in each type of event.

Event Delivery

Consideration must be given to which events need to be delivered synchronously—i.e., those which must be delivered to all interested clients prior to completion, with failed deliveries resulting in synchronous exception delivery and even possible rollback of the transaction. In a very tightly coupled system, clients might even be required to process event notices before acknowledging. This approach might be necessary in a system in which clients must always exactly reflect the current central model.

Generally, most applications do not require synchronous delivery, as long as the application is designed to use some other synchronous mechanism (such as a database locking mechanism) to ensure synchronization of the central model, and clients do not rely on the order of events to ensure correct client view construction. However, wherever events are used to effect synchronization, they must be delivered synchronously. This is actually rare, e.g., if an event signals that a composite object has been checked out for modification, it may not be, at any given instant, actually locked by the database mechanism. There is still no risk of conflicting updates, however, if all clients utilize a protected checkout semaphore for the object. All clients that try to check the object out must, at the start of their transaction, read the semaphore, and if it is not checked out, set it as such. Thus, the event delivery mechanism is more like a messenger of news, rather than a handshaking mechanism.

If synchronous delivery is required, a single queue can be used to synchronize event delivery. (This is discussed in the chapter on JavaBeans.) It should also be possible for an event listener to peek into the queue, and prune events destined for it, in a protected manner. On the other hand, using a nonsynchronous strategy frees us to implement notification with polling, and avoid all these complexities.

Defining the Events

An entire object system can be usually viewed as the construction, promotion, modification, and deletion of composite objects. Each of these processes is a logical transaction. During that transaction, the object in question needs to be guarded, to ensure that only one party has control of it. If other transactions read the object, they need to know if the object's state is tentative; and they may register themselves as listeners for any change in the state of the object, such as constructed, promoted, or approved. These changes of state can be signaled by event objects.

The granularity at which objects can notify listeners of these change events is up to the application. In general, fine-grained notification is complex to implement, and must be weighed against the potential number of listeners registered at any one time (which must have open connections or listener linkages of some type for callback), and the extra code and resources required to provide notification capabilities into those objects. A superior alternative is to put the notification mechanism into the database engine itself, but there are few products that do this. Replicated databases provide this, but that is not the model we seek—our replication is granular and transient, based on transactions. The model we need is more analogous to a caching system with the primary data existing within a database, and replicated content distributed temporarily to a variable and potentially large number of clients for display or processing.

Furthermore, in many systems a hybrid approach is required, in which some clients receive synchronous notification, while others rely on an optimistic policy. For example, an administration application may want to use a synchronous approach, to make changes in real time, while data query clients may not need this and use an optimistic approach. Our methodology must therefore allow for both.

This leads to a modified use of the model-view-controller (MVC) pattern first popularized in the Smalltalk community, and now widely accepted as a standard design pattern for user interfaces. In this pattern, the three primary components are the "model", the "view", and the "controller." The model provides the single interface to a data source. The model presents three kinds of interface: a command interface for requesting changes to the model's data; a data access interface for requesting data from the model; and a notification interface for notifying other components when the model's data has changes as a result of external events (such as other transactions). In the MVC concept, the view component displays data to the user, by requesting it from the model; and it receives input from the user and forward the input to the controller. It is the job of the controller to decide what to do with the input, and to coordinate actions made against the model. The view also receives notification from the model of changes to data.

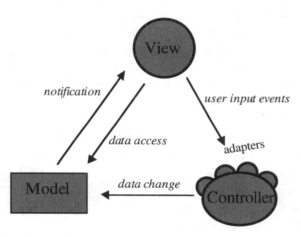

Figure 5–9 The Model-View-Controller paradigm

When programming in Java, the controller component is often implemented as a coordinating component containing a series of event adapters, which receive events from the view and respond by making model changes. What is missing from this design is a clear-cut strategy for dealing with higher-order application-level events. User interface events such as mouse clicks are explicitly handled by the adapters, but there is no model for translating these into events which have meaning in the context of the model. There also must be a clear demarcation of the transaction layer for interacting with the model.

A driving motivation behind MVC is that model changes may occur asynchronously, and a view cannot anticipate the detailed nature of these changes. The view therefore needs a generalized mechanism for being notified of changes, and needs to be able to refresh itself in response. The granularity of notification and refreshing is the major issue in such a design, as it has a major impact on performance and usability.

The MVC model works well in the context of remote transactional applications if we merely address the issue of event delivery, and distinguish between local and remote events; and if we also distinguish between two kinds of "model"—the data local to the application, which may be replicated from a shared database, and the centralized data model consisting of one or more centralized databases. (The centralized database may be distributed for performance reasons as long as it appears to the client to be centralized.)

The four primary categories of events I will introduce in our MVC model are:

1. *Database application events*—These are the large-grain events that represent application-level changes of the state of composite objects. These events fall within the broader category of model change events, if the database is viewed as the central model. An example would be the commit of an intermediate or final flight reservation for an airline customer. If the change represents an intermediate state, this implies an optimistic or checkout-based application-level locking model. Within this category, we have these very prevalent subcategories:

> *Obtain (checkout)*: An object's ownership is assigned.
>
> *Release (checkin)*: An object's ownership is relinquished.
>
> *Change policy (e.g., from exclusive to nonexclusive)*: Access rights to an object are modified.
>
> *Construction* (of composite): A new composite object is instantiated.
>
> *Promotion*: An object is approved in some way, verified, or processed, resulting in it being considered to have transitioned to a new status or level of recognition, or role.
>
> *Modification*: An object is modified (atomically, of course).
>
> *Deletion*: An object is deleted from the system, or marked for deletion.

2. *Database physical events*—These are the small-grain events that represent physical insertions and deletions in a database. These are also model-change events. A single physical event does not signify a logically complete (or consistent) change to the database, and any application that reads changes based on physical events has the risk of reading incomplete or tentative data. An example is the addition of an item to an online product order, prior to committing the order. Another example is the entry of the order's bill-to address. In these two examples, the changes must be made persistent, and so they need to be committed as physical transactions against the database; however, until the order is complete and committed as a unit, most clients would not be interested in these changes. The distinction between physical events and application events becomes more important in applications that are work process in nature, such that users work on changes for a long period before forwarding them to the next stage of processing or approval.

3. *Transaction status events*—These are client-level events that signal changes in the status of transactions initiated by the client. An example would be the successful (or unsuccessful) completion of the commit of changes to the database.

4. *GUI events*—These are purely client-level events, and are not represented in the system's data model. Nevertheless, GUI events are often used in the user application to signal user view changes in response to user input. An example of a user event would be a GUI component signaling a user action, such as the click of a button.

The first category, database application events, are those that carry information about model state changes, usable to other transactions, and these are the events that are of most use in synchronizing replicated data between client and server components, and multiple client application views, as I will now discuss.

Model synchronization v. view synchronization

Most modern multi-tier applications provide the user with a windowing interface, freeing the user to engage in multiple simultaneous activities. Within such an end-user application, especially a workflow application which is usually highly concurrent by nature, there are two inherent data synchronization problems that must be addressed:

- **Inter-view synchronization**—UI depictions of an object's data which appear in more than one view at a time must be synchronized.

- **Inter-model synchronization**—If it is possible that there can be more than one local instance of an object representing an actual database persistent object, these multiple local references must be synchronized.

The need for "inter-model" synchronization may arise if two different parts of an application each perform a read on a database object, into a local instance. Depending on the implementation of the underlying persistence mechanism, these references may point to the same cached object, or they may point to different instances, each acting as a distinct proxy for an actual database object. The model synchronization problem can therefore exist within a single application. It also exists across applications and user sessions, and in this case is the traditional optimistic locking synchronization problem.

Both varieties of inter-model synchronization can be addressed by the same techniques: the data being viewed can be locked (not the best approach); it can be checked out; it can be verified upon commit; or the application can be notified when an externally-initiated change occurs. All of these strategies have already been discussed in detail, except for notification, which is being addressed here.

In contrast to inter-model synchronization, the need for "inter-view" synchronization, which is limited to the client platform, can be eliminated by designing the application so that the user can only do one thing at a time, as in traditional transaction-oriented single-screen applications. With the widespread use of multi-window applications, however, users can be engaged simultaneously in several ongoing work processes and even transactions. If the user changes something in one view, the change needs to be reflected in all other views that are considered to participate in the view's transactions. This is true regardless of whether the user has yet committed the change. In addition, once a change is committed, all applications for *all* users need to reflect the change, including their local copies of the object.

Achieving view synchronization

Inter-view synchronization can be achieved by designing a control architecture that allows application components to register interest in certain events, for the objects that they are currently using or displaying. The controller keeps a list of such interested parties (listeners). When one of those parties makes a change to an object, it notifies the controller, which dispatches a notification event to all listeners who are interested in that particular object. For this to work, *the objects should be large-grain objects,* rather than individual Java objects—that is, *they should be object compositions*—otherwise, the number of objects and complexity would be unmanageable. Thus, when an application view displays data associated with a particular object composition, it should register itself as a listener on the composition, which must have some keyed root object that the object composition can be identified by.

For example, in the diagram below, suppose Q represents an object composition, consisting of a root object, say a person's employee ID number, and all the demographic data uniquely associated with that employee. The composition Q is therefore a set of objects (not shown, to avoid clutter in the diagram), all owned by the root employee persistent object or record (also not shown—only the Q aggregation is shown).

In the figure, Q is depicted on client views A and B. Each of these views may show different aspects of Q: for example, one view might show the employee name and address, and the other view might show only the employee's age and marital status. Regardless, each view shows some data owned by the logical grouping we are calling "Q", identified by the employee's ID. This logical grouping is the basis for composing logical transactions against the object model, and for dispatching application events to those interested in changes to Q. Obviously, views which depict data owned by Q will be interested in changes to Q, and so they should register as listeners for application events that involve Q. Note that such a listener registers its interest in the specific instance Q, rather than merely indicating an interest in all Q-type objects.

Events of any type which change the composition Q go through the MVC controller, and the controller can easily determine all views that need to be updated, based on its list of registered listeners. If a particular view is not visible, a refresh of its contents can be postponed, or done in the background at lower priority.

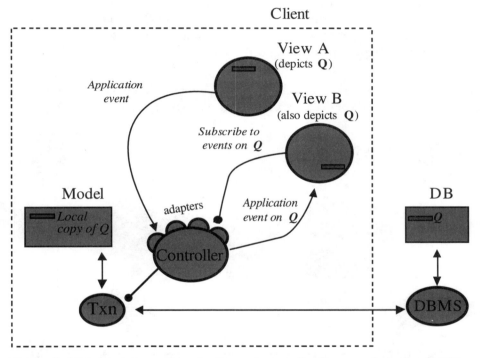

Figure 5–10 Interview synchronization using application events and an MVC design. (UI events have been omitted for simplicity.)

One important modification to the normal MVC paradigm is that we are not assuming the existence of a connection between the model and the views that represent the model. Most multi-user persistent store implementations do not provide automatic notification of model changes. Instead, they provide locking techniques, to protect against changes. The problem is that a typical application spends most of its time in between transactions, rather than in a transaction, and it is this in-between time that the user is actually examining the data and making a decision. We therefore need an explicit architectural role for a component which provides notification to a view when model data changes, and we need to provide for this capability in our design, since it is not automatically provided by most systems. To handle local model changes, we need a local component and protocol for subscribing to changes, and for implementing change notification to subscribers. For remote model changes, e.g. changes made to a central database by other transactions, we need a central change notification component.

Achieving model synchronization

Synchronizing one or more client views with a remote data model requires either using a passive strategy such as optimistic locking, or an active strategy such as pessimistic locking or asynchronous change notification. Since the optimistic and pessimistic strategies have already been discussed in an earlier section, I will now look at a technique for implementing active change notification, for multiple distributed clients.

Consider the following modified scenario, which focuses on the interaction between a client view, controller, and transaction layer, and a remote DBMS.

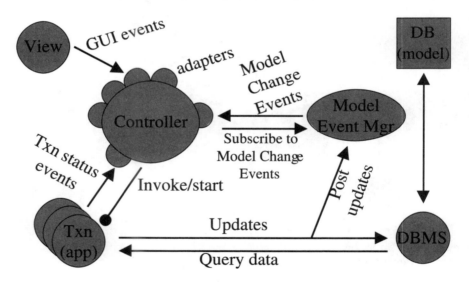

Figure 5–11 Using events to notify clients of remote data model changes.

The view component, which executes on each client, represents the client's view of the system. It communicates with a controller, which also executes on the client, via UI and other bean-type events. The transaction layer is implemented by a set of transactional components—possibly Enterprise JavaBeans—and can be invoked either on the client or on the server, although more likely they would be remote method calls to the server.

The component labeled "Model Event Manager" is an object that executes on the database server. There should be one such service per database, although there is no reason why this object cannot be replicated, since the order of event delivery is not defined. If clients are designed not to rely on notification (i.e., event delivery is not guaranteed), then the Event Manager object need not even be persistent or durable with regard to system failure. This allows for easy replication and relocation, preventing it from becoming a bottleneck.

A multitier Event Manager design is also possible, in which a local server serving a cluster of workstations or network computers maintains a local distributed Event Manager, maintaining a single connection to one or more primary event managers. The workstations and NCs then only need to maintain callback connections to the local Event Manager.

Events could be propagated based on relevance to the needs of the local clients, thereby filtering events that are not of interest. This may be important for some event delivery implementations, and in most implementations a single event channel may actually be used for all events, and the client-side controller filters events not of interest. Providing filtering at a middle event tier would reduce the event traffic, much the way that a network bridge filters packets not of interest to a network segment.

An advanced design could even use multicast for callback notification. This could be implemented by assigning clients compact callback IDs that they can listen for, and then query for the actual message after they hear their ID broadcast—sort of like a pager combined with voice mail.

All transaction atomicity semantics are encapsulated within the txn components, including multidatabase or two-phase transactions. This architecture integrates well, therefore, with the Enterprise JavaBeans framework, which isolates transactional operations from application code.

As you can see, there is a potentially fragile link between the transaction components and the Event Manager. It is fragile because it relies on the applications to design their transactions such that they always post changes to the Model Event Manager. It would be much better if the DBMS or persistence layer provided an event manager as a built-in service, integrated with the DBMS's transaction control system. This would allow clients to register interest in objects, directly with the DBMS, freeing applications from the need to post changes whenever they make them, since the DBMS would handle the posting and notification. This would also make it possible for the event callback connection to piggyback on the database connection. Perhaps some object-oriented database vendor will do this.

Model change events should not convey model information—only that the model has changed, and possibly identify what parts have changed. The model (database) itself should always be consulted for verification. Model change events should be treated as hints only.

If event delivery is implemented asynchronously, then model change adapters must deal gracefully with stale or out-of-order events, and with references to database objects that no longer exist; and the model event manager should also deal gracefully with listeners (client adapters) that no longer exist.

Replicated Code Deployment Issues for Database Applications

Replicating code to clients solves a big problem, in that valuable bandwidth can be saved in downloading code dynamically to clients. The "push" model provided by products like Castanet provide for dynamic distribution of application code, relieving a system administrator of the problem of distributing updates to users, and worrying about version control issues. For mission-critical applications, a problem remains, however: The Castanet protocol, called Distribution and Replication Protocol (DRP), is "transactional" in that it guarantees that a client will receive an update in a correct manner, and never a partial update—the client's integrity is protected. However, it is possible for different clients to update at different times, and so some clients may have obsolete versions of code. This is an important concern for database applications, or any application in which the client code needs to be absolutely in sync with the server code and schema.

The problem is not with DRP; rather, it indicates that single-client transactional software update is only part of the problem; at present, the rest of the problem—client/server update—must be dealt with by your application. There are many types of solutions.

Four client/server code synchronization strategies are

1. *Coordinated shutdown and restart of server*—No explicit syncing is embedded in the application or protocol. Users rely totally on administrative procedures and the design of client and server.

    - Clients must interpret an unexplained connection exception or loss to possibly mean that an update is needed.

    - Whenever a client starts/restarts, it performs an update.

    - A client will never connect to a service unless it has successfully updated since starting or restarting, unless it knows from other means (e.g., administrative procedure) that an update is not needed.

•This approach works particularly well with servers that integrate DRP support with database connectivity. An example of such a product is the Weblogic Tengah application server.

2. *Explicit code versioning*—The application explicitly requests version number as part of every transaction. Each remote request must be in the context of a transaction. Server code updates must be transactional, and done in such a way that transactions in progress are allowed to complete first, and new transactions disallowed until the code update is complete. For CORBA and RMI applications, the client can send a version number with every remote request.

A solution which uses code versioning is as follows:

- Client prefaces every query with a version no. query, as part of the same transaction. If the remote version does not match the client version, attempt an update repeatedly until successful.

- When client starts,

```
if update available,
    update();
else
    connect to database, and accept query requests from user
when update complete,
    restart();
```

- On server, to update code or schema,

    a. wait for all client transactions in progress to finish; do not accept any new client transactions.

    b. publish new code, and make any schema changes; restart db if necessary.

    c. update version number in db.

    d. begin accepting remote transactions again.

3. *Active client notification*—Clients should always update when they start/restart. Here are two implementations.

- Use multicast to notify clients that connection will soon be lost, and that they should update themselves and restart; new db connections should be refused until the new version is published.

Or,

- Bind client db connection to a "control" connection that can asynchronously call back the client (using RMI or CORBA, for example); this connection can be used to notify clients that db connection will soon be lost, and that they should update and restart. New control connections should be refused until the new version is published.

4. *Passive client notification*—The driver or middleware takes responsibility for versioning and/or update notification, and throws an exception when out of sync or when an update and restart is needed, e.g., update notification could be embedded in the JDBC driver (vendors take note!). If the middle tier is custom built, upgrade notification can be built into the protocol in the form of upgrade events. Here is a sketch of a simple single-threaded server example, using Castanet.

Client:

```java
public class Client
    extends marimba.channel.ApplicationPlayerFrame
    implements java.awt.events.ActionListener
{
    public void start() throws Exception
    {
        context.update();
        server = java.rmi.Naming.lookup("Server");
        setLayout(new FlowLayout());
        java.awt.Button button = new java.awt.Button("Get Customers");
        button.addActionListener(this);
        add(button);
        show();
    }

    public void actionPerformed(ActionEvent e)
    {
        try
        {
            Vector customers = server.getCustomers();
        }
        catch (RemoteException reme)
        {
            context.update(); // connection lost - update - this forces
                              // a restart if channel is configured
                              // to restart after an update
        }
```

```
     catch (SQLException sqle)
     {
        sqle.printStackTrace();
     }
     catch (RestartException rese)
     {
        context.update(); // we are being instructed to restart -
                        // perform an update and restart
     }
     ...do whatever with customers, e.g. display them...
   }

   public void stop() { server = null; }// allow remote reference to
                                                be GC'd
   private Server server;
}
```

Server:
```
public class RestartException extends Exception {}

public interface Server extends java.rmi.Remote
{
   public Vector getCustomers()
      throws java.rmi.RemoteException, SQLException,
   RestartException;
}

public class ServerImpl
   extends java.rmi.server.UnicastRemoteObject
   implements Server, java.awt.events.ActionListener
{
   public static void main(String[] args) throws
      java.sql.SQLException
   {
      java.awt.Frame f = new java.awt.Frame();
      setLayout(new java.awt.FlowLayout());
      java.awt.Button b = new java.awt.Button("Shutdown in 10
   seconds");
      add(b);
      ServerImpl si = new ServerImpl();
      b.addActionListener(si);
      show();
   }
```

```java
   public void actionPerformed(ActionEvent e)
{
   notifyClientsAndShutdown(10);
}

public ServerImpl()
{
   String dbURL = args[0];    // the URL of the database
   con = DriverManager.getConnection(dbURL);
   ServerImpl si = new ServerImpl();
   java.rmi.Naming.rebind("Server", si);
}

public Vector getCustomers()
   throws java.rmi.RemoteException, SQLException, RestartException
{
   if (shutdown) throw new RestartException();
   incrementCount();
   try
   {
      Statement s = con.createStatment();
      ResultSet rs = s.executeQuery("SELECT * FROM CUSTOMERS");
      Vector v = new Vector();
      for (; rs.next();)
      {
         Customer c = new Customer(rs.getString("NAME"),
         rs.getInt("ID"));
         v.addElement(c);
      }
   }
   finally
   {
      decrementCount();
   }
   return v;
}
```

```
/**
 * For all remote requests, throw RestartException.
 * When maxSecondsToShutdown has elapsed, exit the server
 * process.
 */

public notifyClientsAndShutdown(int maxSecondsToShutdown)
{
   shutdown = true;
   try { sleep(maxSecondsToShutdown * 1000); } catch
     (InterruptedException ex) {}
   for (;;)  // wait until all transactions in progress are done
   {
     synchronized (this)
     {
       if (count == 0) system.exit(0); // stop server
     }
     try { sleep(1000); } catch (InterruptedException ex) {}
   }
}
protected synchronized void incrementCount()
{
   count++;
}
protected synchronized void decrementCount()
{
   count--;
}
private boolean shutdown = false;
private Connection con;
private int count = 0;
}
```

The most sophisticated approach would be to add application update notification to the type 3 or 4 driver, by extending the JDBC protocol (e.g., by defining the RestartException to extend from SQL Exception). Thus, the driver would notify clients directly when the clients of that database need to refresh their code. If clients access more than one database, they are presumably going through a single middle-tier driver, which would be the control point for application synchronization. This is, in general, not supported by the current generation of JDBC drivers. It is, however, in effect supported by many object-oriented database products, which will throw an exception when they detect that the client code is out of sync with the server's object model. An example is SQLObjectFactory's (made by Poet) Java SDK: ODMGException "index definitions are changed, the database must be updated."

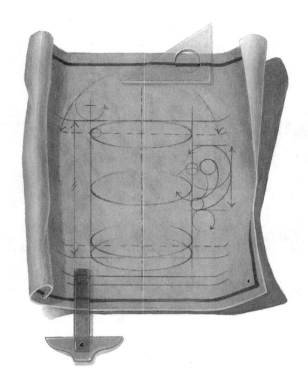

CHAPTER

6

- **Architectural Overview**
- **Internet Server Protocols**
- **Remote Method Invocation**
- **Java and CORBA**
- **Distributed Transactions and Messaging**

Distributed Computing Protocols

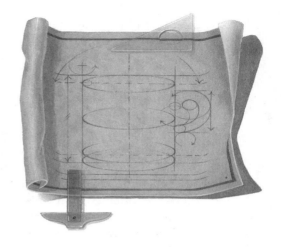

Increasingly, isolated applications within organizations need to be pulled together, providing uniform information sources, processes, and business rules to all business units or branches of an organization, and even between an organization and its customers, and between organizations. The Internet makes this possible, because for the first time there exists a worldwide wide area network with open protocols for implementing this new level of connectivity. The mere availability of this level of integration now makes such connectivity necessary if an organization wants to keep abreast of its competition.

Within most organizations, and certainly between organizations, different needs mandate different technology choices, so the task of integrating applications across a wide area network and the Internet almost always involves tying together equipment and software from varied sources. The heterogeneous nature of cross-business unit computing makes a platform-independent language necessary, so that applications of this scope can be developed in a single language and ideally with a single set of open APIs and standards. Java is such a language.

Interestingly, the penetration of NT into the server market is sometimes cited as a reason for using NT-specific solutions. Yet NT is one of the driving forces within organizations for employing Java. The existence of NT as a newcomer side-by-side with large and trusted UNIX servers makes platform-independent solutions more attractive and critical, since while NTs use in large server environments will increase, it is unlikely to completely displace ever-increasingly capable UNIX servers. This means that while UNIX-only solutions were viable a few years ago, IT managers are now faced with NT as a new low end entrant that must be integrated with their UNIX systems. This major factor fuels the move to platform-independent solutions in server applications.

Java offers many advantages as a development language for server applications. These include its built-in and platform-independent multithreading; a built-in and platform-independent network API, flexible and standardized server application deployment models, including servlets, RMI, CORBA, and Enterprise Java-Beans, and a standardized client deployment model for browsers, along with other client deployment choices from many sources. Java's simplicity, portability, and object-oriented nature also has made many object-oriented choices practical which were much less so prior to Java, including the use of object-oriented databases and the mainstream use of CORBA.

Newer Java API features, including Enterprise JavaBeans, the Java Naming and Directory Interface, and the Java Messaging Service, promise to revolutionize the development of server applications. These features will provide framework for integrating applications of all kinds within and without organizations and create a highly reliable, maintainable, and accessible distributed information infrastructure.

Architectural Overview

A multi-user computing system design must address many issues. The primary architectural issues that drive a design are typically methodology (e.g., object-oriented vs. procedural), interoperability with existing systems, performance and scalability. These last two are sometimes overlooked until deployment, especially if the system is designed by application programmers who do not have experience with large scale systems. Performance and scalability are especially important in a distributed system design, because there are so many potential bottlenecks. Design methodology is important for programmer productivity and maintainability, and compatiblity with toolsets. Interoperability is fundamental to systems which link existing systems into a larger whole.

Some other important considerations for the system include

- Usability for endusers—This applies to any system.

- Security—A distributed system often transports data over wide area networks, possibly external to the organization. (The issues associated with this are addressed in the security chapter.)

- Management of the deployed system—This is often overlooked until deployment.

- Reliability of components—An important issue with now ever-changing technologies.

- Deployment—Distributed objects mean distributed code.

- Evolution—Part of the total cost of the system is the cost of making changes.

- Maintainability—Ability to get technical talent.

Some additional prominent architectural issues often include

- Transaction design and transaction isolation—The amplication must be carefully partitioned into atomic operations, and those operations designed using the chosen products, and technologies.

- Integrating multiple middleware and database brands—When integrating components from different sources, a strategy is needed to make them work together and produce correct results. This requires using components that expose the primitives or facilities needed to integrate them. (Many of these issues are discussed in the database chapter.)

- Integrated transaction monitoring—There may be preferred tools used by administrators with which the final system must integrate.

- Messaging vs. real-time processing—Two very different approaches, discussed below.

- Change propagation to clients; event notification—Distributed processing means distributed data, including persistent data on a server and transient data on a client.

- End-to-end acknowledgment—A way to make an unreliable system reliable.

- Multicomputer-language integration—Making systems of different origin and technology work together.

- Multiple networks—Ability of the application protocols to work on different transports. This usually boils down to having TCP/IP gateways for packet services such as news wire data feeds and server programs to bridge non-TCP/IP network services.

- Firewalls—Getting in and getting out. (Discussed in the security chapter.)

This chapter discusses the fundamental tools and protocols available to build distributed systems using Java. While I use particular implementations to develop examples, I will focus mainly on the open protocols and general techniques relevant to the above considerations. As pointed out, some issues important for distributed systems are addressed in other chapters, especially the chapters on databases and on Javabeans.

Multiprocessing, Performance, and Some Scalability Concerns
Multithreading Issues

Many servers have multiple processors. A server with multiple processors can perform better if applications are designed with multiprocessing and multithreading in mind. However, there is a limit to this, and it is one of rapidly diminishing returns. An application which creates ten threads on a system with two processors simply in order to increase performance is defeating itself, since at any time at most two of those threads can actually be executing. In fact, using two threads or two processes on such a system will not achieve twice the throughput, but something less than twice. Even if the system sports 20 processors (which is not uncommon for high volume UNIX servers), the other processors may be busy serving other tasks.

The fact that Java has multithreading built into the language often is cited as an advantage for building high performance multithreaded applications. This is a true advantage, but the greatest benefits of multithreading occur when you do things while other activities are in a wait state. Having two nonwaiting threads execute at the same time does not buy you anything unless there are processors available to execute those threads.

If there are only two processors and there are six threads, at least four of them will be waiting at any instant. If a thread is chronically waiting because its process is waiting for the system to read pages back in from virtual memory, the system is wasting much effort just switching back and forth between its various tasks. You are probably familiar with this phenomenon, called "thrashing."

Many types of middleware, including Enterprise JavaBean middleware (discussed in the chapter on JavaBeans), constrain server-side user-written application components to be singlethreaded. However, this does not mean that high concurrency cannot be achieved. Consider Figure 6–1.

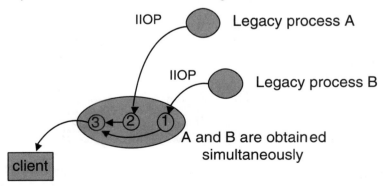

Figure 6–1 Performing operations concurrently without explicitly using multithreading.

In the above figure, a server-side application must perform three activities: 1, 2, and 3. Activity 3 cannot be performed until 1 and 2 are—they are data retrieval activities, and activity 3 processes that data to produce a combined result. Activities 1 and 2 can therefore be performed concurrently. The problem is that the application deployment environment requires the application to be single-threaded.

To get around the singlethreading limitation, suppose that the application server API supports nonblocking calls to legacy processes A and B. For example, if we are using CORBA, the Dynamic Invocation Interface could be used. Or, if we are using the Java Messaging Service (discussed later in this chapter), messages could be dispatched to these processes. The application can then rendezvous with the two non-blocking calls after it has dispatched each one, by performing a blocking wait. APIs that support no-blocking calls invariably have such a rendezvous method. The application achieves concurrency by dispatching the nonblocking requests, and then waits for both to complete. The deployment server environment (EJB, CORBA, JMS, etc.) is then providing and managing the multi-threading, so the application does not have to be concerned with it.

Designing with concurrency such as this does not necessarily increase application throughput, as already discussed, although it may. It will likely reduce latency, however—the time delay between a user request and the delivery of a final result.

Too Many Objects

Application servers have to route requests received over a network to application components targeted by the requests. To do this they must perform a lookup of some type to identify the application component. This lookup is called "demultiplexing." CORBA ORBs perform object demultiplexing to identify the target object of an incoming remote method call. Messaging systems perform demultiplexing to identify the target message channel for an incoming message. Do not assume that this lookup is always efficient, as it is not, even in mainstream products. In particular, does the lookup time increase with the number of server components, or is it relatively constant? A linearly-increasing lookup time would indicate a linear search algorithm is employed.

In addition to this application-level demultiplexing, the communication system must perform demultiplexing to map incoming packets to the application's port. The combination of this and additional communication overhead can add considerably to the latency of an application that uses remote protocols for data exchange between components, as opposed to the traditional approach of linking components within a single application. Some application deployment implementations have the ability to discover dynamically which remote references actually represent local objects, and handle those more efficiently. This is the case for many CORBA implementations, as will be discussed. In general, the performance penalty of remote invocation overhead must be weighed against the flexibility and maintainability advantages of using protocols to decouple application components.

Session overhead

Since most applications access data, some system components will need to establish connections to data repositories, usually relational or object databases, and often legacy application systems including messaging systems and others. The latency of establishing these connections is usually quite large—several hundred milliseconds typically. For this reason, most multitier systems use connection pools to maintain these connections and make them available as required to incoming requests. Application servers differ in their abilities to accommodate such pooled connection resources. This is discussed further in the discussion of Enterprise JavaBeans in the JavaBeans chapter.

Some applications have a need to maintain client session state between requests. A common source of this need is incremental queries—queries that sometimes return results that are too large to accommodate at once, and so are broken up into pieces. One approach is to maintain a connection so that each request can pick up where the previous one left off. This requires a persistent connection with a client, however. If the system is multi-tier, this can develop into a need to maintain a session between each tier all the way from the data source to the client—a very unscalable approach. In the chapter on databases, and in the Enterprise JavaBeans section of the JavaBeans chapter, I discuss connection pools and products that provide connection pool management.

Data Transformations of Middleware

Data transformations are expensive when done on a server—even a local server. Data should be delivered to the client essentially the same way it is stored on the server. When using object-oriented languages such as Java, there is sometimes a tendency in programmers to create many layers of abstraction, and the project architect must be careful to make sure that each layer adds maintainability value that is greater than the actual economic cost of any performance penalties it incurs.

Many applications have a third tier which does nothing but determine where the requested data resides, and then forward the request to a second tier to actually perform the retrieval. If the lookup can be encapsulated into a client-side component, which is kept up to date using a replication protocol, an entire tier can be eliminated. An alternative is to treat the lookup as a redirection server, and after performing the lookup, pass the connection information to the client and allow the client to connect directly, instead of having the lookup tier make the connection and pass all the data through it.

Data should also be stored with the main purpose of the application in mind. For example, if the application's success will be its response time for queries, don't optimize it for data loading.

More Scalability Issues

Thin Client Means Heavy Server

A Java client is not a thin client. A Java client is sometimes referred to as a thin client because it often executes in a browser, which is associated with a thin-client design. Browsers are portrayed as thin clients because in their short history, they have primarily served HTML-based applications, which are thin-client. Browsers are anything but thin, however—laughably, perhaps.

Within the context of this book, I'd like to define the following terms

> thin client—HTML only; all logic on the server
>
> heavy client—native code on the client; traditional client server
>
> portable client—Java and Active-X clients, which contain application logic but are deployable across networks using a Web, publishing, or other model

The term "thin client" is also used to describe enduser computing platforms that consist of network computers with no user-accessible local storage, and which maintain even the user's desktop configuration on a central server. Network computers are discussed in the chapter on Java platforms.

The lines between these categories are extremely blurry. For example, an application which makes heavy use of Javascript can be considered a thin-client application, because it is primarily HTML-based, if Javascript is viewed as dynamic HTML. On the other hand, Javascript is a full-blown computing language, which is interpreted by a browser. I have seen very heavy Javascript applications, which maintain state on clients through the use of persistent frames containing Javascript objects. Such a design is not "thin," although it uses technology usually associated with thin clients.

A portable client, on the other hand, can be either thin or heavy. A useful distinction is that portable clients which keep most business rules on a server are "thin," and those which maintain business rules within the client are "heavy," regardless of the amount of code involved. With this interpretation, a thin portable client is one which provides a generic capability—perhaps a very advanced one—which can access server-based applications or business processes. A heavy portable client is then a portable design which is mostly self-contained, except perhaps for a remote data repository. Be forewarned, however, that people use the terms "thin" and "heavy" in different ways.

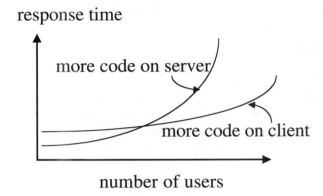

Figure 6–2 Response time tradeoff of code execution on a client versus code execution on a shared server.

Assuming your application has at least some code on the client (i.e., a heavy client or a portable client), the above figure compares the tradeoff of two extremes: having more code on the client and less on the server, vs. having more code on the server and less on the client. The crossover point, at which server-side functionality becomes too burdensome, depends on the nature of the application, and on most systems can only be determined by measurement.

The point of this diagram is that when designing a multitier system, programmers often think, "Well, the server is faster, so I'll put more code on the server, and the application will run faster." Initial tests bear this out, but when the system is tested at full load, it crumbles. The reason is that the server is burdened with application processing that the client should be doing. The server is a shared resource, whereas the client is a dedicated resource, and so there is inevitably a point at which the server runs out of resources as the number of clients increases. Therefore, put only critical operations on the server, and leave all the fluff for the client. The result will be a wider distribution of load. This is not an argument for heavy clients, nor is it a justification for embedding business rules within client applications. It is possible to have critical business rule functionality on a server, and making it available to clients using server-based code deployment techniques, or by tightly encapsulating business rule methods, and still leave most of the manipulation and transformation of data on the client.

Testing Under Load

Another phenomenon is that bugs often do not show up until a system is tested under load. Memory leaks (or simply poor memory utilization) and flaws in synchronization may start to cause instability when throughput and concurrency cross a threshold. Some problems also do not show up until data sets become large. While these issues can be addressed through tuning, they can sometimes have an impact on the entire system architecture; for example, if the architecture is dependent on the choice of a key third party component, which turns out to have scalability flaws.

Load Balancing and Replication

At some point, as usage increases, it may be inconvenient to simply add more processors and IO cards to a system to meet demand. In addition, system availability and on-line maintainability is improved if the load is spread among multiple replicated components. Server scaling can be achieved by replicating the server process, and providing a front end to allocate service requests to processes. In the context of a web server, there are many load balancing products that provide this redirection, including Cisco's LocalDirector, HydraWEB, and RND Networks' ServerDirector. These products sit between the external WAN or Internet router and the organization's external web servers, and map a virtual IP address to a pool of server IP addresses. The allocation policy can be round-robin or a more sophisticated load-based policy, which uses information about the current load of each server.

For services other than conventional web service, including custom services, web-based redirection can still be used if the services are wrapped in HTTP, which is often the case for many non-HTTP protocols. If the service is not wrapped in HTTP, the provider of the protocol may have a load balancing product specifically designed for replication of its servers. Many CORBA products, for example, provide for server object replication and load balancing, as do some of the new Enterprise JavaBean servers. The WebLogic Tengah application server provides transparent routing to replicated Enterprise JavaBean server objects, with automatic failover and reassignment of a connection to a different server object if a connection is lost. (See the chapter on JavaBeans for more on this.)

Messaging vs. Real-Time Delivery

A large scale application often involves connecting multiple software components from different vendors. Single-source technology often is built to provide fail safe operation, with support for backup and recoverable transactions, even for distributed components. When one interconnects components from multiple vendors, however, some of these features may be lost, and must be added back in. The designer is faced with the challenge of making pieces of software obtained from different sources operate as a unified system. In particular, application operations must fail or recover in a clean and atomic manner, when one system component fails.

The two predominant approaches to achieving reliable transaction completion are:

Guaranteed message delivery—In effect, you are delegating the system interconnection and handshaking responsibility to an integrated messaging component. You assume each component of this glue layer obtains acknowledgment from the next recipient along the message's route, and that each component will keep trying until it sends a message successfully.

Real-time transaction—You are requiring that your message or request gets to its final destination right away—you will wait while it tries—and you require immediate acknowledgment as confirmation.

The term "real-time" must be clarified. Real-time programs are programs which are responsive to real-world timing constraints, usually of a short-duration. For example, a device driver must respond in real-time to an interrupt, so that the device it is servicing can be returned to a non-interrupt state as quickly as possible and handle more requests. In a business application, "real-time" means while a user waits. It does not necessarily imply that the system handles the user exclusively, but it does imply that a response normally will be given before the user proceeds with his or her next activity.

A real-time implementation requires more resources than one which is not real-time, just as a phone call ties up more resources than an e-mail. It is inevitable that some activities in the system will have to wait while the real-time request is serviced. Sometimes an application has to be performed in real time, however, especially if customers are in front of you, wanting confirmation that their holiday reservation has been changed from one airline to another.

The messaging versus real-time transaction distinction divides entire classes of middleware. Products such as IBM's MQ Series and Active Software's ActiveWeb are message-oriented products. Such products are often referred to as "Message Oriented Middleware (MOM)." (Note: the MOM community should try not to schedule conferences on Mother's Day, to avoid confusion.) Javasoft's new Java Message Service API is a standardized interface to message-oriented products. These systems provide alternatives to building on-line distributed transactions when multiple data sources or business processes are involved. In such applications, using a reliable message delivery service greatly simplifies the application design. The act of creating a message is implemented as a transaction, but the user does not get immediate end-to-end confirmation of the completion of all processes that the message will ultimately trigger. Instead, the user either receives confirmation later, or more likely, receives a report of those which did not complete, and which need further attention. In general, message-oriented systems are not intended to be used in applications in which the user needs immediate confirmation of end-to-end completion of activities triggered by the user's transaction.

Some considerations in the choice a messaging or real-time approach are:

- Response time requirements, versus response time characteristics of middleware

- Fail-safety requirements versus fail-safety characteristics of components

- Middleware integration with data sources

- All the other issues listed earlier

Helping you choose between these two approaches is beyond the scope of this book, since I am trying to focus mainly on the Java- and Java technology-related aspects of enterprise applications. However, this is a case in which technology choice can affect the entire architecture of the system. For example, if a middleware product provides tight and reliable integration with data sources that you need to access, you might choose that middleware and its associated transaction or message approach because of the mission-critical data source integration requirement. Your computing platform may also influence the decision, since some products, such as MQ, are available on a wide range of server architectures, but others are available only for a few. (Of course, if the middleware is written in Java, it is probably available for almost any platform.) If the application is inherently real-time in nature, however, such as an airline reservation system, the architecture needs to be transactional in nature, and a message-oriented approach is not likely to be viable for that aspect of the system's functionality.

Building correct multi-component transactional systems is extremely difficult, and the APIs and products that provide the required reliable multi-phase commit protocols are complex. Further, no multi-phase commit protocol is completely reliable, despite vendor claims to the contrary, and there are error conditions that must be mapped and dealt with, since in a high volume system, if anything can possibly go wrong, it eventually will. In general, it is best to find open-protocol-based middleware that meets your infrastructure needs as completely as possible and hides or encapsulates the multi-system interactions, and devote most of your resources to your application. The Enterprise JavaBeans products provide this, and shield your application from the complexities of dealing with multiple heterogeneous data sources and processes in a reliable way. Enterprise JavaBeans is discussed further in the chapter on JavaBeans.

Doing-it-yourself—Network Programming in Java

If You Must Build Your Own Protocol

A custom protocol has the opportunity to be faster and more efficient than a general purpose remote invocation or messaging protocol, such as CORBA's IIOP, or RPC. With a custom protocol, you can avoid general purpose overhead, and send just what is needed, and know exactly what to do with each message received. You can reduce the number of layers of software, and establish a direct connection between a client object and server object, avoiding application-level routing between the two. The disadvantage is that the protocol will be specific to that application, and you will have the burden of maintaining it. In choosing to build a custom protocol, you must also consider if the quality of service of the underlying network is sufficient to provide the desired performance, even if the application protocol is extremely efficient. For example, a real-time multi-player game implemented over today's Internet will suffer from unpredictable and sporadic transmission and routing delays, especially if players are far apart.

It seems as if every major corporation I have worked with has at one point developed its own remote object protocol, analogous to CORBA. Now that standardized technologies like CORBA have become real, these home-grown solutions are being shelved. However, the fact that these organizations went to the trouble to create re-usable solutions for the remote invocation problem shows that there are significant advantages of a general purpose protocol that outweigh use of a custom one.

In some applications, however, a custom protocol is necessary. A real-time control application with severe performance or reliability constraints justifies a custom solution. Even if you use a general purpose solution like CORBA or RMI, it is useful to understand the underlying Java network model and how these technologies work.

Sockets and Server Sockets

There are many types of network transport protocols in use today. A transport protocol provides application-to-application delivery of data, usually in sequence and with a fairly high degree of reliability. A transport protocol API (in combination with its underlying network protocol) provides an abstraction for applications to use, to send data from one application to another, without worrying about physical device characteristics such as device addresses and the path to the destination machine. I am tempted to say that issues like flow control and retransmission are taken care of also, but in a practical sense they are only taken care of up through the network transport level—application programmers must still allocate buffers (unless a buffered API is used for reading data), and worry about end-to-end acknowledgment. (See also the notes at the end of this section about the TCP reset problem.) Still, at least you don't have to find out the Ethernet address of the network card on the machine with which you are trying to communicate! What a transport service does provide, is routing to the final destination and application, and automatic retransmission of pieces that don't make it on the first try, with all data arriving in the correct sequence.

With most protocols, however, it is still up to you to define things such as message record boundaries (how does the receiver know when it has read the entire message? It cannot check for EOF, since the connection is still open, and more data may arrive as part of the next message).

Java provides a built-in binding for TCP/IP, which is the protocol used by the Internet. Other protocols may be used from Java, but if you want to use another protocol, you will have to import a package that implements it, and it will likely require loading some native code to access the native communication services. An alternative is to use a TCP/IP gateway.

Implementations of TCP normally use two kinds of logical connection: a client socket, for transmitting and receiving data, and a server socket, sometimes referred to as a "passive socket," for receiving connection requests. A server socket is actually just a socket that has bound itself to a port so it can receive connection requests. Most TCP APIs, however, encapsulate the socket creation and bind into one operation. Java goes further and uses a separate object class for server sockets.

A server socket is opened by a server application, and responds to connection requests from prospective clients by creating client sockets. The server program waits on a server socket read (in UNIX implementations this is often a "select()" function), and when a request comes in, creates a new client socket to service the client and then returns to its blocking read. Usually, the server will also allocate a thread or process to service the new socket, although an alternative approach is to service it right away (or at least read and enqueue the data), and combine the server socket read and all client socket reads into one read operation in a loop. This is not usually the approach of Java programs, because the Java socket API does not lend itself to this design, since sockets and server sockets are implemented by separate objects.

The Java socket API specifies a Socket object type for servicing client socket connections, and a ServerSocket object type for handling connection requests. I will first discuss the Socket class, and then the ServerSocket class.

The Socket Class

The Socket class encapsulates creation of a socket. There are two instances in which a Socket is created—by a server socket for the purpose of servicing a client connection, and by a client application, wishing to communicate with a server program.

Once you create a Java socket, it is already open and ready for use—the act of creating it establishes the connection. With a Socket instance, you can perform reads and writes using the input stream and output stream associated with the socket.

Thus, one socket services communication in both directions, unlike some TCP APIs in other languages, which associate a separate socket object or structure for each direction.

When you write a socket program in a language such as C, you have to worry about an important issue called "network byte ordering." Different computer architectures order bytes differently, the two schemes being "Big-Endian" and "Little-Endian." The Big-Endian scheme, which is used by the Java VM, gives the high order bytes of a multi-byte numeric value a lower address in memory than the low order bytes. This ordering is also referred to as "network byte order," and is the standard ordering used by Internet protocols for transferring numeric values such as protocol part numbers between different machines. (Actually, values usually are transferred as they are, and re-ordered if necessary when they reach their destination.) Intel machines use Little-Endian byte ordering. The Java socket layer takes care of byte order conversion for you and re-orders received bytes when needed, so your application does not have to worry about it—a big relief in comparison with socket programming with most Unix socket libraries.

Here is an example of creating a client socket from a client program to communicate with a server:

```
Socket socket = new Socket("myhost.com", 1000);
```

This attempts to open a bidirectional socket to host "myhost.com," on port 1000. The port is not a physical port with wires coming out of it—it is a logical port, as defined by TCP/IP. The port routes the connection to the server application on the specified host; this number is specified by the server application when it starts accepting connections, as will be seen below when I discuss server sockets.

If you were writing this in C, you would also have to worry about name resolution—obtaining the IP address for the destination host, based on the domain name "myhost.com." In BSD UNIX, a client application calls the gethostbyname() function to do this. The Java socket layer takes care of this for you too—it automatically calls the hosts's name resolution API, which will either use a local name directory, or go out on the network to a name server to look up the specified host. It is all transparent to your application. You can also specify an IP address, thereby avoiding name resolution, e.g. by creating a socket with

```
Socket socket = new Socket("127.0.0.1", 1000);
```

To read from the socket you have created, you can do something like the following:

```
BufferedReader br = new BufferedReader(new
  InputStreamReader(socket.getInputStream()));
String s = br.readLine();
```

One advantage of using BufferedReader is that it is buffered: its readLine() method will read all the data that is available at any moment and block until it finds a line terminator sequence (CR-NL, CR, or NL—whichever it finds), which it treats as a record boundary. This is very useful for many Internet application protocols, such as HTTP, which use CR-NL as a logical record boundary.

To write to the socket, you can call getOutputStream(), and construct a more convenient output writer object, exemplified by the following:

```
PrintWriter pw = new PrintWriter(socket.getOutputStream());
pw.println("hi there");
```

The ServerSocket Class

A Java server socket exists to create client sockets. That is its role. By itself it does not participate in client communication, but merely acts to respond to connection requests from remote clients, and to create local client sockets to actually service those requests. Here is an example:

```
ServerSocket ss = new ServerSocket(1000);
for (;;)
{
    Socket s = ss.accept();
    SocketServiceThread t = new SocketServiceThread(s);
    t.start();
}
```

In this example, we have assumed that the programmer has defined a class called SocketServiceThread, which extends Thread and implements the functionality required by the application to actually communicate with the client and service client requests. The basic flow of control is this: the main server program sits in an endless loop, blocked on a ServerSocket.accept(), waiting for a connection request. When a connection request comes in, the ServerSocket manufactures a client Socket, which can be used to communicate in duplex mode with the new client. In my example, I then create a separate service object specifically for that new connection, and I implement this service object with a new thread, so that it will run concurrently with other service objects. I then return to the accept() call, and wait for the next connection request.

It is possible to extend the Socket and ServerSocket class to provide your own implementation, for example to add encryption to a socket stream. In the security chapter, I provide an example of doing so.

The TCP Reset Problem

Consider a situation in which a client sends a request to a server, and instead of waiting for a response proceeds to send more requests, assuming that the server will handle the first request successfully. If the server fails on the first request and closes its connection, unread data will be left in the TCP buffers, and the TCP connection may be reset by the server ("connection reset by peer"), causing all the data on the server side to be discarded, including any response sent by the server. The problem is that the client does not know if the first request succeeded or if the connection was closed for other reasons. In this case, the client has no choice but to retry the original request, and this process happens all over again. The client and server can end up in an endless loop of tr ying and not succeeding.

While it is true that TCP provides a reliable transport mechanism that delivers all data while two entities are connected, anomalies like this can occur when connections are broken unexpectedly. To prevent this problem, one should avoid using the data transport mechanism as an application queue, and send only the data required for the current operation. You can relax this restriction if you are sure that you handle all possible error conditions.

If you have written the server program, you can also control the reset behavior by setting the "linger" interval, by calling setSoLinger(true, <delay>) on the socket. This is the time (in milliseconds) that the socket will remain open after a close if there is still data that has not been processed. When the linger interval is expired or all data has been processed (whichever comes first), the socket is reset. Not all platforms support this feature, so use it with care.

Internet Server Protocols

Internet server protocols include those Internet protocols that provide application-level services requiring a server. These protocols are important generic utility layers that can be used to move data between applications and between users. They provide a common set of client-server building blocks available ubiquitously within the Internet, and are the means by which most work is done on the Internet today.

Javasoft has added support for many important Internet server protocols to the Java core API, but in such a way as to allow third parties to provide their own implementations. Thus, most of these protocol APIs are specified with interfaces, abstract classes, and factory methods, rather than concrete implementations. In nearly every case, however, Sun has provided a built-in implementation that you can use at no cost; or you can use an implementation that provides features important to your application, for example, SSL encryption, or particular implementations of generic services such as e-mail.

Internet services use URLs to identify resources. The prefix of a URL specifies the protocol to be used to obtain the resource. For example, in the URL "http://www.somewhere.com/abc.txt", the protocol "http" is specified, indicating that the server providing the resource is an HTTP server (i.e., a web server). The java.net package contains a base class URLConnection which contains behavior common to all connections to URL-based services.

HTTP

Hypertext Transfer Protocol (HTTP) is probably the most important Internet server protocol. It is the protocol that sparked the tremendous growth and popularization of the web, and it serves as a backbone protocol on which many diverse kinds of services depend. The Java core API provides built-in support for HTTP, in the form of classes that can open connections to HTTP servers and parse HTTP messages. Let's take a look at some of these classes.

The HttpURLConnection class is an HTTP-specific class that extends URLConnection, and provides functionality specific to HTTP-based resources. This is an abstract class, but the factory method URL.openConnection() returns a concrete implementation. The standard JDK release returns an instance of sun.net.www.protocol.http.HttpURLConnection, which has the signature

```
public sun.net.www.protocol.http.HttpURLConnection
(
    URL url,              // the URL
    String proxy,         // if there is a proxy
    int proxyPort         // the proxy port
);
```

Let's consider an example:

```
import java.net.*;
import java.io.*;

public class C
{
    public static void main(String[] args) throws Exception
    {
        HttpURLConnection c;

        //
        // Writing to a URL
        //
```

```
// Construct an HttpURLConnection object - no connection
// exists yet
c = new sun.net.www.protocol.http.HttpURLConnection(
    new URL(args[0]), null, 0);
c.setRequestMethod("PUT");
c.setDoOutput(true);
c.connect();
OutputStream os = c.getOutputStream();
if (os == null) throw new Exception("os is null");
PrintStream ps = new PrintStream(os);
ps.println("hi");
InputStream is = c.getInputStream();
if (is == null) throw new Exception("is is null");
DataInputStream dis = new DataInputStream(is);
String s = dis.readLine();
System.out.println("response body=" + s);
c.disconnect();
```

For the Apache 1.1.1 server, if the specified URL is a CGI program, the response body displayed on the terminal window will simply be the contents of the specified URL, minus any HTTP header fields. This is somewhat puzzling, since that release of the server does not support HTTP 1.1 or the PUT method. It probably should return a message saying "Not Supported." This is what happens if the URL is a static file.

Now let's see how we would read from a URL. Note that

```
//
// Reading from a URL
//
// Now let's construct a new connection object, for reading
// what we wrote:
c = new sun.net.www.protocol.http.HttpURLConnection(new
    URL(args[0]), null, 0);
c.setRequestMethod("GET");
c.connect();
is = c.getInputStream();
if (is == null) throw new Exception("is is null");
dis = new DataInputStream(is);
s = dis.readLine();
System.out.println("response body=" + s);
c.disconnect();
```

The output of this is the contents of the specified URL.

Now let's try a POST. Note that the URL must specify a CGI program, or we will get a "Not-Supported" message from the server.

```
//
// Writing to and reading from the same URL, via a POST
//
c = new sun.net.www.protocol.http.HttpURLConnection(new
  URL(args[0]), null, 0);
c.setRequestMethod("POST");
c.setDoOutput(true);
c.connect();

os = c.getOutputStream();
if (os == null) throw new Exception("os is null");
ps = new PrintStream(os);
ps.println("Here is some data to write");
ps.flush();

is = c.getInputStream();
if (is == null) throw new Exception("is is null");
dis = new DataInputStream(is);
s = dis.readLine() + s.readLine();// just read two lines
System.out.println("response body=" + s);

// Get header data for the fun of it...
for (int i = 1;;i++)
{
  String k = c.getHeaderFieldKey(i);
  if (k == null) break;
  String f = c.getHeaderField(i);
  System.out.println(k + ": " + f);
}
c.disconnect();
  }
}
```

If the specified URL is a CGI program, the response body display is the output of that program. If that program is an echo program, it will echo the output written to the output stream ("Here is some data to write"). If the URL is not a CGI program, the server will generate a "Not Supported" message.

The request methods supported are:

GET

POST

HEAD

OPTIONS

PUT

DELETE

TRACE

You can, of course, simulate the function of the HttpURLConnection by creating your own socket connection and implementing the HTTP protocol yourself, by sending request headers and data and parsing the responses headers.

SMTP, IMAP, and POP

E-mail plays a large role today in business and the activities of any large organization. More information is exchanged by e-mail than by any other means. In many cases, the recipient of an e-mail is not even human; it might, for example, be a list server, to which a person sends an e-mail in order to subscribe to a mailing list. E-mails can also be generated by non-human agents, such as mailing list servers, the most well-known being a product called Majordomo. Besides these mainstream mechanisms, e-mail can also be used to implement a conduit of information in an automated business process. For example, changes to a database object could trigger an e-mail to all "interested parties." In this situation, the e-mail establishes an important link in a system, for change notification. In such a system, e-mail features need to be integral to the application, in particular because a human is not generating (or perhaps even receiving) the messages, so an ordinary e-mail client program cannot be used; the application has to directly interact with an e-mail infrastructure.

Building basic e-mail capability into an application is not difficult. I will focus on Internet e-mail protocols, since those are open protocols that are rapidly growing and will likely subsume other e-mail protocols. These protocols have evolved from very simple mechanisms into a rich set of standards for sending data of many different kinds. The protocols are also extensible, so one can create new kinds of data to send, and even submit the new type as a proposed standard if desired.

The type of data in an e-mail message is called its "MIME" type—for Multipurpose Internet Mail Extension. When a message is constructed by an e-mail program, it is given a header which describes information such as the recipient's e-mail address, the MIME type, and other information. A receiving e-mail program examines the MIME type in the header, and uses that to determine how to view the message content. If the program cannot handle the MIME type, it will usually save the message data to a file and tell the user where the file is. Most e-mail programs also allow you to identify a program to be used to view a specific MIME type. Such programs are called "content handlers," "viewers," or "plugins."

There are three primary protocols for the transport and receipt of e-mail messages within the Internet: Simple Mail Transfer Protocol (SMTP), Post Office Protocol (POP), and Internet Message Access Protocol (IMAP). There are many supporting protocols as well, such as RFC 822, which defines the Internet mail message header structure. I will discuss these protocols very briefly, spending the most time with IMAP, and then introduce JavaSoft's e-mail client package, JavaMail. JavaMail is a large and complex package, so here I will only discuss its main features. It is an extensible framework that can be used to easily build mail functionality into an application, or to construct an entire e-mail client application.

SMTP

The SMTP mail transport standard is defined in Internet RFC 821, and a series of service extension RFCs that follow it. The primary purpose of SMTP is to define how mail messages are entered into or provided to an e-mail server, and how e-mail servers cooperate to deliver a message to the host on which the recipient resides. In practice, SMTP servers are very complex programs, because they must interface between different incompatible mail systems in a way that is transparent to the user. I recently experienced a real-world nonelectronic analog to this: I had to send a letter to Thailand, and I discovered that if I addressed it in English, it would not get to its destination; so I had to find out how to write the address in Thai. To my amazement, the letter got there; and it made me reflect on how we take for granted issues such as the compatibility of mail systems that we deal with. Sometimes the translation is not straightforward.

To send an e-mail to a local SMTP network service, there are two techniques. One way is to make API calls directly to an SMTP library. This library will interface to the SMTP program running on your system. The other way is to send a message directly to the SMTP port on which the SMTP daemon is listening. If your SMTP server is not on your host, you will have to use the second technique. You basically need to send these command lines:

```
HELO
MAIL FROM: <your email address>
RCPT TO: <email address of sender>
<data> (this should be prefixed with a mail header)
     .     (single period on a line by itself)
```

Here is a snippet that does this:

```
// Open connection to SMTP server
String smtpHostName = ...
int smtpPort = 25;// the SMTP standard port
socket = new Socket(smtpHostName, smtpPort);

// Send an email message to an SMTP server
rina = socket.getInetAddress();
lina = rina.getLocalHost();
ps = new PrintStream(socket.getOutputStream());
dis = new DataInputStream(socket.getInputStream());

// Send message
sendline("HELO " + lina.toString());
sendline("MAIL FROM:" + senderEmailAddress);
sendline("RCPT TO:" + recipientEmailAddress);
sendline("DATA");
sendline(...message data...);
sendline(".");

// Close connection
socket.close();
```

This snippet uses a sendline() method, for sending a line and receiving a response in one step, defined as follows:

```
String sendline(String data) throws IOException
{
  ps.println(data);
  ps.flush();
  return dis.readLine();// we should check these responses
}
```

Conceptually it is quite simple, and you can implement very basic mail-sending functionality in this way. Note that no password is required; however, most ISP routers will only grant you access to their SMTP server if your IP address is part of their subnetwork, to prevent every Tom, Dick, and Harry from using their mail server.

POP3

The POP protocol, now at revision 3, is defined in Internet RFCs 1957 and 1939. I will not go into all the details of the protocol, but instead show a basic usage example before proceeding to discuss IMAP, which is a more advanced protocol.

The purpose of the POP protocol is to provide a means for users to access their mail remotely. Originally, Internet e-mail was oriented toward user account names, because most users had time sharing "shell" accounts on UNIX systems, and each account had an e-mail directory associated with it. SMTP routed e-mail to the host that contained the account for the user appearing in the e-mail address, and delivered it to that user's e-mail directory. Using the UNIX mail program, a user could then read his or her mail. POP makes it possible to access your mail even if you are not logged into your account, by providing a remote service for perusal and transfer of your own mail messages between the system containing your account and any e-mail client program that supports POP (Netscape, Eudora, etc.). Nowadays, most e-mail users do not have real shell accounts; they have e-mail accounts instead, so while the user cannot log on and get a shell, their POP client can connect to the system's POP server and transfer their e-mail.

For example, here are the commands that your e-mail client would send to a POP server to query how many messages you have:

```
USER  <user-id>
PASS  <password>
STAT
```

The first two lines log you into the POP server. The last line asks for status information (how many messages). There are other commands to list, transfer, and delete messages.

One problem with POP is that it allows for two levels of operation: one in which some servers can give messages permanent identifiers, which never change over time and are never (or, not for a long time) reassigned, and another in which messages are identified by their sequence in the user's mailbox or mail directory. The problem is that if messages are identified by sequence number, it is easy for a remote client to get out of sync with the mailbox. For example, suppose the client tells the mailbox to delete message 3, and there are 10 messages total. When 3 is deleted, 4 becomes 3, 5 becomes 4, and so on. The client has to know to reorder its own list of messages as well. This works fine until you start the practice (as I do often) of connecting to your POP server with more than one e-mail client. When a client connects, it has to get a list of the messages on the server, determine which it has, and transfer those it does not have. If message identifications can move around, this is very difficult. I have not disassembled their code, but I strongly suspect, based on observed behavior, that programs like Eudora and Netscape actually transfer all messages and compute a checksum to determine which they don't have yet—and then wastefully discard the rest. On the other hand, if the POP server supports the capability to identify messages by permanent ID, the e-mail client does not have to struggle with this ambiguity.

Here is a snippet to ask a POP server how many messages we have; note that I am using my sendline() method again:

```
String popHostName = ...
int popPort = 110;
String userid = ...
String password = ...
Socket socket = new Socket(popHostName, popPort);
ps = new PrintStream(socket.getOutputStream());
dis = new DataInputStream(socket.getInputStream());


// Check for messages
sendline("USER " + userid);
String response = sendline("PASS " + password);
if (response.charAt(0) != '+') throw new Exception("Incorrect password");
response = sendline("STAT");


// Parse result
int r = Integer.parseInt(response.substring(4,
response.indexOf(" messages")));
System.out.println("User " + userid + " has " + r + " messages
on host " + popHostName);
```

IMAP4

The IMAP protocol, now at version 4, revision 1, is a more advanced protocol than POP. It provides authentication, and a richer command set than POP. The Java-Mail model is based largely on IMAP, so I will go over the standard in more detail than for POP.

An IMAP server listens for connection requests on port 143. The standard does not define mail transport; that is handled by SMTP. In the IMAP protocol, client and server streams are asynchronous; that is, when you send a command, you do not, except for some commands, block on a response. For this reason each command sent by the client is tagged, so the server can reference a particular client command in response messages. For example, in the following, the client sends a SELECT command, tagged with the identifier "A391;" and some time later the server sends a response to that command, identifying the original command by its tag:

    Client: `A391 SELECT INBOX`

    . . .

    Server: `A391 OK [READ-WRITE] SELECT completed`

The IMAP protocol defines six standard "flags" that a message can have set. These are:

    \Seen—The message has been read.
    \Answered—The message has been replied to.
    \Flagged—The message is "flagged" for urgent or special attention.
    \Deleted—The message is marked for deletion by later EXPUNGE.
    \Draft—The message is incomplete - i.e. is marked as a draft.
    \Recent—The message has recently arrived; set until notification has been made.

These flags are used by commands such as SEARCH to filter messages based on the flag value. A server tells the client which flags it supports by sending the FLAGS message (in response to a SELECT or EXAMINE command; commands are discussed below), such as

    Server: `* FLAGS (\Answered \Flagged \Deleted \Seen \Draft)`

=When a client first connects to an IMAP server, it can connect as a pre-authenticated client if the server supports client authentication by other means, or a client can connect and enter a nonauthenticated state from which it will be required to log on. Once authenticated, the client can perform a SELECT or EXAMINE command to select a mailbox, and enter the "selected" state. The states for a client are shown in Figure 6–2.

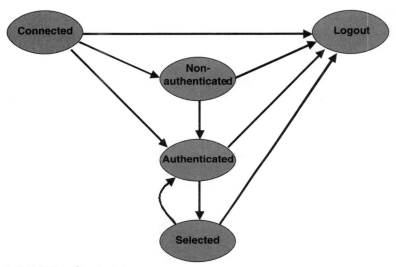

Figure 6–3 IMAP4 client states.

The client commands supported by IMAP4, and the states from which they can be invoked, are as follows

> *Universal*
>
>> **CAPABILITY**—Request a listing of supported features ("capabilities"). The server must indicate if it has IMAP capability, and the types of authentication mechanisms and specification extensions supported.
>>
>> **LOGOUT**—Disconnect from the server.
>>
>> **NOOP**—Merely cause the server to respond, but take no specific action.
>
> *Nonauthenticated:*
> (all Universal commands)
>
>> **LOGIN**—Connect to the server.
>>
>> **AUTHENTICATE**—Initiate a specified client authentication protocol. Certain commands can only be performed if the client is authenticated.

Authenticated

(all Universal commands)

SELECT—Select a specified server mailbox.

EXAMINE—Select a specified server mailbox, but for read-only access.

APPEND—Add a new mail message to the specified mailbox.

CREATE—Create a mailbox.

DELETE—Delete a mailbox.

LIST—List the contents of a mailbox.

LSUB—Return the list of subscribed mailboxes for this user.

RENAME—Rename a mailbox.

STATUS—Request status information for a mailbox, including number of messages, number of messages with the \Recent flag set, number of unread messages, and others.

SUBSCRIBE—Add a specified mailbox to the user's list of subscribed mailboxes, as returned by the LSUB command. The client can use this list to decide which mailboxes to display automatically in its UI.

UNSUBSCRIBE—Unsubscribe a specified mailbox.

Selected state

(all Universal and Authenticated commands)

CHECK—Request a checkpoint of the current mailbox; implementation-dependent.

CLOSE—Permanently remove all messages marked for deletion from the current selected mailbox, and unselect the mailbox.

EXPUNGE—Permanently remove all messages marked for deletion from the current selected mailbox.

COPY—Copy a specified message from one mailbox to another.

FETCH—Retrieve portions of or an entire specified message.

STORE—Modify the flags for a specified message.

UID—Perform a COPY, FETCH, STORE, or SEARCH command, but using unique message IDs instead of message sequence numbers.

SEARCH—Search for messages matching a specified search criteria.

JavaMail

The JavaMail API, represented by packages javax.mail and the subpackages therein, provide a very powerful and flexible framework for adding e-mail capabilities to applications. The framework abstracts e-mail functionality, and separates protocols like POP, IMAP, and SMTP from the application by wrapping them in a service provider layer. Protocols are selected dynamically, depending on the type of e-mail address and selections made by the client. New protocols can be added simply by updating configuration files.

Unfortunately, JavaMail suffers from the deficiencies that exist in the POP and IMAP protocols, in particular that messages are allowed to be identified by message sequence number, and the sequence of a message can change over time. This is not the fault of JavaMail, but rather of the e-mail protocols. The impact is that client design is complicated by the situations that can arise when multiple clients access the same mailbox, or if the client is multithreaded.

JavaMail defines the concept of a "store"—a user mailbox. To connect to a store, you must first establish a session object, as follows:

```
// Create a session
Properties p = new java.util.Properties();
p.put("mail.store.protocol",
p.put("mail.transport.protocol",
p.put("mail.host", <my-email-host>);
p.put("mail.user", <my-user-name>);
p.put("mail.from", <my-email-address>);
Session session = Session.getInstance(p, null);
```

Having created the session, you connect to a store by specifying which kinds of mail protocols you want to use. For example, you might want to access IMAP mailboxes and use SMTP as your mail transport mechanism. To specify this, you get a Provider object that describes each protocol and pass it to the session, as follows:

```
// Query which implementations are available
Provider[] providers = session.getProviders();

// Decide which protocols to use
...you might use a UI, or options panel, for the user to select
   protocols...
Provider[] userChosenProviders = ...

// Pass the list of protocols to the session
for (int i = 0; i < userChosenProviders.length; i++)
session.setProvider(userChosenProviders[i]);
```

Now you can obtain a store object, which you can use to access mail services using the chosen protocols. The store is a proxy for dealing with the mail servers on the specified host (as set by your session). To obtain a store, call the session's getStore() method, and then connect to the store:

```
// Get an store implementation of each protocol. The
// implementations are defined
// in mail.store.protocol
try
{
  Store store = session.getStore();
  store.addConnectionListener(...adapter for responding to
    ConnectionEvent's...);
  store.addFolderListener(...adapter for responding to
    FolderEvent's...);
  store.addStoreListener(...adapter for responding to
    StoreEvent's...);

  store.connect();// the Store implementation will probably
     // display a password dialog
} catch (MessagingException mex) {}
  ...
```

As you can see, once a store is created, it generates events, which you must handle. The event types defined by JavaMail are:

ConnectionEvent—Generated by a store or folder when the store or folder is opened or closed, respectively.

FolderEvent—Generated by a folder when it is created, deleted, or renamed. A folder listener can register with the store, or with a particular folder; in either case, it will receive all events for the folder.

MessageCountEvent—Generated by a folder when the number of messages in the folder changes as a result of an addition or a removal.

MessageChangedEvent—Generated by a folder when a message has been modified.

StoreEvent—Generated by a store to signal alerts and notices to be displayed to the user.

TransportEvent—Generated by a session's transport implementation (i.e., its mail sender); supports status returned by SMTP or another mail sender interface, indicating if a message was successfully sent.

Figure 6–3 shows which JavaMail components generate these events.

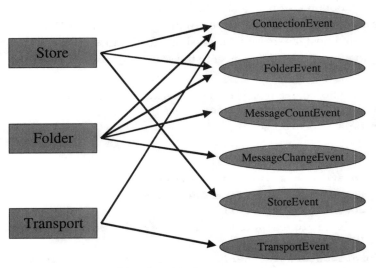

Figure 6–4 Events generated by JavaMail components.

As we saw in the IMAP4 protocol, you must connect to a particular mailbox folder in order to perform certain operations. To connect to a folder in a JavaMail store, first get the root folder for the store using getDefaultFolder(), and then use that object to list folders and connect to specific folders. Connecting to a folder involves creating a proxy object for the folder, from which you can receive events and to which you can issue commands.

```
Folder rootFolder = store.getDefaultFolder();
Folder[] folders = rootFolder.list();
...display list of folders...

inFolder = rootFolder.getFolder("INBOX");
if (! inFolder().exists()) throw new Exception("You don't have
    an INBOX!");
myCurrentFolder = inFolder;

myCurrentFolder.addConnectionListener
(
   new ConnectionListener()
   {
     public void opened(ConnectionEvent e)
     {
       if (e.getSource() == myCurrentFolder)
```

```
                refreshFolderDisplay();// (see below)
        }

        public void closed(ConnectionEvent e)
        { ...folder closed; clear display; attempt to recover by
          reconnecting... }

        public void disconnected(ConnectionEvent e) { ...folder
          disconnected... }
    }
);


myFolder.addFolderListener( ...my FolderEvent adapter... );


myFolder.addMessageCountListener( ...my MessageCountEvent
    adapter... );


myFolder.addMessageChangedListener( ...my MessageChangedEvent
    adapter... );


myFolder.open(Folder.READ_WRITE);
```

The above-referenced refreshFolderDisplay() method could be implemented as follows:

```
protected void refreshFolderDisplay()
{
    Message[] messages = myCurrentFolder.getMessages();
    // This does not actually transfer messages, just as an IMAP
    // LIST command does not transfer messages

    // Now get the header information for each message, so we can
    // display in on the client
    FetchProfile fp = new FetchProfile();
    fp.add(FetchProfile.Item.ENVELOPE);
    fp.add(FetchProfile.Item.CONTENT_INFO);
    fp.add(FetchProfile.Item.FLAGS);
    myCurrentFolder.fetch(messages, fp);// Get the information
                                        // for each message
```

```
      // Display information for each message - this may either
      // fetch the information
      // dynamically, or use information retrieved in the previous
      // fetch() operation
      for (int i = 0; i < myCurrentFolder.getMessageCount(); i++)
      {
         Message m = messages[i];

         Address[] from = m.getFrom();
         String subject = m.getSubject();
         Flags[] flags = m.getFlags();
         Date receivedDate = m.getReceivedDate();
         Address[] recipients = m.getAllRecipients();
         Address replyTo = m.getReplyTo();
         Date sentDate = m.getSentDate();

         ...display this information on a line in the client's
         display...
      }
   }
```

In the above, I first get an array of message objects from the folder; these are lightweight proxies for the actual messages; no message content is transferred in this operation. I then define a message information retrieval profile object, and perform a fetch using this profile—an implementation will normally use this profile to retrieve the kinds of information specified in the profile object for each message, and store that information in the message objects. In this way, the information can be retrieved in one step, instead of going back to the server for each message one by one. Some implementations may implement this more efficiently than others. After this, I then iterate through each message in the folder and display the message information, presumably in a scrollable list of messages. Most likely the user would be able to select a message from this list and retrieve the message content, or the content for all messages could be retrieved automatically.

Note that in the above example, I retrieve each message's flags: the JavaMail predefined flag values are ANSWERED, DELETED, DRAFT, FLAGGED, RECENT, and SEEN; these are exactly the flags defined in the IMAP protocol. User-defined flags are also supported by the API, although not all stores may support this feature.

To actually get the contents of a mail message, you can use the getContent() method. This returns an object of a type that depends on the MIME type of the content. Some of the possible object types returned are:

- Multipart, MimeMultipart—These are nested objects which contain message parts; when you get this, you must handle each nested content type recursively.

- Message, MimeMessage—Use the getContent() method again.

- String

- InputStream

- Image

or potentially any other kind of object for which a MIME type exists. Alternatively, if there is a viewer included with the mail application for the message's MIME type, you can use the data handler for that MIME type:

```
DataHandler dh = message.getDataHandler();
CommandInfo ci = dh.getCommand("view");
Component c = dh.getBean(ci);
...add and show the viewer component...
```

See the Java Beans chapter for more information on data content handlers, and how to create and install viewers.

To send a newly composed message, use the static Transport.send() method:

```
Transport.send(message);
```

The default transport implementation is used to send the message to all the recipients in the message's recipient list. The javamail.providers property file identifies the transport and store provider implementations that are available; and the javamail.address.map property file maps transport address types to transport protocols. For example, the providers property file might contain the line

```
protocol=smtp; type=transport;
  class=com.sun.mail.smtp.SMTPTransport;
```

and the map property file might contain

```
rfc822=smtp
```

This maps an RFC822-style address to the SMTP mail transport protocol. This makes it possible for the Transport class to determine that an RFC822 message requires an SMTP transport, and that the available implementation exists in com.sun.smtp.SMTPTransport, which of course must be in the classpath.

The JavaMail API encapsulates a broad set of e-mail functionality so that applications which need e-mail features do not have to wrestle with protocol details or protocol dependencies. Furthermore, the use of the Java Activation Framework for the incorporation of content viewers makes it possible to support new kinds of content without modifying the application.

LDAP and the Java Naming and Directory Interface (JNDI)

The Lightweight Directory Access Protocol (LDAP), defined in RFC 1777, defines a simplified protocol for accessing X.500-style directory services. The LDAP specification defines the messages supported by an LDAP server. A standard C-language API binding for LDAP is defined in RFC 1823. Netscape has now proposed a standard Java LDAP binding to the IETF. This is the binding used in their LDAP server products (although their own implementation has additional methods not included in the proposed standard).

At the same time, JavaSoft has defined the Java Naming and Directory Interface (JNDI) API, which, in my opinion, obviates the proposed LDAP Java binding, at least for client applications, because it accomplishes the same purpose and more.

JNDI uses X.500 distinguished names to identify entities according to the conventions for representing those as strings, as specified in RFC 1779; for example

```
CN=Frank N. Stein, O=MyCompany, U=Body Parts, C=RO
```

where the keywords preceding the "=" are standardized X.500 keywords, including Common Name (CN), Organization (O), Organizational Unit (OU), and Country (C).

Two primary ways to obtain an object using JNDI are to ask for the object by name using the lookup() method, and to search for it based on attributes using a search method. To find an object by name, construct an InitialContext object, and then provide the name of the object you want to find to the lookup method. For example, to look up a persistent CORBA object with the COS Naming JNDI implementation

```
ORB orb = ORB.init(args, null);

Properties p = new Properties();
```

```
p.put("java.naming.factory.initial",
 "com.sun.jndi.CosNaming.CNCtxFactory");
p.put("java.naming.corba.orb", orb);

Context context = new InitialContext(p);

Object o =
context.lookup("iiop://myhost:900/MyPersistentCorbaObject");

MyCorbaObjectType =
MyCorbaObjectTypeHelper.narrow((org.omg.CORBA.Object)o);
```

In the above, I pass the COS Naming JNDI provider implementation and the ORB to the context constructor as properties. I then perform a lookup, which finds the object, and then I do the obligatory CORBA narrow operation.

Let's look at a sample LDAP search application, first implemented with the Java-soft Naming API, and then at an equivalent application written with Netscape's LDAP API. This program opens a connection to an LDAP server, and searches for all occurrences of the name "Frank N. Stein" within the country "US" and the organization "My Company." Here is the JNDI version:

```
import java.util.*;
import javax.naming.*;
import javax.naming.directory.*;

public class DemoNaming
{
   public static void main(String[] args) throws NamingException
   {
     Properties p = new Properties();

     // Specify the initial context implementation to use
     p.put("java.naming.factory.initial",
       "com.sun.jndi.ldap.LdapCtxFactory");
```

This specifies the JNDI provider implementation to use—in this case Sun's Java LDAP client implementation, which is included with JNDI.

```
     // Specify the directory service's host and port number
     p.put("java.naming.provider.url", "ldap://myhost:389");
```

Above, I specify the host that contains the LDAP server to which I want to connect. Here I have specified the port explicitly; 389 is in fact the default value for the LDAP service.

```
DirContext c = new InitialDirContext(p);

// Specify search constraints
SearchControls sc = new SearchControls();
sc.setSearchScope(SearchConstraints.ONELEVEL_SCOPE);
```

I have specified that it should only look immediately within the country and organization context, and not subcontexts. To cause it to look deeper, specify SUBTREE_SCOPE.

```
NamingEnumeration se = c.search
(
    "o=My Company,c=RO",           // searchbase
    "cn=Frank N. Stein",           // filter
    sc                             // constraints
);
```

Above I have specified a search filter, "cn=Frank N. Stein." Search filters are defined in RFC 1558. The can include complex LISP-like expressions, such as, "(&(objectClass=Person)(|(sn=Stein)(cn=Frank*)))." The "&" indicates that a match occurs if *all* criteria following it within the same parentheses are met; and the "|" means that a match occurs if *any* criteria following it within the same parentheses are met. Continuing with the example, let's now print the search results.

```
// Print name and atrributes for each entry
while (se != null && se.hasMoreElements())
{
    SearchResult sr = se.next();
    System.out.println("name=" + sr.getName());

    Attributes as = sr.getAttributes();
    if (as == null) continue;

    for (AttributeEnumeration ae = as.getAll();
     ae.hasMoreElements();)
    {
        Attribute a = ae.next();
```

```
            String id = a.getId();
            System.out.println("\t" + id);
            for (Enumeration e = a.getAll(); e.hasMoreElements();)
            {
            System.out.println("\t\t" + e.nextElement());
            }
        }
      }
    }
}
```

For comparison purposes, here is the same program, but implemented with Netscape's LDAP API. I have used both of these programs to contact Netscape's Suitespot LDAP server, and both produce the same results:

```
import java.util.*;
import netscape.ldap.*;

public class DemoLDAP
{
    public static void main(String[] args) throws LDAPException
    {
        LDAPConnection connection = new LDAPConnection();
        connection.connect("myhost", 389 /*port*/);

        // Authenticate to the directory, as nobody
        connection.authenticate("", "");

        // Search for all entries with the specified surname
        LDAPSearchConstraints constraints =
         connection.getSearchConstraints();
        constraints.setBatchSize(1);
        // Note: specifies the number of results to retrieve with
        // each request;
        // a value of 0 specifies to retrieve all results in one
        // request.

        LDAPSearchResults r = connection.search
        (
          "o=My Company,c=RO",// search base
          LDAPConnection.SCOPE_ONE,
          "cn=Frank N. Stein",// filter
```

```
            null,
            false,
            constraints
        );

        // Retrieve and display results
        while (r.hasMoreElements())
        {
            // Next directory entry:
            LDAPEntry e = (LDAPEntry)r.nextElement();
            System.out.println("name=" + e.getDN);

            // Get entry attributes
            LDAPAttributeSet as = e.getAttributeSet();
            Enumeration ea = as.getAttributes();

            // for each attribute...
            while (ea.hasMoreElements())
            {
                LDAPAttribute a = (LDAPAttribute)ea.nextElement();
                System.out.println("\t" + a.getName());
                Enumeration ev = a.getStringValues();
                while (ev.hasMoreElements())
                {
                System.out.println("\t\t" + ev.nextElement());
                }
            }
        }

        connection.disconnect();
    }
}
```

An important use of directory servers today is to centrally store an organization's user names with corresponding distringuished names, and possibly digital certificates as well (although the latter is not usually done unless required by security or VPN software). That way there is a central repository for retrieving user distinguished names for comparison with authenticated names. Just because a user presents a valid signed certificate saying they are John Smith does not mean they are the John Smith you think they are—there could be two John Smith's in an organization. The distinguished name stored in a certificate serves to uniquely identify an entity, and if it is possible to look that entity up in an LDAP or other database, then it can be verified and compared, possibly using other information in the database. Common aliases and computer user-id's can be stored as well to serve as a cross-reference.

FTP

The interhost File Transfer Protocol (FTP) is defined in Internet RFC 959. It is a protocol for the transfer of files between hosts, under the control of a client program. An FTP client can initiate the transfer of data between itself and an FTP server, or between two FTP servers (peer-to-peer transfer).

Transfer between the client and server is the mode implemented in most personal FTP client programs that people use to obtain data from FTP sites. Remote peer-to-peer transfer is important, however, for back-end services that need to effect file transfer without user intervention; for example, a program which must periodically make fresh data available from an external system to another application, such as a Castanet Publish tool, or to a data mining application.

Most systems that support FTP have an FTP client program which can be invoked from a script. Using a script however, has the disadvantage that FTP command scripts vary from one system to another, and therefore scripts tend to be somewhat nonportable. A program is also more flexible, and can be integrated with other functions, and even implemented in a transactional manner; this is difficult to do with scripts in a portable way.

I will not go into the details of the FTP protocol here. However, the accompanying CD has an implementation of an FTP client program that has peer-to-peer transfer capability. An example of its use is also provided there. It can be used to remotely effect the transfer of files between any two machines that each have an FTP server running.

SNMP and the Java Management API (JMAPI)

Simple Network Management Protocol (SNMP) is a messaging protocol for building interoperable systems management applications. Such applications are normally in the computing system domain, but the protocol is general purpose and can be used to build any type of application which sends and receives status messages. SNMP is currently in version 3, and is described in RFC's 2261-2265.

The Java Management API (JMAPI) is an application interface for building such applications, and as such has direct support for SNMP. Many of JMAPI's components are redundant (although nicely done) with regard to other Java packages, but some of the unique features include:

- Managed Container Interfaces

- Managed Notification Interfaces

- Managed Data Interfaces

- Managed Protocol Interfaces

- SNMP Interfaces

- Applet Integration Interfaces

The API is still undergoing revision at the time of this writing.

JMAPI is intended for system and server vendors who need to provide operational management features for their products, and want to do so using a browser-based application. However, the API is accessible enough that it can be used by application developers as well to build application management functionality into their applications.

Remote Method Invocation

Remote Method Invocation (RMI) is Java's built-in distributed object protocol. With RMI, you can define objects that export their interface, so that they can be called remotely from other applications in a network. The RMI mechanism handles all the details of packaging method parameters (this is called "marshalling"), sending them across the network to a remote object, unpackaging ("unmarshalling") the parameters at the other end, invoking the correct method with the parameter values, and finally returning the method return result, if any, back to the caller.

Later in this chapter, I will discuss using CORBA from Java. RMI is analogous to CORBA, but it is lighter-weight, and provides a much simpler and standardized model for establishing and managing connections between callers and callees.

All mechanisms of this kind require a facility to handle the packaging of data into a stream. An object-oriented language like Java will require a packaging facility which can package objects. Java's facility for this purpose is the serialization API, which is used by RMI for marshalling and unmarshalling objects. Thus, to understand RMI, we must first look at serialization.

Object Serialization

Java object serialization is a general purpose mechanism for converting an object's state into an encoded form that is independent of the virtual machine context in which the object was created. An object converted in this way can be saved to a file or sent across a network, and later reconstructed in a different virtual machine, to yield a new object equivalent to the original. The process of serializing an object is often referred to as "freezing" it, and the process of reconstruction is often referred to as "thawing."

For an object to be serializable, it must implement the java.io.Serializable or java.io.Externalizable interface. Objects are written to a java.io.ObjectOutputStream and read from a java.io.ObjectInputStream, using the writeObject() and readObject() methods, respectively. First let's discuss the Serializable interface.

There are no methods in the Serializable interface - it is only used as a flag to indicate that the developer of the class intends that users of the class will be able to serialize objects of that type, and can do so without difficulty. Thus, to make an object serializable, simply do this:

```
public class MyClass implements java.io.Serializable
{
  . . .
}
```

You can also do this:

```
public interface MySerializableInterface extends
java.io.Serializable
{
  . . .
}

public class MyClass implements MySerializableInterface
{
  . . .
}
```

In this case, the class MyClass will be serializable, because it implements an interface that is.

To serialize a Java object, use the ObjectOutputStream.writeObject() method. In this example I start with a ByteArrayOutputStream, but you could use any OutputStream subclass:

```
OutputStream anyOutputStream = new ByteArrayOutputStream();
ObjectOutputStream objectOutputStream = new
ObjectOutputStream(anyOutputStream);
objectOutputStream.writeObject(myObject);
```

To unserialize an object, use the ObjectInputStream.readObject() method:

```
InputStream anyInputStream = new
ByteArrayInputStream(objectOutputStream.toByteArray());
ObjectInputStream objectInputStream = new
ObjectInputStream(anyInputStream);
myObject = (MyObjectType)(objectInputStream.readObject());
```

Note that you have to cast the unserialized object to the type you expect or determine it to be, so that you can then make method calls on it; if it is not of that type, a class cast exception will result.

You can write a sequence of objects to a stream, and in that case, you must read them back in the same order you wrote them. When you write an object, all of its attributes—objects and primitive types—are written automatically, except those that are either unserializable or which have a transient modifier. Static attributes are not written either. Giving an object attribute a transient modifier is like saying, "Don't serialize this, and don't save it in any persistent stores." The serialization process is recursive—all member objects (attributes) are serialized, and all members of the member objects are serialized, and so on, except for the exception cases identified. Object instances are not serialized redundantly, however once an object is added during a serialization operation, it is not added again within the same operation, even if it is referenced by multiple components.

If an object attribute is an object type, and the attribute type is not serializable, the attribute will not be serialized with the referencing object. Instead, when the referencing object is reconstructed, the default constructor for the attribute type will be used to provide a value for the attribute. This is a normal behavior mechanism, and is not considered an error. It is an error, however, if a default constructor needs to be called to initialize a transient attribute or nonserializable class, and no public default constructor exists.

Another caveat is that if a class is serializable, but its superclass is not, none of the attributes of the superclass will be serialized when the object is serialized. This is an important point to remember when extending classes and making them serializable. For this reason, you should consider implementing Serializable in all classes you develop which you intend to be reusable, and which might potentially be serialized or passed using RMI in a future application. RMI can only pass object values that are serializable.

Serialized data is "clear"—anyone can read it by writing a simple program. Therefore, if your program saves or transports serialized objects, you must consider the security ramifications of others intercepting those objects. If there are attributes which should not be serialized for this or another reason (e.g., they may be attributes that have no meaning outside of the originating VM's context, such as a database handle or a socket reference), you can either make the attribute transient, or refrain from making the attribute type serializable, and provide initialization in the type's zero-argument constructor.

Another approach for handling sensitive attributes is to encrypt them. You can accomplish this by overriding the default implementation of the object serialization mechanism. This is not as difficult as it sounds, since you can use default behavior for all but the sensitive attributes. The serialization mechanism automatically looks for a readObject() and writeObject() method in the class of each object that gets serialized, using object reflection. If it finds methods with these signatures, it uses them instead of the default mechanisms. Simply implement a readObject(ObjectInputStream in) and writeObject(ObjectOutputStream out) method for your class, and call in.defaultReadObject() and out.defaultWriteObject() at the beginning of your readObject() and writeObject() method respectively—this will take care of all non-transient attributes for that class. Then, in writeObject() implement your own behavior for writing and possibly encrypting the sensitive attributes, and in readObject(), implement behavior for performing an inverse operation, perhaps decryption. The readObject() and writeObject() methods only operate on their own class, and not on superclass or subclass attributes.

The Externalizable interface provides a way for a class to completely take control over the way it is serialized, including all of its superclass attributes. The Externalizable interface has two methods: writeExternal() and readExternal(). If the object implements Externalizable (either directly or through a superclass), its writeExternal() method is called whenever the object is serialized. To reconstruct the object, the class's default constructor is called, followed by its readExternal() method. The writeExternal() and readExternal() methods are responsible for all object attribute serialization, including superclass attributes. If the object does not implement Externalizable but does implement Serializable, the object is written and read using the object stream's default serialization mechanism.

Note that if you write serialized objects to a file, and then make modifications to the corresponding class definitions as part of a system upgrade, the data written previously will be obsolete, and you will probably not be able to read it back in. In general, therefore, serialization should not be used for long-term data storage. I discuss this in the lifecycle and database chapters.

The object reconstruction mechanism automatically loads classes referenced by objects in the stream. It looks for the first non-null class loader on the current thread's stack—normally the class loader of the calling class. Thus, classes are only loaded as needed to represent the objects that get thawed. This is an important feature that is used by RMI, as will be discussed later in this chapter.

How RMI Works

To use the RMI mechanism, you define a Java interface that constitutes the remote interface you want to export over the network. You then implement that interface with a server object class, and use a special compiler ("rmic") to process that server class to generate what are known as "stub" and "skeleton" classes. These classes serve as the glue that links your remote clients with your server objects.

When your client makes a remote call, it is not actually calling the server object; it is calling a method on a stub class that is deployed with the client code. This stub is a proxy for the server object, and knows how to marshall the input parameters onto an RMI stream and send them to the server using the RMI protocol. At the server end, the skeleton code, through a connection set up by the RMI registry service, receives the stream, unmarshalls its contents, and calls the method identified in the stream. Since the skeleton is actually making the call to your server code, it is the recipient of any return value, and it marshalls this value and sends it back to the client as a stream, where the stub unmarshalls it and creates a new Java object to contain its value. This new object is then returned to the calling routine on the client side. Each method invocation on the server object occurs in its own thread. Your remote methods, therefore, must be thread-safe.

Calls made by your server-side code are local or remote, depending on what they are operating on. If they are operating on the the local server object instance, the calls are local. If they are operating on a remote object passed in as a method parameter from a remote client, or if they are operating on a remote object returned from another remote call, the call to that object will be remote—regardless where the associated object actually resides.

Note that the client does not call "new" for a remote object. It obtains remote objects by using the RMI name registry service to get an initial reference, and all subsequent remote references are obtained as return values in remote calls.

Passing or Returning Objects By Reference and By Value

Java passes and returns all objects by reference—a Java object reference is always a local reference, in the context of the local Java VM. There is no remote referencing built into the Java VM.

When referencing a remote server object, an RMI client is actually referencing a local Java object which serves as a proxy for the server object. RMI will return or pass objects "by reference" or "by value." In this context, we are referring to what is marshalled—a remote reference object, or the contents of the actual object. Do not confuse RMI's remote passing by reference with the Java VM's pass-by-reference semantics. The Java VM always passes objects in and out of methods by reference. With regard to RMI, the difference between passing by value and by reference is what is being referenced—a local proxy for a remote object, or a local copy of an the object. Objects passed by value must be serializable so that they can be converted into a stream by the marshalling mechanism, which uses Java serialization.

In a non-remote Java program, when you compare two objects using the "==" operator, you are comparing their identity—that is, you are determining if two references refer to precisely the same instance in memory. In effect, you are comparing their pointer addresses. Since there are no remote semantics built into the Java VM, and Java does not have operator overloading, the "==" operator continues to have this specific meaning even when comparing two references to remote objects. What you end up comparing is the pointer values of the two references, which, for a remote object reference, is actually a reference to the local proxy. Thus, comparing two remote references with the "==" operator determines if the two proxies are identical objects—not if the referenced remote objects are identical, which is probably what you want (in most cases).

Java RMI therefore generates an equals() method for the proxies, and guarantees that this method determines if two remote references refer to the same remote object instance. Thus,

```
remoteObjectA.equals(remoteObjectB)
```

returns true if and only if remoteObjectA, which is actually a local proxy for remote object A, refers to the same remote object (i.e. A) as remoteObjectB—that is, if A and B are the same object. Note that this use of the equals() method carries different semantics than a local equals method, which ordinarily is defined to return true of the contents of two objects are equal. The equals() method for two remote references does not call equals() for the remote object itself to check for the equality of contents of two remote objects—there is no remote call.

In addition, RMI provides a hashcode() method for proxies, so that the value returned by hashcode() for two proxies (stubs) return the same value if the proxies refer to the same remote object.

Basic RMI

To create an RMI application, these are the things you must do:

- Define a remote interface
- Write the server-side implementation of that interface
- Write a server that instantiates and registers that implementation
- Generate stub and skeleton classes, using the RMI compiler (rmic)
- In your client, bind to ("lookup") the remote object
- In your client, make remote calls against the remote object

I will now explain each one with an example.

Defining The Remote Interface

Declare a Java interface that contains the methods you want to export as remote methods. When you declare this interface, extend java.rmi.Remote. The Remote interface has no methods, so this is trivial:

```
interface Server extends java.rmi.Remote
{
public String getStuff() throws java.rmi.RemoteException;
}
```

All remote methods must throw java.rmi.RemoteException. You may want to also throw Exception, because you cannot always anticipate what the actual implementation will throw, and if you only declare your remote methods to throw RemoteException, the implementations will not be able to throw anything that does not extend from RemoteException. When a remote method throws an exception, the exception object is marshalled just like any object and sent back to the client.

Implementing The Server Object

The easiest way to implement the actual server object is to extend UnicastRemoteObject, as follows:

```
public class ServerImpl
extends java.rmi.server.UnicastRemoteObject
implements Server
{
```

```
public ServerImpl() throws java.rmi.RemoteException { super(); }

public static void main(String[] args) throws Exception
{
    System.setSecurityManager(new
     java.rmi.RMISecurityManager());
    Server server = new ServerImpl();
    java.rmi.Naming.rebind("MyServer", server);

}

public String getStuff() throws java.rmi.RemoteException
{
    return "hi!";
}
}
```

In the above example, we create a security manager, because this program will run as an application, so it does not automatically have a security manager unless we create one; and we will be servicing remote clients on the network, which exposes our VM to attack. It is therefore necessary to install a security manager to provide a security sandbox for remote methods to execute in. RMI requires it.

We then create an instance of the server object, and register it with the RMI name registry, so that client programs can perform a lookup to find it and get a remote reference to it. This method call blocks, and so if you want to register more than one object in the same main program you will have to perform the registration in a thread.

The server object must export itself using the exportObject() method. This makes it available to be called remotely. The UnicastRemoteObject constructor does this automatically, as well as other housekeeping things that remote server objects must do, so you will find it convenient to simply extend this class. (If for some reason you must extend another class and so cannot extend UnicastRemoteObject, you can implement the server object functionality yourself by calling the exportObject() method in the constructor for your class, and implementing the hashcode(), equals(), clone(), readObject(), and writeObject() methods, using the UnicastRemoteObject implementation as a guide. Usually you will not have to do this, however, since server objects are usually delegators, and do not typically extend from other classes—but this depends on your design.)

Note also that the main method simply exits after the server object registers itself. You might think that this would cause the entire application to terminate, but it does not, because the program is blocked waiting for incoming requests, and this keeps the program alive. Therefore, you do not have to make any special provisions to make the program block, waiting for requests, as this is taken care of. (This is not the case with CORBA applications, as you will see later.)

To generate stub and skeleton classes, run the rmic compiler, as follows:

```
rmic -d . ServerImpl
```

If your server object class is in a package, you would specify the package root after the -d option, and give the fully qualified name for the server class.

The Client Must Find The Server

A remote client can use the lookup method to find a server object registered with the naming registry. To look up an object, call the static lookup() method in the RMI Naming class, and specify a URL that identifies the registered name and optionally the host of the object you are trying to find:

```
Server server = (Server)(java.rmi.Naming.lookup(
    "//myhost/MyServer"));
```

If the object is on the same host, you can omit the leading hostname, and just use,

```
Server server = (Server)(java.rmi.Naming.lookup
    ("MyServer"));
```

Now we can make remote calls:

```
String s = server.getStuff();
```

Making Callbacks, and Local Object Resolution

In the example above, the remote call getStuff() returns a String. The String class is serializable (it is declared serializable in java.lang.String) so RMI can marshall it and pass it across the network. What the client gets when it makes this call is a copy of the actual string that exists on the server.

If our remote method returns an object whose class implements java.rmi.Remote, the object will be returned by reference—the client will get a proxy (stub) for the actual remote result, and the result object will remain on the server. The proxy can be used to then make calls to the remote object it represents. This is how your remote object methods can return objects that themselves are remote, and so the client does not usually have to call the name registry more than once at the start of a program to get the first reference.

The client can allow the server object to make callbacks to it by passing the server a remote object generated on the client. In this case, the client is sending back a server object, which must itself implement java.rmi.Remote. The main server object (or any other) may use this object sent from the client to make callbacks to the client.

Now suppose a client makes a remote call to the server, and is returned a remote object as a result. The client can pass this same remote object, generated on the server, back to the server, by using it as a parameter in another remote call. What will the server actually get—a remote object, or a reference to its own local object?

RMI does not automatically resolve remote references that are passed back, so the server object's method will receive a stub, even if the actual object represented by the stub exists in the server's VM. Unfortunately, Java 1.1 does not have a mechanism to find the local object. Java 1.2 solves this, by adding a getImpl(RemoteStub) method:

```
class ServerImpl ...
{
    public void doMoreStuff(RemoteSomething  passedBack)
    {
        // passedBack is a remote object stub, even if the
        // corresponding object

        // really exists in this VM; we can use the getImpl() method
        // to get the actual local object, if it is local

        RemoteSomething rs =
            (RemoteSomething)(passedBack.getImpl(passedBack));
        // Now any methods we invoke on rs are merely local calls
        ...
    }
}
```

Most CORBA implementations perform this local resolution automatically. For example, Visigenic uses what it calls "smart stubs," which know how to find a local object corresponding to a remote reference if the local object exists within the process space.

Codebase Issues

If your server program is going to be accessed remotely by client programs (which is normally the case!), and the stub classes are not resident on the client, the machine hosting the server program will have to have a web server running on it, so that the remote classes can be retrieved by the client as needed. This is true regardless of whether the client program is an applet or not, since RMI uses the HTTP protocol to retrieve classes dynamically. (For testing, you can use a file URL—see below.) Note that analogous to an applet security manager, RMI will restrict downloads to the host to which the RMI connection exists.

An important fact to understand is that the RMI registry will only encode a class's URL in a returned object stream if the registry itself obtains the class via a URL (i.e. the class is not in the registry process classpath). If the class is in its classpath, it will not encode the URL, and remote client's will not know where to download the object's class from. Thus, when you run the registry, you should make sure that only the JDK classes are in its classpath. (In particular, do not put "." in its classpath; or, don't run the registry from a directory containing any classes that will need to be transported to clients.)

When you run your server program, you must set the codebase property for the program. When the server object registers itself with the registry, the registry will use the codebase property to find classes for that server object. To set the codebase property for a server program, do something like this:

```
java -Djava.rmi.server.codebase=http://myhost/mydir/MyServerClass
```

If you prefer to test your program without a web server, you can use a file URL instead. On NT, use a URL of the form "file:/c:\mydir\"; on UNIX, use "file:/mydir/". (All forward slashes may work in a later JDK NT release.)

Remote Reflection

You can remotely perform Java reflection on a remote interface to find out what methods it has, and then call those methods dynamically using the reflection API. This is a rough equivalent to CORBA's Dynamic Invocation Interface, discussed briefly later.

If you have a remote reference to an object, what you really have is a stub for that object. You can get the stub class by calling

```
currentClass = remoteObject.getClass();
```

From this class, you can traverse the interfaces implemented by the class, and determine which ones implement java.rmi.Remote, again using reflection. For those that do, you can obtain their method signatures using the getMethods() call, which will return a list of Method objects describing each method, including its name and the types of its parameters and return type. This is enough information to allow you to find the corresponding method for the stub class, and then perform an invoke() on the stub object. This invoke results in a remote call, just as if you had called it statically.

Automatic Invocation

Java is an object-oriented language, but most operating systems are not. Operating systems deal in terms of programs, and to create a Java object, you must first start a program. A Java program has a static entry point—main—which is not object-oriented at all. The main() method is just static code, like in any C program. At some point, the main() method may decide to create one or more objects.

RMI is a protocol that acts on objects, so to use it, your program must create some objects, which must implement one or more remote interfaces. In Java 1.1, you first had to start a program by hand, to give it a chance to create some objects to export, before you could start making remote calls to those objects. This works fine if you have just one program and a few objects. If you have lots of RMI applications, however, and they create a lot of objects, it is impractical, because if the system needs to be restarted (gee, that never happens!), all these programs need to be restarted as well. Further, if there are lots of remote applications, not all of them may be needed at any one time, and it is inefficient to have all of them running, with all their objects created, just waiting to be invoked. It would be better if the programs could be started automatically when their objects are needed. That way, the system administrator would not have to worry about keeping all these RMI programs running.

CORBA from the beginning has had the concept of automatic object creation and activation, which the OMG refers to as a "persistent" object. Java 1.2 adds this feature to RMI, and the component that automatically starts object programs (called server programs) is the object activation daemon, "rmid."

The activation daemon integrates a name service, as performed by the RMI registry, with a new service for automatically starting server programs when their objects are called for.

To be automatically activatable, an RMI server object must have a constructor of the following form:

```
public ServerImpl(ActivationID id, MarshalledObject data)
throws java.rmi.RemoteException;
```

The abstract class Activatable provides some default behavior you can use to build activatable objects. You can extend this class, or you can do it yourself. Here is an example that shows how, for both cases:

```
public interface MyServer extends java.rmi.Remote
{
    public String ping() throws RemoteException;
}


import java.net.URL;
import java.security.PublicKey;
import java.security.CodeSource;
import java.rmi.activation.*;
public class MyServerImpl implements MyServer
{
    public static void main(String[] args)
    {
        URL codebase = new URL("http://myhost.com/myservicedir/");
        PublicKey pk = null;
        CodeSource cs = new CodeSource(codebase, pk);

        // You can provide an initialization object that
        // encapsulates the object's state.
        // For this to work, "AnyObjectType" must be a serializable
        // class.
        AnyObjectType initObject = data;

        MarshalledObject object = new MarshalledObject
            (initObject);
```

Above, I first create a code source; a code source is essentially a code base, with an identity associated with it. (This is discussed fully in the security chapter.) The code source is needed to construct an activation descriptor for reactivating the object later—it is used to locate the object's classes. After this, I create a marshalled object, which is used to initialize the server object whenever it is reactivated. This is an optional step, and is useful for server objects that have a customizable or configurable initialization state, such as the name of a database dataset to use. A marshalled object is essentially an object wrapper for a serialized object; the original object can be reconstituted by calling the marshalled object's get() method.

Below I construct the activation descriptor, and then register this descriptor with the activation daemon.

```
ActivationDesc ad = new ActivationDesc( "MyServerImpl", cs,
  initObject);
MyServer server = (Server)Activatable.register(ad);
// The server is now ready to be activated - you can do so just
// by invoking a method on server, or from anywhere just by
// looking up "MyServerImpl"
// and then invoking a method on the object returned.
}
```

Next I define the constructor that gets called by the activation daemon whenever the object must be reinstantiated. This constructor must have the argument signature (ActivationID, MarshalledObject), and it must export the object to the RMI system, after which it can receive RMI calls.

```
public MyServerImpl(ActivationID id, MarshalledObject data)
throws java.rmi.RemoteException
{
    // If this class extends Activatable:
    super(id, 0);

    // If this class does not extend Activatable:
    this.id = id;
    Activatable.exportObject(this, id, 0);

    // Use the marshalled object data to reconstruct the
    // object's state:
    this.data = (AnyObjectType)(data.get());
}

public String ping() throws RemoteException { return "ping"; }

private AnyObjectType data;

// If this class does not extend Activatable:
ActivationID id;// use this if you want to call inactive() or
    // unregister()
}
```

Java and CORBA

CORBA Overview

CORBA is the acronym for Common Object Request Broker Architecture. CORBA is a standard developed by the Object Management Group, headquartered in Framingham, Massachusetts, a consortium of over 700 companies at the time of this writing. CORBA defines a standard set of protocols and services for building distributed applications using an object model.

CORBA is important because it provides software glue that can be used to tie together different sources of information in an enterprise, regardless what technologies those components are based on. It is a widely supported and open protocol, and implementations from different sources are interoperable. One therefore has a choice of sources, and can choose a CORBA implementation for a platform based on its advantages for that application without worrying that the choice will have to propagate to other platforms. Of course, this assumes that vendor-specific additions and features are used sparingly.

This makes CORBA solutions extremely flexible, and is a reason why CORBA is the architecture increasingly used by third party middleware. CORBA also defines many useful services, including distributed transactions for cooperating middleware, an event service, a name service, and many, many others.

Java and CORBA are extremely synergistic. Java has given CORBA a tremendous boost, because Java solves the problem of code distribution; CORBA solves the problem of intercommunication between distributed components. This means that combined they provide an architecture for creating distributed applications that can deploy themselves and run in a cooperative fashion across a network. It is hard to solve one problem without the other; therefore, CORBA and Java are very synergistic.

ORBs

The central architectural component in a CORBA implementation is the Object Request Broker (ORB). The ORB is the component which manages the communication between a system's CORBA objects and objects on other systems.

Generally, each system has an ORB. This is not a requirement, however. The only requirement is that client stubs be able to bind to an ORB, and that server object adapters be able to bind to an ORB. In practical terms, the ORB is usually within the same computing system; in fact, there may be multiple ORBs within the system. For example, a Java client may have a lightweight ORB, downloaded as part of the applet; this ORB may communicate with the applet host for services, which for a non-applet would be obtained from the execution host.

Netscape bundled the Visigenic Visibroker 2.5 applet ORB with Navigator 4, and Visigenic's server ORB with some of its server products. Thus, if you want to use a more recent version of that ORB product, you must override the built-in Java properties to point to the desired ORB. This is not hard to do, and Visigenic's documentation addresses this issue.

Most CORBA architectures require at least one ORB per machine. However, as in the case of an applet ORB, it may be a component that does not require installation, and which is simply linked with the program (dynamically in the case of Java, or as a shared library with C++).

The Object Adapter

Conceptually an object adapter (OA) is a plug-replaceable component that implements most of the ORB functionality, and can be selected based on OA-specific features and advantages. For example, a vendor may supply two OA's—one that implements thread pooling for requests, and another that implements a thread-per-connection policy. A server object interacts with an OA, which provides specific deployment and activation functionality, and the OA in turn interacts with the ORB, which provides generalized ORB-to-ORB connection functionality for the platform.

Two important categories of OA are the Basic Object Adapter (BOA) and the Portable Object Adapter (POA). The BOA has long been a central component in CORBA implementations. The CORBA specifications define the methods and features of the BOA, but the CORBA Java binding does not include it. This is because it was realized that a new kind of object adapter was needed to satisfy web deployment, and so the Portable Object Adapter (POA) was conceived.

The Java CORBA binding will include POA features when they are finalized. In the meantime, the binding specifies an ORB connect() method, for binding an object to the ORB directly, without invoking an OA. This is intended for binding transient objects. The POA includes an entire object lifecycle architecture for implementing object persistence and different invocation policies. At the time of this writing, POA implementations are still pending.

Stubs and Skeletons

When you write an application with CORBA, you define a remote interface that defines the interaction between a server object and its clients. This specification is written in a language called Interface Description Language (IDL), and is compiled into a set of software modules that implement that interface. While IDL is language-neutral in the sense that the IDL is the same regardless if the ultimate application is in Java, C, or COBOL, the generated modules are in the implementation language. These modules are called the "stub" and "skeleton."

The stub implements the interface between a client and its ORB, and a skeleton implements the interface between a server object and its ORB and object adapter. The interface serves as the linkage between application code and the application-independent ORB module. These components serve similar functionality to the stub and skeleton components in RMI, except that in the case of RMI, the stub is a component that actually communicates with the remote server, whereas with CORBA, it is ORBs that communicate, and the stub is just an interface layer to the ORB.

Repositories

An implementation repository is the ORB's collection of information about an object type, including how to activate it. There is no public API defined for this repository—it is implementation dependent. It is more of a concept defined by the CORBA specification—the features and policies of object activation are specified, but different implementations provide these features and policies in different ways.

In contrast, an interface repository is a collection of information about the method signatures of objects, so that the objects can be introspected and invoked dynamically at run time by remote clients. The interface repository provides a public API for doing this remotely. The API for introspecting and invoking CORBA objects dynamically using the interface repository is called the Dynamic Invocation Interface (DII). In contrast, the "normal" way—invoking an object using statically-compiled stubs and skeletons—is called the Static Invocation Interface (SII).

Information about your objects does not automatically get put into the interface repository. To get something into the interface repository, you have to put it there explicitly, using the interface repository API, or a utility.

Many people anticipate that DII is the wave of the future. Perhaps, but my own feeling is that while DII may be useful for integrated tools, it is too inappropriate for mainstream business applications to use directly. One advantage is the ability to perform non-blocking calls, since DII has this feature. However, since Java is multi-threaded, and it is possible to make multiple requests on a connection or create multiple connections, this advantage is not important in client-side Java applications, because there are other ways to accomplish it that are easily encapsulated, for example, by performing a blocking call in a separate thread. (See "Implementing Nonblocking Calls Using Java" below). In addition, some of the leading implementations (e.g., Visigenic Visibroker and IONA Orbix) appear to have at present some interoperation incompatibilities in DII, especially with regard to the way they implement the CORBA "pseudo-objects" needed for DII—objects that are built-in.

Implementing Nonblocking Calls Using Java

It is easy to implement nonblocking method calls using Java threading. Consider the following sequence, which invokes a nonblocking call which encapsulates the operations of starting a thread to run a method.

```
MyRequest r = new MyRequest();
r.start();        // starts a thread, which performs some long
                  // operation we don't want to wait for

...continue doing other stuff...

...later...when we finally need the results of the async
   request,
r.waitTilDone();// this blocks
...now we continue, knowing the async request has completed...
```

The MyRequest class could extend a base class as follows:

```
public class MyRequest extends Request
{
public void doStuff() throws Exception
{
   ...do some stuff that takes a long time...
}
}

/**
 * Re-usable base class for implementing non-blocking requests
 */
public abstract class Request implements Runnable
{
private Object o = new Object();// a semaphore
private boolean flag = false;

public void start()
{
   Thread t = new Thread(this);
   t.start();
}

public void waitTilDone() throws InterruptedException
{
   synchronized (o)
   {
     if (flag) return;
     o.wait();
```

```
    }
  }

  public void run()
  {
    synchronized (o)
    {
      // Do stuff that takes a long time...
      try
      {
        doStuff();
      }
      catch (Exception ex)
      {
        handleException(ex);
      }

      // Signal we're done
      flag = true;
      o.notify();
    }
  }

  public abstract void doStuff() throws Exception;

  public void handleException(Exception ex)
  {
    ex.printStackTrace();
  }
}
```

How CORBA Sends Information Over the Wire: GIOP and IIOP

In order to send a remote invocation request from a client to a server object, CORBA uses a stream protocol to encode such requests and the returned results. CORBA allows ORBs to use vendor-specific protocols, but requires that all implementations provide a common protocol defined in the standard, called Internet Inter-ORB Protocol (IIOP).

The actual messages used by IIOP are defined in a CORBA standard called General Inter-ORB Protocol (GLOP). IIOP is merely GIOP, with TCP/IP specified as the transport mechanism. Other transports can be used to communicate with GIOP, and as long as a gateway can bridge two transport protocols, two applications can communicate using GIOP over different transports. In practice, IIOP is almost always the protocol used.

All implementations of IIOP must be compatible (i.e., it must be possible to use a VisiBroker-based client with an Orbix-based server object, perhaps even written in different languages), and vice versa. This is possible if the two ORBs communicate using the same protocol, such as IIOP. Here is a taste of the GIOP specification; you do not actually need to know this to build CORBA applications, but it may help to visualize the basic nature of what is being sent when you make remote calls:

```
module GIOP
{
enum MsgType
{
   Request, Reply, CancelRequest,
   LocateRequest, LocateReply,
   CloseConnection, MessageError
};

struct MessageHeader
{
   char magic [4];
   Version GIOP_version;
   boolean byte_order;
   octet message_type;
   unsigned long message_size;
};

struct RequestHeader
{
   IOP::ServiceContextList service_context;
   unsigned long request_id;
   boolean response_expected;
   sequence <octet> object_key;
   string operation;
   Principal requesting_principal;
};

enum ReplyStatusType
{
   NO_EXCEPTION,
   USER_EXCEPTION,
   SYSTEM_EXCEPTION,
   LOCATION_FORWARD
};

struct ReplyHeader
{
```

```
            IOP::ServiceContextList service_context;
            unsigned long request_id;
            ReplyStatusType reply_status;
      };
      };
```

A request consists of a message header, request header, and request body. A reply consists of a message header, reply header, and reply body. The request body contains input parameters according to formatting rules defined in the specification. Similarly, the reply body contains parameter and method return values (CORBA allows out parameters).

The specification defines rules for the representation of primitive types (octet, char, etc.) and composite types (struct, arrays, etc.). These rules define the Common Data Representation (CDR). Thus, the entire format of requests and replies is defined, to the byte level.

IDL

Without providing a detailed treatment of IDL grammar rules, let's look at an example, which has most commonly used features all rolled into one. I will then explain how these features map to Java.

```
module n                      // declare a module
{
    const long c = 3;         // declare a constant
    typedef long T[c];  // declare a new type - an array of three int's
    enum KindsOfThings { A, B, C };// an enumeration type definition
};


module m
{
    struct s                  // declare a struct - analogous to a
                              // C struct
    {
        long i;
        string s;             // an unbounded string with no max
                              // size
        string <5> zipcode;       // a string with a max size
        sequence <char, 10> xyz;    // a sequence of 10 char's
    };

    exception SomethingTerrible// declare a new exception type
```

```
    {
         string whatHappened;
    };

    interface b;              // a forward interface declaration

    interface a               // declare an interface - a remote type
    {
         float m(in float x) raises (SomethingTerrible);// a remote
                                                         // method
         oneway void castaway(inout n::T q);// a non-blocking method
         b getB();                  // uses the forward declaration
         any getWhoKnowsWhat();;// returns an "any" type
         readonly attribute n::T a;// generates a _get_a() method
    };
};
```

An IDL module is a scoping mechanism analogous to a Java package. In fact, the Java binding maps a module to a package. Using modules is optional, just as using packages is optional in Java.

An IDL interface is a declaration of a remote object type. All interface methods are remote methods. An interface is analogous to a Java interface that extends Remote. An IDL interface maps to a Java interface. If the IDL interface has attributes, these map to accessor methods, which are generated to set and get the associated values. A readonly attribute only generates a get accessor. The accessor methods have the form

```
    _get_<attr-name>()
    _set_<attr-name>(<attr-type>)
```

For example, the readonly attribute "a" in the above example would generate an accessor with the signature _get_a(long[3]).

A struct is analogous to a C struct. A struct can have no methods—it just contains elements, which may be primitive types, other structs, and interfaces. When a remote call is made that includes a struct type in a parameter or return result, the struct is passed by value—its contents are marshalled and passed in entirety. This is not equivalent to passing objects by value, however, since a struct has no behavior. A struct maps to a Java class that has no methods.

The CORBA Any type is conceptually a typeless object for representing objects that can be of multiple incompatible types, somewhat analogous to void* in C++. The Java binding automatically generates helper classes that have methods to convert objects to and from the Any type.

IDL has "out" and "inout" parameters, but Java effectively has only "in" parameters. Therefore, the mapping defines holder classes for the built-in types, and generates holder classes for the types you define (except those defined with typedefs). You must use these holder types to pass parameters that can be returned as results. Here is an example using the predefined Int holder type:

```
IDL:

interface MyRemoteInterface
{
    void myRemoteMethod(inout long p);
};


Generated Java interface:

public interface MyRemoteInterface
{
    public void myRemoteMethod(IntHolder p);
}


Java using the remote object type:

...
MyRemoteInterface remoteObject = ...
...
IntHolder ih = new IntHolder(5);
remoteObject.myRemoteMethod(ih);
int returnedValue = ih.value;
...
```

An enumeration type defined in IDL generates a Java class, which contains static instances with names that match the enumeration values. For example

```
enum MyEnumType { A, B, C };
```

results in a class called "MyEnumType," with static instances MyEnumType.A, MyEnumType.B, and MyEnumType.C. Thus, in your Java code you can do this:

```
MyEnumType met = MyEnumType.A;
if (met == MyEnumType.A) System.out.println("All is well");
```

Note that you should not need to create instances of MyEnumType—in fact, you cannot anyway, because its constructor is private.

IDL has a list of primitive types (see table below), which, as you might expect, includes strings. There are actually two string types: one ("string") that consists of 8-bit characters, and another ("wstring") that can handle Unicode characters. The Java binding maps the string type to a Java String object, but if the characters within the Java String are not within the ISO Latin-1 character set, a runtime exception will result during marshalling. Therefore, you should use the wstring type in your IDL if you are writing an application that will process Unicode characters.

Table 6-1 JDL-to-Java Type Mapping.

IDL Type		Java Type
boolean	→	boolean
char, wchar**	→	char
octet	→	byte
string, wstring**	→	String
float	→	float
double	→	double
long double	→	(not supported)
[unsigned]* long	→	int
[unsigned]* short	→	short
[unsigned]* long long	→	long
fixed	→	BigDecimal

*Unsigned values are not range-checked; if the IDL type is unsigned, you are responsible for making sure that large unsigned values map correctly to the corresponding Java signed type.

**Use wchar and wstring for Java programs that may contain nonextended-ASCII characters, since the IDL char and string types cannot handle 16-bit characters, but the wchar and wstring types can.

An IDL "sequence" is a variable length array, with elements all of a single type, and whose length is available at runtime. The Java binding for IDL maps an IDL sequence to a Java array. If a sequence bound is not specified, it is assumed nevertheless that the sequence represents an object that has a fixed bounds, and it is the programmer's responsibility to make sure bounds are not exceeded. IDL also has an array type, whose dimensions are fixed at compile time, and declared like a Java array. An IDL array maps to a Java array.

The RMI community often points out that RMI can pass objects by value, whereas CORBA 2 cannot—actually it can, sort of. CORBA passes structs by value, which are analogous to C structs, and have no methods. A struct only has attributes. However, a struct can have an attribute that is a CORBA interface (i.e., an object, on which remote methods can be invoked. So, it is really not so limited).

I am not sure this limitation is a major drawback for most applications. There may be sophisticated applications (e.g., tools) which can benefit from passing objects that have behavior, but most business applications are message-oriented, and the things that get passed either adhere to a known command pattern or a message pattern. Remote interfaces are used typically as control interfaces for exporting a service and providing transaction control in the context of that service. Passing objects by value is potentially an important capability for toolbuilders, but not for most internal organizational applications. In any event, the issue will be rendered moot with CORBA 3, since it will add the ability to pass interface objects by value, which is addressed in the Objects-by-Value Submission (98-01-18).

Another advantage of RMI over CORBA is RMI's ability to deploy code as needed. However, even this advantage is not typically realized, since deployment is usually addressed explicitly by other techniques.

The most important advantage of RMI over CORBA in typical organizational applications is its simplicity. RMI is a smaller, simpler mechanism, and does not require learning IDL (or how to use a Java-based IDL such as Visigenic's Caffeine) or the intricacies of the CORBA services. If you have something you want to do quickly and economically, you can whip it up with RMI, and not have to go through the trouble of an ORB vendor selection. Of course, you get what you pay for. Following this route, you are likely to forego performance gains made by commercial ORBs, having a range of service implementations to choose from, as well as object management and monitoring tools. In the near future, by using the new class PortableRemoteObject, it will even be possible for RMI applications to directly interoperate with CORBA ones by using the IIOP protocol.

How Does a Program Find CORBA Objects

Normally remote method calls return object references, which you can use to get additional object references, and so on. However, you need a way to get the first object. You can do this in a variety of ways. Here are four:

- Create the object yourself

- Use a persistent reference you stored yourself at an earlier time

- Identify the type of object, and use a service that knows how to create an object of this type

- Look the object up in a directory service of some kind, such as a name service

I will now discuss each approach.

Creating the Object Yourself

To create a CORBA object that you have defined with IDL, assuming you have run your CORBA toolkit's IDL processor and generated stubs and skeletons, you need to connect to the ORB, and create an instance of the object. Here is an example:

```
// Get an ORB
org.omg.CORBA.ORB orb = org.omg.CORBA.ORB.init();

// Construct the object
MyServer myServer = new MyServerImpl();

// Register the server object with the ORB.
orb.connect(server);// Resulting object is not persistent - cannot
             // be automatically activated later just from a
             // reference to it
```

The object can now receive remote calls through its ORB. These calls can originate from within the same process. If you want the object to be available to objects in other processes, you will have to use one of the techniques discussed next to publish the object's reference in some way so other processes can find it.

Using a Persistent Reference

A persistent reference is a reference to an object that can be transported and used across process boundaries. (This is not to be confused with persistent objects, which will be discussed shortly. Here I am only talking about the object's reference.) For CORBA objects, a commonly used way to create a persistent reference is to convert an object reference to a string, store the string or pass it to another process, and then convert it back to an object reference. For this to work, the corresponding object either must exist, or must be a "persistent" object, as discussed under Object Activation below.

Use the ORB's object_to_string() method to convert the reference to a Java String, and string_to_object(String) to convert the String back to a CORBA object reference. The string representation is standardized so that ORBs from different vendors can interpret each other's stringified references.

Identify the Object From Its Type

Some Implementation Repository implementations provide an API to find an object (or an object on any cooperating ORB within a subnet) based on an object's type—in other words the name of its IDL interface. That technique is implementation dependent, and is sometimes used by services that support object replication and create object instances dynamically on demand.

Finding the Object with a Name Service

Object references can be stored in a name service or other kind of service that provides a lookup or search capability for persistent objects. Only objects that the ORB recognizes as persistent can be stored in this way. (Making objects persistent is discussed later.) Using a name service is the most important variation of this technique, and now will be discussed in detail.

Using a Naming Service

In using a name service, the first problem is to find the name service itself. There is a slight problem in that the resolve_initial_references() is the method you call to get the name service. However, this method returns a NameContext object—but you cannot create a NameContext until you have a NameContext obtained through the name service—a catch-22! In other words, the CORBA specs do not say how the initial name context is created. One can imagine that a name service might automatically create an anonymous root context, and return this.

It is up to ORB vendors to provide a means of creating and managing root name contexts for a system. For example, VisiBroker allows you to specify a root context name, and the name service creates this root context automatically when you start it. The downside is that you must specify the root context name as a property when running applications that use the name service—a minor inconvenience. The application component which creates the root context is a Java class (ExtendedNamingContextFactory), so you can use it programmatically if desired.

Example: Finding a Server Object Via a Name Service

Get our local root naming context...

```
org.omg.CORBA.Object ns =
orb.resolve_initial_references("NameService");
org.omg.CosNaming.NamingContext rootContext =
     org.omg.CosNaming.NamingContextHelper.narrow(ns);
```

Construct name service name path for the object we want...

```
org.omg.CosNaming.NameComponent ps =
     new org.omg.CosNaming.NameComponent("MyObject", "");
org.omg.CosNaming.NameComponent path[] = { ps };
```

Find the object, using the name path, and an automatically-generated helper class...

```
// Use the constructed name to locate the object
remoteObject = MyObjectHelper.narrow(rootContext.resolve(path));
```

To use a remote name service, set the org.omg.CORBA.ORBInitialHost property to point to the remote host.

Object Activation

CORBA defines four modes in which object instances may be activated (i.e., instantiated and started). Normally, a server program creates a server object. Thus, in these four invocation models, it is assumed that a server process is invoked to create a server object (a server object is often called a "servant"). The process of starting the server process if necessary and instantiating a server object is called "implementation activation". Activating an object may therefore require the ORB's implementation repository to start a server program which knows how to instantiate the required object or objects.

The four activation modes are:

1.   Persistent process (server)

2.   Shared process (server)

3.   Process per connection ("unshared")

4.   Process per request ("per-method")

Let's look at an example of each mode.

Persistent Process (Server)

In this mode, the server program (process) is started manually. A manually-started server program is referred to as a "persistent server." This is not to be confused with a "persistent object," which is a server object which can be automatically re-created, perhaps by automatically restarting the associated server program.

As an example of a persistent server, I will create a simple ping server that is registered with a name service so that it can be found by a client as long as the server is running.

Here is the IDL for the ping service:

```
module pingservice
{
    interface Server
    {
        string ping();
    };
};
```

Here is the server class, which implements the ping service. Notice that it extends the _ServerImplBase abstract class, which is generated by an IDL-to-Java compiler. (In the past, this generation was vendor-specific, but now it must contain a minimum standard set of Java methods.)

```
package pingservice;
public class ServerImpl extends pingservice._ServerImplBase
{
    public String ping()
    {
        return "ping";
    }

    public static void main(String[] args) throws Exception
    {

        // Get an ORB; here we are choosing to explicitly select
        // Visigenic's ORB
        java.util.Properties p = new java.util.Properties();
```

```
p.put("org.omg.CORBA.ORBClass",
  "com.visigenic.vbroker.orb.ORB");
org.omg.CORBA.ORB orb = org.omg.CORBA.ORB.init(args, p);

// Construct the ping server object
Server server = new ServerImpl();

// Register the server object with the ORB.
orb.connect(server);

// Find the naming service's root naming context
org.omg.CORBA.Object ns =
  orb.resolve_initial_references("NameService");

// Narrow the reference - all objects must do this
org.omg.CosNaming.NamingContext nc =
    org.omg.CosNaming.NamingContextHelper.narrow(ns);

// Now construct a NameService name path for our own ping
// service object
org.omg.CosNaming.NameComponent ps =
    new org.omg.CosNaming.NameComponent
    ("PingService", "");
org.omg.CosNaming.NameComponent path[] = { ps };

// Register our ping service object, under the newly
//      constructed Name Service
// name path
nc.rebind(path, server);

// Now block forever, so this server process remains
// persistent
Object t = new Object();
synchronized (t)
{
    t.wait();
}
    }
}
```

Here is a client that locates and invokes the object:

```java
package pingservice;
public class Client
{
    public static void main(String[] args)
    {
        try
        {
            org.omg.CORBA.ORB orb  = org.omg.CORBA.ORB.init();

            // Get the name service
            org.omg.CORBA.Object ns =
             orb.resolve_initial_references("NameService");
            org.omg.CosNaming.NamingContext nc =
                org.omg.CosNaming.NamingContextHelper.
                  narrow(ns);

            // Construct a name path to the object we want
            org.omg.CosNaming.NameComponent ps =
                new org.omg.CosNaming.NameComponent
                  ("PingService", "");
            org.omg.CosNaming.NameComponent path[] = { ps };

            // Get the ping server object - this should start it
            // if necessary
            Server server = ServerHelper.narrow(nc.resolve(path));
            System.out.println("Bound to server");

            //
            // Now see if we can make calls to our service
            //

            String s = server.ping();
            System.out.println("ping succeeded: " + s);
        }
        catch (Exception ex)
        {
            ex.printStackTrace();
        }

    }
}
```

Shared Process (Server)

A shared server is started in response to a request for a persistent object that that server knows how to create. A persistent object is an object which has a name and can be located automatically (and created if necessary) by an ORB in response to an invocation request. The object is located using a locator service, or by using an object reference obtained at an earlier time (which may even have been converted to a string and stored on disk). Once created, the same server object services all requests made to it until it terminates. If a shared server program does not make provisions to stay alive, it will terminate when its invocation is completed. Normally a shared server arranges to stay alive, as will be shown below.

As an example of a shared server, I will modify the above ping server example, and show how you can make it persistent and register it with VisiBroker's implementation repository (which is called the "Object Activation Daemon," or OAD). Having registered it in that way, a client (also shown below) can request the object at any time—as long as the OAD is running—and (transparently) cause the program that knows how to create the object to be automatically started.

```
package pingservice;
public class ServerImpl extends pingservice._ServerImplBase
{
    public String ping()
    {
        return "ping";
    }


    public ServerImpl(String n) { super(n); }

    /**
     * For creating a persistent server object, as a shared server.
     */
    public static void main(String[] args) throws Exception
    {

        // Get an ORB
        java.util.Properties p = new java.util.Properties();
        p.put("org.omg.CORBA.ORBClass",
          "com.visigenic.vbroker.orb.ORB");
        org.omg.CORBA.ORB orb = org.omg.CORBA.ORB.init(args, p);
```

```
// Get a server object adapter
org.omg.CORBA.BOA boa = orb.BOA_init();// For Visigenic

// Construct the ping server object
Server server = new ServerImpl("MyServer");
// With the Visigenic product, a server object becomes
// persistent if it is given
// a name when it is conctructed. This also makes "automatic
// rebinds" possible.

// Register the server object with the ORB.
boa.obj_is_ready(server);// Visigenic's technique for
                                    creating
            // persistent objects - this is vendor-
                    specific
//orb.connect(server);// Can be used only for
    //non-persistent objects

// Find the naming service's root naming context
org.omg.CORBA.Object ns =
 orb.resolve_initial_references("NameService");

// Narrow the reference - all objects must do this
org.omg.CosNaming.NamingContext nc =
    org.omg.CosNaming.NamingContextHelper.narrow(ns);

// Now construct a NameService name path for our own
// ping service object
org.omg.CosNaming.NameComponent ps =
    new org.omg.CosNaming.NameComponent
    ("PingService", "");
org.omg.CosNaming.NameComponent path[] = { ps };

// Register our ping service object, under the newly
// constructed Name Service name path
nc.rebind(path, server);

// Now don't block - just exit
    }
}
```

This program creates the server object as a persistent object, and gives it a name—both in the persistent object store (via the constructor) and in the name service (via the rebind() method). It terminates without blocking, because whenever the server object is needed the object activation daemon will create the object, using the program that follows.

The program performs the same functions as the one above, except that it does not bother to register the object with the name service. I could have consolidated these, but I kept them separate the emphasize that the purpose of these programs is different—one is to create the object, and another is to restore it.

```
package pingservice;
public class SharedServer
{
    /**
     * For restoring persistent server object, as a shared server.
     */
    public static void main(String[] args) throws Exception
    {
        // Get an ORB
        java.util.Properties p = new java.util.Properties();
        p.put("org.omg.CORBA.ORBClass",
        "com.visigenic.vbroker.orb.ORB");
        org.omg.CORBA.ORB orb = org.omg.CORBA.ORB.init(args, p);

        // Get a server object adapter
        org.omg.CORBA.BOA boa = orb.BOA_init();// For Visigenic

        // Construct the ping server object
        Server server = new ServerImpl("MyServer");
        // With the Visigenic product, a server object becomes
        // persistent if it is given
        // a name when it is conctructed. This also makes "automatic
        // rebinds" possible.

        // Register the server object with the ORB.
        boa.obj_is_ready(server);// Visigenic's technique - this is
        // vendor-specific

        // Now block forever, so this server process remains
        // persistent
        Object t = new Object();
```

```
        synchronized (t)
        {
            System.out.println("Waiting...");
            t.wait();
        }
    }
}
```

The client is the same as in the Persistent Process case. Note that the client uses the name service to make reference to an instance that may no longer exist; in that case, the above program will automatically be called by the activation daemon, recreating the object. This program can perform any object state restoration that might be required, although in the example above there is no state to be restored.

Here is the command sequence that you could give to VisiBroker to tell it to register the persistent object so that it knows how to start the process that creates the object when needed. Different CORBA products will have different means of accomplishing this:

```
start oadj -path \MyImplementationRepository
oadutil reg -i pingservice::Server -o MyServer
    -java pingservice.SharedServer -p shared
```

The first line starts the activation daemon, which provides the persistent object activation service. "pingservice::Server" identifies the repository id —the name by which the implementation repository knows this type of object. "MyServer" identifies the name under which the object was registered as a persistent object. "pingservice.SharedServer" identifies the Java class that contains the main routine to run when starting the server. "shared" specifies that the server be run as a shared server—this affects what the implementation repository does when it receives additional requests for this same object (i.e., whether it will start another process just like this one, start a new process only if the requestor is different, or simply invoke the specified remote method on this object instance).

For the ping service example developed above, which uses the CORBA Name Service, you will also have to start Visigenic's (or any) name service; for example

```
vbj -DDEBUG -DORBservices=CosNaming -DJDKrenameBug
    com.visigenic.vbroker.services.CosNaming.ExtFactory
    Root MyNameLog.log
```

You must run the ServerImpl program to create the server object, and register it with the name service.

```
java -DORBservices=CosNaming -DSVCnameroot=Root
    pingservice.ServerImpl
```

Now try running the client, even though the server has exited.

```
java -DORBservices=CosNaming
    -DSVCnameroot=Root pingservice.Client
```

The client finds a reference to the server object from the name service, but the object no longer exists, so the activation daemon starts the SharedServer program to re-create it. You should get a message that says, "ping succeeded: ping", indicating the client succeeded.

Process Per Connection ("unshared")

In this mode the server program is also started automatically in response to a request for a persistent object. However, each client connection gets its own server object instance and process. The process dies when the connection is closed. Since the server object serves a single client, and is dedicated to the client for the life of the connection, the server does not ever have to keep a list to correlate clients with state; it maintains state automatically for that client between method invocations.

To demonstrate the process-per-connection mode, I will modify the above program so that the server object contains state, which can be shown to persist between invocations. I will add a variable i, which contains the number of times the ping() method has been called, and each call to ping() will return this value and increment it.

Here is the modified IDL. It merely replaces the ping() return type with an IDL long (an int) instead of a string.

```
module pingservice
{
    interface Server
    {
        long ping();
    };
};
```

Here is the modified server class. Notice that it contains a class variable i, which constitutes state information for the object. If the server is run in process-per-connection mode, this value will be unique for each client, regardless of whether it is declared static or not in Java, since each client gets its own VM.

```
public class ServerImpl extends pingservice._ServerImplBase
{
    private int i = 0;
    public int ping()
    {
        return i++;
    }
}
```

All we have to do is change the client so that it loops and calls ping() repeatedly, each time printing out the returned value. It should increase because the server stays connected to us, and can maintain state about our connection (i.e., the current value of the server variable i). If the server object is running in a process-per-connection mode, it will behave the same way regardless how many other clients connect to it, because each clients gets its own instance of the server object.

```
        //
        // Now see if we can make calls to our service
        //

        for (;;)
        {
            int i = server.ping();
            System.out.println("ping succeeded: " + i);

            // Give it a chance to catch its breath!
            Thread.currentThread().sleep(1000);
        }
```

To specify a process-per-connection activation mode for VisiBroker, we can use the oadutil command as in the previous example, but specify an activation mode of "unshared" instead of "shared."

Process Per Request ("Per-method")

In the per-request mode, the server program is started automatically in response to each remote method call on an object. The connection is closed and the process dies at the end of the call. Thus, each request gets its own process. This is somewhat analogous to CGI, in that each CGI request executes in a separate process.

To demonstrate the process-per-request invocation method, we can run the same program as above, but each invocation by the same client will obtain the same value returned by ping() - 0. That is because each invocation results in a new process being started to service the request.

To specify a process-per-connection activation mode for VisiBroker, we can use the oadutil command as in the first example, but specify an activation mode of "per-method" instead of "shared."

Object Cleanup

The Java VM takes care of disposing of Java objects when they are not needed. However, this does not relieve you of the need to consider the disposal of non-Java resources. Sometimes you even have to think about Java object disposal, and make sure to set references of unused objects to null so they can be collected (or use Java 1.2's weak reference facility, which provides a way to define caching references which do not inhibit garbage collection).

CORBA objects are not Java objects. However, from a Java program, you access them using Java objects. This means that you have to make sure you follow CORBA's guidelines for collection of CORBA objects. Also, since a CORBA ORB keeps references to the objects that are exported, it will have a list that references your Java object proxies. If you do not inform CORBA when you are done with its objects, it will never release your Java objects.

If you used the ORB.connect() method to connect to the ORB, instead of an OA adapter bind() or other method, you should use the disconnect() method on the object. If you connected through an OA with activate_object() or a generated helper method, you should call the OA's deactivate_object() method (some implementations use the name deactivate_obj()) to dispose of a server object. This is needed to release ORB resources associated with the object—Java GC will not release these, since they are owned by another object (the BOA or ORB).

When a shared policy is used, you normally want the server program (process) to continue execution after a client connection closes so that other connections can access the server object without having to reinstantiate it. When an unshared policy is used, you want the server process to terminate when the client connection closes. When a per-method policy is used, you want the server process to terminate when the method invocation completes.

In the preceding examples, I use the technique of blocking in a wait() call, to force the server program's main thread to suspend itself so that the process will remain and be ready to service incoming requests. There are no provisions for getting the process to terminate based on the invocation policy. Since the actual implementation of the object persistence mechanism is OA-specific, different products have different ways of providing process termination. The Visigenic BOA provides the method impl_is_ready(), which can be called at the end of the server program. It forces the program to block, and at the same time implements the appropriate process termination, depending on the activation policy that was used. For example, if instead of

```
Object t = new Object();
synchronized (t)
{
    System.out.println("Waiting...");
    t.wait();
}
```

we use

```
boa.impl_is_ready();
```

the server program will terminate appropriately, depending on the policy under which it was activated.

Connection Models

There is considerable variation in the client and server connection models provided by CORBA products. There are two predominant approaches to client connection management, and two for server connections. For client connections, these are:

Multiplexed use of connection on client—Multiple client threads can make simultaneous requests across a single connection. Requests from multiple threads get forwarded to the server, even if pending requests on other threads have not completed. Thus, each client thread does not need its own connection. Since a single socket connection is used, this also results in less communication resources being used overall.

Single blocking call per connection—A connection can only process one request at a time. Requests made by other threads block until the request currently being processed is completed.

For persistent server, shared server, and process-per-connection ("unshared") servers, the predominant approaches are:

Thread pool on server—Each incoming request is assigned a thread from a thread pool. This avoids the overhead of thread creation and destruction, and reduces the number of thread resources that are needed if there are many client connections.

Thread per connection on server—Each client connection is assigned a thread that is dedicated to it for the duration of the connection, and this thread is used to process all requests on that connection. This approach is not scalable for lots of client connections.

It is up to the implementation to provide any or all of these models (or alternative models), and currently both Iona and Visigenic provide all of these approaches.

CORBA also provides a facility for defining a Connection context, which allows a shared server to be used for transactional applications. This permits the reestablishment of transaction context from one method call to the next if an unshared activation policy is not being used. This feature is used by the CORBA Transaction Service.

Object Management

Most CORBA implementations now provide facilities for object management. Ideally you should not have to do any object management. You need to if:

- Objects need to be moved, to balance load.

- Objects need to be replicated, and require dynamic assignment to requests and fail-over capabilities.

- Objects can get stuck: deadlocked, or hung.

- Objects need to be checked (e.g., if they are running or not).

- Objects need to be created manually for replication or for starting.

- Objects need to be installed and uninstalled.

- Objects need resources assigned to them, and those assignments need to be configured or moved if the objects are moved.

- Objects need to be configured (e.g., startup parameters, properties, etc.)

- You need to collect statistics on object utilization.

Since most of these conditions exist in a real system, you will probably need object management tools. If a site has many CORBA objects, a common facility for monitoring and configuring them is essential. The facility should conveniently identify which objects are installed, their types (repository IDs) and published names, which are replicatable, each object's activation style, and system resources such as CPU usage, memory, and communication sockets currently used by each.

Some products provide features that include automatic reconnection to an alternate server if a connection is lost due to system failure (failover), and also object replication and automatic selection based on use or a round-robin policy for load balancing. Object migration—the ability to move objects dynamically—is addressed by the CORBA Lifecycle service, and has been implemented by some vendors.

Using CORBA with Castanet

Castanet has a sandbox security model, just like an applet, and so it will need a server-side proxy to forward requests to other hosts if it needs services from server objects residing on hosts other than the transmitter host, and to proxy server objects that the channel exports (for callbacks). A problem is that a channel is not (necessarily) an applet, and so the ORB.init(Applet) method cannot be used, and even if it could (if the channel were an applet), the applet would not have a proper codebase which the applet ORB could use to locate the host of origin—where the proxy is. For example, Visigenic's proxy is called "gatekeeper," and Visigenic's applet ORB attempts to locate the gatekeeper.ior file in the codebase directory.

Different CORBA products will have different approaches to the host access problem. If you are using VisiBroker, there are two solutions:

1. Sign the channel. This eliminates the security sandbox, allowing the channel to contact other hosts. If your CORBA channel does a bind(), run VisiBroker's OSAgent daemon in the same subnet where the channel is deployed, or set the ORBagentAddr property to point to the host where the OSAgent is running, and so the gatekeeper will not be necessary (unless you need to penetrate a firewall).

2. Tell the channel program where the gatekeeper is. Note that the gatekeeper provides redirection to the OSAgent for binding (locating); for redirection from the transmitter host; and for firewall penetration using HTTP.

```java
public static void main(String[] args)
{
    String myGatekeeperHost = "<your-host's-IP-address>";
    java.util.Properties props = new java.util.Properties();
    props.put( "ORBagentAddr", myGatekeeperHost);
    props.put( "ORBagentPort", "14000" );
```

```
props.put( "ORBdebug", "true" );
props.put( "GATEKEEPER_ADDR", myGatekeeperHost );
props.put( "ORBgatekeeperIOR",
     "http://" + myGatekeeperHost + ":15000/gatekeeper.ior");
org.omg.CORBA.ORB orb = org.omg.CORBA.ORB.init( args, props );
...now do a bind(orb, "ServiceName");
```

IONA has a proxy product as well, called Wonderwall. Similar to gatekeeper, it provides IIOP redirection, allowing applets to access CORBA services from other hosts. In addition, it also acts as a firewall which provides IIOP tunneling based on an administator-chosen list of which objects and methods to make visible to the external network.

Note that the Castanet transmitter is available for Solaris, NT, and AIX (there may be others when you read this; check with Marimba), and so if your server objects are on some other architecture, you will either need a proxy such as gatekeeper to forward your ORB requests, or you will need a signed channel that can reach hosts other than the transmitter host. See the security chapter for an explanation of how to create a signed channel.

Distributed Transactions and Messaging

The increased use of extranets and organization-wide networks has led to attempts to integrate data sources and applications in place within those organizations, to create a larger integrated application framework and improve information flow. Departments can often justify keeping existing processes and data as they are, because they are proven and trusted, and operations depend on them. Therefore, instead of fixing systems that are not broken, wider integration may mean tying together these systems as they are.

Nowadays, most systems are transactional and multiuser. Integrating two transactional systems, however, is not merely a matter of getting data from one system and sending it to another—the integrated process must be transactional for the same reasons that the individual systems are transactional. Transactional operation provides quality of service characteristics that are critical to enterprise level applications, including atomicity, data integrity and isolation during a transaction, and usually recoverability after failure.

Integrating separate transactional systems requires that the separate systems are designed such that they can be integrated. Proprietary systems that support distributed transactions provide their own mechanisms for implementing a cross-system two-phase commit protocol; in order for such systems to cooperate in multi-system transactions in a nonproprietary way, they must open up their mechanisms for performing transaction control.

Many open transaction protocols exist. Predominantly used is the X/Open XA standard, developed by the X/Open consortium. This protocol is used by many popular transaction managers including such as BEA Systems' Tuxedo. Systems that have components called "transaction managers" which support this protocol can participate in integrated transactions, to tie together separately developed applications.

As discussed earlier, integration of separate applications can be approached using a transactional approach or a messaging approach. Even if a messaging approach is used, often the act of sending or receiving a message is incorporated into a distributed transaction. Thus, the reliable nature of the messaging operations (which may themselves have a local transaction context) cooperates with a reliable distributed transaction mechanism that ties together other components that do not use messaging, to create a more comprehensive end-to-end reliable system. For this to be possible, the messaging system itself (as opposed to the applications using it) must be able to participate in distributed transactions.

End-to-End QOS

Quality of service (QOS) refers to the reliability and performance characteristics of a system. These are often the features that distinguish two implementations of a standard. For transactional and messaging systems, quality of service considerations are very similar, and can be grouped as follows.

- Durability—The effect of a committed transaction is persistent, or at least is recoverable. Includes loss of operations performed while connected, and loss of operations performed while not connected.

    - Prevention of repeat operations or duplicates.

    - Correctness (garbled messages or data are detected or prevented)

    - Detection and appropriate notification of unresolved problems; no unnecessary notification if problems are handled by the system.

- Atomicity—Either all aspects of a transaction complete, or none of it completes. this is very important for ensuring correct results if a system fails, needs to be rolled back and redone, or recovered. Atomicity can apply to:

    - A send or store operation

    - A receipt or retrieve operation

    - An acknowledgment or receipt or storage

- An end-to-end send or store, receipt or retrieval, and acknowledgment of receipt or retrieval (atomicity of this is not typical for messaging systems, by definition)

- Ordering—Preservation of sequence. Can the application assume that the order of records or messages it obtains from the system represents the order in which they were actually created or sent? Ordering can be relative to:

  - A particular sender or writer. For example, if you receive two messages from a sender, you can be sure that the second message was actually sent subsequent to the first.

  - All senders or writers, and universal time. For example, if A and B both send messages to C, and at the same time send the same messages to D, will C receive all messages in the same sequence that D does? And if A's messages are sent a moment before B's, will both C and D receive A's messages before B's?

- Throughput—How quickly does data pass through the system, in real time?

- Latency, delay—either to send, or to send and receive acknowledgment of receipt; and time to establish a connection.

- Responsiveness to priority

Java Message Service

Java Message Service (JMS) was developed by JavaSoft, IBM, Modulus, NEON, OpenHorizon, Oracle, TIBCO, and Vitria, to provide a common Java interface to the messaging products offered by those vendors and others. A messaging middleware vendor wishing to provide a Java interface implements a provider layer which plugs into the JMS application layer, thereby making the underlying system specifics transparent to the calling application. Further, because JMS specifies standard protocols for transaction and messaging services, JMS can bridge message services transparently—even those for which there is no JMS provider implementation. JMS is designed for Java 1.2, and a 1.1-compatible version is not planned.

Point-to-Point vs. Publish/Subscribe

JMS supports two models of operation: Point-To-Point (producer/consumer) and Publish/Subscribe (broadcast). In the point-to-point model, applications send and extract messages from named queues. In the publish/subscribe model, applications publish messages to named "topic" channels, and listen asynchronously for arriving messages on those topics.

Message producers and consumers are independent—a sender or publisher does not need a receiver or subscriber to be connected in order to send or publish messages, and a receiver or subscriber can request or wait for messages even if there are no senders or publishers connected.

Sessions

A JMS session represents a connection to an underlying messaging service provider. A session provides:

- An interface for creating messages.

- An interface for creating message producers (QueueSenders and TopicPublishers) and message consumers (QueueReceivers and TopicSubscribers).

Message delivery from a session to its message listeners (discussed below) is serialized for the session's listeners. Therefore, consumers implemented as listeners can safely share session resources. To implement a producer and consumer within a single client, use separate sessions.

A transactional session maintains a local transaction context for all operations on the session, including its producers and consumers.

Transactions and Quality of Service

A session may be transactional; that is, queue and publish/subscribe operations can participate in local transactions. Any unacknowledged messages received during the course of the transaction will be redelivered if the transaction is rolled back, or acknowledged automatically if the transaction is commited, and any messages sent will be discarded and not actually sent if the transaction is rolled back, or dispatched if the transaction is committed. A transactional session always has a current transaction in progress—you do not have to explicitly start a transaction.

If the JMS provider layer supports Java Transaction Service (JTS) distributed transactions (discussed later, and also under Enterprise JavaBeans in the Java Beans chapter), the JMS system can transparently incorporate its JMS transactions into larger JTS distributed transactions, under the control of XA transaction management. The application code is not specifically affected by this choice, except that if a session is transactional, and the server is using JTS, then the JMS application should refrain from calling commit or rollback on its JMS transaction. Doing so will result in an exception.

Thus, while JMS transactions are like any other simple transaction on a single resource, and define an atomic unit of work for their own resources, a JTS transaction is a composite unit of work that combines several simple transactions across the same resource or multiple resources into one transaction. In contrast, a JMS transaction applies only to the session of which it is a part, and does not extend to other message consumers or producers, even if they make use of the same messages. JTS or underlying XA support is not required by a JMS provider implementation.

JMS defines these message delivery modes:

> PERSISTENT—Guaranteed delivery. Messages will be delivered at least once, and after a receiver acknowledges it, never again to that receiver.

> NON_PERSISTENT—Delivery is not guaranteed. The message will be delivered at most once.

If a JMS messaging session is transactional, the session automatically acknowledges all messages received upon a commit. Non-transactional sessions may use one of these modes for acknowledgment:

> AUTO_ACKNOWLEDGE—Message receipt is acknowledged automatically by the system when a message is received.

> CLIENT_ACKNOWLEDGE—Message receipt is not automatically acknowledged, and applications must explicitly acknowledge them. When a message is acknowledged, all messages received before it are also acknowledged.

A session maintains consumed messages until they have been acknowledged by the session, so unacknowledged consumed messages will be redelivered after a rollback. This is the primary purpose of acknowledgment. There is no notification back to the sender of a message when a message is acknowledged; it is merely a way to notify the messaging system that the message has been received, processed, and will never need to be redelivered.

Message Filtering

Both the point-to-point model and publish/subscribe model support automatic message filtering, in which the underlying messaging system selects incoming messages based on the values of header fields and application-specific message property values. The header fields defined for JMS messages are:

JMSDeliveryMode—Whether delivery is PERSISTENT or NON_PERSISTENT.

JMSPriority—The urgency of the message; 0 is lowest, 9 is highest; a value greater than 4 is considered urgent.

JMSMessageID—A unique ID that identifies a particular message after it has been sent. This field is set by the underlying system when a message is sent, and can subsequently be read by the sender or receiver.

JMSCorrelationID—Optionally used by message senders in an application-specific way to refer to other messages.

JMSType—An application-specific message type. In general, all messages should have this set, since some messaging providers require that each message have a type. However, JMS does not require any particular types be used.

Message properties are defined by the application, and are set by the sender or publisher by creating a Java Properties object and calling the message's setJMSProperties() method:

```
Properties properties = new Properties();
properties.put("Region", "North America");
message.setJMSProperties(properties);
```

At the receiving end, the JMS system extracts the properties set by the sender, and makes them available for filtering.

Message filters, called "selectors," are expressed using a subset of SQL92, and can make direct references to message header fields or message properties. Filters cannot reference data included in the message body itself. As an example of a selector, suppose the message has a property called "Region," and we are only concerned with urgent messages—those with priorities greater than or equal to 5. We could then filter out all messages that do not meet the criteria specified in our selector expression:

```
String selector = "(Region = 'North America') AND (JMSPriority >= 5)";
```

is a selector for selecting only those messages in which the "Region" property is equal to "North America" and the message priority is greater than or equal to 5. When we create a point-to-point queue receiver, we pass in the message selector String. For example, a queue receiver could be created with this selector, using

```
QueueReceiver receiver = session.createReceiver(queue, selector);
```

To create a filtered topic subscriber, pass in the message selector String in a manner analogous to the queue selector:

```
TopicSubscriber subscriber = session.createSubscriber(topic,
  selector);
```

A more complete example that includes this selector is shown below.

Message Content Types

The message content type variants supported by JMS are:

StreamMessage—A stream of data, consisting of supported data types. Data can be retrieved in the sequence written. Retrieval of data can be done using type-specific methods, or using the general object retrieval method readObject().

MapMessage—Named values can be stored and written, using type-specific methods, or using the methods setObject(String name, Object value) and getObject(String name).

TextMessage—For text-based messages, including text consisting of XML.

ObjectMessage—For messages containing a serialized Java object.

BytesMessage—For messages that must have specific byte and numeric formatting in order to interoperate with an external messaging system. The methods specify the exact format in which data values are written and read.

An example

Let's look at an example of a point-to-point queue which accepts product orders.

```
import javax.jms.*;

javax.naming.Context nameContext = new
    javax.naming.InitialContext();
Queue orderQueue = (Queue) nameContext.lookup("OrdersQueue");
QueueConnectionFactory factory =
    (QueueConnectionFactory)nameContext.lookup("MyJMSProvider");
```

The above code performs a JNDI lookup of the orders queue and the local JMS provider. The orders queue object encapsulates access to the orders queue as implemented by the message service being used. The factory object encapsulates access to connection creation to the message service. Once we have the factory, we can use it to create a queue connection, from which we can in turn create a queue session.

```
QueueConnection connection = factory.createQueueConnection();
QueueSession session =
    connection.createQueueSession(false,
    Session.AUTO_ACKNOWLEDGE);
```

The boolean parameter in createQueueSession(boolean, int) is a flag indicating whether the session should be transactional or not. If we had wanted this session to be transactional, we would have specified instead in the last line "...create-QueueSession(true, ...)".

From the session, we can create a sender object specific to the queue we are interested in:

```
QueueSender sender = session.createSender(orderQueue);
```

We now have a sender object we can use to send messages to the orders queue. Here I create a map message containing the attributes needed for a customer product order, and then dispatch the message to the queue using the send() method:

```
MapMessage orderMessage = session.createMapMessage();
orderMessage.setString("CustomerName",  "Big A. Spender");
orderMessage.setString("ProductName",  "L. V. Wallet");
orderMessage.setDouble("Price", (double)(340.00));
sender.send(orderMessage);
```

The basic scenario is shown in the Figure 6–5.

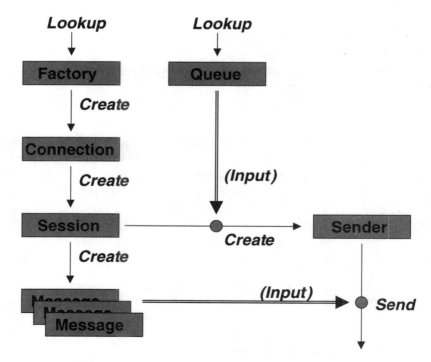

Figure 6–5 Sending a point-to-point message.

On the receiving end, the receiving application would use the same procedure to connect to the orders queue, and then instead of creating a sender object it would create a receiver, and issue a receive() request whenever it wants another message from the queue. The receive() request blocks until a message arrives.

```
QueueReceiver receiver = session.createReceiver(orderQueue);
Message message = receiver.receive();
```

Thus, the receiving application connects in the same way as the sending application, and the only difference is that the receiver uses a receiver object and calls a receive() method.

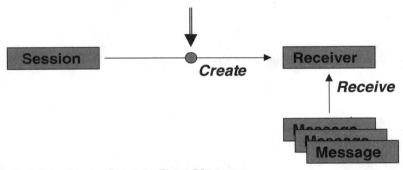

Figure 6–6 Receiving a Point-to-Point Message

If the receiving application wants the messaging system to automatically filter messages for it, it can provide a selector expression when it creates the receiver:

```
String selector =
"(Region = 'North America') AND (JMSPriority >= 5)";
QueueReceiver receiver =
session.createReceiver(orderQueue, selector);
Message message = receiver.receive();
```

Using the publish and subscribe broadcast model is very similar to using the point-to-point queueing model. The main difference is that instead of using a queue, we use a "topic" to publish and subscribe to:

```
javax.naming.Context nameContext = new
javax.naming.InitialContext();
Topic orderTopic = (Topic) nameContext.lookup("OrdersTopic");
```

```
TopicConnectionFactory factory =
     (TopicConnectionFactory)nameContext.lookup("MyJMSProvider");
TopicConnection connection = factory.createTopicConnection();
TopicSession session =
     connection.createTopicSession(false,
Session.AUTO_ACKNOWLEDGE);
```

To publish to this topic, create a publisher object:

```
TopicPublisher publisher =
  session.createPublisher(orderTopic);
```

Now we can use this publisher object to publish messages to the topic, as follows:

```
MapMessage orderMessage = session.createMapMessage();
orderMessage.setString("CustomerName",  "Big A. Spender");
orderMessage.setString("ProductName",  "L. V. Wallet");
orderMessage.setDouble("Price", (double)(340.00));
publisher.publish(orderMessage);
```

Figure 6–7 shows the basic scenario.

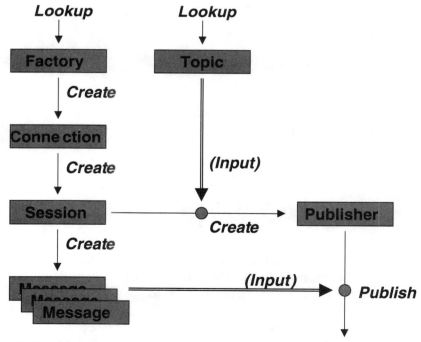

Figure 6–7 Publishing a broadcast message

Other applications can subscribe to this topic by creating a subscriber object for the topic:

```
TopicSubscriber subscriber =
    session.createSubscriber(orderTopic);
```

Having subscribed is not sufficient, however. You must define a callback for the JMS system to call when topic messages actually arrive. To do this, you create a message listener—an adapter object which implements the JMS MessageListener interface—and register it with the subscriber object. Whenever a message arrives for the subscribed topic, the listener's onMessage() handler method is called:

```
subscriber.setMessageListener
(
    new MessageListener()
    {
        void onMessage(Message orderMessage)
        {
            // Retrieve data from message
            String customerName =
                orderMessage.getString("CustomerName");
            String productName =
                orderMessage.getString("ProductName");
            double price = orderMessage.getDouble("Price");
            // Respond to message with actions...
        }
    }
);
```

This is depicted in Figure 6–8.

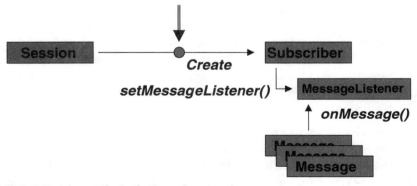

Figure 6–8 Being notified of a broadcast messagearrival.

QueueReceivers can also add message listeners in the same way, for receiving messages asynchronously, instead of calling the receive() method, which blocks. There is also a receiveNoWait() method which does not block, and returns null if there is no message. If you need to control the flow of messages, the connection has methods stop() and start() to temporarily pause and resume incoming message delivery to the associated session's receivers and listeners.

If the application wishes the messaging system to filter topic messages automatically, it can pass a selector expression to the session when it creates the subscriber:

```
String selector =
"(Region = 'North America') AND (JMSPriority = 5)";
TopicSubscriber subscriber =
  session.createSubscriber(orderTopic, selector);
```

CORBA Event Service

The CORBA Event Service defines a mechanism for the asynchronous dispatching of messages between multiple senders ("suppliers") and multiple interested parties ("consumers"). Unfortunately, the specification does not specify a required quality of service (QOS), so users of the service cannot be sure that if they change vendors, their application will still have the same performance or reliability characteristics. Primary QOS considerations include durability, response time, and the preservation of message order. The service does not require atomicity, and some subscribers may receive messages while others do not. Loss of messages can occur, for example, if an implementation uses queues, and the queue size is reached, causing messages to be discarded—either the oldest or the newest, depending on the implementation. The event service specification leaves it completely up to the vendor to address or not address such QOS issues.

With a minimal QOS implementation, the Event Service is therefore useful mainly as a non-critical notification or advisory system; a design cannot rely on it for correctness, unless acknowledgment and other required QOS features are added by the application. Still, this may be sufficient for many information delivery applications or applications that use notification as a "hint" and do not rely on it for correctness. Also, the Event Service is here today, and Java implementations of it are available from the major CORBA vendors.

The Event Service defines two models: "push" and "pull". They are really the same, in that one is a negative analog of the other. In the push model, a consumer sits and waits for units of work to arrive. In the pull model, it sits and waits for requests for work. In either model, there can be any number of suppliers and consumers. You decide which model you want to use, and then define a supplier and a consumer using interfaces for that model. For example, if you choose a push model, you define a push supplier and a push consumer. If you choose a pull model, you define a pull supplier and a pull consumer.

You can create an event service object in a separate process, or embed its creation in a server program that uses the service. Event channels can be named, but they don't have to be, and if you create a channel in your program, you can just use its reference, instead of having to obtain it by name.

The mechanism for finding event channels is not defined. However, since an event channel is an object, you can register it with the CORBA Name Service, and use that service to look it up from other processes.

Event channels can either be typed or untyped. An untyped event channel dispatches objects of type Any, and your application must convert these objects to the expected application type. You can also define typed event channels, in which the channel type is defined using IDL.

An important issue is how many channels to create. Should you create a separate channel for every kind of event or message in your system, and let clients subscribe to very specific channels? Or should you create a smaller number of generic channels, and effectively broadcast event notification on those channels, and require clients to listen to those for the ones they are interested in? The answer to this depends partly on the implementation of the event service, and how much overhead is involved in creating a channel. In general, you probably do not want to create a separate channel for every kind of event, but you may want to create channels for specific types of important events, to provide notification of application-level events, as described in the Database chapter.

Example: A Loan Approval Application

To demonstrate the Event Service, I will create a Loan object, and allow interested parties to register to be notified when the loan is approved. It is assumed that a fallback notification mechanism also exists, possibly less timely but more reliable, perhaps in the form of an approval notification checklist. The event notification is therefore an auxiliary mechanism, used to alert people at the very moment of approval. Here is the code:

```
import org.omg.CosEventComm.*;
import org.omg.CosEventChannelAdmin.*;
import org.omg.CORBA.SystemException;

import com.visigenic.vbroker.orb.*;
import com.visigenic.vbroker.services.CosEvent.*;
```

```
public class SingleProcessTest
{
    /**
     * Main program, for demonstrating this. This program creates
     * an instance of a Loan, and
     * an instance of an InterestedParty.
     */
    public static void main(String[] args)
    {
        org.omg.CORBA.ORB orb = org.omg.CORBA.ORB.init();
        org.omg.CORBA.BOA boa = orb.BOA_init();

        // Create the event channel right here - that way we won't
        // have to give it a name and expect the objects to find it
        EventChannel channel = EventLibrary.create_channel(boa);
        boa.obj_is_ready(channel);

        // Create an instance of a server that generates events
        Loan loan = new Loan(orb, boa, channel);

        // Create an object that will subscribe to the server's
        // events
        InterestedParty interestedParty = new InterestedParty(boa,
         channel);

        // Now approve the loan
        loan.approve(true);
    }
}

public class Loan extends _PushSupplierImplBase
{
    public Loan(org.omg.CORBA.ORB orb, org.omg.CORBA.BOA boa,
     EventChannel channel)
    {
        this.orb = orb;
        this.boa = boa;
        this.channel = channel;
        boa.obj_is_ready(this);

        // Create consumer proxy for the supplier to talk to
```

```
            consumerProxy =
             channel.for_suppliers().obtain_push_consumer();
            try { consumerProxy.connect_push_supplier(this); }
            catch ( org.omg.CosEventChannelAdmin.AlreadyConnected ex)
            {}
        }

    public void approve(boolean b)
    {
            try
            {
                org.omg.CORBA.Any message = orb.create_any();
                String s;
                message.insert_string(s = (b ? "Approved" :
                  "Disapproved"));
                consumerProxy.push(message);
                System.out.println("Approval message sent: " + s);
            }
            catch(Disconnected e)
            {
                System.out.println("Disconnected");
            }
            catch(SystemException e)
            {
                e.printStackTrace();
                disconnect_push_supplier();
            }
        }

    public void disconnect_push_supplier()
    {
            try { boa.deactivate_obj(this); }
            catch (org.omg.CORBA.SystemException ex) {}
        }

    private org.omg.CORBA.ORB orb;
    private org.omg.CORBA.BOA boa;
    private EventChannel channel;
    private ProxyPushConsumer consumerProxy;
}

public class InterestedParty extends _PushConsumerImplBase
{
```

```java
public InterestedParty(org.omg.CORBA.BOA boa, EventChannel
  channel)
{
    this.boa = boa;
    this.channel = channel;
    boa.obj_is_ready(this);

    subscribeToChannel(channel);
}

public void subscribeToChannel(EventChannel channel)
{
    // Create a supplier proxy for the subscriber
    ProxyPushSupplier supplierProxy =
        channel.for_consumers().obtain_push_supplier();

    // Connect the subscriber to the channel
    try { supplierProxy.connect_push_consumer(this); }
    catch ( org.omg.CosEventChannelAdmin.AlreadyConnected ex)
    {}
}

public void push(org.omg.CORBA.Any data) throws Disconnected
{
    System.out.println("Loan was: " + data);
}

public void disconnect_push_consumer()
{
    try { boa.deactivate_obj(this); }
    catch (org.omg.CORBA.SystemException ex) {}
}

private EventChannel channel;
private org.omg.CORBA.BOA boa;
}
```

The issue of persistence is not addressed in this example.

CORBA Messaging Service

The CORBA Messaging Service is a standard under development by the OMG to address MOM requirements in the context of CORBA. The companies actively involved in developing the standard are BEA Systems, Borland (Visigenic), Expersoft, ICL, IONA, IBM, Nortel, Novell, Oracle, PeerLogic and TIBCO.

The standard is being completed at this writing, and a Java binding does not yet exist. It is not clear exactly how this new CORBA service and JMS will interoperate, but they certainly will. CORBA Messaging is a fairly complex standard. It is likely that, just as RMI provides a Java-friendly interface to IIOP, and JNDI provides, through the CosNaming JNDI provider, a Java-friendly interface to CORBA Naming Service, that similarly JMS will provide a Java-friendly interface to the CORBA Messaging Service.

CORBA Transaction Service

The CORBA Transaction Service defines a mechanism for coordinating operations occurring on separate systems, to provide atomicity. It defines a distributed transaction model, based on IIOP and CORBA objects, and also incorporates support for the X/Open protocol, and its associated XA API.

The CORBA Transaction Service API is very difficult to use directly, and is aimed mainly at middleware vendors who wish to incorporate interoperable transaction management into their products.

Java Transaction Service

The Java Transaction Service (JTS) is Javasoft's binding for the CORBA Transaction Service and X/Open XA Transaction standard. It is an API intended to be used primarily by middleware vendors, to implement Enterprise JavaBean application servers. You might consider using the JTS API directly if your application needs to integrate data from multiple sources, and you have decided not to use a middleware solution that provides the transaction management required to integrate these sources. Another reason you might use JTS is to provide client-side demarcation of transactions, rather than rely on the Enterprise JavaBeans framework for declarative transaction specification (see the Java Beans chapter.)

Using JTS correctly, however, is very challenging, since there are many non-obvious issues to consider, including what happens if a two-phase commit appears to succeed but actually fails; or, what if one component does not support XA transactions but the others do? You will also have to deal with the issue of transaction logging. There are many complex issues that must be considered to create a reliable system, and that is why the developers of the Enterprise JavaBeans specification felt that middleware vendors were in a better position to deal with those issues than application developers, since a middleware product can solve these issues once for all the interfaces they support, and make those interfaces reliable. The cost of doing this for an end-user application is prohibitively high in all but the most sophisticated systems.

CHAPTER 7

- **Developing Beans**

- **Bean Frameworks**

- **Javasoft's Enterprise JavaBeans Framework**

JavaBeans for the Enterprise

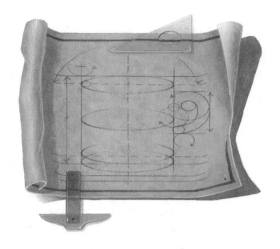

Beans are the emerging foundation of all Java application frameworks. Beans address important issues such as application packaging and deployment, reuseability, and customization. New additions to the bean specifications provide frameworks for application development, to enable cross-compatibility of components created by different vendors and adaptability to different deployment environments. All of these aspects are extremely important issues for enterprise applications, which need to have a long life cycle and be compatible with all the environments and components with which they may be combined over time.

I will begin with some bean fundamentals, and then discuss the various bean frameworks that now exist that are of particular relevance to enterprise applications, a notable one of which is the Enterprise JavaBeans specification. I will not spend much time on bean issues that pertain mainly to end-user interfaces, as is the case in most books on beans. What is of interest here are the issues in server-based and large-scale client and server application development. We are concerned about issues of reliability, maintainability, reuseability, scalability, and transactional integrity.

Developing Beans

What Are Beans?

A Java Bean is a class or set of classes designed as a reuseable component. Components designed as beans can be assembled with minimal programming to create larger systems, typically via a drag-and-drop development tool.

A bean is the software equivalent of an electronic integrated circuit, which has self-contained and well-defined behavior, and adheres to some design framework. Anyone who has worked with electronic ICs knows that such components come in "families" which consist of components designed to work together. Components within a family share a set of protocols for communicating with each other. A protocol between electronic components consists of a set of signals with a time-dependent behavior, which carry information. In an analogous fashion, beans communicate via signals in the form of EventObject objects, which may contain information within them.

In the same way that parameterized micro-electronic circuit library components are instantiated and customized for an application within an integrated circuit, beans may be customized with each use, and the customization parameters are referred to as "properties."

How Beans Work

Beans are extendable and customizable components. However, there is no "bean interface" that must be implemented, and no bean "base class" that must be extended. Rather, the way that bean features are identified are through a bean component's adherence to a set of design rules, or "patterns," for defining the "bean-like" features. For example, if a bean has methods of the form getXyz() and setXyz(), these are assumed to be accessors for a property called "Xyz," and that property will be identified within a bean development tool's property sheet.

In order to identify the properties of a bean, as well as all the other kinds of information that is needed to instantiate a bean, customize it, and hook it up to other components, a bean development tool uses a special bean API called the introspection API. A bean developer can provide a bean with descriptive information about the bean, in particular detailed textual descriptions of its methods and method parameters, and the introspection API is the API for accessing this information when the bean is later used. If such information has not been provided or is incomplete, the introspection API automatically resorts to a foundational API called the reflection API, which is a set of methods for discovering information about any Java class, including the names of all methods and the types of any method's parameters. Thus, there is always a way to discover at runtime what the method names and signatures are within any class, and therefore there is always a way a bean development tool can find methods that adhere to bean design patterns. It is even possible for a development tool to dynamically invoke any method at runtime—for example, an accessor method—by calling the Method.invoke() method and passing a reference to the target object.

The most important part of designing a bean is choosing the event model that the bean will use. The event model defines the signals that the bean will use to communicate with other components, whether they are beans or not. Normally when a programmer instantiates a bean, the programmer identifies which of the bean's events neighboring components will respond to, and conversely which events from other beans this bean will respond to. A response takes the form of a method invocation.

There is no built-in mechanism for dispatching bean events. That is, there is no central event system that beans must hook into. It is therefore up to the bean's developer how the bean will dispatch events to objects which are interested in those events; that is, the bean itself decides how the response methods of interested components will be invoked. Normally, invocation occurs in the same thread that generates the event: the bean simply calls the response methods of all interested components. However, the bean is free to implement an event dispatching queue. The AWT implements such a queue for dispatching its own events in a separate dispatching thread.

A bean has special packaging requirements. Beans are transported in Java Archive ("JAR") files. A JAR file is a PKZIP file, which may optionally have some special files in it for describing its contents. One of these is the manifest file, which is an attributed index of the archive's contents. Any index entry which has the attribute "Java-Bean: True" is understood to be a bean. Once a bean is instantiated into a system, however, it can take any form; beans do not have to retain their identity as beans once they are used, although they may.

What You Should Implement

This all sounds rather complicated, and you are probably wondering if you need to do all this just to create a bean. More fundamentally, you may even be wondering if you are a bean developer or a bean user. The answer, if you ever share your work with other programmers, is probably both: you will probably use beans made by others, and you will probably create beans for others to use.

What should you make a bean? Should all your organization's objects be made into beans? Where do you draw the line? In general, you should consider making a class into a bean if there is a good chance that the class will be reused by others, and, in particular:

- Those which encapsulate a macro service or function

- Utility classes which need customization in order to use

Once you decide you need to develop a class as a bean, is it necessary to do all the things outlined?

You would probably document software differently if you were creating it for internal use than if you were putting it in a shrink-wrapped package for sale. The same is true for beans. Just because you are developing a bean does not mean you have to add all of the self-documenting and customization features that a bean can have. For an internal-use enterprise bean, you need some level of reuseability, and you need good documentation so that other programmers don't have to call you to ask you how your bean works. Most likely your bean will not need a customizer, or custom property editors, but it may have these if the property data types are programmer-defined (e.g., enumeration literals). If your organization is multinational, the bean may also need to be designed for localization. For a commercial bean, you would include everything already mentioned, and localization is probably more important.

Documentation, localization, and packaging can easily be delegated to a specialist in those areas. A senior designer should choose or design the event space and framework for your beans. Otherwise, you will have a proliferation of partly compatible components.

Bean Design

In all likelihood you will use a tool to help you construct a bean. However, the tool cannot design the bean for you; unless your bean is a trivial UI bean, design is something that you will likely do "off-line." You are ready to sit at the tool only after the design is essentially complete. (Of course, people work differently. Some people get good results by "hacking"—designing by adding a little here and a little there, the way a chef might experiment with a new recipe. It is a very gifted person, however, who can produce good results this way for a complex design.)

Define the Events

The first step is to select an event model for the bean. The event model consists of the set of events that the bean will generate and respond to. This can be either an existing event model, such as the AWT component event model, or one of your own design. If your bean will be part of a larger set of reuseable components within your organization, you will want to give careful thought to this model. This step should be done by a senior designer. You are, in effect, defining the "information bus" of your and all interrelated applications and components.

Any events you use or define must extend java.util.EventObject. Event objects carry information about the event. This information is for you to define, and generally constitutes the message passed from the event source to objects that will receive and respond to the event. You should write accessor methods for setting and retrieving this information in the event object, and these methods should follow the get/set design pattern. The event class must have a constructor that takes a single Object parameter (the event source), and it must have a getSource()

method—although in practice it will simply inherit the getSource() method from the EventObject class. Here is a whimsical example of an event type that signals an increase in temperature:

```
/**
 * An event for notifying interested parties that the
 * temperature has suddenly jumped!
 */
public class ItsHotEvent extends java.util.EventObject
{
  /**
   * The source-argument constructor; all events should have
   * this.
   */
  public ItsHotEvent(Object source) { super(source); }

  /**
   * An additional constructor for the convenience of event
   * sources.
   */
  public ItsHotEvent(Object source, float t) { this(source);
    temperature = t; }

  /**
   * Setter method; follows the setXyz() design pattern.
   */
  public void setTemperature(float t) { temperature = t; }

  /**
   * Getter method. Follows the getXyz() design pattern.
   */
  public float getTemperature() { return temperature; }

  /**
   * Private property of this event type.
   */
  private float temperature;
}
```

Define a Listener Type

When you define an event type, you should define a type which listens for events of that type. This is an interface, containing event notification methods. The event notification methods are the methods a bean will call when it dispatches events to other components that are interested in those events. An event notification method should take a single argument of your event type, and return void. It may throw checked exceptions: those that extend java.lang.Exception, and don't extend RuntimeException. It should not knowingly throw other kinds of exceptions.

All of your event notification methods for a particular event type should be defined in an event notification interface, called a listener interface, and this interface should extend java.util.EventListener. Here is an example of a listener type for our ItsHotEvent event type:

```
/**
 * Those who are interested in rising temperature should
 * implement this interface, and
 * register themselves with all heat sources.
 */
public interface ItsHotEventListener extends
  java.util.EventListener
{
  public void temperatureRaised(ItsHotEvent e) throws
  ThermometerBrokenException;
}


/**
 * An exception needed for this bean.
 */
public class ThermometerBrokenException extends Exception {}
```

Define Your Bean Class

A bean class should implement java.io.Serializable so that its customized state, as configured in a bean development tool, can be made persistent and packaged into a JAR file. In addition, all bean properties should be based on serializable types (all the built-in Java classes are serializable; when in doubt, see the definition for any class in question). The Serializable interface has no methods, so you don't need to do anything other than simply add the words "implements java.io.Serializable" to your class—it is just a tag, indicating that this class grants the right for others to serialize it. (Any classes it extends from should also be serializable, or their data will not be saved.) Your bean class should also have a zero-argument constructor so that a development tool can dynamically instantiate it without needing to know how to construct it. Your bean may optionally implement the Visibility interface so that environments which use the bean can determine if the bean needs a GUI environment to function, and also tell the bean whether or not it is okay to use a GUI if the bean so desires.

Write Listener Registration Methods

Other components that are interested in receiving events from a bean register their interest in a specific event type by calling a registration method of the form add<listener-interface-type>(<listener-interface-type>) on the bean from which it wants to receive events. This method must maintain a list of interested components ("listeners") for the bean, normally as a java.util.Vector object. The listener list should be labeled with the "transient" modifier so that when the bean is packaged into a JAR file, other attached components which are not part of the bean are not inadvertently taken with it. It is the responsibility of the instantiating component to programmatically recreate the listener hookups (by calling the addXyzListener() methods) of any embedded beans on initialization.

Properties

Bean properties are the parameterized values that a bean development tool will use to allow a programmer to customize your bean when using it in a project. Normally these are simply class variables, but they need not be. The distinguishing feature of a property is that if it is of an object type it implements java.io.Serializable (all built-in types do), and that it has accessor methods of the form getXyz() and setXyz(Xyz's-type). This naming convention is very important because it is used by bean tools to identify property accessor methods.

Note the mixed case capitalization. The actual rules for capitalization are implemented in a method called Introspector.decapitalize() which, when in doubt, you can call to obtain the "correct" capitalization for any method. Using the correct capitalization is important, because the bean introspection methods will search for features in your bean based on naming patterns. (A sequence of capitals, such as "ABC," does not become "Abc," but rather remains "ABC.")

For array properties, define methods of the form

```
void setter(int, xxx[]) throws ArrayIndexOutOfBoundsException
XyzType getter(int) throws ArrayIndexOutOfBoundsException
void setter(XyzType[])
XyzType[] getter()
```

Property accessor methods may also throw other checked exceptions.

Here is an example of a bean class that has a "temperature" and "period" (between events) properties, and which allows ItsHotEvent listeners to register for notification:

```
/**
 * A bean which generates heat, and notifies interested parties
 * when the temperature rises.
 * This is an invisible bean - it has no visual appearance to
 * the end user.
 */
public class MyHeatGeneratorBeanClass
{
 /**
  * A bean should have a zero-argument constructor.
  */
 public MyHeatGeneratorBeanClass()
 {
    ...here you may initiate autonomous behavior for this bean
 }

 /**
  * Getter method for the temperature property.
  */
 public synchronized float getTemperature() { return
  temperature; }

 /**
  * Setter method for the event period property.
  */
 public synchronized void setPeriod(long p) { period = p; }

 /**
  * Getter method for the event period property.
  */
 public synchronized long getPeriod() { return period; }

 /**
  * Method that interested parties (listeners) call to register
  * interest in itsHot events.
  */
 public void addItsHotEventListener(ItsHotEventListener
 listener)
 {
    itsHotListeners.addElement(listener);// this is sync'd,
                        // because Vector is
```

```
    }


    /**

      * Method for unregistering interest in itsHot events.

      */

    public void removeItsHotEventListener(ItsHotEventListener
      listener)

    {

        itsHotListeners.removeElement(listener);// sync'd by the
                      // Vector class

    }


    /**

      * The itsHot event listener list. These are the parties to
      * call back when there are

      * "itsHot" events. This list, like all listener lists, should
      * be transient, because it is the

      * responsibility of the listening components to create event
      * hookups on initialization -

      * hookups (i.e. listeners) should not be automatically
      * carried with the bean when it is saved.

      */

    private transient Vector itsHotListeners = new Vector();


    /**

      * The temperature property. Properties must be serializable -

      * this is, because all intrinsic types are.

      */

    private float temperature = (float)0.0;


    /**

      * The period property.

      */

    private long period = 1000;// default to once per second

    }
```

Event generation

The actual behavior of this bean could be such that the bean reacts to external events, and is itself an event listener; or it could generate its own events spontaneously. Here is an example implementation of the constructor which does the latter, using the "period" property to determine the time interval between events:

```java
public MyHeatGeneratorBeanClass()
{
    class R implements Runnable
    {
        public void run()
        {
            for (;;)// ever
            {
                try
                {
                    Thread.current.Thread().sleep(period);
                }
                catch (InterruptedException ex) {}

                // Generate a random temperature change
                double d = Math.random();
                float f = (float)d;
                synchronized (this)
                    // temperature is accessible to other threads
                {
                    float prev = temperature;
                    temperature = f;
                }
                if (f > prev)
                {
                    // Fire an itsHot event to each listener
                    Vector v = (Vector)(itsHotListeners.clone());
                    for (int i = 0; i < v.size(); i++)
                    {
                        // Generate an itsHot event
                        ItsHotEvent e = new ItsHotEvent(
                        MyHeatGeneratorBeanClass.this, f);
```

```
                 // Note 1: We used the outer class this as
                 // the event source, since that is the bean.
                 // Note 2: we used "f" instead of
                 // temperature, because f is private to this
                 // thread, and so it need not be
                 // synchronized.


                 // Fire event to listener
                 ItsHotEventListener listener =
                    (ItsHotEventListener)
                       (v.elementAt(i));
                 listener.temperatureRaised(e);
            }
         }
      }
    }
  }


    Runnable r = new R();
    Thread thread = new Thread(r);
    thread.start();
}
```

In the above implementation, I defined a local class and made the local class runnable. The asynchronous behavior of the bean is encapsulated in the member class. An alternative would have been to make the bean class itself runnable. In the above implementation, however, there is the possibility of constructing the bean behavior by composition such that a runnable class is passed as a property, thereby defining the behavior at customization time.

Examine Reentrance for Synchronization Requirements

It is hard to anticipate how your bean will actually be used by other programmers, so it should be robust enough to handle all situations. One consideration is that the end application might be multithreaded, so there may be multiple concurrent threads running through the bean, causing it to generate events in several threads at the same time. The bean therefore needs to be designed to be thread-safe. I have therefore made all of the accessor methods synchronized, since these methods access and modify the object's state.

One area which requires special consideration is that the bean's event dispatching mechanism, which maintains a listener list and needs to access that list in a synchronized fashion. It is possible that the end application might call the addXyzListener() or removeXyzListener() methods as part of its response to event notification. You don't need to synchronize the add...() and remove...() methods, because the above implementation uses single-line addElement() and removeElement() operations on a Vector, and Vector operations are synchronized. The other section of code in this bean that accesses this list is the section that performs the event dispatching, where the event is actually generated and the list of listeners is traversed. What if someone removes a listener when we are in the midst of traversing this list?

An obvious solution is to synchronize the section of code that performs the dispatching. The difficulty is that *we don't know ahead of time what the code we are dispatching to will do*. The receiver of the bean's events is code that uses the bean, long after the bean has been designed and built. If that code attempts to access the listener list (e.g., by calling add...Listener()), we will have a deadlock situation.

A solution to this potential problem is to clone the list immediately prior to delivering events, and not synchronize the event delivery mechanism. Instead, deliver events based on the cloned list, which there will be no contention for since the only operation that needs to be synchronized is the brief cloning operation, which occurs prior to event delivery. This solves the potential deadlock problem, but you should be aware that an implication is that listeners should expect that they may sometimes be invoked even if they have just been removed from the source's list of listeners, since the cloned list might be a little bit out of date.

Note: The example presented here defines an event type that is not an AWT event. AWT events extend from java.awt.AWTEvent. (I am not talking about Java 1.0 events - I am trying to forget about those!) If your event type extends from AWTEvent, you can use a utility class in package java.awt, AWTEventMulticaster, which performs the listener list management and event dispatching functions for you, so you don't have to worry about these considerations. This is pure UI-related stuff, so I won't go into it, because this book is not about UI development; if you are interested, see the example shown in the AWTEventMulticaster class javadoc documentation.

Bean Visibility

If your bean may be run in a variety of environments (e.g., in a servlet or an applet), you will want to implement the java.beans.Visibility interface. This allows the application to control whether the bean will attempt to make itself visible. To make your bean sensitive to visibility considerations, implement these methods:

- needsGui()—Returns true if the bean cannot be run without a GUI

- dontUseGui()—Tells the bean not to use a GUI, assuming it is optional

- okToUseGui()—Tells the bean it can use its GUI, if it has one

- avoidingGui()—Returns true if the bean is not using its GUI

Bean Metainformation—"BeanInfo"

All Java classes expose metainformation about their methods and variables with the reflection API, available through methods in the Class class. However, this information is incomplete, because it lacks certain details such as parameter names, and, more important it lacks descriptive information that only the programmer can provide. A developer who wishes to use a bean needs to have metainformation available about the beans methods, parameters, properties, and for what they are intended to be used. The beans "introspection" API is designed to provide this information.

The table below summarizes the introspection methods that a bean can use to publish information about itself, and conversely the methods that a bean development tool can use to obtain information about the bean. When you create a bean, you may define these classes in order to make this information available to users of the bean.

Table 7-1 BeanInfo and FeatureDescriptor Methods

BeanInfo methods:
- **BeanDescriptor** getBeanDescriptor()
  - *BeanDescriptor methods:*
    - Class getBeanClass()
    - Class getCustomizerClass()
    - \<FeatureDescriptor methods - see below\>
- Image getIcon()
- **MethodDescriptor**[] getMethodDescriptors()
  - *MethodDescriptor methods:*
    - Method getMethod()
    - ParameterDescriptor[] getParameterDescriptors()
      - *ParameterDescriptor methods:*
        - \<FeatureDescriptor methods - see below\>
    - \<FeatureDescriptor methods - see below\>
- **PropertyDescriptor**[] getPropertyDescriptors()
  - *PropertyDescriptor methods:*
    - \<FeatureDescriptor methods - see below\>

- **EventSetDescriptor[]** getEventSetDescriptors()
  - *EventSetDescriptor methods:*
    - Method getAddListenerMethod()
    - **MethodDescriptor[]** getListenerMethodDescriptors()
    - Method[] getListenerMethods()
    - Class getListenerType()
    - Method getRemoveListenerMethod()
    - boolean isInDefaultEventSet()
    - boolean isUnicast()
    - void setInDefaultEventSet(boolean inDefaultEventSet)
    - void setUnicast(boolean unicast)
    - <FeatureDescriptor methods - see below>
- int getDefaultEventIndex()
- int getDefaultPropertyIndex()
- **BeanInfo[]** getAdditionalBeanInfo

FeatureDescriptor methods:
- Enumeration attributeNames()
- String getDisplayName(), void setDisplayName(String)
- String getName(), void setName(String)
- String getShortDescription()
- void setShortDescription(String)
- Object getValue(String), void setValue(String, Object)
- boolean isExpert(), void setExpert(boolean)
- boolean isHidden(), void setHidden(boolean)

To get a bean's BeanInfo object, you call the static method Introspector.getBean-Info(Class), and you pass it a Class object that describes the bean's class. (You can obtain a Class object for any object instance by calling the Object.getClass() method; or, if you don't have an instance yet, Class.forName, "<class-name>", will return a Class object.) The getBeanInfo() method returns a BeanInfo object, which completely describes the bean. The information used by getBeanInfo() to construct the returned BeanInfo object is obtained by a combination of looking for BeanInfo classes and using the reflection API, with the former taking precedence. A BeanInfo class should be named according to the following convention: "<bean-class-name>BeanInfo", and it should be placed in the same package as the associated bean class. The same rule applies to bean superclasses if the super-classes have BeanInfo objects.

Thus, if you want to provide explicit information about your bean, for other developers to have access to, you need to create a BeanInfo class, describing your bean class. To do this, you can create your own BeanInfo from scratch, according to the naming convention described above, and implement all the methods in the

BeanInfo interface; or you can take the somewhat easier path of extending the SimpleBeanInfo class, which has an empty default implementation for each of the methods in the BeanInfo interface. In that case, you only need to override the methods you want to provide explicit information for, above and beyond what the Introspector will automatically derive through reflection. Once you create your BeanInfo object, you don't have to hook it to anything: just put it in the same package as your bean. Introspector.getBeanInfo(Class.forName("<bean-class-name>")) will then be able to find the bean info object for your bean.

The BeanInfo.getBeanDescriptor() method returns a BeanDescriptor object, which has a method called getCustomizerClass(), which should return a Class object for the customizer if you have created one. The implementation of this method should perform a Class.forName("<your-customizer-class>"). Other BeanInfo methods include getEventSetDescriptors(), getMethodDescriptors(), getProperty-Descriptors(), getIcon(), and others which can be seen in the table.

Here is an example of a bean info class for the heat generator bean:

```
/**
 * BeanInfo class, for a bean which generates heat and then
 * notifies interested parties when the
 * temperature jumps.
 */
public class MyHeatGeneratorBeanClassBeanInfo extends
  SimpleBeanInfo
{
  public EventSetDescriptor[] getEventSetDescriptors()
  {
    EventSetDescriptor[] descriptors = new
     EventSetDescriptor[1];
    try
    {
      descriptors[0] = new EventSetDescriptor
      (
        Class.forName("ItsHot"),// source class
        "itsHot",        // eventsetname
        ItsHotEventListener.class// listenertype
        "temperatureRaised"// listenername
      );
    }
    catch (Exception ex) { ex.printStackTrace();
    return descriptors;
  }
}
```

Localization of Descriptive Information

If the developers who will be using your bean to build applications will be in different locales, you will want to localize the descriptive information that your bean info class provides. In particular, you should localize the setDisplayName() and setShortDescription() in the FeatureDescriptor class, and the getDisplayName() and getShortDescription() methods of the BeanDescriptor class. You will also want to localize the toString() method of your classes.

Setting the Icons

To implement the BeanInfo.getIcon(int) method you can use the SimpleBean-Info.loadImage() method, which obtains an image from the bean's codebase. Note that you should be prepared to deliver icons with different sizes, appropriate for different purposes and display types. Here is an example:

```java
/**
 * BeanInfo class for my bean - "MyBeanClass".
 */
public class MyHeatGeneratorBeanClassBeanInfo extends
  SimpleBeanInfo
{
  ...
  public Image getIcon(int iconKind)// applications call this
                                    // if they want the bean's
                                    // icon
  {
    switch (iconKind)
    {
    case BeanInfo.ICON_COLOR_16x16:
        ResourceBundle bundle =
          ResourceBundle.getBundle(
          // "MyResourceNames", Locale.getDefault());
          // E.g., I have a file called
            MyResourceNames_us.properties,
          // and "us" is my default locale.
        String imageName =
          bundle.getString("ICON16x16_IMAGE_FILE");
          // Gets the image file property specified in the
          // bundle property file
      Image image = loadImage(imageName);// inherited from
                                          //   SimpleBeanInfo
      if (image == null) throw new Error("Unable to load " +
        imageName);
```

```
        return image;
    case BeanInfo.ICON_COLOR_32x32: return null;// unsupported
    case BeanInfo.ICON_MONO_16x16: return null;// unsupported
    case BeanInfo.ICON_MONO_32x32: return null;// unsupported
    default: throw new RuntimeException("Unrecognized icon kind");
    }
  }
  ...
}
```

Packaging

A bean is packaged in a JAR file. JAR files are discussed in detail in the "Platforms" chapter. What makes a bean's JAR file implementation unique is that JAR manifest entries which represent bean classes must be identified as such, with a "Java-Bean: True" attribute. For example, here is a manifest file containing two entries: a class file called "DirectoryLister.class," which is a bean, and an HTML file, called "a.html." Note that the bean class has a "Java-Bean" attribute following the name of the entry (actually, it need not immediately follow the Name attribute).

```
Manifest-Version: 1.0

Name: DirectoryLister.class
Java-Bean: True
Digest-Algorithms: SHA MD5
SHA-Digest: cjV76hByRA20074NyfgGdWCwrCY=
MD5-Digest: 0vpuJ65q4Y0c3JmceRp9FQ==

Name: a.html
Digest-Algorithms: SHA MD5
SHA-Digest: DqxOMKKyU0DPoSM20jt3cJ0ICEk=
MD5-Digest: l3rHu7ylacxe+s+XkCyncA==
```

If there is no manifest file, every class and .ser file in the JAR file is assumed to be a bean. If there is a manifest file, only entries with the property "Java-Bean: True" will be recognized as beans. If the bean is packaged with its serialized state (see the discussion below about applet beans), the serialization file must have a ".ser" suffix. (If there is a .ser file, it will internally contain a reference to the bean's class name.)

The "jar" tool used to create JAR files automatically creates a manifest file for you and puts it in the JAR file. At present, this tool does not know how to add a bean attribute (this may change by the time you read this). However, a manifest file is just a text file, so you can edit it with a text editor to add the "Java-Bean: True" attribute. Hopefully you will have a bean development tool so you will not have to do this, but if you have to, all you need to do is extract the manifest, add the "Java-Bean" attribute, and reinsert the manifest. For example, if you used the jar tool to create your JAR file, you can extract its manifest file with a command such as

```
jar xvf DirectoryLister.jar "META-INF\MANIFEST.MF"
```

You can then edit the manifest, and reinsert it with

```
jar cvfm x.jar META-INF\MANIFEST.MF <your-files>
```

This will recreate the JAR file, but use the manifest created earlier with your edits included.

Another important attribute is the "Main-Class" attribute, added by Java 1.2. If this is set to True in the JAR file, the JAR is an "executable" JAR, and it can be executed by the java.util.jar.Exec program or directly by specifying the -jar option to java:

```
java -jar <jar-file-name>
```

This is how you can create an "executable bean." The class identified as the main class must be a valid Java application class, with a public static method called "main" and a string array argument. The Java Runtime Environment (see the chapter on deployment platforms) is also able to automatically invoke a main class packaged in a JAR file in this way. This makes it possible to encapsulate an executable program with all its resources. Note, however, that a main program cannot be run in a browser as an aÿlet unless it extends the Applet class.

HTML 2.0 Documentation in a JAR File

A bean JAR file may contain HTML 2.0 files for documentation. These files must have names of the form "<locale>/*.html" if they are localized, or simply "*.html" otherwise, and the top-level file must have the name of the bean, for example, "us/mypackage.MyBean.html" or "mypackage.MyBean.html." The top-level HTML file may have relative links to other HTML files within the JAR file, or absolute links, for example, to a web site. Note, however, that most browsers cannot extract HTML content from JAR files, so the documentation feature is currently of most use to developers using beans to create applications (as opposed to applets deployed as JAR files); a bean development tool can extract the HTML documentation and either present it, or simply extract it and copy it to a place where the programmer's browser can access it.

Instantiating a Bean

You should not instantiate a bean by calling the "new" operator. Instead, you should use one of the instantiate() methods in the java.beans.Beans class:

```
static Object instantiate(ClassLoader cl, String beanClassName
   bcn);
static Object instantiate(ClassLoader cl, String
   beanClassName, BeanContext bc);
static Object instantiate(ClassLoader cl, String, BeanContext
   bc, AppletInitializer ai);
```

The last two were introduced with Java 1.2, and their differences will be explained later when BeanContexts are discussed. For now, let's concentrate on the first one. The main difference between using instantiate() and using "new" is that the instantiate() method allows for the creation of a bean instance from a serialization file. This allows any property values that were set when the bean was saved to be restored to their prior values. If there is a serialized object file (a file ending in ".ser") which matches the name of the bean, it uses that and unserializes it instead of creating a new instance. If the bean name has a package prefix, it looks in that package, just as it would do for a resource name (see the chapter on resources and internationalization). To get the class loader, just use the getClass().getClass-Loader() sequence to get the class loader which loaded the class that wants to instantiate the bean; this will try to load the bean from the same codebase as that class, presumably a JAR file.

If Your Bean Is an Applet

If your bean is an applet, you need to give special consideration to how the applet will be used, and how the bean will be stored for reuse. If the bean is restored from a serialization file, when the applet is used, its init() method will not be called (nor will its constructor). Instead, it will be restored to the way it was when it was serialized, and its start() method will be called. If, on the other hand, no serialization file was stored with the bean, it will be constructed as usual and its init() and start() methods called.

Note that if the bean applet contains other embedded beans, and if a serialization file is included, any listener hookup code placed in the constructor or the init() method will not be invoked. For applets, it is generally preferable to not include a serialization file; or you can deal with the event hookups in the start() method. Note that during unserialization, the class loader will look for classes in the same place from which it got the .ser file.

Bound and Constrained Properties

A bean may generate events which notify all interested parties that a property has changed. Such properties are known as "bound properties." To create a bound property, you need to provide notification of all bound property listeners or property-specific notification. To allow for notification of all bound property listeners, provide methods in your bean with these signatures:

```
addPropertyChangeListener(PropertyChangeListener x),
removePropertyChangeListener(PropertyChangeListener x)
```

To provide property-specific notification, provide these methods for the property:

```
addXyzListener(PropertyChangeListener x),
removeXyzListener(PropertyChangeListener x)
```

where "Xyz" denotes the property name. To provide for the property change event dispatching, use the helper class PropertyChangeSupport, as in the following example:

```
    ...

/**
 * Setter method for the event period property.
 *
 * In this implementation, we use the PropertyChangeSupport
 * helper class, to handle the
 * property change event propagation.
 */
public void setPeriod(long p)
{
   // Change the property value
   synchronized (this)// needs to be synchronized, because long
   {                   // operations are not atomic
     period = p;
   }
```

```
    // Notify all interested parties that the rate has changed
    periodPCS.firePropertyChange("period", new Long(period),
       new Long(p));
}

/**
 * Getter method for the event period property - same as before.
 */
public synchronized long getPeriod() { return period; }

public void addPeriodListener(PropertyChangeListener x)
{
   periodPCS.addPropertyChangeListener(x);
}

public void removePeriodListener(PropertyChangeListener x)
{
   periodPCS.removePropertyChangeListener(x);
}

private PropertyChangeSupport periodPCS = new
PropertyChangeSupport(this);
   // Note: the constructor parameter is the source object in
   // the events that are generated
   // by the firePropertyChange() method.

   . . .
```

Constrained properties are bound properties that must accept vetoes; that is, a listener can prevent the change from occurring by vetoing it. To implement this, the property set methods must throw the PropertyVetoException. Again, you can notify all change listeners when there is a change:

```
addVetoableChangeListener(VetoableChangeListener x),
removeVetoableChangeListener(VetoableChangeListener x)
```

or notify on a property-specific basis:

```
addXyzListener(VetoableChangeListener x),
removeXyzListener(VetoableChangeListener x)
```

You must notify listeners of the proposed change prior to actually making the change, and allow them to veto it. If one listener vetos it, you are required to renotify all listeners that the property is being reverted from the new value back to the old.

You can implement the required behavior yourself, or take advantage of the Veto-ableChangeSupport helper class, which provides this behavior just as for the PropertyChangeSupport class. Here is an example:

```
    . . .

    /**
     * Setter method for the event period property.
     *
     * Notifying that the temperature change period is changing,
     * and then, if it succeeds,
     * notifying all interested parties that it has changed: In
     * this implementation, we use
     * the VetoableChangeSupport helper class, to handle the
     * vetoable change event
     * propagation, and implement the specifics of the vetoable
     * change protocol.
     */
    public void setPeriod(long p) throws PropertyVetoException
    {
        // Tentatively notify all interested parties that the rate
        // is about to change
        periodVCS.fireVetoableChange("period", new Long(period),
            new Long(p));
        // If any of the listeners generate a PropertyVetoException,
        // the periodVCS object
        // catches it, then renotifies all listeners that the change
        // is being revoked,
        // and then rethrows the exception. In that case, we choose
        // to propagate the exception out of this method.

        // Change approved; implement it
        synchronized (this)    // needs to be synchronized, because
        {                      // long operations are not atomic
            period = p;
        }

        // Notify all interested parties that the rate has changed
        periodPCS.firePropertyChange("period", new Long(period), new
            Long(p));
```

```
}

/**
 * Getter method for the event period property - same as before.
 */
public synchronized long getPeriod() { return period; }

public void addPeriodListener(VetoableChangeListener x)
{
   periodVCS.addVetoableChangeListener(x);
}

public void removePeriodListener(VetoableChangeListener x)
{
   periodVCS.removeVetoableChangeListener(x);
}

public void addPeriodListener(PropertyChangeListener x)
{
   periodPCS.addPropertyChangeListener(x);
}

public void removePeriodListener(PropertyChangeListener x)
{
   periodPCS.removePropertyChangeListener(x);
}

private VetoableChangeSupport periodVCS = new
 VetoableChangeSupport(this);
   // Note: the constructor parameter is the source object in
   // the events that are generated
   // by the fireVetoableChange() method.

private PropertyChangeSupport periodPCS = new|
 PropertyChangeSupport(this);
   // Note: the constructor parameter is the source object in
   // the events that are generated
   // by the firePropertyChange() method.

...
```

Property Editors

A property editor is a visual component which allows a user to interactively view and modify the value of a particular bean property. A typical bean development tool will provide a property editor for entering and modifying the values of bean properties. Such a property editor will know how to parse and format values for the standard Java types (e.g. int, String, boolean); however, it would not know how to parse or format a value that was a temperature, such as a Centigrade or Fahrenheit value—the property editor would not know that it had to display a °C or °F next to the value; or perhaps the user should even be allowed to enter an expression (e.g. 10+273 °C).

Another consideration is that the property editor is a component that is built into the development environment, and it must accept and modify changes to values within beans the user is working on; however, the bean ought to remain in control of any changes that are made to its properties. Therefore, there is clearly a need to establish a protocol of interaction between the property editor and the bean; and also a means for the bean to take over the input and display of user-defined property data types.

A property editor provides these capabilities. It is a class that the bean developer provides, for use by property sheets. A property sheet in a development environment will find a property's property editor, if it has one, and employ it to accept and display property values. There are essentially three modes that a property editor can choose to work in: text mode; graphics mode; and it may operate as its own AWT component. Which mode is chosen is up to the property sheet, and which modes are supported by the property editor.

To register a property editor for a type, use the static method.

```
PropertyEditorManager.registerEditor(Class targetType, Class
    editorClass).
```

A property editor can be implemented in any or all of three modes: text-based, graphics based, or component-based. A text-based property editor provides text-based entry and modification of a property value, using a text field provided by the property sheet in which it is embedded. A graphics-based property editor paints the property's value in a rectangular area provided to it by the property sheet. A component-based property editor goes even further—it provides a full-blown AWT component with which the user interacts to view and set the property value.

Here is an example of creating a property editor. It allows the bean user to enter and edit a Centigrade or Fahrenheit value. It supports text, graphic, and custom (i.e., component-based) editor modes.

```
import java.awt.*; import java.beans.*; import java.awt.event.*;
public class TemperatureEditor extends PropertyEditorSupport
{
  public TemperatureEditor(Object source) {super(source); }

  // -------You usually don't override these methods, so I'll
  // leave them commented out------

  // getJavaInitializationString()

  // addPropertyChangeListener(PropertyChangeListener pcl)

  // removePropertyChangeListener(PropertyChangeListener pcl)

  // -------You may have occasion to modify these------

public void setValue(Object o)
{
   super.setValue(o);
      // Sets a local copy of the value, and notifies all
      // listeners.
      // Does NOT set the actual property in the bean - it is
      // presumed that the
      // environment will listen for this event, and call the
      // property setter method
      // in the bean.
}

public Object getValue()
{
   return super.getValue();
      // Returns the local copy of the value.
}
```

```
// -------Usually you customize some or all of this part-------

public void setAsText(String s) throws
IllegalArgumentException
{
    // If this property cannot be represented as text, throw
    // IllegalArgumentException.
    // Here you may want to provide localized parsing of input
    // text strings.

    // super.setAsText(s);
        // This sets the property value to the String object, with
        // no conversion.

    // I will parse a temperature value - remove the " °C" or " °F"
    // symbol, and make sure
    // that the required conversion gets performed.

    float t = parseTemperature(s);     // automatically converts to
                                          Centigrade. As a side
                                       // effect, it sets the
                                          editor's current C or F
                                          mode.
    Float f = new Float(t);
    setValue(f);
}

protected static float parseTemperature(String s) throws
NumberFormatException
{
    try
    {
    // Extract the numeric portion
    int endOfNumber = Math.max(s.indexOf(' '), s.indexOf('º'));
    String ns = s.substring(0, endOfNumber);
    float t = Float.valueOf(ns).floatValue();

    // Parse the rest - if "ºF", convert to Centigrade
    // other than whitespace, throw exception
    int endOfDegree = s.indexOf('º', endOfNumber-1);
    if (endOfDegree < 0) return t;// assume Centigrade
    String m = s.substring(endOfDegree+1).trim().toUpperCase();
```

```
    if (m.equals("C")) return t;
    else if (m.equals("F")) return (float)((t - 32.0) * 1.8);
    else throw new NumberFormatException();
    }
    catch (Exception ex) { throw new NumberFormatException(); }
}

public String getAsText()
{
  // Return null if the property cannot be converted to a
  // String representation, which can
  // be passed back into setAsText(). You may want to provide
  // localized formatting of text strings for display.

  return super.getAsText();
    // This calls toString() on the property
}

public String[] getTags()
{
  return null;// The property is not an enumerated value
}

public boolean isPaintable()
{
  return true;// We know how to graphically display our value.
    // If we don't know how to graph the value, return false.
}

public void paintValue(Graphics g, Rectangle r)
{
  // Graph the property value in Graphics context provided,
  // within the bounds of the provided rectangle.
  // If we don't know how to graph the property,
  // simply do nothing.

  g.clipRect(r.x, r.y, r.width, r.height);
  // Draw a red bar on a white background, on a scale from 0 to
  // 120 - beyond that is off the scale.
  float t = ((Float)getValue()).floatValue();
  g.setColor(Color.white);
```

```
      g.translate(r.x, r.y);
      g.fillRect(0, 0, r.width, r.height);
      int x = ((int)t * r.width) / 120;
      g.setColor(Color.red);
      g.fillRect(0, 0, x, r.height);
   }

   public boolean supportsCustomEditor()
   {
      return true;// We can provide an AWT component for editing
                  // the property.
   }

   public Component getCustomEditor()
   {
      Panel p = new Panel()
      {
         // A component that lets the user select a new temperature
         // graphically.

         // Hook up the panel
         {
            // Add this component as a PropertyChangeListener
            TemperatureEditor.this.addPropertyChangeListener
            (
               new PropertyChangeListener()
               {
                  public void propertyChange(
                     PropertyChangeEvent evt)
                  {
                     update(getGraphics()0;
                  }
               }
);

            // Handle panel events

            addMouseListener
            (
               new MouseListener()// a new anonymous adapter class
```

```
        {
          public void mouseClicked(MouseEvent e)
          {
            // Convert the x-position of the click
            // into a float temperature value
            int x = e.getX();
            float t =
            ((float)x * 120.0) / ((float)getSize().width);

            // Set the new temperature and notify
            // listeners
            setObject(new Float(t));
          }
        }
      );
      . . . other MouseListener methods . . .
    }


    // Render the component
    public void update(Graphics g)
    {
      Rectangle r = new Rectangle(0, 0, getSize().width,
        getSize().height);
      paintValue(g, r);
    }
  };
  return p;
  }
}
```

Customizers

A customizer is a property sheet developed specifically for a bean. It can take any form; it need not use a property sheet metaphor. It is an AWT component that a bean development tool can instantiate to allow the bean user to modify the bean's property values in a totally unique way for that bean.

To get the customizer, the bean development tool calls the BeanInfo.getCustomizerClass() method. A development environment can (should) choose to use the customizer instead of the environment's built-in property sheet if a customizer is provided by the bean. Following is an example of creating a customizer:

```java
public class MyHeatGeneratorBeanClassBeanInfo extends
 SimpleBeanInfo
{
  private BeanDescriptor descriptor;

  public MyHeatGeneratorBeanClassBeanInfo()
  {
    descriptor = new BeanDescriptor(new Customizer.class());
  }

  ...

  public BeanDescriptor getBeanDescriptor()
  {
    return descriptor;
  }

  public class BeanDescriptor extends java.beans.BeanDescriptor
  {
    public BeanDescriptor(Class beanClass)
    { super(beanClass); }

    public BeanDescriptor(Class beanClass, Class
      customizerClass)
    { super(beanClass, customizerClass); }
  }

  public class Customizer extends java.awt.Panel
  implements java.beans.Customizer, ActionListener,
   PropertyChangeListener
  {
    public Customizer()
    {
      setBackground(Color.white);
      setLayout(new BorderLayout());

      // The environment will set the size, and validate

      // Create title
      Panel p = new Panel();
      add("North", p);
```

```
      p.add(new Label("Set the Period and Temperature Property
       Initial Values..."));

      // Create control for setting initial period
      p = new Panel();
      add("South", p);
      p.add(new Label("Period:"));
      p.add(pField = new TextField(10));
      pField.addActionListener(this);

      // Create control for setting initial temperature; we
      //   elect to use our own temperature editing conrol.
      add("Center", tControl = new TemperatureEditor(this));
      tControl.addPropertyChangeListener(this);
   }

   public Customizer(Object b)
   {
      super();
      setObject(b);
      pField.setText((new Long(period)).toString());
      tControl.setValue(new Float(temperature));
   }

   public void actionPerformed(ActionEvent e)
   {
      // A new property value has been entered.
      // Signal the change
      pcs.firePropertyChange(
         "period", e.getOldValue(), e.getNewValue());
   }

   public void propertyChange(PropertyChangeEvent e)
   {
      // A new property value has been entered; rebroadcast the
         event
      pcs.firePropertyChange(
         e.getPropertyName(), e.getOldValue(), e.getNewValue());
   }
```

```java
    public void setObject(Object b)// gets called by environment
                                   // upon instantiation
    {
      bean = (MyHeatGeneratorBeanClass)b;

      // Get initial property values
      period = bean.getPeriod();
      temperature = bean.getTemperature();
    }

    public void addPropertyChangeListener
    (PropertyChangeListener x)
    {
      pcs.addPropertyChangeListener(x);// delegate notification
    }

    public void removePropertyChangeListener
    (PropertyChangeListener x)
    {
      pcs.removePropertyChangeListener(x);// undelegate
                                          // notification
    }


    private MyHeatGeneratorBeanClass bean;// the bean whose
                                   // properties we are setting
    private long period;           // temp proxy for the real property
    private float temperature;     // "
    private TextField pField;      // text field for setting the
                                   // period property
    private TemperatureEditor tControl;// component for setting
                                   // for temperature property
    private PropertyChangeSupport pcs = new
      PropertyChangeSupport(this);
  }


  ...

  }
```

Understanding Bean Event Dispatching

A client once asked me if the bean event mechanism was reliable enough for transactional applications. The challenges to relying on bean events in a transaction are:

- Nonatomicity: When a component receives an event it cannot be sure if other components have been notified, so the system is not in a well-defined state. Furthermore, listeners may have transitioned to another state by the time they get the message.

- Reliability: Event delivery is not guaranteed, so events cannot be used to deliver information reliably. For example, if an event source looks at its list of listeners and decides to message a listener, it cannot be sure that the message will get there unless it makes provisions to monitor or synchronize the delivery process, that is, synchronize the event generation with the capture of the listener list.

In other words, event delivery and handling are not *atomic*, and the *quality of service* of event delivery is *best-effort*. Event delivery has nondeterministic semantics, and event delivery is not necessarily serialized or guaranteed.

This does not disqualify beans from transactions by any means. However, the burden is on the application to add the required level of reliability. If bean events are used to send messages as part of a transaction, your application should treat all bean events as advisory. In other words, event delivery should not be relied on for correctness: sending a message does not mean it gets there, so your application must have another means for ensuring that all initiated transactions are completed satisfactorily.

One solution is to use a single event queue (as in a discrete event simulator) or a group of event queues (e.g., one per recipient) for a class of events. Simply obtain all queues and recipient lists as part of event generation and delivery, which must be synchronous. This makes guaranteed delivery possible. Event delivery (producer role) is then decoupled from event processing (consumer role) by the queue. Thus, once an event handler begins to process an event it retrieves from a queue, it knows that the event has been delivered to the queues of all interested parties; therefore, events are serialized, and the sequence within each queue is preserved. Optionally, you may enforce that a party cannot remove its event queue from a source's interested party list unless it first scans the queue and makes sure there are no events from that party, and it must do this synchronously. This guarantees that event generation and delivery will have a well-defined effect—event sources can trust that whenever you tell them to stop sending you messages, you will have responded (and reacted) to all their prior messages.

A problem with implementing this is that present-day bean development tools implement extraneous bean adapter "glue code" according to nontransactional policies. Most of these tools are oriented toward developing UI-based application code, and these kinds of issues are not considered.

Incidentally, the AWT uses a single queue for all GUI events; this queue is the object returned by Toolkit.getSystemEventQueue(). This works fine until a recipient needs to suspend its thread—its thread is the shared AWT queue processing thread. Suspending the current thread in an event adapter will likely cause the UI thread to be suspended and freeze the UI. For example, modal dialogs do this, and to avoid a freeze the workaround is very complex. This is, of course, not a problem if you know that your beans are well behaved (don't call suspend(), wait(), stop(), or sleep() in their event handling code).

Bean Frameworks

BeanContexts

All programs execute within some kind of environment, which provides services to the application, the most fundamental of which are application loading and unloading. Some services are implicit in the application language and standard APIs. For example, a Java application implicitly makes use of memory management services from the underlying system. A Java application may also make use of network services, for example, when it creates a socket connection. Even though a socket request is explicit, it uses the core Java API and so is considered an implicit service, since the programmer does not have to explicitly request or locate an environment-specific service.

Some kinds of Java platforms provide other standard services, which are standard for that class of platforms. An example of this is an applet context, which represents an environment interface that is unique to browsers but standard across all browser-based Java implementations. The applet context provides services to an applet that are of special use to a browser-based application (an applet), such as the showDocument() method, which allows the applet to request that remote content be retrieved and displayed in the browser.

Besides browsers, there are different ways of deploying programs, many of which are discussed in the "Platforms" chapter, and more are evolving all the time. It is therefore useful to define a generic environmental context type, with a standard set of operations for interrogating what services are available and requesting services. This will allow programs to be developed somewhat independent of their deployment environment, and also to be flexible with regard to the environment they are deployed in and what services they require. This is an important feature for enterprise applications, because enterprise applications are often deployed in multiple environments, and environments change over time.

Another consideration for component-based applications is that sometimes the application needs to override the services provided by the environment. For example, suppose a component uses a print service, but a new use of the component deploys it in an environment (such as a mobile computing platform) that does not support printing, but has faxing, E-mail, and a host-based backup service. It is not possible for the component to anticipate all these new services. The application may therefore need to *interpose* itself between the component and the default service context supplied by the environment, to in effect trap print operations and reimplement them with other methods. The context framework therefore needs to allow applications to create their own context objects, and insert them between components and the native environment's context. In a more general case, we need the ability to insert arbitrary contexts between a component and another context, thereby—in sophisticated cases—creating a context hierarchy.

Java 1.2 introduces a new package to package java.beans, called java.beans.beancontext, which attempts to address the need for a core application context API. (Note: this API is not frozen at this writing, and may still change slightly when Java 1.2 is officially released.) It provides features for interposition and nesting of contexts, and for service interrogation and access.

The Context Hierarchy

The base type of all bean contexts is BeanContext. This type, which is an interface, extends java.util.Collection, which has methods add(), remove(), and other collection-oriented methods. By virtue of this extension, and a set of context-insertion and removal rules, BeanContext provides a means for creating context hierarchies. The rules for managing contexts are very complex, but there is a helper class, BeanContextSupport, which a context may extend to provide the behavior for adding and removing contexts, and notification of contexts of the associated events.

How a Bean Gets Its Context

In order for a bean to know what its context is, the environment has to have a way to pass the context to the bean when the bean is instantiated, and there has to be a method for the bean to call to get this context. When a context's add() method is called, the object passed to it can be another context, or it can be any bean. If this object implements the BeanContextChild interface (strongly recommended), the context will automatically call the object's BeanContextChild.setBeanContext() method, and the object will implement a getBeanContext() method to retrieve this context. Otherwise, it is up to the instantiating application to know how to pass the object its context.

If the bean implements BeanContextChild, it is required to obtain its resources from its owning context instead of through the class loader. Thus, the bean would call these BeanContext methods on the context in which it is instantiated.

```
InputStream getResourceAsStream(String name, BeanContextChild
  requestor);
URL getResource(String name, BeanContextChild requestor);
```

The context can then provide the resources from an application-specific source, or from the class loader in the standard way, using the Class.getResource() or Class.getResourceAsStream() methods.

Defining a Context that Adds a Service

You can define your own context class that provides a service you want to make available to beans you plan to instantiate. The context must implement the Bean-ContextServices interface, which extends BeanContext; if it does not, the context is not able to provide services to its subordinate objects. For example, if we have a print service that we want to make available, to override the built-in print service available in the native environment we can define a context and instantiate our beans in that context. Our context class might look like this:

```
public class MyContext extends BeanContextSupport
{
  public MyContext()
  {
    super();
    addService(PrintJob.class, new MyPrintServiceProvider());
  }
}
```

Once that context's beans have a reference to the context, they can request that context for services. A bean requests a service from its context by calling the Bean-ContextServices.getService() method. This method takes a service class as a parameter, in addition to some other parameters, and returns an object that represents the requested service. For example, to request a print service,

```
public class MyBean
{
  public void setBeanContext(BeanContext bc) { beanContext = bc;
  }
  public BeanContext getBeanContext() { return beanContext; }

  ...
```

```
protected PrintJob getMyPrintJob()
{
   return (PrintJob)(getBeanContext().getService
   (PrintJob.class, null, this, this));
}
...
private transient BeanContext beanContext;
}
```

In the above, note that the private reference to the bean's owning context is marked transient. It is required that references to any outer context, and any services, be market-transient so that if the bean is serialized it does not take the environment with it!

If the context does not have a requested service, it may (but does not have to) propagate the request to its own containing context until either it is at the top level or the service is obtained.

How to Create a Context and Install It under an Existing Context

Your application may create a context object to make a set of services available to beans the application plans to create. The application may itself be installed under a context, or it may be the "top level," and not have a context. Regardless, to make services available to beans, it will have to create a context. For example, the following application creates an instance of MyContext and adds it to its own context:

```
public class MyApplication
{
     public MyApplication(BeanContext nativeContext)
     {
          BeanContext myContext = new MyContext();
          nativeContext.add(myContext);
     }
```

Now it can create a bean and add it to the context

```
     protected void addMyBean()
     {
          MyBean b = (MyBean)(myContext.
              instantiateChild("MyBean"));
          b.setContext(myContext);// unnecessary if MyBean
                                  // implements
                                  // BeanContextChild
          ...the bean may now request print services, and
           our context will attempt to serve them...
```

The overall scenario is shown in Figure 7–1.

The instantiateChild() method is a convenience method that invokes the appropriate java.beans.Beans.instantiate() method. (Note that all beans must have a default constructor.) You could instead invoke the Beans.instantiate() method directly. These are the Beans.instantiate() methods:

```
static Object instantiate(ClassLoader cl, String
      beanClassName bcn);
static Object instantiate(ClassLoader cl, String
      beanClassName, BeanContext bc);
static Object instantiate(ClassLoader cl, String,
      BeanContext bc, AppletInitializer ai);
```

The last two variations of this method are new in Java 1.2, and allow you to pass in a bean context. The third version is intended for browsers to use so that a browser can instantiate an applet as a bean, using the same instantiation interface as other beans use and allowing an applet to be created with a bean context in addition to an applet context. There is no correspondence between an applet context and a bean context; the two have conceptual similarities, but the definition of applet context exists for historical reasons, and will likely remain as it is for backward compatibility. To instantiate an applet bean using the above instantiate(..., AppletInitializer) method, the browser must construct an object that implements the AppletInitializer interface, which has methods for initializing the applet (i.e., setting its AppletStub and AppletContext)—as well as activating it (calling the applet's start() method).

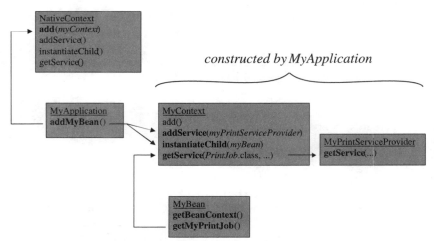

Figure 7–1 Instantiating a bean with an interposed context that supplies a service.

Adding a Context that Is a Component

If a bean context is intended to be associated with an AWT container object, it should implement the BeanContextContainer interface. This has a single method:

```
Container getContainer();
```

This allows other objects to query to find the associated container from the context.

The InfoBus

The Lotus/Sun InfoBus is a generic application data controller framework intended for building application components that can be assembled completely without programming. The framework uses a producer/consumer model for implementing data flow between components.

To coordinate that data flow, the framework defines a generic set of events and a generic controller class, called the "InfoBus." Producers of data make it available by broadcasting its availability via the bus, and consumers listen for data by registering their interest with the bus.

Data items exchanged between producer and consumer components are identified by name. The names can be obtained at runtime, (e.g., via applet parameters). This makes it possible to hook producers and consumers to the InfoBus using HTML. All that is required is that the consumer understand the data—the "flavors" (MIME types)—available from the producer of the data. It is up to a producer to decide which flavors it will make its data available in. For compatibility there is a set of canonical types, which are discussed below.

The fact that data is shared using canonical types, and identified by names which can be configured without programming (e.g., by HTML), makes it possible to create true plug-in compatible families of software components.

A powerful use of this is to use the data producer to encapsulate a query that requires an optimistic transactional policy. All users of the query can use this producer object as their gateway to a database or application server. The data source would make use of transactional remote queries or calls to obtain any data it needed from any number of actual sources, and broadcast change events on the InfoBus.

Component Role Interfaces

The InfoBus API is defined in a Java standard extension package, javax.infobus. The interface types defined in this package are

InfoBusMember—All producers and consumers must implement this.

InfoBusEventListener—The base type of all InfoBus event listeners.

InfoBusDataConsumer—A consumer, which listens for data availability.

InfoBusDataProducer—A producer, which listens for requests for data.

DataItemChangeListener—A consumer that wishes to be notified when a data item has changed must implement this.

InfoBusDataController—For implementing custom controllers. This is only used when there are special control requirements that cannot be satisfied by the default InfoBus behavior.

In addition, there is a concrete class, "InfoBus," which implements the InfoBus.

There may be multiple InfoBus instances per VM; each must have a unique name, however. InfoBuses are normally attached to by calling the InfoBusMemberSupport.joinInfoBus() method. This method in turn calls the static method InfoBus.open() method, followed by join(). The fact that the open() method maintains a static list makes it possible for different applets on a web page to join the same bus and communicate.

JavaSoft has also defined the InfoBus as service that can be requested from a BeanContext in the following way:

```
import javax.infobus.InfoBus;
...
InfoBus infoBus =
  (InfoBus)(getBeanContext().getService(InfoBus.class, null,
  this, this));
```

Having obtained an InfoBus instance in this way, you can join it with the join() method.

An InfoBus consumer can obtain data from InfoBus producers in three ways: by explicit request, by subscribing for notification when a data item becomes available, and by subscribing for notification of changes to data items.

Explicit Request

A consumer may at any time explicitly call

```
InfoBus.findDataItem(
  String dataItemName, DataFlavor flavors[],
  InfoBusDataConsumer consumer)
```

In this case, the InfoBus calls the dataItemRequested(InfoBusItemRequestedEvent) method of each data producer in turn, and passes it an InfoBusItemRequestedEvent object. The producer obtains the name of the requested data item from this event object by calling the event's getDataItemName() method. If the producer has the named data item, it passes it back to the InfoBus by calling the event's setDataItem(Object) method with the data item value, and then returning from the dataItemRequested() call. The InfoBus stops looking for the data item when it first receives a non-null value for the data item. It then returns this value to the consumer that made the findDataItem(...) request. In Figure 7–2, fully contained inner boxes represent interfaces, and the tinted rectangular regions represent object instances.

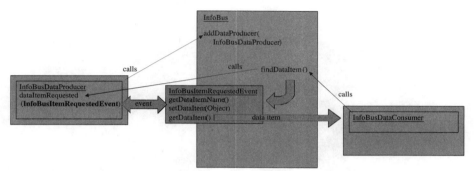

Figure 7–2 A consumer making an explicit request to the InfoBus for a data item

Subscribing to Data Availability

A consumer can subscribe to be notified when data items become available. It does this by calling

```
InfoBus.addDataConsumer(InfoBusDataConsumer consumer)
```

After this point, the consumer's dataItemAvailable() method is called whenever a producer makes a data item available by calling the InfoBus's fireDataItemAvailable(InfoBusItemAvailableEvent) method. The consumer may then respond by calling the findDataItem(...) method, as above, to actually retrieve the data item. See Figure 7–3.

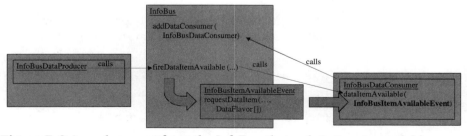

Figure 7–3 A producer notifying the InfoBus that a data item is available

Subscribing to Change Notification

Once a consumer has obtained a data item, it may want to be notified when that data item changes. If the data item implements the DataItemChangeManager interface as shown in Figure 7–4, the consumer can subscribe to changes by implementing the DataItemChangeListener interface, and registering itself with the data item change manager, by calling its addDataItemChangeListener() method.

```
DataItemChangeManager.addDataItemChangeListener(DataItemChange
    Listener)
```

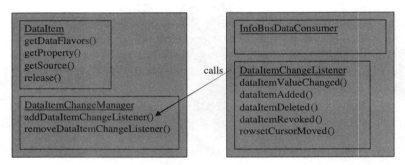

Figure 7–4 A consumer subscribing to a data item for change notification.

Data Item Wrapper Interfaces

All named data items passed on the InfoBus must implement at least the DataItem interface. This has a method, getDataFlavors(), which allows a consumer to query in which data flavors the data item is available. Any valid Java transferable data flavor is permissible. However, the following new types are defined by the InfoBus:

> ImmediateAccess—A data item may implement this to provide String and Object access.
>
> ArrayAccess—A data item may implement this to provide N-dimensional array access functionality to any nested elements it may have.
>
> RowsetAccess—Intended for relational database data. Provides a simplified interface similar to a JDBC ResultSet.
>
> ScrollableRowsetAccess—A RowsetAccess that can be scrolled backwards.

Any of the Java 1.2 Collection types are recommended as well for aggregate objects

Java Activation Framework

The Java Activation Framework (JAF) is a set of classes, interfaces, and standards for creating reusable object viewers and handlers. It is considered a JavaBean extended framework, and is distributed as a standard extension package, javax.activation. It is important for enterprise development because it allows you to create applications that very effectively decouple objects from the ways those objects are used, allowing for object publishing. An enterprise can create viewers for its objects, and clients have a standard way of invoking those viewers.

The architecture defines these components:

Client—Any application class that makes use of the framework.

DataSource—An interface, that must be implemented for the kind of physical data stream from which the data is served. Implementations included with the JAF are FileDataSource and URLDataSource. You create a data source instance for accessing a particular data stream.

DataHandler—A concrete class that provides clients with a single point of access to a data source. You create a data handler instance for providing access to a particular data source. The data handler's means of communicating with the data source is through the methods defined in the DataSource interface.

DataContentHandler—An interface that defines methods for constructing data objects from the data stream. The kind of object created depends on the nature of the stream; there needs to be a data content handler for each MIME type the client needs to access.

DataContentHandlerFactory—An interface, that data content handler factories must implement.

CommandMap—An abstract class which defines a mapping between MIME types and operations which can be performed on the data, (e.g., View and Print operations).

CommandObject—An interface for objects that implement the operations defined in the command map. A command object is usually a "viewer" for a particular type of data; for example, there might be a GIF file viewer, for data of type "image/gif," and the viewer might handle "View" and "Print" operations. A command object may be interactive, or not.

CommandInfo—A descriptor returned by a command map, which can be used to obtain a command object for performing an operation.

These are depicted in Figure 7–5.

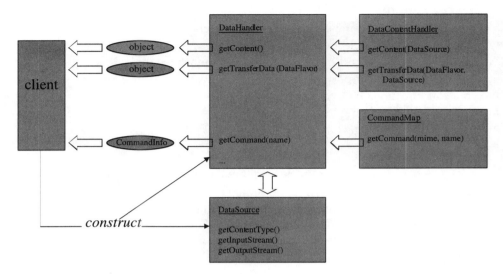

Figure 7–5 How a client uses a DataHandler to get and put objects from and to a DataSource *(Note: not all methods are shown)*

DataHandler provides a full set of methods for accessing the data by flavor (MIME type), and the command types and objects available to process this MIME data type. Thus, you can get the data by flavor or get a viewer for it.

Getting an Object from a Data Source

When a client has a data source for which it wishes to obtain the object representation, it uses a data handler to perform the object construction. The data handler is the client's total interface to a data source. The data handler performs its task based on a determination of the MIME type of the data source. For example,

```
DataSource ds = new URLDataSource(new
   URL("http://somehost/somefile.gif"));
DataHandler dh = new DataHandler(ds);
Image image = (Image)(dh.getContent());
```

Notice that you just call the data handler, and it reads the actual data as necessary to find out what kind it is, and based on that it constructs the appropriate object. To do this, the data handler obtains a DataContentHandler object from the statically installed DataContentHandlerFactory. A data handler has a built-in content handler factory, but you can set your own (once only per VM) by calling the setDataContentHandlerFactory() method.

If the client already has a constructed object and wishes to use a data handler's services on the object (e.g., to get command beans or write the object back to a data source), it can construct the data handler with the following constructor:

```
DataHandler(Object object, String mimeType)
```

For example,

```
DataHandler dh = new DataHandler(image, "image/gif");
```

In other words, in this case a data handler is constructed from the object itself, instead of from a data source (such as a file). Having done this, the client can the do things like the following:

```
dh.writeTo(new FileOutputStream("MyNewImageFile.gif"));
```

You can even do this:

```
InputStream is = dh.getInputStream();
```

In this case, the data content handler writes the object in its appropriate MIME format (in this case "image/gif") to a stream, and that stream is piped back to an input stream, which is returned by the getInputStream() method.

The DataHandler class implements java.awt.datatransfer.Transferable, so you can use the Transferable methods: getTransferData(DataFlavor), getTransferDataFlavors(), and isDataFlavorSupported(DataFlavor).

Getting a Viewer

When a client has a data source and wishes to perform a command on the data, it uses the data handler to return it a CommandInfo object; the client then calls the data handler's getBean() method with the returned CommandInfo object as a parameter, and this returns a command bean which automatically performs the command. In many cases the command operation requires user interaction; for example, a Print command bean may pop up a print dialog. Here is an example of performing the View command ("x-java-view") on our earlier GIF data source:

```
com.sun.activation.viewers.ImageViewer iv =
  (com.sun.activation.viewers.ImageViewer)
  (dh.getBean(dh.getCommand("x-java-view")));
```

If the returned command bean (in this case a viewer object) implements the CommandObject interface, its setCommandContext() method will automatically be called, and passed the command name and data handler as parameters. In this example, the call automatically made would be

```
iv.setCommandContext("x-java-view", dh);
```

This establishes a calling context for the command bean in case it is a general-purpose implementation that implements multiple command types. If the command bean does not implement CommandObject but implements Externalizable, its readExternal() method will be called to reconstitute the object.

To find out the available commands for a data source, the client can call the data handler's getAllCommands() or getPreferredCommands() methods. The getAllCommands() method will return a list of all the command beans that can handle the data source's MIME type. (Actually, it returns a list of CommandInfo objects, from which the CommandObjects can be obtained.) The getPreferredCommands() method will limit the list to one command bean per MIME and command name combination.

Who Creates the DataContentHandler

If you provide a data content handler for your application, you can make it available via a data content handler factory or a command map.

When you call the DataHandler's getContent() method, it first sees if there is a statically installed DataContentHandlerFactory that it can use to obtain a data content handler, using the factory's createDataContentHandler() method. If this fails, it sees if a command map has been set for the data handler, and, if so, uses that, using the command map's createDataContentHandler() method. (Note: this sequence is not documented, so it may change in subsequent releases.)

You can use the default command map, MailcapCommandMap, or create your own and set it for the data handler with the setCommandMap() method. The way in which a command map associates MIME types with data content handlers is up to the command map implementation. However, MailcapCommandMap uses a mailcap file to map between MIME types and commands. It also defines the command "x-java-content-handler" for the purpose of associating a content handler class with each MIME type. Thus, if you want to create your own data content handler for a MIME type, make an entry in the mailcap file you distribute with your application.

Here is the default mailcap file included with the JAF:

```
image/gif;;   x-java-view=com.sun.activation.viewers.ImageViewer
image/jpeg;;x-java-view=com.sun.activation.viewers.ImageViewer
text/*;;      x-java-view=com.sun.activation.viewers.TextViewer
text/*;;      x-java-edit=com.sun.activation.viewers.TextEditor
```

Just create your own mailcap file (called "mailcap") and put it in the META-INF directory of the JAR file in which you distribute your application. For example,

```
image/tiff;; x-java-content-handler=com.me.MyTIFFImageHandler
```

You can also use this form, which specifies the "Viewer" program according to the the RFC 1524 mailcap file definition; JAF will consider the viewer to be the content handler

```
image/tiff;com.me.MyTIFFImageHandler
```

In this example, whenever a TIFF image is encountered, the MyTIFFImageHandler will be used as the content handler.

The META-INF directory may also contain a mime.types file. The default one distributed with the JAF contains these types:

```
text/html               html
text/plain              txt text
image/gif               gif GIF
image/ief               ief
image/jpeg              jpeg jpg jpe JPG
image/tiff              tiff tif
image/x-xwindowdump     xwd
application/postscript  ai eps ps
application/rtf         rtf
application/x-tex       tex
application/x-texinfo   texinfo texi
application/x-troff     t tr roff
audio/basic             au
audio/midi              midi mid
audio/x-aifc            aifc
```

```
audio/x-aiff          aif aiff
audio/x-mpeg          mpeg mpg
audio/x-wav           wav
video/mpeg            mpeg mpg mpe
video/quicktime       qt mov
video/x-msvideo       avi
```

Javasoft's Enterprise JavaBeans Framework

In the previous chapters we saw some of the tremendous practical difficulties in designing and implementing correct multiuser multitier applications. Intuitively, you should feel that these difficulties should not be necessary; somehow, the tools are not right, or are too complicated. After all, all you want to do in most cases is get data in and out, in such a way that you don't conflict with what someone else is doing. It should be very simple.

As we saw, the challenge is that despite an attempt by the industry to create a standard query language and semantics, vendors have gone in their own directions, each implementing slight but insidious differences with far-reaching consequences, thereby making applications nonportable. In addition, the options available to application programmers are too complex and subtle; and there is no clear architecture for separating code that implements transaction control from code that implements business logic.

Enterprise JavaBeans (EJB) attempts to remedy these problems by defining a standard architecture for creating multiuser applications based on a three-tier approach. The architecture drastically simplifies the choices the application programmer needs to make, and delegates most of those concerns to an infrastructure layer that is the responsibility of the middleware vendor. The EJB specification has very good timing, because the market for middleware is entering a tremendous growth phase, and having a standard architecture that requires interoperability, as the Enterprise JavaBeans framework does, will greatly enhance the value of these products.

One interesting omission from the specification is event delivery, which is a central aspect of ordinary beans, and is not addressed by EJB from a transactional application point of view. This is because messages, which are similar to events, are addressed by the Java Message Service (discussed in the distributed computing protocols chapter).

Client and Server

The EJB model is a client/server model based on remove method invocation on server objects using RMI. EJB defines an object framework for a set of server object roles and implementations. The model is symmetric, however, in that server objects invoke each other in the same way clients invoke them (i.e., there is no distinction between a local and a remote client). This provides a high degree of object relocatability. (Of course, under the covers, an implementation is free to implement local calls differently, as long as it is transparent to the application.)

Client sessions with server objects are either stateless or stateful. A stateful object retains value between transactions (but not necessarily between client connections). If a connection is stateful, the server object can be either persistent (retains value between client connections) or not persistent. A nonpersistent server object is called a "session" object, and a persistent server object is called an "entity" object. Entity objects are available to all clients, and a server which provides entity objects in effect provides an object database. Session objects, however, are available only to the client for which they were created, and they do not persist after the client connection is terminated.

Even through client/server connections are based on RMI, they are free to use either RMI's native stream protocol (JRMP), IIOP, or any protocol that can bridge to either of these. This, of course, means that EJB objects can interoperate with non-Java clients. Many vendors are also planning EJB-based gateways to their server products, including many mainframe-based applications.

Transaction Management

Transactions are therefore manifested as remote calls. You can either take charge of transaction management in your client or server beans, or leave it up to the middleware. The latter is recommended, since that is one of the main advantages. I will assume that unless otherwise specified.

A remote call automatically starts a transaction. The transaction is committed (or aborted if necessary) when the call returns. If the call itself makes other calls, they all automatically use the same transaction by testing whether a transaction is in progress. This is even the case if the operation spans multiple databases and multiple EJB middleware implementations; a two-phase commit protocol is used if available (i.e., if all middleware involved provides open-protocol transaction management) to implement an atomic transaction from the client's point of view. The EJB server takes care of the implementing of object caching, synchronization, and locking based on the isolation level specified for the object. Isolation levels are those defined by SQL2. What a wonderful design!

This is significant for portability reasons as well, because a problem is brewing with the way JDBC is being used and implemented. JDBC leaves transaction control in the hands of the client; but the transaction and locking facilities available to an application depend on the driver and the database, so users are resorting to using database-dependent SQL and hard-wiring their applications for specific drivers. (The JDBC 2 RowSet extension will help to address this problem.) The EJB framework puts the burden back in the lap of the database and middleware vendor to make all these things transparent. EJB server implementors are free to use native APIs to achieve this—the application code does not know or care.

One shortcoming is that there does not appear to be a way for an application to request intention locks on entity objects. (See the chapter on databases.) This has performance and scalability implications. Another issue is how an enterprise bean caches non-Java resources, such as connections to other (non-EJB) servers. Entity objects can persist, but they do not retain context across invocations; instead, they are restored as necessary. This means that these objects cannot maintain resource connections, but they must reestablish them. This would make it hard to maintain a socket pool, for example. Some EJB servers, such as WebLogic's Tengah server, have solved this by providing a persistent connection cache object.

How It Works

Let's look at the sequence of events that normally occurs, as depicted in Figure 7–6. When a client wants to use a server service, it first establishes a connection by looking up the container object in some directory service via a JNDI interface and performing a create(). This creates (or allocates from a pool, if the object is stateless) an instance of the requested enterprise bean. It does not return a reference to this object, however; it creates a server-side proxy, called an "EJB Object" (an unfortunate name, since everything is an object; a better name might have been "EJB Proxy" or "EJB Facade"), and returns a reference to that. The proxy object fields calls from the client, and in turn makes identical calls to the e-bean,

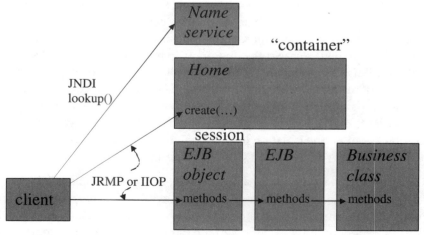

Figure 7–6 Client and EJB interaction.

which in turn makes identical calls to the actual user-written class that implements the business logic. In addition, the proxy object acts as a checkpoint, and performs checks with the container environment regarding security policies.

Deployment

An enterprise bean is packaged with a deployment descriptor. A deployment descriptor is itself a serialized bean. Its state contains the deployment attributes, which may apply to the entire enterprise bean or be specific to particular remote methods. The deployment descriptor contains a security descriptor, method descriptors, a transaction attribute, and an object JNDI name.

The security descriptor specifies access rights on a per-user basis. The deployment descriptor may have a set of method descriptors, which specify a security descriptor and transaction attribute on a method-specific basis. The transaction attribute may be one of the following:

> BEAN_MANAGED—The bean uses JTS to manage transactions itself. It can obtain the current JTS transaction by using java.jts.Current-Transaction.

> MANDATORY—If the client is not in a transaction when the bean is called, an exception will be thrown.

> NOT_SUPPORTED—The bean must not be invoked within a transaction.

> REQUIRED—The EJB server starts a transaction for each method invocation (and commits on return), unless one is already in progress for that client.

> REQUIRES_NEW—The EJB server always creates a new transaction for the call. If the client was already in a transaction, that transaction is temporarily disassociated from the caller's thread until the new call (and new transaction) completes.

> SUPPORTS—The call executes in the context of the client's transaction, if there is one; otherwise it executes without a transaction.

An EJB server registers an enterprise bean via JNDI, using the object name obtained from the deployment descriptor. This provides object location independence, because other beans can find the object simply by using the JNDI API.

Context

When an EJB server instantiates an enterprise bean, it passes it a context object (SessionContext for Session beans and EntityContext for Entity beans) which the bean can use to obtain various services and information. The methods available from the context include:

getCallerIdentity()—Returns the java.security.Identity of the client.

isCallerInRole()—Returns true if the client has the role specified in the server's identity database.

getCurrentTransaction()—Returns the current JTS transaction.

setRollbackOnly()—Marks the current transaction for rollback so that the transaction will not be allowed to commit after this call returns, even if the transaction is distributed and was started by another bean.

getEnvironment()—Returns a Properties object that contains the properties for the bean environment seen by the client.

getEJBHome()—Returns a reference to the EJBHome proxy.

Creating an Enterprise Bean

To create an enterprise bean, you have to create three things: a Home interface, which defines methods for creating instances of the bean (actually, proxies for the bean); a remote bean interface, which defines the transactions or services the bean provides; and a class that implements the business logic of these transactions or services. The only implementation code you have to write when doing this is the code that implements the business logic; all the rest is generated by an EJB development tool provided by the middleware vendor.

The restrictions on business code include:

- It cannot use multithreading or monitors.

- All static fields must be final.

- Unless the bean's deployment defines its transactions as BEAN_MANAGED, it cannot directly access the transaction management services or perform a commit or rollback.

- It cannot change its java.security.Identity.

The middleware tools generate an implementation of the Home interface, which maps the create() calls to the bean create methods with corresponding signatures. The middleware tools also generate a bean class and a proxy class. The generated bean class has methods which correspond to methods in the remote interface, and maps these to corresponding methods (which must be present) in the business logic class you have written. The generated proxy has the methods defined in the remote interface, and maps these to the corresponding methods in the bean class.

Obviously there must be agreement between all these method signatures. The driving definitions for the method signatures are the home interface and remote interface you have defined. All this is depicted for a session bean in Figure 7–7.

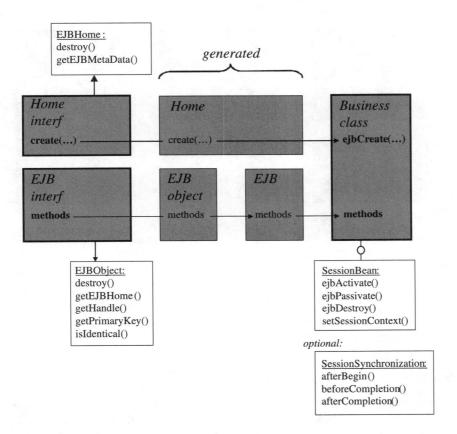

Figure 7–7 Session Bean code generation.

For an entity bean, the code generation is shown in Figure 7–8.

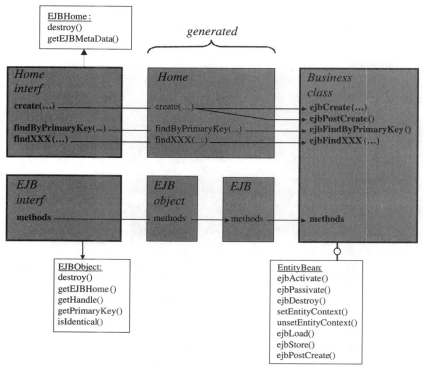

Figure 7–8 Entity Bean code generation.

Who, When

At this writing, many EJB products have appeared, including WebLogic, Sybase, IBM, Sun, Gemstone, BEA Systems, and Oracle, among others. It is anticipated that most middleware vendors (except for Microsoft for awhile) will support EJB. One notable early robust implementation is WebLogic's Tengah Application Server (a 30-day evaluation version is included on this book's CD, and is also available from http://www.weblogic.com). Tengah is a pure Java product, and WebLogic has been a leader in the early implementation of Java standards, including JDBC and RMI. This experience has given them an edge, and their JDBC drivers are among the most sophisticated. Tengah is a multipurpose application server, which supports HTTP, Java Servlets, SSL, JDBC (with full-featured multitier drivers for Oracle, MS SQL Server, Sybase, Informix, DB2), and IIOP. Tengah also supports the Java Message Service, which allows interoperation with message based systems such as IBM's MQ Series and others. The Tengah server is Java 1.1 compatible, but clients can either use Java 1.1 or 1.02.

Tengah has implemented the Java Transaction Service, with built in transaction management and support for client-demarcated transactions, and can interoperate with any JTS-compliant implementation, including Tuxedo and others. This means that you can manage multiple Enterprise Beans transactionally, regardless of which server they reside on, and cooperate in multiple simultaneous database transactions using WebLogic's JTS-compatible JDBC drivers. Tengah also implements its own high performance JNDI naming provider (JNDI is discussed in the chapter on distributed computing protocols), and can interoperate with any JNDI-compliant provider, including LDAP implementations and others.

The EJB and Servlet services support clustering, such that multiple Tengah servers can cooperate to distribute requests to replicated EJB objects or servlets transparently to the end-use application. Clustered failover protection reconnects clients to replicated objects when a connection is lost and a server becomes unavailable. The JNDI and RMI services support clustering as well.

Tengah implements both session beans as well as entity beans, which presently are an optional feature in the EJB specification. Entity beans can be made persistent using a variety of means, including file-based persistence and database-based persistence. Persistence management is automatic, according to the EJB specification for passivation and activation.

On the subject of passivation and activation, Tengah has an extremely interesting and useful feature. When an Enterprise bean is passivated, its state is stored using serialization. If the bean manages a resource connection pool, the resource connections, such as database connections, will be lost. The whole point of a connection pool is to have connections ready instantly to avoid latency when a request arrives; having to restore the connections defeats this. Tengah deals with this by supporting persistent connection pools, which live beyond passivation. When an entity bean is reactivated, it merely reconnects to the connection pool, and finds all of its database connections still there, waiting to receive SQL requests.

The feature of Tengah I like most of all is something called Zero Administration Client (ZAC). WebLogic has developed their own implementation of DRP—Castanet's software deployment protocol. A Tengah-based client application can receive software and content updates from a Tengah server automatically. Whenever a connection to a Tengah server is established, ZAC automatically checks if the client needs an update, and transports the update if required. There is an important aspect to this, however: since a client uses one server for access to all of Tengah's services, that means that it is impossible for a client to get out of sync with regard to a server application, because if the server is stopped to update it, all client connections to that server are lost, and when they reconnect, they automatically perform the update. The fact that a single server is used guarantees client/server software version synchronization, a topic with which I dealt extensively in the distributed computing protocols chapter, as it is a real problem.

Tengah comes with command line tools for generating the code infrastructure required for an Enterprise Bean. WebLogic's philosophy is that developers usually have development tools and component libraries that they prefer, and do not want to have to switch to be compatible with a brand of middleware. Thus, Tengah applications can be developed with Borland JBuilder, SymantecVisual Cafe, and even MS Visual J++.

Tengah also has a management console, for object, service, and transaction management, shown in Figure 7–9. The version of Tengah that comes on the book's CD has two EJB demo programs included, "bank" and "trading." The bank example is shown as a deployed Enterprise Bean in the Tengah console.

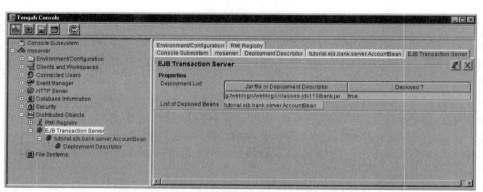

Figure 7–9 The bank example, deployed in a Tengah server.

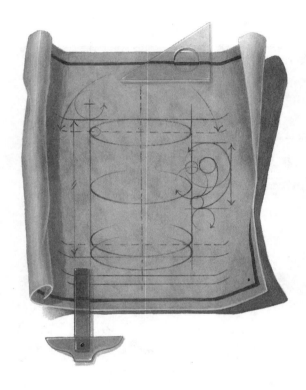

CHAPTER

8

- **Java Threads vs. System Threads**

- **Creating and Starting a Thread**

- **Reentrancy**

- **Adding Synchronization**

- **Synchronized Code Can Be Preempted**

- **Synchronized Methods in Package Java**

- **Threads of Execution Are Independent of Thread Object Instances**

- **Thread Groups**

- **The wait() and notify() Methods**

- **Waiting for Another Thread to Terminate: The join() Method**

- **Handling External System Interrupts**

- **Avoiding Thread Deadlock**

- **A Simple Multithreaded Server Application**

- **Implementing a Thread Pool**

- **Implementing a Thread-Based Service Scheduler**

- **Thread-Local Variables**

Threads in Server Applications

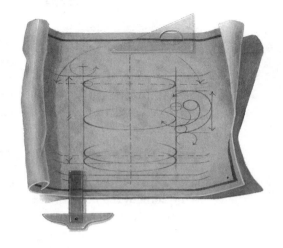

Most operating systems today provide threads. The purpose of threads is to allow programs, executing within the context of a single process, to provide concurrent execution of separate activities. Multiple threads within a process share the same space for static and heap data, so interthread communication is achieved simply through the sharing of variables.

Threads are increasingly important for modern applications. For example, most user interface environments operate under the control of a separate thread or group of threads dedicated to delivering GUI events to application code. Web applications, such as Netscape Navigator, use multithreading to allow multiple content files to download simultaneously instead of sequentially; the net effect is that multiple images are painted at the same time instead of one at a time.

One of the most challenging aspects of thread programming is that the specifics of thread programming APIs vary from one operating system to another. Traditionally, a programmer needs to be experienced in the thread programming models of various systems in order to avoid relying on thread primitives unique to an operating system. Java, on the other hand, defines a generic yet powerful thread programming model, with well-defined semantics, which is portable from across operating systems Sophisticated multithreaded programs can therefore be written in a portable way.

Nevertheless, designing a well-behaved multi-threaded application, even in Java, is not a trivial task. Java provides powerful primitives for creating multi-threaded applications, but Java is not a thread "design" language, in that it does not protect you in any way from creating incorrectly designed multi-threaded programs. Creating a correct design is completely up to you. In this chapter, I will demonstrate how to construct correct multithreaded applications in Java.

Java Threads vs. System Threads

Most implementations of Java today use native operating system threads in order to implement the Java thread model. However, it is important to understand the distinction between a Java thread object and an actual system thread. A system thread is a schedulable entity within the operating system. A Java Thread object is merely a Java language wrapper or surrogate for the system-dependent thread. When you create a Java Thread object, a corresponding system thread does not yet exist, and is not created until you call the Thread's start() method. Calling start() for a Thread object causes a system thread to be created and run.

In a Java VM implemetation, a Java thread is an abstraction, and this abstraction is implemented using native system thread facilities. A Java thread has a Java VM execution stack, but a system thread has a system execution stack of its own. The Java thread's execution stack has information about the current Java methods and data visible to the Java thread; the system thread has information about the current VM functions it is executing, and VM data that identifies the associated Java thread and stack. From the Java thread's point of view, it is executing Java application code; from the system thread's point of view, it is executing VM code to service the Java thread. The start() method bridges these two worlds, creating the system thread that will be used to service a Java thread, setting up the VM data structures necessary to establish the link between the system thread and Java VM Thread object, and then launching the system thread.

Creating and Starting a Thread

To create and start an independent thread of execution in Java, you need to create an instance of the Thread class or a subclass and call its start() method.

The start() method will invoke native code to construct a system thread for servicing this Java thread. After constructing the system thread, start() will determine if a target Java object instance has been specified for it. The target object is the object containing Java code that the thread will execute. A target object can be specified when the Java Thread object is constructed as a Thread constructor parameter.

The target object must implement the Runnable interface, which requires a single method with signature "void run()." If there is a target object, the new system thread uses the target object's run() method as its Java entry point.

If no target object was specified when the Thread object was constructed, its start() method will assume that it is itself the target object. Thread itself implements Runnable, so it has a run() method (empty by default, but you can override it), so in this case start() causes the new system thread to begin executing with the Thread object's run() method as the Java entry point. After initiating this sequence, start() returns to its caller.

To execute code in a separate thread, you therefore need to provide a Runnable object for a Java Thread object to execute. You can create a Runnable object by subclassing Thread, which is a Runnable; or you can create a Runnable object by using any other object which implements Runnable and passing that object to the Thread constructor. Let us look at an example of the first approach.

```java
class SleepyThread extends Thread
{
    /**
     * We override run(), which has an empty implementation in
     * the
         Thread class.
     */
    public void run()
    {
        for (;;)// ever
        {
            try
            {
                sleep(1000);
            }
            catch (InterruptedException ex)
            {
                // This executes if another thread calls
                // interrupt() for this thread object.
                System.out.println("Please don't interrupt me!");
            }
            System.out.println("One more time!...");
        }
    }
}
```

Now that you have defined this Thread class, you can use it as follows:

```
public class RunMyThread extends Applet
{
     SleepyThread sleepyThread;

     public void start()
     {
          sleepyThread = new SleepyThread();// Create a Java
                              // SleepyThread object.
          sleepyThread.start();// Creates a system thread, with
                         // sleepyThread.run() as its entry point.
     }

     public void stop()
     {
          sleepyThread.stop();// Destroys sleepyThread permanently.
          sleepyThread = null;// Allow sleepyThread instance to be
               // garbage collected.
     }
}
```

The second way of executing code in a separate thread is to create a Runnable object by using any other object that implements Runnable, and passing that object to the Thread constructor. For example:

```
public RunMyThread extends Applet implements Runnable
{
     Thread thread;

     public void run()// We must implement this, because Runnable
                    // requires it
     {
          for (;;)// ever
          {
               try
               {
                    sleep(1000);
               }
               catch (InterruptedException ex)
```

```
            {
                    System.out.println("Please don't interrupt me!");
            }
            System.out.println("One more time!...");
        }
    }
    public void init()
    {
        thread = new Thread(this);// Pass it the Runnable - this
            // object.
        thread.start();
    }

    public void destroy()
    {
        thread.stop();
        thread = null;
    }
}
```

Reentrancy

A section of code is "reentrant" if it can be safely executed by multiple threads at the same time, without any external provisions for controlling access to data. (This property is also referred to as being "thread-safe.") There are two forms of reentrancy, which I will call "concurrent" and "guarded." (I don't like these terms much, but they are consistent with the current UML definitions of concurrent and guarded.) A section of code is concurrent reentrant if it is reentrant without using any internal provisions for synchronizing access to data. In other words, it contains no constructs that may cause it to block in order to wait for access to shared data. In contrast, a section of code is guarded reentrant if it uses synchronization mechanisms for accessing shared data, which may cause it to block on occasion.

Concurrent reentrancy can be achieved by not using global data, and not using any data that has a lifetime which extends prior or subsequent to the lifetime of the code section's execution; and if any data created by the section of code is not accessible by other sections of code or other threads. In practice, in the context of Java programming, a concurrent reentrant routine is one that does not use either static or instance variables unless they are constant. Concurrent reentrant methods are usually static. Guarded reentrancy is usually achieved using the Java synchronized modifier.

A Java method that is reentrant by either technique is completely thread-safe—it can be executed by any number of threads without concern for protecting the simultaneous access of data by multiple threads.

To illustrate, in this code the method setX() is not reentrant:

```
class C
{
    char[] x = new int[5];
    void setX(int i, char value)
    {
        x[i] = value;// we are changing data accessible to other
        // threads
    }
}
```

However, in this code setX() is concurrent reentrant:

```
class C
{
    void setX(char[] x, int i, char  value)
    {
        x[i] = value;// no inherent problem here - as long as we are
            given parameter
                // objects that are not shared by multiple threads;
                // protecting against that is a matter of making
                // the calling routine thread-safe

    }
}
```

Each thread has its own execution stack; however, class instance variables are on the shared heap. Therefore, local variables, including object references, which are created on the thread's stack exist only for the lifetime of the scope in which they are created, and so cannot be accessible to other threads. Data and object references which are part of a class's scope are accessible to any thread executing a method belonging to that class, and so are a potential source of non-reentrancy.

If a section of code cannot be concurrent reentrant because it must access a shared item of data, and it is possible that multiple program threads might access the shared item, it must be made guarded reentrant in order to protect against simultaneous access to the shared data. A section of code labeled "synchronized" is guarded reentrant and can be accessed by only one thread at a time for a given object instance; the virtual machine ensures this.

Adding Synchronization

You can synchronize access to instance variables by making the code that accesses them synchronized. For example, in the following code the method setX() is declared synchronized, so only one thread at a time can execute this method *for any instance of class C.*

```
class C

{

    char[] x = new int[5];

    synchronized void setX(int i, char value)

    {

        x[i] = value;      // only one thread at a time can execute
                           //    this

    }

    void m() {}


    synchronized void n() {}

}
```

The existence of the synchronized keyword on any method or section of code in the class causes a lock to be created for each instance of the class. Threads that want to enter *any* synchronized code belonging to the object instance must obtain this lock, and automatically release it when they exit the synchronized code. Using the example above, if there is an instance of C called "c," and a thread is executing c.setX(), then another thread attempting to execute c.setX() *or* c.n() will be forced to wait until the first thread is done or otherwise releases its lock on instance c. However, threads wishing to execute c.m() will not have to wait, since that method is not synchronized. An object that uses a lock to guard itself in this way is called a "monitor."

On the other hand, if there is another instance of class C, called "d," a thread wishing to execute a synchronized method in this instance will not have to wait for threads using "c" to finish, even though "c" and "d" are instances of the same class. The monitor is therefore the object, not the class. (Below we will see that a class monitor can be created as well.)

The actual VM instructions that implement synchronization are the monitorenter and monitorexit instructions. Here is their definition.

monitorenter: (assumes an objectref has been pushed on the stack)

The interpreter attempts to obtain exclusive access via a lock mechanism to objectref. If another thread already has objectref locked, then the current thread waits until the object is unlocked. If the current thread already has the object locked, then continue execution. If the object is not locked, then obtain an exclusive lock.

monitorexit: (assumes an objectref has been pushed on the stack)

The lock on the object is released. If this is the last lock that this thread has on that object (one thread is allowed to have multiple locks on a single object), then other threads that are waiting for the object to be available are allowed to proceed.

Thus, if a thread already has a monitor's object when it tries to get it, it simply proceeds without waiting. Conversely, it does not release control of the object until it has released its last lock—exited all synchronized sections of code for that object.

The "synchronized" modifier is not considered part of a method's unique signature, and can therefore be overridden. That is, if a method is synchronized in a base class and is not in a subclass, instances of the subclass will not need to obtain a monitor in order to enter the method. The "synchronized" keyword is therefore a modifier that applies to a particular implementation of a method signature. You cannot even specify "synchronized" in an interface.

In general, it is necessary to synchronize access to any data that might possibly be read or updated by more than one thread at a time. A synchronized section of code can be viewed as "atomic": it executes until it completes, and cannot be entered by another thread until then. To other threads, it is *atomic*—logically uninterruptible (even though it might be preempted by the scheduler so other threads can execute for a time—but they won't be able to execute this same code for this object instance; that is, enter this monitor).

The built-in Java operations on the Java intrinsic types and object references are defined by the Java language specification to be atomic, except for the double and long types, which will be discussed shortly. For example, arithmetic operations on a Java int value are atomic. In other words, you can be sure that when the VM begins to perform an arithmetic operation on an int, it will get all the way through once it starts. Since an int is composed of four bytes, this is important, because it would be disastrous if one thread started to read an int value when another was in the midst of incrementing it—the thread reading the value would get a corrupted result. The atomic nature of Java arithmetic operations on ints, however, makes such a corrupt value impossible. Operations on the intrinsic types double and long are not atomic, and therefore accessor methods for these types need to be synchronized if access might occur from multiple threads.

Accessor methods for object attributes may or may not need to be synchronized. In particular, if a class defines an immutable object type—one which has no public methods or attributes that can modify the object—accessors to the object do not need to be synchronized, since the state of the object can never change. A good example of this is the String class. To change the value of a String object, you must create a new String, so the String's length can never change once created, and there is no reason to synchronize the length() method. On the other hand, if the object type is mutable and its internal state can change, attribute accessors—and possibly all the object's methods—should be synchronized unless the design of the application ensures that only one thread at a time will access a given object instance.

A synchronized section of code need not be an entire method. For example, in the following, the code within the synchronized block can only be executed by one thread at a time, and that thread obtains (if it does not already have it) the monitor for the object represented by *this* when it enters the synchronized section:

```
...
synchronized (this)      // synchronize access to this object instance
{
     // synchonized code section: the thread that is executing it has
     // the object's monitor

     ...
}
// end of synchronized section: the monitor is now released by the
// thread
...
```

Like object instance data, static data must also be synchronized if it might be accessed by more than one thread at a time. Consider this problematic example:

```
class C
{
     static char[] x = new int[5];
     static void setX(int i, char value)
     {
         x[i] = value;
     }
}
```

In the above example, the static array x is accessed inside of the method setX(). If more than one thread at a time might be entering setX(), we must make sure access to x is protected so that it does not get corrupted by simultaneous accesses occurring in random order. We can do this as follows:

```
class C
{
    static char[] x = new int[5];
    synchronized static void setX(int i, char value)
    {
        x[i] = value;
    }
}
```

In this case the monitor belongs to the class, instead of an instance of the class. A class monitor is distinct from any class instance monitors. If we do not want to synchronize the entire method, we can synchronize a block in a static method by synchronizing on a static object as follows:

```
class C
{
    static char[] x = new int[5];
    static void setX(int i, char value)
    {
        synchronized (x)
        {
            x[i] = value;
        }
    }
}
```

You may be wondering what overhead synchronization imposes on an application. The overhead was significant in early versions of Java—as much as a factor of ten just to make a single synchronized method call versus a non-synchronized call in Java 1.0. However, Java 1.2 and newer VM's such as the HotSpot VM drastically improve this, making a synchronized method call almost as efficient as a regular method call. Regardless, it is merely good programming practice to be judicious about where you use synchronization. Rather than simply synchronizing every method that might be called by a multithreaded application, it is wise to think the design through carefully and isolate the places where multithreaded access to objects needs to occur.

Synchronized Code Can Be Preempted

Synchronized code is often likened to a critical section. From the point of view of a typical application, the comparison is correct. There is one important difference, however: synchronized code can be preempted by the thread scheduler. The Java thread model allows low-priority threads to get some time, even if higher-priority threads are running. (Contrary to what is published in some early books, the rule is that a higher-priority thread receives at least as much time as a lower-priority thread.) However, if a thread has an object's monitor, it can be guaranteed that, even if it is preempted for awhile, no other thread will be able to execute synchronized code belonging to the object (or class, if any static code is synchronized) for which the preempted thread has the monitor. Nevertheless, there might be periods of time when a thread is preempted right in the middle of a synchronized section of code. The synchronized keyword is therefore not sufficient to guarantee immediate execution, as is required for a device driver or code that must respond immediately to a request. Sun's JavaOS™ portable operating system delegates this function to C language routines for hardware interrupt handling (this is sometimes referred to as the "lower" portion of a device driver); the application-oriented part of each JavaOS driver (sometimes referred to as the "upper" portion) is always written in Java.

Another ramification of preemption is that thread priority cannot be used in place of synchronization. Just because one thread is a higher priority than another does not mean that it will execute first, so you cannot use priority to effect any kind of scheduling. (In fact, threads of different priorities may even execute concurrently on some multiprocessor systems.) Thread priority is merely a mechanism for allowing more important activities to have more CPU time. Furthermore, the Java thread priorities, which have values 1 through 10, map to different native thread priorities on different operating systems; and some Java thread priorities actually map to the same value: for example, Sun's Windows Java VM maps Java thread priorities 4, 5, and 6 to the same Windows thread priority value, so decrementing priority by one or even two will sometimes have no effect.

Synchronized Methods in Package Java

At this point you might be wondering, if synchronization is so important, why is it not more prevalent in code in the standard Java packages? For example, how come many methods in the AWT, such as the Component paint() method, are not synchronized, since the UI event thread needs access to these routines, which can also be called by the application's main thread?

In fact, synchronization is used heavily within package java, including the AWT. It is usually encapsulated at a low level, however, out of sight. It is good practice to synchronize as small a section of code as necessary, to minimize the time other threads have to wait.

Here is an example, from MComponentPeer.java, which includes methods that get called when a component is repainted:

```java
public void repaint(long tm, int x, int y, int width, int height)
{
    addRepaintArea(x, y, width, height);
    ScreenUpdater.updater.notify(this, tm);
}


private synchronized void addRepaintArea(int x, int y, int w, int h)
{
    if (updateX1 == updateX2)
    {
        updateX1 = x;
        updateY1 = y;
        updateX2 = x + w;
        updateY2 = y + h;
    }
}
```

Threads of Execution Are Independent of Thread Object Instances

A Java Thread is merely a Java object, and it is important to recognize the distinction between a Java thread object and a thread of program execution. If you define a thread class by extending Thread, any execution thread can call any of the public methods in that class—not just the thread started by your Thread object. For example, consider this class, which extends Thread:

```
class T extends Thread
{
    public void run()
    {
        // The execution thread associated with this Thread object
        // will execute this code
        ...
    }

    public void doStuff()
    {
        // However, any execution thread may execute this code
        System.out.println(Thread.currentThread);
    }
}
```

When you create an instance of T, for example, with

```
T myThread = new T();
```

and then start the thread, with myThread.start(), the VM will create an execution thread and give it myThread's run() method as an entry point. However, there is nothing to stop *any* execution thread from calling *any* of T's methods, e.g. doStuff(), or even run(). Figure 8–1 depicts three separate threads of execution calling myThread's doStuff() method.

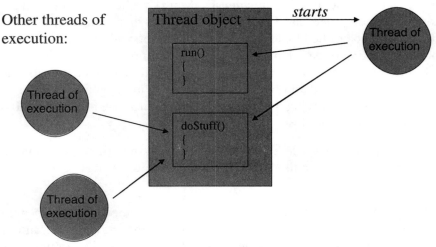

Figure 8–1 Three threads of execution entering a Thread object.

Thread Groups

A thread group is an aggregation of thread objects. Threads within a thread group can be managed as a unit. For example, you can add new threads to a thread group, set the maximum priority that any thread within the group may have, list the threads in a thread group, and interrupt all threads within the group with a single method call. A thread group can also contain other thread groups, forming a hierarchy.

Often, a thread group is used to collect together client threads of some kind under the management of a server or framework application. For example, the Java Commerce Client framework uses thread groups for managing commerce beans so that the independently developed commerce beans can create their own threads, but the set of threads they create can be stopped or interrupted by the Commerce Framework.

In order to perform operations on a thread group, you have to have permission, since all thread group operations invoke a checkAccess() operation. The default security policy allows a thread to access and modify (e.g., add new threads to) its own thread group, but not modify or access information about the thread group in which its own thread group belongs.

The wait() and notify() Methods

The object synchronization feature of Java allows you to protect access to critical data. In addition, a means is needed for releasing a monitor in a controlled way such that it can be obtained again later. The wait() method allows a thread to release its monitor, place itself into a wait state, and then resume later at the same point when notified to do so. The notify() method allows another thread to inform the waiting thread that it should resume and reclaim the monitor. This allows the creation of producer-consumer designs, in which one thread waits for service requests, and another performs the function of generating the requests or at least notifying the service thread when a new request has arrived. The basic model is as follows:

- A synchronized object calls wait(), causing the current thread to temporarily release the object's monitor, putting the thread into a wait state (in effect hibernation).

- A different thread later calls the object's notify() method to notify the thread waiting for the monitor that the object's monitor may be available, and that it should reenter the runnable state. If more than one thread is waiting for the object's monitor, it is undefined which will get notified.

- If there may be more than one waiting thread, use notifyAll()—all threads waiting for this monitor will attempt to reobtain the monitor.

Figure 8–2 illustrates an example.

When a thread goes into a wait state, it is waiting for some external condition to become true; the monitor is the mechanism used to represent this condition. Subsequent notification of monitor availability is in effect notification that the waited-for condition has become true; whether it stays true for long is uncertain. The notify() method does not guarantee that the thread which gets notified will actually get the object next; if there are many threads another thread may get it first, because threads that are notified compete on an equal basis with all other threads vying for the object, including those that were not in a wait state. When a thread returns from a wait state, it should therefore not assume anything about the condition that caused it to be notified, unless it knows it is the only thread that could have been notified.

The notify() and notifyAll() methods must be called from synchronized code, and any threads that are notified will of course wait until the notifying thread releases its lock (leaves the synchronized section). Therefore, while notify() is often called at the end of a synchronized section, it does not have to be—it could safely be called in the middle.

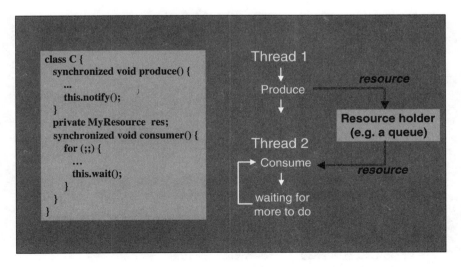

Figure 8–2 A class that allows creation of producer–consumer thread relationships.

Notifying all threads waiting for an object with the notifyAll() method makes it possible to implement an application-specific policy about which thread should get the object after notification. In this scenario, a thread that returns from a wait() call would execute code which decides if it should go back into a wait state or not.

Waiting for Another Thread to Terminate: The join() Method

You can use the join() method to suspend the current thread until a specified target thread object stops. The join() method will cause the calling thread to block until the target thread has stopped, and then resume; at this point, you can issue another join() on a different thread, terminate, or do anything you want.

This can be useful for gracefully coordinating the termination of threads when a program needs to exit. For example, if a user clicks the Exit button of an application while the application is performing a calculation, the button's handler should not just call System.exit()—that might corrupt data, perhaps persistent data. Instead, it should set in motion a termination sequence, perhaps as this button click adapter does:

```
public class Terminator implements java.awt.event.ActionListener,
    Runnable
{
    public Terminator(ThreadGroup g)
    {
        groupToTerminate = g;
        terminate = false;
    }

    public synchronized void
        actionPerformed(java.awt.event.ActionEvent e)
    {
        terminate = true;

        // We use a new thread, because we don't want to block the
        // UI thread
        if ((terminatorThread != null) &&
            terminatorThread.isAlive()) return;

        terminatorThread = new Thread(this);
        terminatorThread.start();
    }
```

```
public synchronized void abortTermination()// called from other
    // threads
{
    terminate = false;
    if (terminatorThread == null) return;
    terminatorThread.interrupt();// interrupt this thread
     // object
    terminatorThread = null;
}

public void run()
{
    // We are now on our way to the gallows...

    int ac = groupToTerminate.activeCount();
    Thread[] threads = new Thread[ac];
    int n = groupToTerminate.enumerate(threads);
    // Note: we should take care of the possibility that
    // more threads could join the group during this process.
    // That is omitted for simplicity.

    for (;;) try
    {
        for  // each service thread
        (int i = 0; i < threads.length; i++)
        {
            // Perform code to cause thread i to terminate
            MyThreadType t = (MyThreadType)(threads[i]);
            t.setTerminate(true);

            threads[i].join();// blocks until this service
                // thread terminates
            // ... on to the next...
        }

        // Exit the VM - you might choose to put this call
        // elsewhere
        System.exit(0);// "release the lever!"
    }
    catch (InterruptedException ex)
```

```
        {
                // Check if termination has been aborted
                System.out.println("Reprieve?");

                if (! terminate) return;// reprieve from the
                    // Governor!!!
        }
    }


    private ThreadGroup groupToTerminate;
    private Thread terminatorThread;
    private boolean terminate;
}
```

When you instantiate this adapter, you have to pass it the thread group corresponding to the set of service threads that need to be terminated when the user clicks Exit. When the button is clicked, the adapter's actionPerformed() method is called, and the adapter then constructs a thread in which to execute a termination sequence. It is important to do this in a new thread and not the current thread, because the current thread is the UI thread, and we do not want to cause the UI thread to block.

The new thread then obtains a list of all the threads in the thread group that it was passed when the adapter was constructed. This is the list of threads it will terminate before exiting the VM. It loops through the list and performs an application-specific method on each thread, which signals that thread to terminate. I have used the method name "setTerminate()" for illustration. Such a method would be a method implemented by the thread class of the threads to be terminated. In some cases, you can just call stop() for each thread, but if you do, you must be certain that it will not have undesirable consequences, since stop() will abort whatever the thread is doing midstream, release all its locks, and terminate the thread. Its use can therefore lead to inconsistencies. (For this reason, stop() has been deprecated in Java 1.2.)

A better approach would be to have a setTerminate() implementation which sets a flag that the thread checks periodically, and stops itself if the flag is true; or, if the thread is in a wait state, setTerminate() could call interrupt() on the thread. The interrupt() method causes the target thread to throw an InterruptedException if it is in a sleep, wait, or join state. This method did not work in Java 1.02; you had to simulate it with the stop() method as a workaround. Thankfully, though, that is history. If a thread is not in a wait (or join) state, interrupt() will merely set the isInterrupted flag in the thread, which can be tested by calling isInterrupted().

Consider this implementation of MyThreadType:

```
public class MyThreadType extends Thread
{
    public void setTerminate(boolean t)// called from another
        // thread
    {
        terminate = t;
        interrupt();// interrupt this thread object
    }

    public void run()
    {
        for (...)
        {
            try
            {
                if (terminate) return;
                wait();
            }
            catch (InterruptedException ex)
            {
                if (terminate) return;
            }
            ...do stuff...
        }
    }
    private boolean terminate;
}
```

When a thread calls setTerminate() on this thread instance, the thread instance's interrupt() method is called. This does not act on the calling thread—it acts on the *called* thread instance. After all, it would not make sense to interrupt your own thread! This is a way for another thread to interrupt this thread. If the thread object that is interrupted is in a wait state, it catches the InterruptedException and checks its terminate flag; if the flag is true, it terminates itself by returning from run().

This brings me to another issue: what if you want to abort the termination? It is easy to implement an abortTermination() method by simply calling interrupt() on this Terminator thread. This will change the terminate flag back to false, and interrupt the join() method the terminator thread is in, if any. When it resumes from the join as a result of the interrupt, it checks the flag, and, if the terminate flag is false, returns from the terminator thread's run method. Of course, by this time it may already have terminated many threads in the thread group, but at least the program has been prevented from exiting and is in a somewhat well-defined state.

Other implementations are, of course, possible, depending on the thread structure of an application; this example is intended to be illustrative.

If the number of service threads can grow during the above operations, you must iterate, checking that all threads have actually completed before you exit. Another consideration is that the above procedure will wait for child threads of the service threads as well; this should be harmless in most cases, since if a service thread terminates a child thread, the worst that can happen is that a join() will be issued on a thread that is stopped, which will have a null effect—the join will instantly return.

Thread States

Figure 8–3 shows the thread states and transitions between states that are possible. Note that if a thread enters a wait state, it can only leave that state by an interrupt() or a notify(). In general, for each blocked state, there is a single way of entering that state and a corresponding method for exiting that state. For example, the sleep() method causes a thread to sleep for a specified period of time;[1] the sleep state can only be left by the elapse of that time or by an interrupt() call—not by any other means. Similarly, a thread that is blocked on an IO operation can only exit that blocked state by successful or unsuccessful completion of the IO operation.

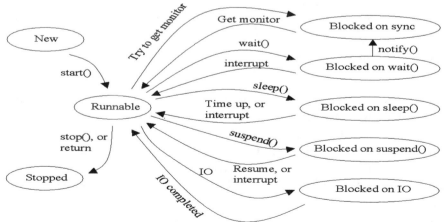

Figure 8–3 Thread state transitions

---

1. Note that the granularity of time supported by the sleep() method implementation may be different on different systems

Handling External System Interrupts

Java does not have a built-in way to handle external system interrupts. For example, if a server administrator types Control-C at the console to stop a server, the Java program does not normally have a way to respond to this appropriately and clean up before terminating. However, you can provide a native signal handler to do this, which calls a Java method in your code. Here is an example, taken from a news group posting by Mark Gritter of Standford University, showing how to write a native signal handler for Unix, installable from Java:

```java
/**
 *  CatchSignal.java
 */
public class CatchSignal implements Runnable
{
    static { System.loadLibrary("CatchSignal"); }
    public native static void setControlCHandler();
    public static void callback()
    {
        System.err.println("Control-C hit!");
    }
    public void run()
    {
        setControlCHandler();// never returns
    }
    public static void main(String[] args)
    {
        Thread t = new Thread(new CatchSignal());
        t.setDaemon(true);// Allow program to end even through
            // signal-handling thread doesn't ensure signals are
                handled
        t.setPriority(Thread.MAX_PRIORITY);
        t.start();
        // Go about normal business...
        ...
    }
}
```

```
/*
 * CatchSignal.c -- Compile as shared library libCatchSignal.so
 */
int pipefd;
void ctrl_c_handler()
{
    int foo = SIGINT;
    write(pipefd, &foo, sizeof(int));
    signal(SIGINT, ctrl_c_handler);
}
JNIEXPORT void JNICALL
Java_CatchSignal_setControlCHandler (JNIEnv * env, jclass cls)
{
    int filedes[2], sigfd, s;
    jmethodID mid = (*env)->GetStaticMethodID(env, cls,
        "callback", "()V");
    pipe(filedes);
    pipefd = filedes[0];
    sigfd = filedes[1];
    signal(SIGINT, ctrl_c_handler);
    while(1)
    {
        read(sigfd, &s, sizeof(int));
        (*env)->CallStaticVoidMethod(env, cls, mid);
    }
}
```

Avoiding Thread Deadlock

Thread deadlock is an undesirable situation in which two different threads are each waiting for each other, in such a way that they will wait forever. For example, if thread A has a lock for an object and is waiting for a lock held by thread B, but B is waiting for the lock on the object held by thread A, then a deadlock results. This can occur in the real world, say, if you play in a band and are waiting for permission to marry Mary; but Mary's parents are waiting for you to quit the band before they will give permission (this is the old days), but you can't quit until you marry Mary and the two of you can move to Colorado where you can find a new job. This is deadlock—semingly unresolvable!

To avoid deadlock, always obtain locks in the same sequence. In the case of Mary, you joined the band before you asked Mary to get married; but her parents, who apparently have a lock on Mary, have had that lock since Mary was born. You should try to obtain this lock in the same sequence as her parents: get Mary's lock before you get the "band lock." In other words, ask Mary to get married before you join the band. In the case of a Java application, design the application such that in case thread A ever needs access to two synchronized objects, make sure that every other thread accesses those objects in the same order A does. This strategy works if one assumes that each method has a means of completing and will not *explicitly* block for some resource.

Two Thread methods which are deadlock-prone are suspend() and resume(). The suspend() method causes a thread to explicitly go into a blocked state until some other thread calls the resume() method on the blocked thread. In the meantime, the blocked thread holds all of its locks. These methods have been deprecated in Java 1.2, so you should not use them.

The elimination of these methods does not prevent us from using the wait() method to write code that explicitly blocks and cannot be resumed. The wait() method only releases the lock for the object instance on which it is called. If the thread holds locks for other objects, it will not release them while it is waiting. This has nothing to do with calling order; it has to do with going to sleep while someone is waiting, and they can't call to wake you up because your phone is off the hook! Let's look at a Java example:

```
class Outer
{
    Inner inner = new Inner();
    Outer()
    {
        synchronized (this)
        {
            inner.selfishBlock();    // We are now blocked; the
                                     // current thread now holds
                    // this object's lock, but has released
                    // inner's lock
        }
    }
    synchronized void wakeInnerUp()
    {
        // no thread can ever get this lock, because the waiting
        // thread holds it
        inner.notify();
    }
}
class Inner
```

```
    {
        synchronized void selfishBlock()
        {
            wait();// current thread releases inner's lock, but still
                   // holds all other locks - yet it is blocked
        }
    }
```

A waiting thread only releases the lock of the object for which the wait was called. If the wait () call occurs inside synchronized code that holds a lock to another object, the notify () method had better not be called from that other object. In the above example, the class Inner is in a wait state; but it also holds Outer's lock, and Outer is the "telephone"—it has the only method that can be called to release the lock. Thus, no one can call, and Inner sleeps (waits) forever. This situation of an object explicitly waiting for a call to an object it has locked is called a "nested monitor."

A way around this is not to rely on Inner's phone; use the front door. Have an unsynchronized method in Outer that calls a synchronized method in Inner, to wake Inner up, to call notify(). The tip-off of a potential problem in the code above is the fact that wait() is called in an Inner method, and the corresponding notify() call occurs in an Outer method; they are in different classes. Here is a version that does not deadlock:

```
class Outer
{
    Inner inner = new Inner();
    Outer()
    {
        synchronized (this)
        {
            inner.selfishBlock();    // We are now blocked; the
                          // current thread now holds
                              // this object's lock, but has released
                              // inner's lock
        }
    }
    void wakeInnerUp()
    {
        inner.wakeupBuddy();
    }
}
```

```
class Inner
{
    synchronized void selfishBlock()
    {
        wait();// current thread releases inner's lock, but still
            // holds all other locks - yet it is blocked
    }
    synchronized void wakeupBuddy()
    {
        notify();
    }
}
```

Any thread can call the wakeupBuddy() method, because it is not synchronized. This method can then successfully call the wakeupBuddy() method, which is synchronized, because the lock it needs is released.

A Simple Multithreaded Server Application

Threads allow for lightweight servicing of concurrent client requests. The basic approach is to assign a separate thread to service each incoming request. Since threads have access to the same virtual machine, care must be taken in the design of the service applications, and consideration should even be given to writing a security manager specific to the needs of the server application. (This is demonstrated in the chapter on security.)

The following program demonstrates a simple server application using threads. It is a "chat" server, which performs a simple function: it receives incoming text from each of multiple clients, and broadcasts all text received to *all* clients. If you like, you can embellish this program to provide logon identity and other features that are commonly found in real chat programs. The program consists of two classes: the server's main class and a thread class. Let us first look at the main class:

```
import java.util.*;
import java.net.*;
import java.io.*;
public class ChatServer
{
    public static void main(String[] args)
    {
```

```
int port = 0;
try { port = Integer.parseInt(args[0]); }
catch (Exception ex) { System.out.println
    ("Must enter port no."); return;}
ServerSocket ss = null;
try
{
    ss = new ServerSocket(port);
}
catch (Exception ex)
{
    ex.printStackTrace();
    return;
}
ChatServer cs = new ChatServer();

for (;;)// ever
{
    Socket s = null;
    try
    {
        s = ss.accept();// blocks until next connection
            // request
        SocketServiceThread t = new
            SocketServiceThread(s,cs);
        t.start();
    }
    catch (Exception ex)
    {
        ex.printStackTrace();
    }
}
}

Vector instreams = new java.util.Vector();
Vector outstreams = new java.util.Vector();
}
```

The first thing the server program does is attempt to create a server socket on a user-specified port for listening for incoming connection requests. Assuming this succeeds, it then creates an instance of its own class. The only reason it does this is to create a single object on which it will synchronize access to two data structures: a list of input streams and a list of output streams; the need for this will be clear shortly. It then enters an endless loop, in which it repeatedly blocks on an accept() call. The accept() returns when a new connection request has arrived, and the server then immediately allocates resources to service that request: it creates a new Java thread specifically for the request, and starts it. If requests were known to arrive at a high rate, a more sophisticated implementation could first enqueue the request and then reenter the accept(); the enqueued request could then be serviced by a separate queue manager thread. However, connection requests are a small part of the service demands for this application.

The threads that are created to service requests are defined as follows:

```java
class SocketServiceThread extends Thread
{
    public SocketServiceThread(Socket s, ChatServer chatServer)
    {
        setDaemon(true);

        this.chatServer = chatServer;

        dis = new DataInputStream(s.getInputStream());
        ps = new PrintStream(s.getOutputStream(), true);

        synchronized (chatServer)
        {
            chatServer.instreams.addElement(dis);
            chatServer.outstreams.addElement(ps);
        }
    }

    public void run()
    {
        for (;;)// ever
        {
            String data = "";
            try
            {
                data = dis.readLine();
            }
            catch (Exception ex) { data = null; }
```

```
        if (data == null)
        {
            synchronized(chatServer)
            {
                int index =
                    chatServer.instreams.indexOf(dis);
                PrintStream ps =
                (PrintStream)(chatServer.outstreams.
                    elementAt(index));
                ps.println();
                ps.flush();
                ps.close();
                try { dis.close(); } catch
                    (IOException ex2) {}
                chatServer.instreams.removeElementAt(index);
                chatServer.outstreams.
                    removeElementAt(index);
            }
            stop();
        }
        // Write to all clients

        synchronized(chatServer)
        {
            for (int i = 0; i < chatServer.outstreams.size();
                i++) // all clients
            {
                PrintStream ps =
                (PrintStream)(chatServer.outstreams.
                    elementAt(i));
                ps.println(data);
            }
        }
    }
}

private DataInputStream dis;
private PrintStream ps;
}
```

When this thread is constructed, it firsts sets the daemon flag to true, to indicate that it is a daemon thread. This is desirable because if the main program thread terminates, we want all service threads to terminate as well. It then constructs streams to use for input and output on the socket that it is servicing. At this point, it adds these newly constructed streams to two lists. These lists are needed later when the thread needs to broadcast data to all other clients, and also when it needs to disconnect itself from a client. Since these lists are shared objects, used by all service threads, access to them must be synchronized. Furthermore, while it is true that the methods that operate on the Vector class, which is what we are using for our lists, are synchronized themselves, this is not sufficient, because we want operations that we perform on *both lists at the same time* to be atomic; we do not want the two lists to get out of sync, even for an instant. That is why we wrap accesses to both lists in synchronized blocks of code, and synchronize *on the object which owns (contains) the lists:* the instance of ChatServer.

This last point is an important point: you should either synchronize on the object you are trying to protect access to, or you should synchronize on an object that is a single identifiable owner of that object. Many other objects may have references to a protected object, and synchronizing them does not accomplish your goal of protecting access to the object. For example, consider a class D which references a class C:

```
class C
{
    Vector v = new Vector();
    public static void main(String[] args)
    {
        C c = new C();
        D d1 = new D(c);
        Thread t1 = new Thread(d1);
        D d2 = new D(c);
        Thread t2 = new Thread(d2);
        t1.start();
        t2.start();
    }
}

class D implements Runnable
{
    public D(C c)
    {
```

```
            this.c = c;
    }
    public void run()
    {
        // synchronized (this)// Wrong - we are synchronizing on
                             // the wrong thing
        synchronized(c)        // Right - synchronize on the actual
                             // object being changed,

                             // or its logical composite parent.

        {
            c.value++;

        }

    }
    private C c;  // This object does not own this instance of C -
                  // it merely references it.

}
```

Each instance of D merely references a common instance of C. Synchronization therefore should be on the shared instance, since that is what must be protected; or on an object that is the single logical parent of the common instance. In the ChatServer example, the latter approach is used: access to the instreams and outstreams lists is serialized by synchronizing on the single object that owns both lists: the ChatServer object.

Returning to the ChatServer, the thread's run() method merely loops forever, blocking on a read of the socket's input stream. Whenever the read returns data, the thread scans the list of output streams and broadcasts the data to each. This operation must be synchronized, since one of the server sockets could close during this process, and the thread servicing it would then remove it from the list of output streams; this could change the position of elements in the list, at the same time as another thread is broadcasting. There is a flaw in this design, however—can you spot it? In many cases, where service time is short or the number of clients small, this approach is workable. In a high-throughput application with a large number of clients, however, it would be unacceptable to lock the client list while data is broadcast to all clients, which might take a long time compared to the normal time between the arrival of new data. A more scalable approach would be to first make a copy of the client list, in a synchronized fashion, and then release the list and use the copy, and make provisions for the fact that the copy might become out of date while we are using it. Thus, we might rewrite the last section of the class as

```
class SocketServiceThread extends Thread
{
    ...

    public void run()
    {
        for (;;)// ever
        {
            ...
            // Write to all clients

            java.util.Vector outstreams = null;
            //synchronized(chatServer)
            //{
                outstreams = chatServer.outstreams.clone();
            //}
            for (int i = 0; i < outstreams.size(); i++)
                                    // all clients
            {
                try
                {
                    PrintStream ps =
                        (PrintStream)(outstreams.elementAt(i));
                }
                catch (ArrayIndexOutOfBoundsException ex)
                {
                    continue;
                }
                try
                {
                    ps.println(data);
                }
                catch (IOException ex)
                {
                    continue;
                }
            }
        }
    }
    ...
}
```

Thus, we clone the chatServer.outstreams list of client output streams, and then use that list for determining to whom to broadcast. I have even commented out the synchronization specification, since the Vector.clone() method is synchronized and we only need to clone the outstreams list in this operation, not both lists.

The only difficulty lies in taking care of the possibility that the real list of outstreams may change while we are using the cloned list, so some of the outstreams may become invalid and some new ones be added that we will not know about. The price is a small one, since in this application failing to deliver a line of text to a newly arrived client is a very minor and acceptable failure, so we are not worried about not knowing of a new connection occurring during a broadcast. The other situation—that a connection may be terminated after we clone the list and before we complete the broadcast—will potentially result in the list ordering changing, and also a possible attempted broadcast to someone who is already disconnected. The list ordering is not important, since we are broadcasting the same thing to all clients (we might encounter an array index out of bounds exception, which we can catch), and a broadcast to a disconnected client will at most result in an IO exception, which we can also catch.

Implementing a Thread Pool

These improvements work fine, but for large numbers of clients the system will start to run out of resources. A thousand clients would require a thousand connections and a thousand threads. This would not occur in a chat application (at least not in a single chat room—it would be a noisy chat room indeed!). However, it can occur in many transactional applications. Applications that require access to data, often intermittently, from large numbers of clients are designed as transaction-oriented instead of session-oriented in order to improve scalability. The application only needs to retain state about a client for the duration of a single transaction. With this simplification resources can be reused, including system threads.

Transaction-oriented applications may maintain a persistent connection to a server; but the server does not allocate processing resources until the client makes a request, and the resources are freed when the request has been serviced. For example, a DBMS requires the client to maintain a connection to the DBMS, but each transaction is serviced by a thread allocated for the duration of that transaction; or, if the transaction spans multiple queries, it may not even be the same thread. Another example is a CORBA ORB, which maintains connections to a large number of clients, but maintains a thread pool for servicing incoming remote call requests. It is then up to the application to retain any required client-specific state between requests.

A Producer-Consumer Thread Pool Model

One way of implementing a thread pool is to view it as a set of consumer threads which service requests manufactured by a producer. The basic approach is:

- Create a producer: this is the main server object.

- Create *N* consumer thread objects; start each, and put each into a wait state.

- Loop: whenever a request comes in, create a new service object (includes the socket), add the object to a queue, and call notify().

- When a consumer thread object resumes, it attempts to get a single service object from the queue. If it fails, it goes back into a wait state. If it succeeds, it processes that object and then tries to get another object, or goes back into a wait state.

I will now explain an example implementation using this technique. For simplicity, I will assume a pool of a fixed (ungrowable) size. I will also assume that the calling routine manages client connections, and only invokes the pool manager when a new request arrives, that is, there is a new connection, or there is data on a connection. The client manager may be a single-threaded routine, looping until data is available on the socket's SocketImplementation. (There is unfortunately not an equivalent to the UNIX select() call, which blocks until there is either new data, or a new connection request.)

The PoolManager class (makes me think of summer days gone by) provides a server program with the required consumer functionality, to service manufactured (incoming) service requests. The entry point a server program would use is the PoolManager's service() method, which takes a Runnable object as a parameter. When this method is called, the PoolManager takes care of making sure that the object's run method is called in its own thread.

```
class PoolManager
{
    private ServiceThread[] threads;// the thread pool
    private Vector serviceRequests = new Vector();
    public PoolManager(int noOfThreads)
    {
        threads = new ServiceThread[noOfThreads];
        // Create the thread pool
        for (int i = 0; i < threads.length; i++)
        {
            ServiceThread thread = new ServiceThread(this);
            threads[i] = thread;
            thread.start();// this will start a separate thread,
```

```
                         // which will then call getObject() and block
        }
        // We can now be sure that all threads are created and are
        // in a blocked
        // state, waiting for us to call notify(). That is what
        // service() does.
    }


    /**
     * This method is the entry point for the server's main routine,
     * whenever it wants to pass us a Runnable object
     * to service in a thread.
     */

    public synchronized void service(Runnable object)
    {
        serviceRequests.addElement(object);
        notify();
    }


    /**
     * This is the method that our service threads call in order to
     * get new Runnable
     * objects to service; these threads block in this call until
     * the above service()
     * method results in a notify to one of them.
     */

    public synchronized Object getObject() throws InterruptedException
    {
        while (true){
        {
            try { Object o = serviceRequests.firstElement();
            serciveRequests.removalElementAt(0);
            return o;
            } catch (Exception ex) { wait(); }
        }
    }


    /**
     * Gracefully stop the threads in the thread pool.
     */
```

```
    public void finalize()
    {
        // Stop all the threads that are not blocked...
        for (int i = 0; i < threads.length; i++)
        {
            if (threads[i].isAlive()) threads[i].stop();
        }
    }
}
```

The getObject() method is called by service threads waiting in the pool when they want another object to service. This method blocks those threads until a notify() wakes one of them up, at which point the awaken thread can check if an object is available to be serviced; if not, it goes back into a wait state. If an object is available, it returns, and the thread's run() method proceeds and calls the object's run() method. When the object's run() method returns, the thread's run() method loops back to the getObject() call.

The finalize() method above takes care of graceful termination of service threads. A more complete implementation would not call stop(), but would signal the service threads to terminate, and join() on those threads, as illustrated earlier in this chapter.

The ServiceThread class is the thread class for the threads used to service requests. Its run() method contains a loop, as just described. This loop executes forever, repeatedly blocking on a getObject() call, and then calling the returned object's run() method.

```
class ServiceThread extends Thread
{
    private Runnable object;
    private PoolManager poolManager;
    public ServiceThread(PoolManager pm)
    {
        poolManager = pm;
    }
    public synchronized void run()
    {
        for (;;)
            // ever
        {
```

```
            //
            // Wait to be notified; blocks until an object is
            // returned
            //
            try
            {
                object = (Runnable) (poolManager.getObject());
            }
            catch (InterruptedException ex)
            {
            }
            //
            // Do the callback, at the specified priority
            //
            try
            {
                if (object != null) object.run();
            }
            catch (ThreadDeath td)// We simply want the thread to
                                  // go back to the pool
            {
            }
            catch (Throwable t)// Exception "firewall"
            {
                t.printStackTrace();
            }
            finally
            {
                object = null;// Allow runnable object to be
                              // collected and finalized
            }
        }
    }
}
```

A Thread Assignment Model

A problem with the previous implementation is that you don't know if the service request is being handled right away. In particular, if there are not enough threads in the thread pool, there is no way to find out—the notify() method will fall on deaf ears. In that case, the request will not be serviced until another thread is done. You also cannot control or manage priority changes if you want to, since thread allocation is handled completely automatically by the Java VM.

You can take direct control of thread assignment to service requests by implementing your own thread allocation mechanism. Here is an implementation that does not rely on notify() to select a thread. The changes from the previous pool implementation are indicated in bold.

```
class PoolManager
{
    private ServiceThread[] threads;// the thread pool
    private boolean[] allocated;// allocation flag for each thread
    public PoolManager(int noOfThreads)
    {
        threads = new ServiceThread[noOfThreads];
        allocated = new boolean[noOfThreads];
```

Above I have added a set of flags to indicate if a given thread in the pool is assigned or not. The next section of code gets a little more complicated, because we have to take care of the situation in which our threads no longer call getObject(). Instead, we need to cause the threads to start, and then block on a wait() from which we can extricate any particular one of them. We must be careful to know the state of all threads before we allow any of them to be allocated to a service request. To accomplish this, the following code must block after each thread's start() method is called, until the thread signals that it has started and is waiting.

```
    // Create the thread pool
    for (int i = 0; i < threads.length; i++)
    {
        allocated[i] = false;
        ServiceThread thread = new ServiceThread(this);
        threads[i] = thread;
        synchronized (thread)
        {
            thread.start();// this will start a separate
                // thread, which will then call wait() and
                // block (which releases its monitor so
                // we can get past the next line)
            try
            {
                thread.wait();// this blocks until the thread
```

```
                        // calls notify() and then blocks (which
                        // releases its monitor,
                        // allowing this statement to return)
                }
                catch (InterruptedException ex)
                {
                }
            }
        }
        // We can now be sure that all threads are created and are
        // in a blocked
        // state, waiting for us to call notify(). That is what
        // allocate() does.
    }
```

The following method replaces the service() method in the previous implementation. Its purpose is to allocate a thread from the pool, and cause that thread to execute the passed object's run() method. This routine immediately returns with a
reference to the thread used to service the object. This thread reference could be
used in a more advanced implementation to perform thread management functions, such as changing the thread's priority or unscheduling the thread. (These
features will be seen in the next example.) Note also that this routine can throw an
exception type I have defined, InsufficientThreadsException, indicating that there
are not enough threads to service the request. A more complete implementation,
which is left to the reader to implement, would dynamically grow the thread
pool.

```
    public synchronized ServiceThread allocate(Runnable object)
    throws
        InsufficientThreadsException
    {
        // Pick a thread from the thread pool
        ServiceThread thread = allocateAThread();
        if (thread == null) throw new
            InsufficientThreadsException();
        // Allocate that thread
        thread.allocate(object);
        // Return a unique identifier for the thread
        return thread;
    }
```

```
/**
 * Allocate a thread from the thread pool.
 */

protected ServiceThread allocateAThread()
{
    for (int i = 0; i < threads.length; i++)
    {
        if (allocated[i]) continue;
        allocated[i] = true;
        return threads[i];
    }

    return null;
}
```

The following method returns a thread to the thread pool. The service threads automatically call this after they have completed servicing a request.

```
/**
 * Return a thread to the thread pool.
 * This method must be synchronized in case multiple threads in
 * an application
 * call this method for this Scheduler object, and also because
 * threads call
 * this to return themselves to the thread pool.
 */

public synchronized void deallocateThread(ServiceThread thread)
{
    for (int i = 0; i < threads.length; i++)
    {
        if (threads[i] == thread)
        {
            allocated[i] = false;
            return;
        }
    }
}
```

```
/**
 * Gracefully stop the threads in the thread pool.
 */

public void finalize()
{
    // Stop all the threads that are not blocked...
    for (int i = 0; i < threads.length; i++)
    {
        if (threads[i].isAlive()) threads[i].stop();
    }
}
}
class ServiceThread extends Thread
{
    private Runnable object;
    private PoolManager pm;

    public ServiceThread(PoolManager pm)
    {
        poolManager = pm;
    }
```

The following method is the method called by the PoolManager to allocate this thread to a service object. It has the effect of bringing the thread out of the wait state into which it puts itself below in the run() method.

```
public synchronized void allocate(Runnable object)
{
    this.object = object;
    // Now, resume this thread
    notify();
}
public synchronized void run()
{
    notify();// this merely notifies the pool manager, which is
            // waiting
            // to be notified, that it should unfreeze itself
            // in the thread's
            // monitor queue. This helps to ensure that all
            // threads have been
```

```
            // started before the PoolManager starts
            // allocating them.

for (;;)
    // ever
{
    //
    // Wait to be called upon; blocks until a call to
    // allocate() results in a notify()
    //

    try
    {
        wait();
    }
    catch (InterruptedException ex)
    {
    }

    //
    // Do the callback, at the specified priority
    //
    try
    {
        object.run();
    }
    catch (ThreadDeath td)// We simply want the thread to
        go back to the pool
    {
    }
    catch (Throwable t)// Exception "firewall"
    {
        t.printStackTrace();
    }
    finally
    {
        object = null;// Allow runnable object to be
        // collected and finalized
    }

    //
```

```
                // Thread's work is done; return it to the pool
                //

                poolManager.deallocateThread(this);
            }
        }
}

/**
 * If there are insufficient threads in the thread pool.
 */
class InsufficientThreadsException extends Exception {}
```

Implementing a Thread-Based Service Scheduler

A service scheduler is a server application which allows clients to schedule processing to occur at a future time. An example of such a requirement is the UNIX cron utility. Ideally, a scheduler allows you to not only schedule processing, but unschedule it as well if circumstances change. (The algorithm employed for this kind of application is very similar to a discrete event simulator, which schedules and unschedules future events in a synchronous way.)

We can extend the thread pool manager developed in the previous section to provide thread scheduling. We have the basic framework; a thread pool manager is just a special case of a scheduler in which threads are scheduled to service requests immediately instead of at a future time. What we must add to create a true scheduler is delayed servicing, and also the ability to unschedule a service that has already been scheduled. We can also add some additional features to make the scheduler more functional, such as variable service thread priority, an application-specific service argument, and a feature for scheduling services that recur at regular intervals.

To implement this, we only have to make a few additions to the previous implementation. Most of the program is very similar to the previous one, so I will only present the changes. First of all, I will rename the class "Scheduler," since that is more descriptive of its new purpose.

Next, instead of requiring service objects to implement the Runnable interface, I will define a new interface, more appropriate for a schedulable object:

```
/**
 * Callback object interface.
 */
```

```
interface Schedulable
{
    public void onEvent(Object arg);
    public void onAbort();
}
```

The onEvent() method will be called by the scheduler when a future scheduled event arrives; and the onAbort() method will be called when an exception of any type occurs while the event is being serviced.

Next I will rename the allocate() method to schedule(), and give it this implementation:

```
/**
 * Schedule thread to run at a future time.
 * The Schedulable.onEvent() method will be called for object
 * after a real-time delay of "delay" milliseconds.
 * The thread's handle is returned, which
 * we can later use to reschedule the thread.
 * If "recurring" is true, then a new event will be scheduled
 * automatically each time onEvent() is called.
 * This method must be synchronized in case multiple threads in
 * an application call this method for this Scheduler object.
 */

public synchronized EventThread schedule(long delay,
        Schedulable object, Object arg, int priority, boolean
        recurring)
throws
        InsufficientThreadsException
{
        // Pick a thread from the thread pool
        EventThread thread = allocateAThread();
        if (thread == null) throw new
            InsufficientThreadsException();

        // Schedule an event for that thread
        thread.schedule(delay, object, arg, priority, recurring);

        // Return a unique identifier for the event
        return thread;
}
```

As you can see, there are parameters for a time delay and an execution priority. I will also define a "reschedule()" method as follows:

```
/**
 * Unschedule the future event for a thread, and reschedule it.
 */
public void reschedule(EventThread thread, long delay,
    Schedulable object, Object arg, int priority, boolean
    recurring)
throws
    InsufficientThreadsException
{
    thread.reschedule(delay, object, arg, priority, recurring);
}
```

The above method can be used to reschedule future events that have already been scheduled. This is important, since it is often the case that scheduled processing must be unscheduled or moved to a new time. The rest of this class is the same as before.

I will now modify the EventThread class by adding these class variables to it:

```
private long delay;          // wait for this time
private Object arg;              // a parameter for onEvent()
private int priority;            // execute onEvent() at
                                 // this priority
private boolean recurring;       // reschedule the event every
                                 // time
```

and redefining its allocate() method—which I will also rename "schedule"—as follows:

```
public synchronized void schedule(long delay, Schedulable
    object, Object arg, int priority, boolean recurring)
{
    this.object = object;
    this.delay = delay;
    this.arg = arg;
    this.priority = priority;
    this.recurring = recurring;

    // Now, resume this thread to tell it how long to wait for
    notify();
}
```

I will also give this class an unschedule() method.

```
/**
 * Reschedule this Thread object. Note that this will be called
 * from a different thread.
 */
public synchronized void reschedule(long delay, Schedulable
    object, Object arg, int priority, boolean recurring)
throws
    InsufficientThreadsException
{
    // stop(new InterruptedException());// This was the only
                                        // way in JDK 1.0
    interrupt();                        // This is the
                                        // right way

    try
    {
        wait();// wait until the stopped thread blocks
    }
    catch (InterruptedException ex)
    {
    }
    schedule(delay, object, arg, priority, recurring);
}
```

I will re-implement the run() method as follows:

```
public synchronized void run()
{
    notify();// this merely notifies the scheduler, which is
            // waiting to be notified,
            // that it should unfreeze itself
            // in the thread's monitor queue.

    for (;;)
        // ever
    {
        //
        // Wait to be called upon; blocks until a call to
        // schedule() results in a notify()
        //
```

```
try
{
    if (! recurring) wait();
}
catch (InterruptedException ex)
{
}


//
// Sleep until the specified time has elapsed
//

try
{
    // This is the real wait, requested by the
    // scheduler
    wait(delay);
}
catch (InterruptedException ex)
{
    // We are being rescheduled: abort the current
    // sleep
    recurring = false;
    notify();
    continue;
}


//
// Do the callback, at the specified priority
//
int savep = getPriority();
setPriority(priority);
try
{
    object.onEvent(arg);
}
```

```
catch (ThreadDeath td)
{
        try
        {
            object.onAbort();
        }
        catch (Throwable ta)// Exception firewall
        {
            ta.printStackTrace();
        }
}
catch (Throwable t)// Exception firewall
{
        t.printStackTrace();
}
finally
{
        object = null;
}
setPriority(savep);
//
// Thread's work is done; return it to the pool
//

        if (! recurring) scheduler.deallocateThread(this);
    }
  }
}
```

The main change to the run() method is the division of processing into two steps: a delay step, which effects the time delay, and a service step, which actually invokes the service object's onEvent() method. The delay step must accommodate the possiblity that the event gets rescheduled, by catching InterruptedException and performing a continue to go back to the start of the loop and back into a wait state. I have also added a "recurring" feature for events that need to occur at regular intervals: the schudule method has a boolean argument which is set to true for recurring events, and in that case the event occurs again and again after the passage of the specified time period.

Thread-Local Variables

Java 1.2 has a new feature, called "thread local" variables, which provide a convenience mechanism for implementing multithreaded programs that must service an arbitrary number of clients and be stateful. It allows you to defer the replication of your object data until the moment at which a new thread actually enters your code. For example,

```
public class MyClass
{
    private static ThreadLocal myData = new ThreadLocal()
    {
        protected Object initialize()
            // called when a new thread accesses this thread local
        {
            return new SomethingOrOther(...);
        }
    };


    public synchronized void doStuff()// some method that many
                                      // threads may call
    {
        ...

        SomethingOrOther soo = (SomethingOrOther) (myData.get());

        ...

    }
}
```

If we then create an instance of MyClass and call its doStuff() method, then the instance's initialize() method gets called. If we subsequently call doStuff() again from the same thread, initialize() is *not* called. However, if we call doStuff() on the object from a different thread, initialize() will be called, and each thread will have its own instance data—its own copy of SomethingOrOther. Thus, each thread will be operating on a different SomethingOrOther when it calls doStuff, even though both threads access a single instance of MyClass.

The advantage of this approach is that we did not have to anticipate in the design of our thread class that we would want to have a copy of SomethingOrOther for each thread instance—we added that later to the reentrant doStuff() method, just by declaring a ThreadLocal variable.

Index

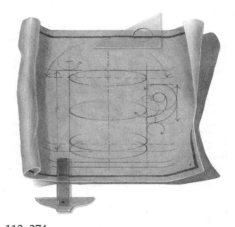

LICENSE AGREEMENT AND LIMITED WARRANTY

Company does not warrant that the SOFTWARE will meet your requirements or that the operation of the SOFTWARE will be uninterrupted or error-free. The Company warrants that the media on which the SOFTWARE is delivered shall be free from defects in materials and workmanship under normal use for a period of thirty (30) days from the date of your purchase. Your only remedy and the Company's only obligation under these limited warranties is, at the Company's option, return of the warranted item for a refund of any amounts paid by you or replacement of the item. Any replacement of SOFTWARE or media under the warranties shall not extend the original warranty period. The limited warranty set forth above shall not apply to any SOFTWARE which the Company determines in good faith has been subject to misuse, neglect, improper installation, repair, alteration, or damage by you. EXCEPT FOR THE EXPRESSED WARRANTIES SET FORTH ABOVE, THE COMPANY DISCLAIMS ALL WARRANTIES, EXPRESS OR IMPLIED, INCLUDING WITHOUT LIMITATION, THE IMPLIED WARRANTIES OF MERCHANTABILITY AND FITNESS FOR A PARTICULAR PURPOSE. EXCEPT FOR THE EXPRESS WARRANTY SET FORTH ABOVE, THE COMPANY DOES NOT WARRANT, GUARANTEE, OR MAKE ANY REPRESENTATION REGARDING THE USE OR THE RESULTS OF THE USE OF THE SOFTWARE IN TERMS OF ITS CORRECTNESS, ACCURACY, RELIABILITY, CURRENTNESS, OR OTHERWISE.

IN NO EVENT, SHALL THE COMPANY OR ITS EMPLOYEES, AGENTS, SUPPLIERS, OR CONTRACTORS BE LIABLE FOR ANY INCIDENTAL, INDIRECT, SPECIAL, OR CONSEQUENTIAL DAMAGES ARISING OUT OF OR IN CONNECTION WITH THE LICENSE GRANTED UNDER THIS AGREEMENT, OR FOR LOSS OF USE, LOSS OF DATA, LOSS OF INCOME OR PROFIT, OR OTHER LOSSES, SUSTAINED AS A RESULT OF INJURY TO ANY PERSON, OR LOSS OF OR DAMAGE TO PROPERTY, OR CLAIMS OF THIRD PARTIES, EVEN IF THE COMPANY OR AN AUTHORIZED REPRESENTATIVE OF THE COMPANY HAS BEEN ADVISED OF THE POSSIBILITY OF SUCH DAMAGES. IN NO EVENT SHALL LIABILITY OF THE COMPANY FOR DAMAGES WITH RESPECT TO THE SOFTWARE EXCEED THE AMOUNTS ACTUALLY PAID BY YOU, IF ANY, FOR THE SOFTWARE.

SOME JURISDICTIONS DO NOT ALLOW THE LIMITATION OF IMPLIED WARRANTIES OR LIABILITY FOR INCIDENTAL, INDIRECT, SPECIAL, OR CONSEQUENTIAL DAMAGES, SO THE ABOVE LIMITATIONS MAY NOT ALWAYS APPLY. THE WARRANTIES IN THIS AGREEMENT GIVE YOU SPECIFIC LEGAL RIGHTS AND YOU MAY ALSO HAVE OTHER RIGHTS WHICH VARY IN ACCORDANCE WITH LOCAL LAW.

ACKNOWLEDGMENT

YOU ACKNOWLEDGE THAT YOU HAVE READ THIS AGREEMENT, UNDERSTAND IT, AND AGREE TO BE BOUND BY ITS TERMS AND CONDITIONS. YOU ALSO AGREE THAT THIS AGREEMENT IS THE COMPLETE AND EXCLUSIVE STATEMENT OF THE AGREEMENT BETWEEN YOU AND THE COMPANY AND SUPERSEDES ALL PROPOSALS OR PRIOR AGREEMENTS, ORAL, OR WRITTEN, AND ANY OTHER COMMUNICATIONS BETWEEN YOU AND THE COMPANY OR ANY REPRESENTATIVE OF THE COMPANY RELATING TO THE SUBJECT MATTER OF THIS AGREEMENT.

Should you have any questions concerning this Agreement or if you wish to contact the Company for any reason, please contact in writing at the address below.

Robin Short

Prentice Hall PTR

One Lake Street

Upper Saddle River, New Jersey 07458

About the CD

Welcome to the *Advanced Java Development for Enterprise* Applications CD! This CD contains:

- The WebLogic Tengah Application Server, for evaluation.
- A page containing links to Object Design Inc. PSE object database system.
- The Java Development Kit 1.2 Beta 3 release.
- Selected source code from the book.
- A page containing links to Marimba's website for downloading the Tuner and Transmitter.

Some notes about the included products: In order to be compatible with US Department of Commerce export controls, all encryption code has been removed from Tengah. Otherwise, the products are fully functional. The version of Tengah included is 3.03, and is a 30-day trial version.

There are instructions in each product's directory for installing and using the product.

System requirements: Any Java-capable system. Recommended memory: 32Mb or greater. Required disk space: The largest product on the CD is the Java 1.2 Development Kit Beta 3 (JDK 1.2b3). It requires approximately 68Mb unextracted. The Tengah server is the next largest product, and requires approximately 20Mb unextracted. It is a pure Java application, so it is not OS-specific and there is no native code.